HOW TO GROW
A MULTI-MILLION DOLLAR
PROPERTY PORTFOLIO
IN YOUR SPARE TIME
FULLY UPDATED

MICHAEL YARDNEY

Published by:
Wilkinson Publishing Pty Ltd
ACN 006 042 173
Level 6, 174 Collins St
Melbourne, Vic 3000
Ph: 03 9654 5446
www.wilkinsonpublishing.com.au

A catalogue record of this book is available from the National Library of Australia.

ISBN(s): 9781923259119: Printed - Paperback

Cover and page design by Spike Creative Pty Ltd
Ph: (03) 9427 9500
spikecreative.com.au

Printed in Australia by Ligare Book Printers

NOTE TO READER

This publication contains the opinions and ideas of the author. It is sold with the understanding that neither the author nor the publisher is engaged in rendering legal, tax, investment, insurance, financial, accounting, or other professional advice or services. If the reader requires such advice or services, a competent professional should be consulted. Relevant laws vary from state to state.

Additionally, it is important to note that Australian laws and regulations are subject to constant revision and amendment and as such, some of those mentioned in this book may now be out of date. Any opinions, conclusions or recommendations set forth in this book are subject to change without notice.

The strategies outlined in this book may not be suitable for every individual and are not guaranteed or warranted to produce any particular results. Past performance may not be a reliable indicator of future performance.

This book has been written without taking into account the objectives, financial situation or needs of any specific person who may read this book, which means that before acting on the information in this book, the reader should seek appropriate professional or financial advice.

No warranty is made with respect to the accuracy or completeness of the information contained herein, and both the author and publisher specifically disclaim any responsibility for any liability, loss or risk, personal or otherwise which is incurred as a consequence, directly or indirectly, of the use and application of any of the contents within this book.

ACKNOWLEDGEMENTS

In early 2006 I approached publisher Michael Wilkinson with the manuscript for my first book.

He was initially courteous and polite, but not overly enthusiastic – until he read the manuscript. Then his gutfeel gave a new, and then unknown, author (me) a chance.

He initially did a print run of 4000 copies of *How to Grow a Multi-Million Dollar Property Portfolio – in your spare time*, thinking that quantity would last for years. But we had to order a reprint within months and since then this book has become a property investment classic, on the bookshelf of tens of thousands of property investors, catapulting it to best seller status, initially in hard copy and then on Amazon.

This is the fully updated seventh edition.

A lot has happened in the ensuing 16 years to my business and personal life with many new people influencing my life, my thoughts, my values and my business and property investment success. Creating wealth is never a solo effort. Similarly, this book would not have been possible without the support and encouragement of certain people who have contributed to my life in many ways.

In particular, my wife Pam for encouraging me, supporting me in every way and putting up with all my late nights and weekends on the computer. She endures my almost fanatical attitude to business and property investment and continually encourages me through all the good times and through all the things I still need to learn. I am humbled by her love and devotion, which I try hard but never quite succeed to match.

Special thanks go to my family, including our children and grandchildren for their love and encouragement.

Further thanks to my business partners, Ken Raiss, Mark Creedon, Brett Warren and Greg Hankinson and the whole team of property professionals at Metropole. And thanks also to our many clients whose collective inspiration has given me strength.

Over the years I have read almost every book about wealth creation and property investment ever written. I have learned a lot along the way and there are many ideas sprinkled throughout this book that I have learned from others. I guess I had to learn everything from someone at one stage, so I am sorry I cannot acknowledge everyone - I really can't remember where I first came across many of my strategies.

Where I recollect first hearing about an idea I try to give credit where it is due, but if I have omitted mentioning your name, please excuse me as I shamelessly acknowledge borrowing other people's good ideas picked up from observation or from conversation, books, CDs, DVDs, podcasts and seminars. As knowledge about becoming rich and successful investing isn't one individual's sole domain and there are really no secrets, I can only assume that these people also learned from and copied other people's ideas, books, CDs, DVDs, podcasts and seminars.

I have also learned from the many successes, and also the failures, of the over 2,500 property investors I have personally mentored through my 12-month mentorship program over the last 17 years. I am very proud of your successes.

And finally, to you, the reader – thank you for choosing to invest in this book. Please take advantage of the information I have to offer by using it to obtain the financial independence you deserve.

CONTENTS

INTRODUCTION

Whether you have yet to make your first investment or you already own a multi-million-dollar property portfolio, there is something in this book is for you. It will give experienced investors the opportunity to re-evaluate and fine-tune their current approach for the new market reality and new investors will obtain a perspective that normally takes years and years to acquire.

I have been investing for over 50 years now and in that time, I have adapted and fine-tuned my investment strategies from the successes I've had and from the many failures I've endured. In fact, I've often said I've become a real success at failure. I've just kept getting up one more time till I became successful, and in that time, I've grown my wealth substantially, as well as that of thousands of clients, and just as importantly, many readers of my books and blogs and listeners to my Podcast.

In that time recessions, fluctuating interest rates and changes in legislation have all taken their best swing at our property markets. Yet despite all these changes and of contant predictions that our real estate markets will collapse, property prices and rentals have continued to increase. In fact, they've been doing so for more than 200 years.

Having said that, I do see some let's call them "interesting" times ahead considering the current economic and political environment as well as the fact that inflation remains higher than the RBA would like, meaning interest rates will remain longer than many investors would've hoped for.

But early in 2023 our housing markets turned and entered a new property cycle, which will create a new generation of property multimillionaires.

However, one of the many problems that property investors face is that with the advent of the Internet and such easy access to almost unlimited information and instantaneous news, change seems more prevalent and economic cycles seem shorter. This has led to a band of fortunetellers trying to predict our property markets and property spruikers selling "get rich quick through property" schemes, suggesting new techniques for our changing market conditions.

While there's a lot of information out there, much of it is *misinformation*. That's one of the reasons why the majority of people who become involved in property investment are not successful in building the financial independence they are seeking.

The fact is most property investors fail.

Statistics show that about half of those who buy a property investment sell up within five years. And most (93%) of those who hang in only manage to buy one or two properties and less than one in a hundred investors ever buy six or more properties. In fact, the latest A.T.O statistics show there are less than 20,000 property investors in Australia who own 6 or more properties.

Of course owning one or two properties isn't really enough. You will run out of money before you run out of life! To become financially free you need to own a multi-million dollar property portfolio.

This means that most Australian property investors won't achieve financial independence. It also means that if you do what most property investors do, if you invest the way most Australians invest and if you listen to who most investors listen to, then you will get the same results most Australian property investors get!

And you want better than that don't you?

That's why I wrote the first edition of this book way back in 2006. My aim was to give ordinary Australians a system to become wealthy through residential property investment – a strategy that would allow them to survive changes in the market. As you will discover, this book offers a different approach to property investing than is found in most writings about this topic. Interestingly since I wrote the first edition of this book a swag of "property gurus" have come and gone, leaving a wake of failed property investors behind them. In contrast my strategic approach has stood the test of time and while I embrace many of the classic methods used by professional investors, you'll find this book contains many ideas and techniques not widely used or understood, but which can dramatically affect your results.

While I don't know everything about real estate, having invested for decades I now have a clue about what works and what doesn't. And while I've become a very successful investor, I would have given anything to have had the benefit of the information in this book earlier in my investing career. Getting the right ideas and then putting yourself in the right environment with the right mentors is a huge shortcut to success.

If you're like most readers you've bought this book because you have a dream. A dream about what your life could be like in the future if you were financially independent. And you're looking for a plan to fund your dream. Most people want to wake up in the morning and be able to do what they want to do, when they want to do it and with whom they want to do it. The way to achieve this is to have more money.

Unfortunately, most Australians use their money to buy more "stuff." On the other hand, successful investors use their money to buy themselves more time – but I'll explain this in more detail later.

My aim in writing this book is to put down a strategy to help you achieve your dream. One that has not only worked for me but for many others who have read earlier editions of this book and the many clients of my company, Metropole Property Strategists, who've been involved in over $6 billion worth of property deals. This way all Australians can at least get some insight into a successful wealth-making property formula – one that is reproducible and has stood the test of time.

Over the years I've been humbled at how many people have approached me in the street, in shopping centres or at airports to specifically thank me for the information they have learned from this book and how it has given them a clear path to their own financial freedom.

The highlight of many of my business days is when I receive emails from people I've never met telling me they have read this book and it takes pride of place on their bookshelf. They tell me that now they "get it" – how it all makes sense now that I've outlined a financial blueprint for them.

Remember ... all the strategies in this book have been proven in real life. They actually work. They are not some theory a property "guru" preaches but does not practice. Of course, the power of all this information is not in the information itself; it's in the implementation of the knowledge. It's in taking action.

Both my wife Pam and I remain active property investors and developers, and we still use exactly the same techniques I will teach you to grow our already substantial property portfolio.

But back to this updated edition...

As I write this introduction in mid 2024 we are living in interesting times. There are volatile social, political and economic issues all around the world. Australia has lived through a stage of rising inflation and interest rates. Our property markets have moved from the downturn of 2022 caused by concerns about the rising interest rates, into the beginning of a new growth phase of the property cycle.

Yet this has not quietened the perpetual property pessimists who will tell anyone who is prepared to listen that real estate Armageddon is around the corner, we've taken on too much and that property is too unaffordable.

Interestingly the current market reminds me of the times we experienced when I wrote the first edition of this book, a time when some ridiculed me for suggesting it was a great time to think long term and buy well located properties countercyclically.

It's the same today – those investors who head the lessons in this book, think long term and take advantage of the great property opportunities available today will look and smile at the naysayers.

However, we are in a time of change. Let's be honest: most of us don't like change – we'd rather have a nice predictable environment for our job security, our businesses and our investments. Unfortunately, all these are subject to the whims of the markets and the economy, and therefore are not predictable.

I felt compelled to update this book when I realised how much the property markets have moved in the couple of years since I penned the last edition. In this edition I clarify some strategies, expand on others and in fact completely change my opinion on one or two.

The game of property investing is a little like the game of chess. We all have the same pieces on the board. But those players who can see three or four steps ahead are the ones who are going to win.

As our markets move through the next property cycle and properties in Australia increase in value by millions of dollars, the properties themselves won't care who owns them. You should be one of these owners. Somebody is going to make money – so why not you? And I'm giving you the knowledge to do that.

I'm going to teach you a system that is well rooted in the real world of property and, while it is not a get rich quick scheme. It has helped me, hundreds of my clients and many readers of earlier editions of this book grow very substantial property portfolios.

While the majority of people will sit on the sidelines, waiting for all the signs to improve before they make their move into property, strategic investors are taking a long-term view. They're not worried about where interest rates or the economy will be in six months' time. They're making their plans based on where our housing markets will be in 5- or 10-years' time.

As you read this book, I will be your property mentor and give you the perspective you will need to **build your own multi-million-dollar property portfolio** – one property at a time. And don't worry, it will be easier than you think.

Why do I say that? I'm glad you asked. Read on to find out...

Michael Yardney
July 2024

LET ME BE YOUR MILLIONAIRE MENTOR

Would you like to become rich by investing in real estate — possibly very rich? Then this book is for you.

You should be aware from the outset that there is no safe way to get very rich from real estate quickly. It takes time, but most Australians who simply have owned their own home for more than a few years have made money. This rise in real estate values means that many home owners have seen their household wealth increase substantially.

But another group of Australians discovered how to profit in ways other than just owning their own home. They became real estate investors and bought additional properties.

Most investors recognise that the performance of real estate as a financial asset is astonishing.

Through this book I am going to be your property mentor and will argue that over the next decade almost every reader will be able to build themselves a multi-million dollar property portfolio because I am going to give you an insider's view of how the professionals invest in property. This means you will be able to grow your property portfolio faster, yet more securely, than most and in a way that will have the banks support you.

And the real benefit is that you will be able to become financially independent. You may be able to replace your day job with your property income and only go to work if and when you choose.

As your mentor I will show you how to get set for, and take advantage of, this new property cycle, which will create a new group of property multi-millionaires in Australia over the next decade.

You see, in Australia we are witnessing a confluence of a number of fundamental factors that will ensure that, in general, property values around Australia will increase significantly in the medium to long term. We have:

1. Robust **population growth** fueled by immigration and to a lesser extent strong natural population growth. Now that our borders have reopened as we've moved out of our Covid Cocoon, Australia's population will increase dramatically. There's now more than 25.5 million of us, and while population growth stalled during the Covid pandemic, Australia has a business plan to increase our population to 40 million people by the middle of this century. This means we'll be adding equivalent of another Melbourne, Sydney and

Brisbane in that time, meaning we'll need to add one new dwelling for every three houses already in existence.

2. **An economy** which will rebound strongly from the current slump and remain the envy of much of the Western world.

3. **A sound banking system** with tight lending practices, low default rate and even if interest rates are rising, they are still low by historic standards.

4. **Business confidence** and **consumer confidence** is positive but tends to fluctuate with the vagaries of our Federal and State governments.

5. **A healthy level of household debt**. While we are borrowing more, this debt tends to be in the hands of those who can afford it. Over the last few years the banks' responsible lending criteria have ensured that those taking on loans, and particularly property mortgages will be able to keep up their repayments even if interest rates rise a few points.

6. **A culture of home ownership** – just under 70% of us own or are paying off our homes. In contrast to some overseas markets Australians have high equity in their properties and a conservative debt position. In fact, half of all homes have no debt against them.

And at the time of writing this edition it's a time of great opportunity for investors and home buyers to get a foot on the property ladder or to add to their portfolio.

Sure there are some headwinds including rising interest rates, yet there is still a large demand for housing – people are still getting married, having babies, getting divorced and coming from overseas. And if they can't afford to buy their homes they are going to rent and this will force rentals up.

I can see little impetus for wages growth for the average Australian over the next few years, and the gap between the wealthy Australians who already own property or have multiple streams of income and ordinary Australians will only grow wider, meaning that moving forward our property markets will be more fragmented than they ever were as some locations increase in value significantly more than others.

What I mean by this is that lack of affordability is likely to affect suburbs where the average worker lives, regional locations and first-time buyer locations. On the other hand, property values are likely to increase in the more affluent, gentrifying inner and middle ring suburbs of our major capital cities where the locals' income is less dependent on CPI rises in wages.

So my top picks for locations that will outperform include suburbs where people have higher disposable incomes and are able to, and prepared to, pay a premium to live there the because of the amenities in the area.

As your mentor I want to persuade you to take advantage of the opportunities that will arise in Australia's property markets over the next few years.

AN INSIDER'S PERSPECTIVE INTO THE PROPERTY MARKET

Many years ago I made a decision about my future that I've never regretted. I decided to start exploring ways to become financially independent by investing in real estate.

As I write this today I've been at it for close to 50 years. As a real estate investor and property developer I've personally bought, sold and developed well over $350 million dollars' worth of residential, commercial and industrial real estate transactions. I am CEO of one of Australia's premier independent wealth and property advisory – Metropole Property Strategists – and my team and I has been involved in over four and a half billion dollars' worth of property transactions creating wealth for our clients. So I am not a theorist – I have skin in the game as they say and I've either made or seen almost every mistake an investor can make, so in this book my aim is not only to teach you what to do, but to explain what not to do.

It's been an amazing journey and, while I don't claim to be the world's greatest real estate expert, I have a wealth of experience and knowledge that has created massive profits for thousands of clients. In fact, I've been voted one of Australia's top 50 influential thought leaders.

Increasingly these days I'm dedicating a lot of my time to writing, creating videos and giving commentary to the media about property investment and the psychology of success; and helping others to find their own way on the path that I've taken.

As your mentor and as a property "insider", I'm ready to share this information with you, and have sprinkled this book with exclusive insider tips.

WHY DID YOU PICK THIS BOOK UP AND WHY SHOULD YOU READ IT?

I'm guessing that it's because you've made a decision too.

If you're ready to start a life-changing journey by exploring ways to invest in real estate over the long term then you will find that what you have in your hands is an invaluable guidebook that can help direct you as you take your first steps on what should be an incredible journey. I know this is true because of the successes so many other readers of the previous editions of this book have experienced.

For those of you who already own investment properties there are plenty of advanced property investment strategies in this book including a number of concepts I haven't seen written in property investment books before.

To help you I'm going to share some of my own story and lots of insights into how you can build a multi-million dollar property portfolio. Initially, you will be able to do it in your spare time, while you have a day job. Eventually, you will have a choice of whether you go to a day job at all.

On the other hand, if you don't invest wisely you'll run out of money before you run out of life, but remember that this book is not only about the money. It's about giving you choices. It's about your lifestyle. Ultimately it's about your freedom.

IT'S A BRAVE NEW WORLD FOR PROPERTY INVESTORS

When I wrote the first edition of this book in 2006 there were a lot of people who were too scared to invest in real estate. One of the biggest property booms in recent memory had come off the boil and prices were slumping. Negative talk dominated the media, and many investors were wondering how they could have been so stupid as to have believed in wealth creation through property, and wondered whether prices would ever increase again. Some commentators were suggesting that the property bubble had burst and that it was all over for many years.

At the time I had a clear response: there would be another property boom and it would be even stronger than the property boom of the late 1990s and early 2000s.

A brave call? Not at all!

At the time I'd been in this business for more than 30 years and I'd learned to appreciate the cyclical nature of markets and how to ride the peaks and troughs.

Looking back now, I was a lone voice in the media, predicting our property markets were about to turn. I have since been proven correct with most parts of Australia experiencing an amazing boom in 2006 and 2007. I was right not because I'm so smart, but because that's the way property cycles work. And throughout this book, I'm going to use the lessons of history as our teacher to pave your way for the future, giving you confidence to make your own investment decisions.

Then as I wrote the fourth edition of this book in 2012 the market was coming out of a two-year property slump commencing in 2010. Prior to this slump the price of the average home in some of our capital cities experienced two or three years of strong capital growth, some increasing in value by over 25%. Not long before we experienced the aftermath of world financial crisis and with concerns that the European financial markets could melt down, banks became more conservative and once again property fell out of favour as Australians stashed their cash, saving rather than spending.

It's interesting how the cycle repeats itself. Each property boom sets us up for the next downturn. Each property slump sets us up for the next boom.

Again at that time I encouraged readers to invest in property and many who followed my system and invested in the right properties have built their own multi-million dollar property portfolio.

If you want to become a successful investor you can't afford to wait until the next boom is evident. You should get set for it, because by the time the press and the general public becomes aware of the upward trends in our property markets, the big profits will already have been made.

THREE CARDINAL RULES OF PROPERTY

Here's three thoughts that I'd like to share with you before we start our journey together.

1. If you want to become financially independent through property investing you're going to have to do things differently to most property investors. Don't make 30-year investment decisions based on the last 30 minutes of news in the media — all your investment decisions must be made based on evidence and facts not the prophecies in the media.

2. You will need to find others who have invested successfully over a number of property cycles and have achieved what you want to achieve and who have maintained their wealth, and then use them as your mentors. The road you want to travel on is one many people have travelled before you — find role models and learn how they think and what they do. Follow their footsteps and obey the rules they play by, because there is no need to reinvent the wheel.

3. Property investment is not a get rich quick scheme. To be successful you must treat it like a business using systems that are proven.

A WEALTH OF EXPERIENCE

As your mentor I want to share with you as much of my experience as I can. I've made a lot of money for myself, and for others, and I've lost money too by making foolish decisions. In the past I've also been caught when economic circumstances changed unexpectedly. I know the terrain only too well, and the purpose of this book is to help point out a safe path and uncover some of the pitfalls for you.

I have personally used all the techniques you will read about — I'm not just spouting forth theory. I will show you the way I operate and share knowledge that can save you real money. But more importantly, I can empower you to start on the path to realising your own financial goals and financial freedom, if you're ready to make the same decision that I made myself many years ago.

After I finished writing this book there was still so much content left over, so I've decided to provide this to you as a bonus. You can access this now by registering your copy of this book at www.TheBookOnPropertyInvestment.com.au.

OK... are you ready and willing to get started?

PART 1

WHAT ARE WE TRYING TO ACHIEVE?

> MAN'S MIND, STRETCHED TO A NEW IDEA,
> NEVER GOES BACK TO ITS ORIGINAL DIMENSIONS.
> *OLIVER WENDELL HOLMES*

WHO IS MICHAEL YARDNEY?

This section is really a second introduction. This time it's about me, but don't let that stop you from reading it!

I'm not writing it to impress you or because my life is so interesting. This section is to explain how I learned about wealth creation through investing in property and to show you that if I can do it, so can you.

If I'm going to show you how I got started on the road that **turned $2,000 into a multi, multi-million dollar property portfolio in my spare time,** first we need to flash back for a moment and look at where this journey started.

WORKING CLASS AND WORKING HARD

I was brought up in Melbourne, the son of working-class parents. It was many years before they gave me a baby sister who was born when I was nine. Some people say it was because it took my parents nine years to get over the shock of having me!

Personally, I think the reason it took so long for them to have another baby was that they were struggling financially to make ends meet and they needed both incomes to survive. My mother couldn't afford to give up her job as a clerk in a bank (this was in the days before computers, when you had to enter all the figures manually).

My recollections of my childhood include my parents arguing at the end of each month when it came time to pay the bills. I remember hearing them discussing who would get paid that month and who wouldn't. I remember them struggling to put a few shillings (this was before dollars and cents) aside each week to save up to have some money to spend at Christmas.

Interestingly, while both my parents worked as employees (my father was too afraid to take the "risk" of running his own business), almost all of their friends owned their own businesses and were considerably wealthier than we were. It seemed to me that we were the poorest family in the street and I definitely felt the poorest amongst our friends.

My friends' parents all owned cars — mine couldn't afford one for many years. My friends and their parents went on summer holidays; for many years we didn't. And my friend's parents owned investment properties; mine didn't when I was young.

So while my friend's parents owned their own businesses and invested in property to grow their wealth, I remember my father's financial plan. Every Saturday morning he would sit at the kitchen table smoking his cigarettes, drinking black coffee and daydreaming. He would make a list of how he would spend the winnings when his lottery numbers would come up. Of course he never won the big jackpot. But occasionally he won a small prize, just enough to encourage him to buy a few more lottery tickets in the hope of getting the big one the following weekend.

Clearly the lottery is not a financial plan... it's a tax on those who can't do maths! But it was the only way my father could see himself escaping the rat race.

I learned a lot of very beneficial things from my parents who tried to instil good moral values in me. They wanted me to have a better life than they did. They strongly encouraged me to get a good education, get a secure job, buy a house and pay it off.

On the other hand, when I visited my friends I heard their parents give them very different advice. They said things like, "If you want to get on in Australia," (the "lucky country" as they would call it, as most were European migrants) "you need to go into business and earn money which you should then invest in property — that's the true path to real wealth."

Through my friend's parents I learned you couldn't count on the lottery or your boss to make you rich. I knew from an early age that I wanted to be rich, and I soon realised that if I was going to get rich it was up to me!

WHAT MAKES PEOPLE RICH AND POWERFUL?

While I don't remember exactly when I decided that I wanted to become rich, I do know I was pretty young. I determined that I did not want to struggle when I grew up like my parents were. I didn't want to fight with my wife about money and which bills we could pay and which we couldn't.

Apart from seeing how my friend's parents did it and learning what I could from them by endlessly asking questions, I studied rich and successful people because I wanted to be like them. I read all I could to find out what it was that caused certain men and women to succeed in everything that they did, while others of equal intelligence failed. I wanted to know what it was that set the rich and super successful apart from the rest.

As I studied these people I found that they did not necessarily have a higher education — there were many examples of rich and successful people who did not go to university; in fact many did not finish school. They did not necessarily have more resources; many came from poor or migrant backgrounds.

So I looked for common threads. What I found was that many had made their fortunes in real estate. And those that had made their money in other industries seemed to have invested their money in property.

Now you may say that not all successful people are rich and not all rich people are successful, and you would be right. We've all read of rich people who lead miserable and lonely lives or don't lead a balanced life and enjoy the pleasures that family and friends can bring.

It took me many years to learn that rich people are really poor – all they have is money. To be truly wealthy you need to a lot more than money. But remember I was still young and naive and I wanted to have it all! This led to an unbalanced life and at times, more problems than I care to discuss.

Looking back now, I can see that because of my early childhood experiences I was tainted and angry that we were poor and I felt that I had missed out on many things my friends enjoyed. So for the first half of my life I chased money. I desperately wanted to be "rich" and I went about trying to "prove" myself to the world.

Interestingly, as the size of my property portfolio grew, it wasn't enough. The anger didn't really go away and I still wanted more. It was many years later that I realised that if what drives you to want money is fear or anger or the need to prove yourself, money won't help you. When you get the money, the fear doesn't go away. The anger doesn't disappear. The money doesn't make you a different person.

Chasing money in an unhealthy way led to a very unbalanced life and this, amongst other things, led to me sabotaging the first half of my life. When I was much younger I did some things that I am very ashamed of and this broke up my marriage and ruined my early career. I paid the price for my actions and it made me a very different and much better person.

I came to realise what was really important to me. Over time I realised that there has to be a more significant reason to have money. I then set about building the Metropole business and this became the focus of many years of hard work for my second wife Pam and me. But it wasn't until I found a real purpose for the money that I became truly wealthy.

I'm sorry to say that it took too many years to realise that the true purpose of money for me (and I accept that it will be different for every reader of this book) was contribution.

For many years now I have enjoyed giving back to the community in a number of ways. I have dedicated myself to educating property investors through my blogs, writings, podcasts and seminars. Pam and I donate to many charities – not only money, but also time and energy.

Yes, I've had my challenges in life (mostly self-inflicted) and I've hit rock-bottom, but I got up again, learned from my mistakes and moved forward.

I'm not telling you this because I'm looking for approval. I am explaining this because it highlights the point that a situation is what you make of it. For years I dreamed of giving up my day job, getting off the treadmill and enjoying the lifestyle that could come from being a full-time property investor and developer. I had the knowledge, the contacts and had built up the asset base with my property investments to be able to do this. But I did not have the courage to give up the security of my day job!

Then I was forced to. Losing my wife, my family and much more than half of my assets in a bitter divorce could have broken me. But what I still had was the mindset of success and the knowledge of how to make money investing in and developing real estate. Having the correct mindset was much more valuable than the millions of dollars' worth of properties I had to give up as a divorce settlement and all the money that I had to pay the solicitors.

It enabled me to start all over again. I set about making profits in the property market using the same techniques that I am going to share with you in this book. Now, over 27 years later, my property portfolio is substantially larger and financially sounder than ever. And as I said — I have a much more fulfilling life.

I have found that many of my clients want to copy what I have done and become financially free by owning a substantial property portfolio. They use the services of the property professionals who work with my partners and I at the Metropole Group of Companies — www.metropole.com.au — to create their own story of financial success.

Today I am CEO of the Metropole Group of Companies, with a team of property professionals across our offices in the three biggest capital cities in Australia — Melbourne, Sydney and Brisbane. Together we have bought, sold, negotiated and project managed over $4.5 billion-worth of property transactions to create wealth for our clients (and ourselves).

I have often been called Australia's most trusted property commentator (probably due to the perspective I've gained over the years), I've been voted Australia's leading property investment educator and mentor on numerous occasions and my daily property newsletter www. PropertyUpdate.com.au has been independently raked the **#1 *real estate blog in the world*** for the last four years in a row and in 2019 had over 2.6 million unique readers visit my site.

Over the years the team at Metropole have won multiple industry awards and have helped clients from all over Australia and overseas, who trust us to guide them on their wealth creation journey through property. Some even use our services to research, negotiate for and acquire properties that they have never seen because they live on the other side of the country or the globe. Now that's trust!

I have a beautiful wife, Pam, my partner in life who was one of the significant partners in my business until she retired. I have six children (two inherited through Pam) and we have 11 grandchildren, two cute cats (Bentley and Harley) and a miniature Schnauzer, Lincoln. We own a very substantial property and share portfolio, live in a luxurious penthouse apartment, have many good friends and enjoy a life we could have only dreamed of as we were growing up.

I believe that information without real world context is ineffective at best and irrelevant at worst. So it should give you comfort that all you will read about in this book I have done myself. I am not just spouting forth theory, I'm sharing the system of my property success to assist you in creating your property success.

WHY AM I STILL WORKING?

Recently a prospective client asked me: "Michael, now that your candles cost more than your birthday cake, why are you still working?"

I know others have wondered — is this guy really financially independent? If so why is he sitting here across the table from me wanting to show me how to become financially independent?

I'd like to answer these questions for you because there are some instructive lessons in the answers for anyone who wants to develop financial freedom.

Firstly the answer to the second question is — yes, I am truly financially independent, having over the years built a very substantial investment portfolio of residential, commercial industrial and retail real estate.

But I think the biggest lesson for you will come out of my answer to the question of why I am still working.

Let me explain with a little story...

I recently read that Mick Jagger is on tour again, at the age of 79, turning up at one city performing, leaving, on to the next place. I repeat he's 79 years old and still on tour.

I suppose this should be reassuring — it suggests that years from now I might still somehow or other get on stage and deliver my seminars.

Over the years I've worked hard so that I now don't need to work for financial reasons, but I think I will still enjoy doing it when I'm 77 years old just like Mick does. As far as I know, Mick has no unmet financial needs — he's reportedly worth $360 million. He's still touring largely because he has nothing better to do for which he has comparable enthusiasm.

Why successful people stay at it long after they need to reveals why they became so successful at it.

I guess what I'm trying to say is that what many people don't seem to understand is the reason so many business people, entrepreneurs and investors became so successful and rich is from the enthusiasm they had in their job in the first place.

This is the main reason why I'm still working.

I still get an intense buzz putting deals together, developing training programs, writing my blogs and books, educating investors and more importantly seeing clients become financially independent and successful.

You see... I spend all day talking about property while drinking coffee and dealing with nice people. Why wouldn't I still be working?

And to be honest I am still clearly, unashamedly, intensely enthusiastic about making and multiplying money. I enjoy passing it on and helping future generations including my children and grandchildren and also contributing significantly to charity.

I am very grateful for what I have and believe it's my obligation to repay the world and that's in part why I spend so much time writing and educating. These activities are clearly the least financially profitable of all that I do, but are the most rewarding.

THE FIRST PROPERTY I BOUGHT

Shortly after I purchased my first investment property in the early 1970s in Larch St Caulfield for $18,000, in partnership with my parents, the Labor Party came into power in Australia and over the next few years inflation ramped up significantly. And so did property values and interest rates, but my investment grew so much in value that a few years later I was able to refinance against its new value and borrow the deposit for my second investment property.

When I got married a few years later I sold both these properties. The first of many investment mistakes I made — no one told me I could borrow against them for the deposit for my home.

When I sold my half share of Larch Street to my parents it was worth $32,000. In 2001 I bought the same property back from my mother for $250,000.

A few years later we pulled down the old house and built two two-storey townhouses on the site we still own today. So I still own my first investment property which cost $18,000 but today is worth well over $2.5 million. That's the power of strategic property investment.

WHAT IS REAL WEALTH?

When I speak with investors, I soon discover they all want similar things and it's not actually the properties they're after. Some want the financial security or financial freedom or the lifestyle that comes with wealth. Others want the toys such as imported European cars or holiday homes by the beach.

There is nothing wrong with that. The desire to obtain security and material things is basic to most humans. It's nothing we should feel bad about; it's a reality. These things make us happy.

Think back — as a child it was toys, dolls or bikes we wanted. As teenagers it was computers, mobile phones or the latest fashion clothes. Now as adults we're after new cars, bigger houses, longer vacations and security for our families, or maybe all of the above.

If the last few economically challenging years taught us anything, it's that we need to start taking a different approach to money and how we value it, procure it and use it. In the past many people felt their job was secure and their superannuation would see them through retirement.

But now many realise they're going to have to work longer than they hoped and when they eventually retire they'll find their superannuation will give them a (very) modest living at best. In reality super was never enough; only about 1% of Australians become truly financially free. Most are trying to stretch their savings and superannuation so it won't run out before they die. Some end up taking a part-time job to supplement their pension and superannuation.

WHAT DOES WEALTH MEAN TO YOU?

Most people say wealth means a big salary with a lifestyle to match. Most people equate wealth to money, but that's not how wealth works.

You need a lot more than money to be truly wealthy. You need your health, your friends and family to share it with, you need personal growth, spirituality (this means different things to different people) and contribution.

As you can see, to me wealth is a product of the mind and no amount of money will make you wealthy. To be truly wealthy you have to be grateful for what you have in life and you have to be living a life where you know you are contributing or giving back.

Financial independence is different to wealth. It means you never have to work again to live your life. That's what you're really investing for, isn't it?

My suggestion is that you should be committed to being wealthy as well as financially independent.

Just to make things clear... income by itself does not make you financially free. In fact income is one of the worst predictors of financial freedom. You spend some, maybe you save some, and taxation takes away a portion of it. Most people in Australia never become wealthy; they never develop real financial independence.

For most people the bills keep mounting up and despite working more and more hours they can't make ends meet. So it's not really income you are after. To secure your financial future you need to acquire assets that grow in value and bring in **passive recurring income**.

Having dealt with Australians from all walks of life I've developed a number of models to explain the progression most investors take in their path to developing financial freedom. These models allow you to know exactly where you are heading financially, what stage you are at along the way, and what the key focus areas and leverage points are that you can use to fast track your journey.

But I'm jumping ahead. Let me tell you about how I first started to become aware of these ideas.

Way back in the early 1980s Brian, my business partner at the time, said to me "Michael – I'd like a cash machine!"

"What?" I responded.

Brian explained, "You know a cash machine. I'd like to come to work in the morning, flick the switch and the machine would start working and churn out money. At the end of the day I'd flick off the switch and go home to my family and then come back tomorrow and flick on the switch once more. And the machine would again start working and churn out the money."

As you can imagine I replied: "Sure, I'd like a cash machine too."

Now that you have read about this concept I bet you'd also like a cash machine, wouldn't you?

You know what? I now have a cash machine — my property investment business.

Twice a year Pam and I go overseas on vacation, sometimes for a month or more at a time, but our cash machine keeps churning out the money. Our rent comes in, the property managers look after our tenants and our properties keep increasing in value and we wake up richer in the morning than we went to bed the night before.

Yes, we truly have a cash machine and so can you if you build your own property investment business.

OK now back to my concept of the different levels of wealth. I call it...

THE WEALTH PYRAMID

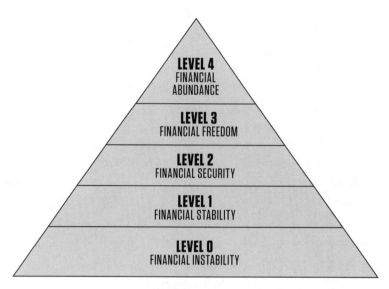

THE WEALTH PYRAMID ©

My financial model – the **Wealth Pyramid** – shows what level you are at on your way to financial independence and what the key focus areas and leverage points are along the way to speed you on your journey.

Like all pyramids it has a wide base and tapers towards the top, in other words most people are at the lower levels of the wealth spectrum and fewer reach the top. Hopefully the knowledge and skills you'll learn from this book will help you work your way up the pyramid, but the solutions you'll need to move from one level to the next will vary depending where you are.

Unfortunately, most people don't really have any wealth and therefore are at...

WEALTH LEVEL 0 – FINANCIAL INSTABILITY

Since most people live from pay cheque to pay cheque, they are what I call Financially Unstable. If they lose their job, or if they have an emergency (you know how these keep cropping up – an illness, the car breaks down, the refrigerator packs up), they have no financial reserves to cope.

Since they have no spare financial capacity, the only way to cope with these burdens is for people at Level 0 to borrow more (and get further into debt) and this only creates more financial hardship. They live their lives with their heads buried in the sand, not really conscious about money and their spending habits.

If they have money they'll spend it, if they don't they'll borrow it because their favourite pastime is shopping and buying stuff they don't really need. This means much of what they own has debt attached to it. They keep doing this and fooling themselves that they'll just work harder and pay off their debt someday.

If you ask them what their problem is, they'll tell you they don't make enough money. They think more money will solve their problems. But that's not right.

Their biggest problem is their money habits, which has nothing to do with how much they earn. It's what they do with the money they earn. As they move on in their lives and earn more, they just spend more. Today, they can't survive on the type of income they would have only dreamed they could achieve five years ago.

There are many high-income earners who fall into this category because they spend as much, or more, than they make. Sure some people at Level 0 Wealth can look rich — they may even have big homes or fancy cars, but they also have huge loans that they struggle to repay.

Unfortunately, they often argue with their spouses about money, being in financial denial and justifying why they bought this or that.

Level 0 Wealth can really be divided into two subgroups:

1. **Casualties** — I call those at the lowest level this because they're casualties of the money game. Each month they seem to find themselves in a worse place than they were the month before — getting themselves deeper and deeper in debt, usually through credit card debt. They're paying high interest rates today to use tomorrow's money now. Of course they blame others for their problems — it's never their "fault". They've often read books about budgeting or been told the trick of cutting up credit cards, but that just doesn't work. They don't know how to "do" money. Then half a level up the pyramid are the...

2. **Survivors** — these are employees, self-employed or even business people who seem to make just enough money each month to have nothing. And if by accident they end up with some money in the bank they spend it or take a holiday. They are just surviving.

While the fact is that at Level 0 people simply live beyond their means, the real cause of their problems is denial of this. Unless they are prepared to change, their financial future is bleak.

The fundamental key to getting out of this level is mindset, education and taking financial responsibility. So first be honest with your personal cash flow position. Then stop the bleeding by changing your financial habits and at the same time get a financial mentor.

Fact is, when you're at Level 0 you can't get out of your problems on your own. You need someone to mentor you and you need to be part of a group — just like getting fit or losing weight — it's just too hard to do on your own. How many people sit on the couch watching diet videos while eating ice cream?

The next rung up is...

WEALTH LEVEL 1 — FINANCIAL STABILITY

This is the most basic level of wealth and gives you some level of financial security.

You have achieved Financial Stability when:

1. You have accumulated sufficient liquid assets (such as money in an offset account, line of credit or savings) to cover your current living expenses for a minimum of six months.

2. You have private medical insurance and some life insurance to protect you and your family's lifestyle should you become permanently ill, disabled, unable to work or if worse comes to worst, you suddenly die. I know that's an unpleasant thought, but in the last year two of our acquaintances died leaving their families in financial trouble.

At this level you will have the peace of mind that should any unexpected challenges come your way, such as retrenchment, a business failure, illness or disability, you and your family's lifestyle will not be unduly compromised. You will have adequate time to look for new sources of income to put you back on track.

The problem at this level is that your cash flow is being controlled by others — your boss who pays your salary or your clients who pay for your services. This means you're still on a treadmill and you don't have the ability to increase your cash flow without working more, and that has its limits. Sure you've got a bit of a financial buffer, but if you stop working for a while you slip back to Level 0.

If you're at Level 1 your goal should be to move more of your cash flow into assets and build that Cash Machine so your income does not depend on you putting in more effort.

At this level your biggest leverage comes from investing in yourself and becoming financially savvy building a solid base of financial and investment skills upon which you can grow your financial future, as well as beginning to build a network of peers you can make your journey with.

You'll also have to choose the first wealth vehicle you are committed to master and become a devoted student learning all you can about this niche wealth vehicle. In my opinion the best place for most people to start is residential real estate investing.

In making the decision on which wealth vehicle to go after, you must cultivate the discipline to say no to the pull of other "great opportunities" and vehicles. I've made more money by saying no to second-rate investment opportunities than I've made by saying yes to them.

Then carefully choose who you'll study with. Contrary to popular belief, the most expensive education isn't "graduate school" like an MBA. The most expensive education is one based on a flawed models and incorrect information. The hardest form of learning is UN-learning all the wrong, mistaken, and flawed things you "learned" from unqualified teachers. So choose to learn from the best. It will save you years of frustration following defective models.

Your aim should be to move up to...

WEALTH LEVEL 2 — FINANCIAL SECURITY

You achieve **Financial Security** when you have accumulated sufficient assets to generate enough passive income to cover your most basic expenses. These would include not more than the following:

- Your home mortgage and all home related expenses such as your utilities, rates and taxes.
- All your tax payments plus the interest payments on your loans and debts.
- Your car expenses.
- Your grocery bills and minimal living expenses.
- Any insurance premiums including medical, life, disability and your house.

When you reach this level of Financial Security you will be able to stop working and still be able to maintain a simple, basic lifestyle. Of course you'll want more than that.

At Level 2 you will be an investor focused on building your net worth by owning assets that appreciate in value and ideally, you'll accelerate the process by "manufacturing" capital growth through renovating or developing residential real estate (I'll get into this in Section 4 of this book).

At the advanced stage of Level 2 you are beginning to make the transition from capital gains investing to investing for passive, residual cash flow. This means you've got to master a whole new skill set. You'll also have to radically upgrade your advisor network and peer group. Being the big fish in a small pond no longer serves you. You need to begin playing with people better than yourself, because you want to move up to...

WEALTH LEVEL 3 — FINANCIAL FREEDOM

You know you have achieved Financial Freedom when you have accumulated sufficient assets to generate enough passive income to pay for the lifestyle you desire (not necessarily your current lifestyle) and all of your expenses, without ever having to go to work again.

Having first built a substantial asset base (of properties, shares or businesses), now you are using your assets to create cash flow, which doesn't mean you won't go to work again, but you will now be able to make the choices you want because you have time freedom.

At Level 3 your focus should be on stabilising your passive income streams and fine-tuning your estate planning and asset protection. Now is also a great time to grow your service to the world by finding ways to expand your contribution.

Level 3 is NOT about "retirement", it's about regeneration and contribution.

WEALTH LEVEL 4 – FINANCIAL ABUNDANCE

A small group of people around the world achieves Financial Abundance when their Cash Machine works overtime. Not only are they free of financial pressures, but they have so much surplus income after paying for their lifestyle, all of their expenses and their contributions to the community (often through charity work or donations) that their asset base just keeps growing and growing.

A COUPLE OF THOUGHTS ABOUT THE WEALTH PYRAMID

There is nothing new about this hierarchy of wealth; it's always been there and we're all part of it. Complaining about where you are won't help, however your level of wealth is your choice. Despite that, most people get stuck at a particular level.

The good news is that everyone can move up the Wealth Pyramid. Understanding where you are empowers you to ensure you do what you need to do to get to the next level. But this never happens by accident, you have to earn you way up through personal development and upgrading your mindset. I discuss this in detail in by book *Rich Habits Poor Habits* (www.RichHabitsPoorHabits.com).

However, in this book I'm going to show you how I created a Cash Machine so that I don't have to trade my time for money. I suggest you do the same – you should have a Cash Machine that feeds you.

And you can achieve this in 15 to 20 years or so by wisely investing in residential property. I will show you how, step-by-step, in this book. But first, I would like to introduce you to some of the important financial concepts that the wealthy have learned and used to make themselves rich.

THE 4-STEP FORMULA TO FINANCIAL INDEPENDENCE

Here are four timeless rules for achieving financial freedom. Please don't dismiss them because they sound so simple:

1. *Spend less than you earn.* This maxim may seem obvious, but many people have difficulty following it. If you're spending more than you earn, you will never become financially independent. You will be paying money to others for the rest of your life. The earlier you start living by this rule, the better. It is never too late to start.

2. *Invest the difference wisely.* It may surprise you but the average Australian, earning between $70,000 and $100,000 a year for 40 years will earn somewhere between $3 and $3.5 million during their working life. Yet most of them will retire poor. Clearly the level of your income has no bearing on the level of wealth you achieve, what is critical is the amount you save and invest wisely.

3. *Reinvest* your investment income so you get compounding growth. As you are beginning to understand, you will never become financially independent on your earnings alone. You need to keep reinvesting. In fact, by the time you become financially free almost all your assets will have come from compounding capital growth, not from your income, your savings or your rent.

4. *Keep doing steps 1 and 2* until your asset base reaches a critical mass so that you have the Cash Machine that gives you the income you desire.

If it's as simple as that why don't more people develop financial independence? Because it requires discipline and delayed gratification — sacrificing today in return for more choices later in life.

IT'S EASY TO BECOME A MILLIONAIRE

In step 3 above I talk about reinvesting. Here's why — it's simple to become a millionaire if you understand the principle of compounding. All you have to do is start with a dollar and double it 20 times.

Since you probably don't believe me, take a moment to figure it out.

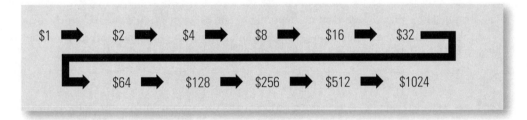

That's 10 times.

See how it starts out slow and then begins to snowball? That's exactly the way your real estate portfolio grows. It starts out slowly and gradually begins to snowball until one day you wake up and realise that you really are a millionaire!

Let's keep going:

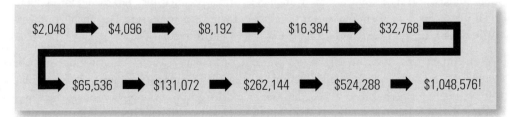

Simple isn't it? Just double a dollar 20 times and you'll have over a million dollars! That's the principle of compounding I was talking about a moment ago — it's the way you'll build your Cash Machine.

Now I said simple, I didn't say it was easy.

The reason that it's not easy to make a million dollars is that very few people know how to double a dollar on a regular basis.

One way to do this is to invest in a high growth asset and then reinvest your income using the magic of compounding. Well positioned residential real estate is such an asset and in the section on tax I'll explain more about why I've used it as my preferred investment vehicle for compounding.

INSIDER TIP

The wealthy understand how the power of compounding, leverage and multiple streams of income can grow their money.

THE WISDOM OF MULTIPLE STREAMS OF INCOME

The wealthy know that you need more than one stream or source of income to be rich today. If you think back to the 1950s when, in most families, only the husband worked, how many streams of income did a family need to survive?

Only one.

Yet today, very few families can survive on less than two streams of income, with both the husband and wife working. And the way things are going, that won't be enough in the future. It would be wise to have multiple streams of income flowing through your adult life.

Wealthy people have always known this. They generate income through wages or their businesses and also from their various investments such as property, shares and managed funds. If one stream dries up, they have many more to support them. If one of their businesses goes broke, they have other sources of income available.

But ordinary workers are much more vulnerable. If they lose their income stream, for example their job, it can wipe them out and it often takes them years to recover. How many ordinary Australians learned this lesson during the Covid lockdowns of 2020–21?

On the other hand, imagine you have a portfolio of income streams — not just one or two, but many streams from completely different and diversified sources, perhaps from a portfolio of investment properties. If one stream of income dries up (for example a property becomes vacant), you'll barely feel the bump. You will be stable. You will have time to adjust. You will be safe.

Do you have multiple streams of income flowing into your life at this time?

Maybe it's time to add another one!

THE POWER OF RECURRING INCOME

So let's look at how you might add another stream of income to your life. You could always get another part-time job, but that's not the kind of income I'm suggesting.

What I am talking about is recurring income that you receive whether you are working or not. Another name for this is passive income because it is money you make when you are asleep.

So, first, it is important to understand that not all incomes are created equal. Some streams are linear and some are recurring. Now here's the question that will determine whether your income streams are linear or recurring: **how many times do you get paid for every hour you work?**

If you have answered only once, then your income is linear.

Income streams from your salary are linear — you get paid only once for your effort, and if you don't show up for work, you don't get paid.

With *recurring* income, you work hard once and you get paid over and again for the same effort. It unleashes a steady flow of income for months or even years. Wouldn't it be nice to get paid hundreds of times for every hour that you work?

Let me explain...

When I sat down to write the first edition of this book, before I earned a cent, I put thousands of hours of hard work over a number of years into compiling it. Now it has been published and is a best-seller and I earn royalties every six months, the cheques flow in no matter where I am or what I am doing. And this has been going on for over 16 years.

That's the power of recurring income!

This is also the way that property investors make their income; they work hard to develop some capital to invest in property, which then goes on working for them, by bringing in rent and appreciating in value.

On the other hand, I see many people trying to obtain multiple streams of income the hard way. They either get themselves another job, or they try to make a go of network marketing or they make hard work out of property by attempting strategies such as managing their own properties or leasing out their properties room by room or on Airbnb in an attempt to increase their cash flow.

They are building the wrong sort of income — they're just getting themselves another job.

What you need is *passive* and *recurring* income – income that comes into your life whether you work or not. This is the type of income that can be deposited into your bank account while you are off holidaying on the other side of the world. The secret of the wealthy is not that they have more money, but that they have more time freedom, because their income is passive, and they can spend time on anything they want.

When you view people's lives through the filter of passively earned recurring income, you find that many people aren't as wealthy as they first appear. Doctors and dentists don't earn recurring income for their work; their income potential is capped by the number of patients they can see. They have to be there for every single one of them. That's linear income.

The same is true for most professionals. They don't enjoy the power of recurring income either. They may appear to be rich but they're on a treadmill just like other workers.

WHAT PERCENTAGE OF YOUR INCOME IS RECURRING?

If you're smart, you will start to develop some streams of passively earned recurring income. Eventually this will give you the time freedom to do what you want when you want.

One way you can do this is to buy an investment property. Whether you're working or not, the rental income will continue to come in and over the years your property's value will increase.

To become truly wealthy, and to have sufficient passive income to indefinitely pay for the lifestyle you enjoy, while covering all your debts, you'll obviously need to buy more than one property. You'll need to build a multi-million dollar property portfolio so that your passive income is substantial. (Luckily that's just what this book is all about!)

It is said that all long journeys start with one small step. You can start by absorbing the knowledge contained in this book, and then committing to putting that knowledge into action by buying your first property or growing your portfolio using the systems we explore.

INSIDER TIP

To become financially independent you are going to need to get another job — but not for yourself. You need to get a job for your money — you need to get it working hard for you making passive income.

ASSETS, NOT INCOME, CREATES WEALTH

While passive income (cash flow) is important in becoming financially free, what I'm trying to explain is that it's your assets that create real wealth; because, if invested wisely, your assets grow and income flows from them.

Unfortunately, most people don't get past the income stage. They don't manage to make their money work for them and quite simply, you can't save your way to wealth with income.

One of the reason most people don't get rich is they invest for cash flow — not asset (capital) growth. I know this message is very, very different to what you'll hear from others, yet it's the way the wealthy all around the world do it. Investing for cash flow is the reason most investors get stuck at Level 2 Wealth. Cash flow gets you through life, but asset growth gets you out of the rat race. You'll see this theme runs throughout this book and I know it will be hard for some to swallow, but the results speak for themselves.

INSIDER TIP

The rich think "Assets", the poor think "Cash Flow". Assets not cash flow creates real wealth.

TRUE WEALTH

Throughout this book I talk about wealth and money as if the two are much the same but, once again, I want to make it clear that I recognise this is not the case. When I went through my divorce and a number of other major personal challenges many years ago, I quickly realised the importance of all those things money can't buy.

So while this book is about making money, I want to remind you that true wealth is not measured in dollars. To be truly wealthy you need much more than money. As I've already said, you need your family, friends, time, health, your spirituality and the ability to contribute back to your community.

Money won't solve your all your problems — of course rich people still have problems, but I've often said that any problem money can solve isn't really a problem. That's interesting, isn't it?

Now I think we're ready, so in the next chapters we'll take a closer look at the details of my philosophy and investing system.

THE FIVE LEVELS OF INVESTING

I would like to introduce you to the concept of the five levels of investing which is another model I've created to explain the progression most investors take in their path to developing financial freedom.

While these don't exactly correlate with the Levels of Wealth on the Wealth Pyramid, as I explain them to you, the relationship between what level of investor you are and your level of wealth will become clear.

Remember — this has nothing to do with your level of income.

I've seen many people who earn hundreds of thousands of dollars a year, yet by spending most of it on a flashy lifestyle they fail to graduate up the Wealth Pyramid. Having said that, I've also seen successful investors build a substantial property investment business while working at what some would call menial day jobs, earning relatively little in their pay packet. In other words, their job becomes something they choose to do, not something they have to do for their primary source of income.

LEVEL 0 — THE SPENDER

Level 0 are really not investors — they tend to be spenders and borrowers and as a result, end up with a high level of debt. They spend everything they earn and often more. Their money runs out before the month does. They usually survive from pay packet to pay packet, using credit cards and store credit where they can.

They're at Level 0 on the Wealth Pyramid. The Level 0 investor lives for today. If they have some money they spend it, if they don't have money they borrow it. These are the people who, when they need some cash, go to the ATM and pay a fee to collect an advance on their own money and then pay interest on it. Their solution to financial issues that arise is to spend their way out of it or to take on more debt.

Do you know any level 0 investors? A large part of our adult population falls into this category and they will never become wealthy unless they do something radically different.

LEVEL 1 — THE SAVER

The vast majority of people who are not spenders will generally be what I call savers. Their main investment is their home, which they aim to pay off over time. Sometimes they save a little, squirrelling away a few dollars of what's left over after paying tax but in general they save to consume, not to invest.

Savers tend to be afraid of financial matters and are generally unwilling to take risks. They're following the plan their parents and grandparents followed — get a steady job, buy a house, pay it off and save a nest egg for retirement. The problem is savings, or even owning your home outright, doesn't make you rich.

What usually happens is that they work hard over their lifetime, diligently save or pay off their home and are left with what will be a modest, most likely old and tired house.

Savers are what I would call *financially illiterate*. They need to focus their efforts on building a solid base of financial and investment skills, upon which they can grow their financial future. They will get the most leverage by investing in themselves and getting a quality financial education and beginning to build a network of peers that they can make the journey with.

LEVEL 2 — THE PASSIVE INVESTOR

Level 2 investors have become aware of the need to invest. They realise their superannuation won't get them through retirement, so they start learning about investment and begin accumulating assets.

While they are generally intelligent people, they are still what I would call financially illiterate — they don't really understand the rules of money. But remember it's not their fault — nobody taught them. If anything, their parents taught them old fashioned, out-dated concepts about money.

Rather than taking responsibility for their financial education themselves, Level 2 investors tend to look for answers to their investment needs from outside sources or "experts". This makes them easy prey for the newest "get rich quick scheme" advertised in magazines or the latest flash-in-the-pan investment strategies spruiked by telemarketers.

Instead, they should refine their financial and investing education and focus their efforts on choosing a specific wealth vehicle that they are going to master. They must unlearn the flawed, incorrect and misguided lessons they have learned about money and wealth from unqualified teachers.

LEVEL 3 – THE ACTIVE INVESTOR

Level 3 investors realise that they must take responsibility for their financial future and become actively involved in their investment decisions. They become financially literate by building a knowledge base of investment strategies and techniques. They are starting to get their money working for them.

These investors *actively* participate in the management of their investments and concentrate on building their net worth. Their main focus is on growing their asset base.

As this is the asset accumulation stage of their investment life, these investors have in general moved to high growth, low yield investments to grow their wealth. This is where residential real estate really shines – it's the best asset class I know for growing your wealth safely.

Level 3 investors usually leverage the time and expertise of a network of industry professionals as they realise that they can't do it all themselves. They also upgrade their network of advisors and peers, often joining a Mastermind group of like-minded people.

LEVEL 4 – THE PROFESSIONAL INVESTOR

A very small group of investors move to the top rung of the ladder and become a Level 4 "professional" investor who has built and now manages a true investment business.

A Level 4 investors' property investment business has a substantial asset base that generates sufficient recurring passive income to pay for their lifestyle costs, plus they keep growing their investment portfolio whether they work in a real job or not.

They are well educated; financially fluent, comfortable with the language of money and understand how the game is played. They understand the "system" of finance, tax and the law and use them to their advantage.

These investors tend to concentrate on optimising the performance of their properties, whilst at the same time minimising their risks. While they are still accumulating assets, they are now more interested in cash flow that will allow them to gain the most out of life.

Rather than investing what is left after they have spent their money, they have the correct tax structures in place that enables them to spend what is left over after their money-making investment machine ploughs more cash back into further investments.

They have a finance strategy and financial buffers to buy themselves time and see themselves through the ups and downs of the economic and property cycles. And they understand the law as it relates to property so that they don't make the mistakes many beginning investors do.

These professional investors don't hand control of their investments over to others; they retain control whilst employing a proficient team: accountants, finance brokers, property managers, solicitors and property strategists who have great systems that achieve repeated and consistent results, which are reliable and predictable.

This gives Level 4 investors the freedom to choose whether they get up in the morning and go to work or not. Many still continue working because they enjoy it, but now they go to work because they choose to, not because they have to. Others find the time to contribute more to their community or to charities.

Neither the state of the economy nor the stage of the property cycle seems to affect the professional investor who makes money in good economic times and bad.

Level 4 investors rarely stop educating themselves. They read, still attend seminars and surround themselves with a team of advisors and mentors. They're prepared to pay for solid advice – not only to increase their wealth but also to protect their assets from opportunistic family members, lawsuits and the government.

You will find that Level 4 investors personally own very little in their own names. But even though they "own nothing", they control everything through companies and trusts. By controlling the legal entities that own their assets, these investors gain considerable legal tax benefits and asset protection.

And a final point about Level 4 investors is that they teach their financial knowledge to their children and pass on their family fortune to future generations as their companies and trusts endure after they have departed this life.

ASSET GROWTH FIRST, THEN INCOME STAGE

Sorry I'm repeating myself, but I want to make this clear because so many investors get this wrong...

The first stage in becoming financially free is to educate yourself; the next stage is that of asset accumulation – your job as a Level 3 investor is to build a sufficiently large asset base to fuel your "cash machine".

Then, only when you have grown a substantial asset base, you transition into the cash flow (income) stage of your life as a level 4 investor. Sure you need income (cash flow) to service your debts as a Level 3 investor, but your focus must be on asset growth rather than income growth.

WHAT IS YOUR LEVEL OF WEALTH?

Now it's time for some home truths... How far up the Wealth Pyramid are you? Where do you currently sit in this hierarchy of investors?

Everyone starts at the bottom – at Level 0 – but not everyone makes it to Level 4. In fact, few do. But you can once you understand why the rich keep getting richer.

Remember, this assessment of your current level of wealth has nothing to do with your income. You can be a "low income" earner when it comes to your day job, but still be a Level 3 investor and have financial security. Likewise, you can be considered "rich" by working income standards yet still be at Level 0 Wealth, spending every dollar that you earn.

What I want you to understand is the pay packet that you work for every day has nothing to do with what level of wealth you are and in fact is one of the worst predictors of wealth.

INCOME IS THE WORST PREDICTOR OF WEALTH

I've come across many clients who earn substantial incomes yet still don't "have" anything and similarly I've seen plenty of clients who earn modest incomes grow substantial property portfolios.

I know Bob, my doctor, has earned hundreds of thousands of dollars a year for the last 40 years. He's in his early 70s now, drives a nice European car but still lives in a rented house and continues to feel like he's on a treadmill. Every day he goes to his medical practice to see patients and at the end of the month, he just manages to pay the bills. (Remember the Level 0 casualty we discussed?)

I have spoken to him about this on a number of occasions. The trouble is, every time he earns money, he seems to spend it. He has never managed to put anything aside in the way of savings or investments, or even as an emergency fund. He said to me a while ago that his car broke down and needed major repairs and even that created some degree of financial hardship for him.

The story of someone like Bob, who probably earns over $300,000 a year, may sound strange to you. But if you're like most people, despite working for around forty years, and having earned millions of dollars in their lifetime very few people become financially free. In fact most retire just above broke.

So the question isn't really can you *make* a few million dollars? My question to you is: are you able to keep a few million dollars? If you're like Bob, in fact if you're like many people, you're going to find it difficult to save and easy to spend.

I asked Bob why he still rents; why despite his income he hasn't managed to save up a deposit for his own home and he told me the following story: each new year he makes a resolution and says to his wife, "This year we're going to take $1,000 out of every week's pay and put it aside for the future." (Maybe $1,000 each week is so much you couldn't even imagine having that amount to save from your wages but that's okay, just follow the story and you'll soon see my point.)

He hoped by putting this money into a savings account it would give them a deposit to finally purchase their own home. When I asked him why that didn't happen he told me, "Life keeps getting in the way." Somebody got sick, or he needed a new TV, or his car broke down. You know what it's like — there are always unexpected expenses.

So he asked me, "How do I do it? How can I do it? What am I doing wrong?"

I explained to him that if he wanted to save but didn't make a firm commitment to pay himself first, it wouldn't work. I suggested he do exactly what the Government does.

"What do you mean?" he said.

I explained that every time we get paid, the Government automatically takes out small amounts of money in the form of taxes. I guess they do it that way because they know that if they didn't take it then, it would be really hard to get it out of us any other time. Therefore, Bob should similarly set aside a small, pre-determined portion of his wage each and every time he got paid. He should take at least 10% of his wage and put it into a form of savings account before doing anything else with a cent of his money.

Now Bob had heard this before, but had just left it very late to change old habits and make a start. You can probably guess what Bob thought when he heard this theory many years ago — "How much difference could 10% of my pay packet really make? How much could I really gain from that?"

We've all heard of the power of putting a small amount of money aside to secure our future, so why doesn't everybody do it? We've all heard of the idea that we should pay ourselves first, yet most of us don't. Although many of us make an attempt, we want to put some money aside to save for a rainy day or we want to invest, why doesn't it seem to happen as we plan?

I've spoken to so many people who've told me the same thing; no matter how hard they try, they just never manage to get ahead. They run out of money before the month is over and regardless of how much they earn, they only ever seem to have enough just to pay the bills and scrape by.

The scary thing is, I hear the same story from people making $45,000 a year as I do from people making over $200,000 a year. Just think of my friend Dr Bob, who earns over $300,000 a year and is still constantly broke.

"That can't be possible," you might think, "If I made that kind of money I'd be rich by now."

But would you? Or would you find more to spend it on? The simple fact is that because Dr Bob does what most people do, spending all the money he makes and then some, and he has no investments and nothing set aside for a rainy day, the fight to get ahead has never worked for him.

The basis of success in moving up the Wealth Pyramid is to:

1. Live below your means so that you have money left over and,
2. Convert your earned income into assets which will generate passive income.

Since there is no amount of money you cannot outspend, managing your cashflow is essential to building wealth. As you can see, it's not what you earn that counts. It's what you spend that makes the difference.

Good cash flow management is going to be critical at every stage of your investment journey. It's so important I devote a significant portion of my book *What Every Property Investor Needs to Know About Finance Tax and The Law* to it. I really suggest you get your own copy at www.MichaelYardneyBooks.com.au.

WHAT LEVEL OF INVESTOR ARE YOU?

Now it's time for some home truths... How far up the investment ladder are you? Where do you currently sit in this hierarchy of investors?

Remember, this assessment of your current investment level has nothing to do with your income. You can be a "low income" earner when it comes to your day job, but still be a Level 2 or 3 investor. Likewise, you can be considered "rich" by working income standards yet still be a Level 0 investor, spending every dollar you earn.

What I want you to understand is that the "active" income you make (the pay packet you work for every day) has nothing to do with what level of investor you are and in fact is one of the worst predictors of wealth.

WHERE ARE YOU HEADED?

If you're like me you believe you have a future waiting for you, so what is in store for you financially? If you think about it it's likely to be one of four possible financial outcomes, so please look at the following graphic and work through this exercise with me.

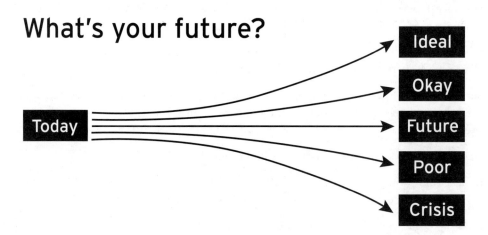

How long until you want to reach financial independence? Ten years? Fifteen years? Maybe longer? If you don't invest wisely you'll run out of money before you run out of life.

Let's face it... it's likely you're facing one of these four possible financial futures:

1. **An ideal future** where your Cash Machine will pour out so much money that you'll have the financial freedom to choose to work or not. You'll also have a sufficiently large asset base to live off the funds that it is generating and there will be a sufficient surplus to keep growing your assets so you'll be able to leave a legacy.

2. **An OK future** where you'll have reasonable income and limited choices and on retirement, you'll and probably have to slowly eat away at your asset base and hope you don't live longer than your income.

3. **A poor future** where you'll still need to keep working.

4. **A crisis future** where you hope there will still be a pension to help you survive.

Looking at the above graphic, which trajectory are you on?

Sometimes it's hard to know because at the beginning of the journey the four paths look much the same, but the further along your wealth creation journey you have travelled the further part the lines become.

Looking at the graphic, which trajectory are you on? Sometimes it's hard to know because at the beginning of the journey the four paths look much the same, but the further along your wealth journey you have travelled, the further apart the lines become.

To reach an ideal future you're going to have to jump lines. Truth is the lines will never be closer together than they are today, which means you must start taking action today. If you are at point 1 in the following graphic it won't take much to move you up a line or two onto a better trajectory and towards a better financial future. However if you're at point 2 it will be much harder to reach the financial future you desire. But that's my aim — that's why I wrote this book for you. And if you already on your way to an ideal future, congratulations. My aim is to get you there faster and safer through the knowledge gained from this book.

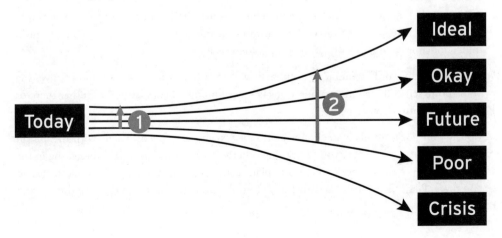

RETIREMENT IS A WORKING-CLASS CONCEPT

"Retirement" will mean something different for everyone. Many investors I speak with don't really want to retire – they don't want to stop working completely.

Most of the investors I mentor want more choices in life and would like to go to work because they enjoy it, not because they have to keep working. Look at most successful business people and entrepreneurs – they're not in a hurry to retire.

So when I use the term "retirement" in this book, I'm using the term loosely, and it's important to remember that more of us are living well into our 90s, so when planning your financial future you need to ensure your money lasts longer than you do.

While most financial planners will suggest you build up a nest egg during your working years and slowly eat away at it during your retirement, my strategy is different. I want you to build a Cash Machine that will fund your future years, your potential medical expenses and possibly aged care and also leave a legacy for future generations.

In other words, you're investing for your future self and not your retirement.

Most people want to wake up in the morning and be able to do what they want to do, when they want to do it, with whoever they want to do it with. The way to achieve that is to have more money. And, of course, the way to have more money is to invest wisely.

But rather than investing, most people use their money to buy more "stuff". On the other hand, successful investors use their money to buy themselves more time by building a Cash Machine.

So as you work through this book I'd like you to think about the following financial goals:

1. When would you like to achieve financial freedom so that you can choose whether you continue working or not? Most people seem to want to achieve this by age 60 which creates the need to fund a further 30 "golden years".

2. How much money will you need in retirement? It's likely to be much more than you think. Most of my clients aim at $100,000 per annum income, but I believe you're going to need much much more than this to enjoy your golden years.

Again I've used the word "retirement", but really what I'm suggesting is you should be investing for your future self and for future generations (your children and grandchildren) rather than for the traditional form of retirement.

Obviously your goals are likely to change along the way, but you need to start with the end in mind. You have to know where you're heading otherwise you won't know if you're going in the wrong direction. Then you need to create a plan using a proven strategy or set of strategies to get you there. Planning is bringing your future into the present so you can do something about it now.

By the way... buying an investment property is not a plan or a strategy. Successful property investing is not an event, it is a process and the property you eventually buy will be the physical manifestation of a whole lot of decisions that you will need to make, and make in the right order, as part of your strategic plan.

That's why my team at Metropole (www.Metropole.com.au) always start by building our clients a Strategic Property Plan. We recognise that attaining wealth doesn't just happen and planning is bringing your future into the present so you can do something about it now.

Your Strategic Property Plan should contain the following components:

1. An asset accumulation strategy

2. A manufacturing capital growth strategy

3. A rental growth strategy

4. An asset protection and tax minimisation strategy

5. A finance strategy including long-term debt reduction and...

6. A living off your property portfolio strategy

I'll explain all these elements further on in this book, but of course your plan shouldn't be set in stone, because things change and it must be reviewed regularly. In fact, I often say you should plan for your plan not to go to plan.

WHY INVEST IN RESIDENTIAL REAL ESTATE?

Property is just one of several investment vehicles that you could choose to try to get from where you are today to where you'd like to be financially in the future. So why choose property?

In my mind if you want to move up the investment ladder and become a Level 4 investor, you need to choose an investment vehicle that will generate wealth producing rates of return. I know of no better option than property based on its reliability and performance advantages compared to the alternatives.

That's why I advocate the purchase of well-located, capital city residential property that will grow in value. Simple, safe and reliable over the long term — as long as you know what you're doing.

BUT INVESTING IS RISKY...

I can understand why some people are worried about getting involved in real estate. They've probably heard about the disasters some of their friends have experienced when they bought property without being prepared or doing the right research and or having a good team around them.

Risk exists everywhere and in everything. In a practical sense, risk is relative and based on your perception of it. The first time your property becomes vacant for a week it can be scary. The tenth time it's no big deal.

But in my mind, the biggest risk a person can take is to do nothing and let inflation erode the spending value of their money. The people who are not "taking risks" are really the risk takers.

Of course, some risks are perceived — education and information can put these into perspective — in other words, risk is a function of your knowledge. Some risks are real and I've developed risk-mitigation strategies to manage these.

What it boils down to is that if you believe that the two main elements of a good investment are:

1. *strong capital growth*, which allows you to grow your net worth, and

2. *secure income*, which increases over time

then residential property must be a key to your wealth-building program. Let's look at the reasons to invest in property in more detail.

1.   More millionaires

If you look at the results others have achieved, you have to say that property makes pretty good investment sense. According to the annually published AFR Rich 200 list, property has consistently been the major source of wealth for Australia's multi-millionaires. And it's the same all over the world. And those that have made their money in businesses other than property generally invest their money in real estate.

If the majority of extraordinarily wealthy people have used real estate profitably, it stands to reason that there's money to be made in property so why not hop on the bandwagon?

2.   Anyone can do it

Property investment is not just for the wealthy. It doesn't really take large sums of money to get involved in real estate. This is because banks will lend you up to 80% or more of the property's value to help you purchase it, which means that most Australians with a steady job and a little capital behind them can afford to buy investment properties.

It has been shown over and over again that careful and intelligent use of real estate can enable ordinary Australians, like you and me, to become property millionaires in about 10 to 15 years.

If you truly intend to become one of the wealthy people in the future, you should probably take a serious look at using property to your advantage.

3.   Security

It's often said that residential real estate offers the security of "bricks and mortar", but let's take a closer look at why I believe it's one of the safest and potentially most profitable investment markets in Australia.

You never hear of houses "going broke" do you? But lots of companies have gone broke. Even companies previously considered blue chip have gone broke. Yet even allowing for the ups and downs of real estate values that we hear about, the underlying trend of property prices in the major capital city residential markets has been steady growth.

You don't have to believe me when I say that residential property is a secure investment. Just ask the banks.

Banks have always recognised residential real estate as an excellent security. The reason they'll lend you up to 80% of the value of your property is that they know property values in our capital cities have never fallen over the long term. In fact, the entire Australian banking system is underpinned by the continual growth of residential property.

Another factor contributing to the security of the residential property market is its size. According to Corelogic there are over 10.8 million dwellings in Australia with an estimated total value of close to $10 trillion dollars. This is by far Australia's largest asset class. It's close to four times larger than the value of all stocks listed on the ASX ($2.9 trillion) and well over twice as large as all the superannuation assets in the country ($3.5 trillion).

But the really special feature of the residential property market is that owner-occupiers (people owning or paying off their homes) own around 67% of these properties. Investors own most of the other 33%.

Yes, home ownership rates have declined over the last few decades as property values soared, and more people have a mortgage against their homes, but it is the Great Australian Dream of home ownership which brings it stability to our property markets.

Think about it... residential property is the only investment market not dominated by investors, and this effectively gives investors a built-in safety net. Even if all the investors were to leave the market at once, it would not totally collapse.

This high level of home ownership is a huge advantage for another reason — the majority of the market in which we invest does not act according to normal investment criteria or motivation. If times get tough the majority of homeowners don't panic and rush to sell as can happen in other sectors such as the share market. In fact half of them no longer have a mortgage against their homes, so they're in it for the long term.

This means that while property prices do fluctuate over time, affected by supply and demand, the large homeowner market will always underpin property values.

4. Income that grows

The rental income you receive from your investment property allows you to borrow and get the benefit of leverage by helping you pay the interest on your mortgage. And over the years the rental income received from property investments has increased at a rate that has outpaced inflation.

Will this continue in the future?

Well, if anything, it's likely that the level of home ownership will slowly continue to decrease in the future. There are a number of reasons for this but, in particular, as property prices keep rising, fewer people are able to afford their dream home. Despite falling interest rates and the first home owners grant, rising HECS debts, high rentals and mounting consumer debt mean that for many first home buyers the great Australian dream of owning a house remains just that — a dream.

Indeed, according to the Australian Housing and Urban Research Institute (www.ahuri.edu.au) up to 40% of Australians are likely to be tenants in the future. That means an entire generation of Australians may never get to own their own home. We know that the government is having difficulty providing public housing, which means there will be plenty of opportunities for landlords to make good money in residential property investment, particularly if you own a property that will be in demand by tenants of the future.

By the way, you'd be excused for thinking that at times when property values go up, rents go up accordingly, but that's usually not the case. In a hot real estate market, when property values increased rapidly rents usually remain stable or may even drop. This is because the prevailing low interest rates allow people who have previously rented to buy properties.

At these times, builders are encouraged to develop new houses and apartments, flooding the market with new stock. Also, investors start buying investments and putting their properties into the rental market. Hence, with more supply of properties and fewer potential tenants, rents usually don't increase during times of increasing property values.

As the cycle moves on and interest rates start to increase, fewer people qualify to buy new properties, and fewer people invest. These factors combine to cause a tighter rental market and rents increase as tenants compete for fewer properties.

It's important to understand these cycles because although rents will increase in the long term, there often will be periods of years when landlords have difficulty increasing their rentals.

By the way... investors get paid in four ways:

1. The cash flow they receive as rent.

2. The capital appreciation of their properties — which I'll explain below.

3. The tax benefits the government offers — there's a whole chapter on this later.

4. A hedge against inflation — just like inflation erodes the value of your savings, it erodes the weight of your mortgage debt balance just the same. Your $400,000 loan today has its "drag" diluted over time as $400,000 won't be worth as much in 10 years' time.

5. Consistent capital growth

Perhaps the most compelling benefit of real estate is its proven performance over time — its capacity to provide those wealth-generating, life-changing rates of return that you need to grow your asset base as a Level 3 investor.

Well located capital city residential property has an unequalled track record of producing high and consistent capital growth. Over the past 45 years the value of the average property in all capital cities has doubled every ten years or so.

To be fair, in the short term the picture is much more uncertain and confusing and at times capital growth stops and even reverses for a time, as we saw in the early 1980s, the early 1990s, in the slump of 2008-09 and is likely to occur in certain locations in the next few years.

But I prefer to assess investment returns over the longer term as this takes into account variables such as property and interest rate cycles and the many political and economic changes that have occurred.

By the way, that's another great thing about property. You can outperform these averages by researching areas of strong capital growth, by buying your properties below market value and then adding value, which increases your capital growth and rental return.

Let's look more carefully at what all this means.

If you decided to buy a median price house in one of our capital cities in mid-2024 this is what you would have paid:

Year	Sydney	Melbourne	Brisbane	Perth	Adelaide	Canberra	Hobart	Darwin
2024	$1,441,957	$937,289	$937,479	$769,961	$811,059	$961,403	$697,770	$584,538

Source: Corelogic

If you had bought that **same property** 18 years earlier, when I wrote the first edition of this book, this is what you would have most likely paid at the beginning of 2006:

Year	Sydney	Melbourne	Brisbane	Perth	Adelaide	Canberra	Hobart	Darwin
2006	$521,000	$358,500	$322,100	$336,000	$278,000	$369,000	$268,500	$295,700

Source: REIA

Interesting isn't it. The value of your property would have gone up significantly over the past 16 years, even though we've experienced the largest property downturn in modern history a few years ago. And these are just averages, meaning that if you had bought a well-located investment grade property, it's likely it would have more than doubled in value. And if you had bought the property back in 1986 here is what you could have paid:

Year	Sydney	Melbourne	Brisbane	Perth	Adelaide	Canberra	Hobart	Darwin
1986	$103,600	$86,200	$59,400	$61,600	$77,000	$87,700		$87,500

Source: REIA

You may have read that some commentators suggest that the strong rate of capital growth over the last few decades have been an aberration and property values can't keep increasing at these levels forever.

Well... a study by AMP Capital shows that after allowing for costs, **since the 1920s residential property has historically returned 11.1% pa** allowing for capital growth and rents. That's a 90-year time period, through recessions, depressions, world wars and almost a century of economic ups and down.

And below leading market commentator Michael Matusik (www.matusik.com.au) charted the growth of "real" (inflation-adjusted) median house prices for 140 years despite all the challenges thrown at them. This shows that all the declines in the property market are temporary, while the long-term in property values is permanent.

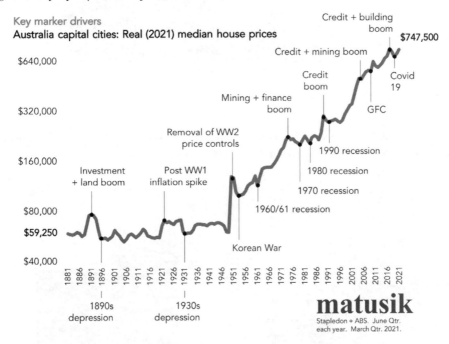

What does this mean for you?

I'll explain it with an example.

If a property increases in value by 7% per annum (averaged out over a number of years) then the value of that property doubles every 10 years. Imagine you owned a property worth $500,000. In 10 years the same property would be worth $1 million and in 20 years it would be worth well over $2 million.

Imagine when you bought your property you had a 20% cent deposit and borrowed the balance ($400,000) from the bank. After 10 years you would still owe the bank $400,000 (assuming you had an interest-only loan) and your net worth would have increased from $100,000 to $600,000. That's an increase in your net worth of six-fold even though the value of the property only doubled.

By the way… the $400,000 you still owe the bank wouldn't be worth as much in 10 years' time, with inflation having eroded away some of its value.

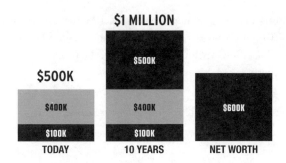

What could happen over the next 10 years?

Your property could once again double in value to $2 million and your net worth would increase to $1.6 million dollars. Your initial $100,000 investment would have increased in value 16-fold while your property only increased in value four-fold. This amazing increase in your net worth is due to the combined effects of compounding and leverage.

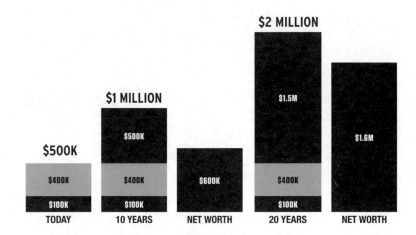

6. You can buy it with someone else's money

The beauty of real estate is that instead of buying it with your own money, you use someone else's money to buy your properties. That is, you put down a small deposit — often 20% — and the bank finances the rest. This is called leverage.

You see, finance is the leveraging tool investors use to get into property, and real estate is the vehicle they use to gain wealth.

The ability to use leverage with real estate significantly increases the amount of profit you can make and, importantly, it allows you to purchase a significantly larger investment than you would otherwise be able to.

Because of its history of security, stable income and proven capital growth, residential real estate is regarded as prime security or collateral for loans, which means that banks may lend you as much as 90% of the value of the residential property.

Banks won't lend this proportion on other types of investments. If you buy shares in the banks themselves, the banks may only lend you 50 to 60% of the value of their own shares, and they only lend 70% or so of the value of commercial properties. This makes residential property an appealing vehicle for building wealth.

Let's use an example to illustrate how this works.

Imagine there are five investors each with $100,000 to invest. Say they all buy an investment that returns 10% capital growth per annum and has a yield (or return) of 4% per annum. I'm using these round numbers more to illustrate a point rather than to suggest this is the type of return you'll get, so bear with me.

Investor #5 doesn't borrow any money at all, but all the others do. Investor #1 borrows 90% of the value of his investment ($900,000) and buys an investment worth $1,000,000. The other investors borrow lesser amounts as shown in the following table.

	Investor #1	Investor #2	Investor #3	Investor #4	Investor #5
Equity (your money)	$100,000	$100,000	$100,000	$100,000	$100,000
Growth + Yield	10% + 4%	10% + 4%	10% + 4%	10% + 4%	10% + 4%
Interest rate	7%	7%	7%	7%	7%
Leverage (LVR)	90%	80%	50%	30%	0%
Debt (other people's money)	$900,000	$400,000	$100,000	$42,857	$0
Value of investment	$1,000,000	$500,000	$200,000	$142, 857	$100,000

At the end of each year all the investors have received their returns and paid their interest as shown in the table below.

	Investor #1	Investor #2	Investor #3	Investor #4	Investor #5
Interest repayment	-$63,000	-$28,000	-$7,000	-$3,000	$0
Yield	$40,000	$20,000	$8,000	$5,714	$4,000
Capital growth	$100,000	$50,000	$20,000	$14,286	$10,000
Net profit	$77,000	$42,000	$21,000	$17,000	$14,000

As you can see, investor #1, who borrowed the most (used the highest leverage), received the highest return. Cash return on the amount invested ($100,000 for each investor) is shown as follows:

	Investor #1	Investor #2	Investor #3	Investor #4	Investor #5
Cash return	77%	42%	21%	17%	14%

Pretty impressive – that's the power of gearing a property portfolio! That's the stuff that makes property millionaires out of ordinary people.

In the technical sense leveraging, or gearing as it is also known, means using a small effort to move a large object, like the gears on your bicycle where you have to pedal a small rotation to turn the large back wheel.

In the financial sense, leveraging is using a small amount of money to control a large asset. You do this by borrowing money and mortgaging your property and using this borrowed money to invest in a larger asset. The more highly you are geared, the more money you have borrowed, and the lower your invested capital is in relation to your borrowings.

As you can see from the examples in the table above, the higher the degree of gearing, the more leverage you achieve and the more your returns are magnified. But be warned, gearing not only magnifies your profits, if the value of your investment falls, your losses are magnified as well.

7. Someone else helps pay your bills

When you own an investment property the tenants go to work to earn a living and then pay you for the use of your property to live in.

Think about that. They get up every day, get dressed and go to work. You don't have to supervise them, pay for their sick leave, holiday pay or superannuation. Yet every month you get a portion of their income in the form of rent. The more of these tenants you employ, the more income you get!

8. You are in control

Property is a great investment because you make all the decisions and have direct control over the returns from your property. If your property is not producing good returns, then you can add value through refurbishment or renovations or adding furniture to make it more desirable to tenants. In other words, you can directly influence your returns by taking an interest in your property and by understanding and then meeting the needs of prospective tenants.

9. Tax benefits

These are so important that I have allocated a whole chapter to this section alone. We'll skip over explaining them here, but we'll examine these in detail later.

10. You can add value

There are hundreds of ways you can add value to your property, which will increase your income and your property's worth. These include little things like giving it a coat of paint or removing the old carpet and polishing the floorboards underneath. Or you could do major renovations or development works.

11. You don't need to sell it

Unlike other investments, when real estate goes up in value you don't need to sell in order to capitalise on that increased value. You simply go back to your bank or finance broker and get your lender to increase your loan.

12. Property is an imperfect market

When I look to invest, I want to invest in an imperfect market. This means that I'm more likely to be able to buy an investment below its true value, or I can sell above its true value. Let me explain this in more detail...

The world of shares is not a completely perfect market, but it's about as perfect as it gets. That's because it is a liquid market where investors are well informed. I can buy stocks at the same price as anybody else can. In general, the overall marketplace has the same information as I have, because for the most part the information is equal. This shared knowledge creates a more "perfect" market.

On the other hand, real estate is what I would call an imperfect market. I know many people who have bought properties at five or even 10% below the real market value. If property was a perfect, liquid marketplace, you would not be able to buy a property considerably below its intrinsic value. I can do this every time, and so could you because information, contacts and expertise help you get an insider's edge in an imperfect market.

13. You can insure against risks

Another factor that adds to the security of residential property as an investment is that you can insure it against most risks. You can insure the building against fire or damage and you can insure yourself against the tenant leaving and breaking a lease.

14. Most forgiving

Even if you bought the worst house at the worst possible time, the chances are good that it would still go up in value over the next few years. History has proven that real estate is possibly the most forgiving investment asset over time. If you are prepared to hold property over a number of years, it's bound to rise in value.

Mind you, I'm not advocating wasting time, money and effort buying not so good properties at the wrong time in the cycle. As your mentor I would prefer you learned how to choose wisely in the first place. If you do this, then even if you are a Beginner Investor, you can buy property and be comfortable that you won't see the value of your asset decline over the medium term.

There's really no other asset class quite like property!

WHAT IS THE RIGHT INVESTMENT AT THIS STAGE OF THE ECONOMIC CYCLE?

One thing is certain: there is no such thing as a perfect investment. If somebody tells you they have found "*the perfect* investment" be very sceptical and ask lots of question, because chances are they're trying to sell you something you just shouldn't buy.

The things I look for are:

1. Liquidity (ability to take my money out by either selling or borrowing against my investment)

2. Easy management

3. Strong and stable rates of capital appreciation

4. Steady cash flow

5. A hedge against inflation, and

6. Good tax benefits.

When you look at the major categories of investments, you will recognise that not many fit the bill when it comes to all six of these criteria. The new era of money we are entering means that to be a successful investor you have to invest in assets that are both powerful and stable.

By **powerful**, I mean that your investments will need to act as a hedge against inflation and have the ability to grow at wealth producing rates, which means you're going to have to be able to borrow against them and use the power of leverage.

By **stability**, I mean your investment should grow in value steadily and surely, without major fluctuations in value.

Many investments are powerful and many are stable, but only a few are both. Well-located residential real estate is one of the few investment vehicles that have both power and stability in spades.

Now this doesn't mean property investment is perfect, because property is not as liquid as some other investments. It can take months to get cash out of your property portfolio, by either selling up or borrowing against it. While some might see this as a deterrent, I would argue that a relative lack of liquidity is one of the virtues of property as an investment vehicle. The only way for an investment to achieve liquidity is to relinquish some of its stability. If it is liquid (easily sold like shares) it is more likely to have wide, more volatile fluctuations in value.

WHAT ARE THE INVESTMENT ALTERNATIVES?

The stock market is another potentially powerful investment vehicle because you can borrow against the shares you own. But in order to achieve the liquidity the stock market provides, you give up some stability. Share prices are volatile and fluctuate up and down and then down and up again. Sure you can get your money out quickly, but you also run a bigger risk of making a loss.

What about putting money into a savings account? This type of investment is very liquid and pretty stable, but it won't give you a wealth producing rate of return.

If I had the choice (and I do), I'll take stability (lack of big swings in price) over liquidity every time.

I would also avoid **"When-to"** investments, the type where you have to know when to buy and when to sell. Timing is crucial with these investments: if you buy low and sell high, you do well. If you get your timing wrong though, your money can be wiped out. Shares, commodities and futures tend to be "When-to" investments.

I would rather put my money into a **"How-to"** investment such as real estate, which increases steadily in value and doesn't have the wild variations in price yet is still powerful enough to generate wealth-producing rates of return through the benefits of leverage.

While timing is still important in "How-to" investments, it's nowhere near as important as how you buy them and how you add value. "How-to" investments are rarely liquid but produce real wealth. Most "When-to" investment vehicles (like the stock market) produce only a handful of large winners (the millionaires), but there tends to be millions of losers. On the other hand, real estate produces millions of wealthy people and only a handful of losers.

Currently, as our property markets enter the beginning of a new property cycle, strategic property investors have an amazing opportunity to get set for the profits this cycle will deliver. The chance to tale advantage of timing such as this only occurs once every decade or so.

It should be fairly obvious by now that I believe income producing residential property is the best option for your Cash Machine. While it's really hard to outperform the long-term averages in the share market (that's why many managed funds try to just track the averages), it's really very easy to outperform the averages when investing in property. You do this by buying well and buying the right type of property, one in a high capital growth area and one to which you can add value.

I've found it's easier to become an expert in property — there are fewer unknowns than with shares. While you might like to think that you can master the world of shares, online trading and corporate legalities and structures, the fact is that it is much easier to gain a sound comprehension of property investment than it is of shares. Sure it will require some learning to become an expert in property, but this is far less daunting for the Beginner Investor than trying to comprehend how the corporate world or the share market works.

HOW LEVERAGE CAN MAKE MOLEHILLS INTO MOUNTAINS!

As you'll recall, we briefly discussed the importance of leverage in the previous chapter, but now we're going to walk through a real-life example and study the specifics of how this concept is a key to building a multi-million dollar property portfolio.

Leverage is often called gearing and, of course, gears are mechanical cogs that interlock with each other and can be set up so that tiny movements in a small cog cause big rotations in larger cogs.

OK, this is starting to sound like a car manual, what does it have to do with properties?

The same effect occurs when you put down a small amount of your money as a deposit and borrow a large amount of money to purchase real estate. In effect you have control of the whole property and entitlement to capital gains that affect the whole, whilst only having partial equity and a large mortgage.

Let's say you bought a property for $500,000 by using $100,000 of your money (your equity) and borrowed the rest from a bank. If the property increased in value by 10% over the next few years this would give you $50,000 in profits. This translates to a 50% profit on your invested money of $100,000 because of the leverage in your investment. You've put down $100,000 and the bank has contributed the rest, but they don't share in the capital growth.

As you can see, leverage can effectively turn molehill gains into mountains of money!

Using the dual concepts of leveraging and pyramiding (or compounding), I am going to show you how to build a multi-million dollar property portfolio. And you can achieve this in your spare time, because other than educating yourself, doing some active research, property hunting and negotiation on the weekends, values will grow all by themselves and you can build it one property at a time.

Effectively this is the blueprint for how you can increase your financial worth by millions of dollars over the next 10 to 15 years using other people's money and then borrowing again using the increasing equity of your investment properties.

To understand the concept of pyramiding you must remember that if you select the right investment property, and I will explain how to do this later in this book, your property should double in value every ten years or so. Pyramiding is borrowing against the increasing value of your properties and using this money to buy more properties.

Don't be discouraged if you look at your current assets and have only $50,000, $60,000 or $70,000. Don't say to yourself: "There is no way this small amount of money can be pyramided into a multi-million-dollar property portfolio." Believe me, it can. But you have to take just one step at a time.

It was a bit like when I started writing this book. I knew I wanted to give investors the benefit of the ideas and techniques I had accumulated over 40 years in property but the thought of trying to combine all this information into a 300-page book was overwhelming. I had to take it one step at a time, one page at a time, then one chapter at a time.

This gets us back to the theory of pyramiding – don't worry about reaching your goal in 10, 15 or 20 years' time. It will happen, but for the moment just concentrate on today.

Here's a good story to illustrate how time and pyramiding can work wonders:

A wealthy man hired a young boy to do some work for him for a 30-day period. He offered him $30 a day. The boy said, "I will make it easier for you – I'll work for a cent on the first day, on the second day my pay is doubled to two cents, the third day it is double again to four cents. Pay me on the same basis for 30 days, doubling my previous day's pay each day".

The wealthy man thought this sounded like a bargain and hired the boy, so let's have a look at how much he made working this job:

The power of compounding					
Day	Amount	Day	Amount	Day	Amount
1	$0.01	11	$10.24	21	$10,485.76
2	$0.02	12	$20.48	22	$20,971.52
3	$0.04	13	$40.96	23	$41,943.04
4	$0.08	14	$81.92	24	$83,886.08
5	$0.16	15	$163.84	25	$167,772.16
6	$0.32	16	$327.68	26	$335,544.32
7	$0.64	17	$655.36	27	$671,088.64
8	$1.28	18	$1,310.72	28	$1,342,177.28
9	$2.56	19	$2,621.44	29	$2,684,354.56
10	$5.12	20	$5,242.88	30	$5,368,709.12

I'm sure you will agree that while he got paid very little in the first few days, the last few days were quite profitable (to say the least). Pyramiding uses the power of *compounding* and it began with only one cent. Compounding is the act of reinvesting your returns — remember how I explained reinvesting for compound growth as the 3rd of the 4 fundamental pillars of wealth creation?

So if you have one dollar and it doubles in value you have then made another dollar. Now you have two dollars and if once again you double its value your profit is four dollars. Double it again and you have eight dollars. As you can see, even though you are only still getting the same investment return your profits get bigger and bigger.

This is an example of money making money and exactly the same thing will happen with your real estate investments. Of course you won't be able to double your equity on a daily basis, or even on a yearly basis, but you will also start a lot further into the above chart with your initial investments.

Rather than look at the dollars you intend to accumulate, look at the number of times you must double your initial investment in order to end up with the desired amount in the future.

THE ADVANTAGE OF REAL ESTATE

One of the great advantages of real estate is by using leverage (other people's money) you accelerate this process of pyramiding

You may begin with $100,000, but you could use this to purchase a property valued at $500,000. If, over the next ten years, your $500,000 property doubles in value to $1,000,000 and your mortgage remains the same you haven't really doubled your equity, have you? It's increased from $100,000 to $600,000! Leverage and time multiply the effect of compounding.

I'm living proof that leverage really works, and to help you see that these are not just pie-in-the-sky figures we're going to walk through a real-life case study.

LET'S GET REAL

Let's begin with a young couple, we'll call them Liz and Gavin, who today are well on the way to achieving their goal of owning a multi-million dollar property portfolio. Remember this could be you!

Liz and Gavin bought a house for $250,000 seven years ago and it has now doubled in value to $500,000 and over the years they have paid down their mortgage to $150,000.

They now want to use the equity in their home to buy an investment property. They'll access their equity by refinancing their home loan and 'draw down' some of this equity to use as a deposit on their new investment property purchase.

As their house is worth $500,000 most banks will advance them a loan of $400,000, being 80% of their property's value. They already have a $150,000 mortgage, so they would take out a separate loan – an investment loan – for an additional $250,000.

There are many loan products on the market but they may choose to use a "Line of Credit", which is a bit like having a big credit card. They have the capacity to borrow up to its limit, in this case $250,000, if they want to.

Just like a credit card, they would only pay interest on any money they borrow on their loan, but not on the un-borrowed limit. Unlike a credit card though, they don't have to find money for their interest payments because any interest due each month can come out of their unused credit limit.

At the end of the month, they pay their interest bill by increasing their loan amount and the next month they pay interest on the new larger loan amount. This means they don't need to find any spare cash to pay the interest until they reach their credit limit.

So what do Liz and Gavin decide to do with their new Line of Credit?

They've read this book and learned the benefit of borrowing other people's money to buy real estate, so they go out and buy an investment property worth $500,000.

They could use $100,000 from their line of credit as a 20% deposit for their new investment and their mortgage broker would arrange for a loan for the balance of 80% of the funds needed to buy their new property. They would probably need an extra $30,000 or so from their loan facility for stamp duty, legal and other acquisition costs. So effectively they are borrowing 105% of the purchase price of their new investment property.

When you add their new acquisition to their present property, they now own real estate worth $1 million.

INSIDER TIP

It's not really difficult to become a property millionaire in Australia. You just have to buy the right property and wait.

Since they now own two well located capital city properties which in all likelihood will, on average, increase in value by around 8% per annum, it is possible that their two properties will have a capital gain of about $80,000 in the first year and this will compound each year.

If they are conservative investors and wait another nine years before investing again, the worth of their real estate (increasing in value at the rate of 8% per annum), would be around $2 million.

Let's assume they took out interest-only loans, which means they only pay the bank interest and don't decrease the amount of their mortgage (the principal). At the end of this nine-year period their borrowings would still be:

Original mortgage on home:	$150,000
Deposit from line of credit:	$100,000
Purchase costs from line of credit:	$30,000
Mortgage on investment:	$400,000
Total borrowings:	**$680,000**

Considering they now own $2 million worth of property, they have grown their equity to $1,320,000 at the end of the nine-year period.

Consider these figures carefully. This couple would now be property millionaires and it all started 14 years ago when they acquired their family home, probably with a deposit of $50,000.

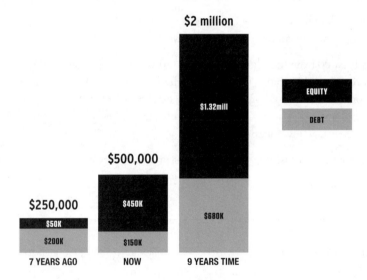

INSIDER TIP

When you grow your investment property portfolio by pyramiding, you don't need to find another deposit. You just use the increasing equity in your properties to borrow the funds for further investments.

Yes, "*But how are they going to pay their interest bills?*" you ask. "*What about the cash flow shortfall?*"

The great thing about their investment property is that paying the interest on this loan will be much easier than paying the interest on their original home loan, because the tenant will pay a large portion of it as rent. Our couple will also have the benefits of the tax savings available to property investors which I'll explain in a subsequent chapter.

Despite this, Liz and Gavin will most likely be in a position of negative cash flow on their property (their expenses will be higher than their income), at least for the first few years until the rent increases sufficiently to cover all of the interest payments and outgoings.

Remember, in essence they have borrowed 105% of the funds to purchase this investment property – they borrowed the deposit (against their home), the balance of the purchase price and all the acquisition costs. After tax, in this low interest rate environment, they're lucky to be out of pocket around $100 a week, which amounts to $5-6,000 a year. How are they going to afford this on their salaries?

THERE IS A REALLY SIMPLE ANSWER

Remember Liz and Gavin obtained a line of credit giving them access to $250,000 using their home as security?

So far they have used $100,000 of this as a deposit and a further $30,000 on the acquisition costs for their investment property. In other words, they still have a further $120,000 available to borrow for whatever purpose they desire.

If they allocated this $120,000 as a financial buffer to pay for any unexpected expenses as well as for their interest and holding cost shortfall they have bought themselves well over a decade's worth of time, haven't they? Remember they don't pay interest on any part of the loan until they "drawn down" the funds, so this safety net costs them nothing until they use it, but gives them security and peace of mind.

INSIDER TIP

Debt is a risk management tool used by the wealthy. Having debt is not risky, not being able to have more is. Set up a line of credit before you need it and have a "big credit card" set aside for a rainy day.

Now don't get too hung up on the details at this point. It's the big picture that's important at the moment.

Obviously their buffer may last less than a decade because interest rates may rise, or it could last longer as their rents will increase. Either way, I have shown you what I set out to explain – a way to set up your property portfolio with a sound financial strategy so that your investment could pay for itself, without relying on your income to service the debt.

CAPITALISING INTEREST

What I have just explained is called capitalising interest payments.

Liz and Gavin have used debt to pay their interest. In essence, they're borrowing money to pay their interest. This is like increasing the debt on your credit card to pay the monthly credit card interest bill.

Now this is a common business principle. Imagine you were planning to buy the coffee shop down the road. You'd ask the bank for money for the goodwill and a further amount for the stock and equipment and you'd also get a loan for working capital, knowing that it would be a few years before your new business venture would be profitable.

Of course Liz and Gavin's debt increases as they capitalise their interest payments, because instead of paying the interest on their debt, they are adding it onto their debt; in effect, they are borrowing more to fund the interest payment.

The following diagram shows how debt increases when capitalising interest. Notice that the interest compounds, because you are being charged interest on the interest that you borrow. For this type of finance strategy to work, obviously the value of their property must grow faster than their debt – but that's why correct property selection is so critical.

But as I said, in today's tighter bank lending environment, Liz and Gavin will still need secure personal incomes to prove they can service their loans.

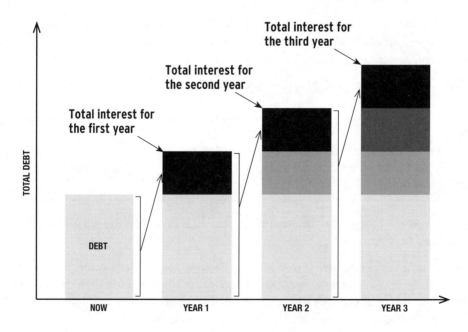

We know that properties increase in value over time, but due to the nature of the property cycle there are some years where the value doesn't increase at all and other years where the value increases significantly.

Having well over a decade of buffer should be more than enough for the investment in their home to double in value, allowing Liz and Gavin to refinance their debt and start the whole process again.

DO THEY REALLY NEED TO WAIT 10 YEARS?

Clearly the answer is no.

So how long do they need to wait until they can access the equity of their properties and buy another investment? Well that depends.

If they have secure jobs and lots of disposable income, they really don't need to buy themselves the security of ten year buffer. On the other hand, if Liz was planning to give up her job and have a baby, thereby decreasing their disposable income, or if they were concerned that interest rates were on the rise, or they wanted the certainty that they could live through a complete property cycle and not need to refinance, maybe this level of financial buffer would be appropriate.

Obviously, what they should not do is spend the available money in their Line of Credit on a holiday, a new car or gamble it on the latest Internet marketing business (and boy have we seen clients lose money on those). By doing this, they would have spent their "time buffer", which means the only method of servicing their debt would be from their salary. This is how some people fall into the debt trap.

UNDERSTANDING FINANCIAL BUFFERS

Now, let's look more closely at how this strategy works and how to use the equity in your property portfolio as a financial buffer to cover its holding costs.

Examining the following table, you'll see that we've used the example of Liz and Gavin's first investment property over a 10-year period. We've assumed their property increases in value by 8% each year (they've read this book and can outperform the averages a little) and that the interest rate on their mortgage remains constant at 5% over the 10 years.

To be fair neither of these will happen; they are just averages and serve the purpose of this exercise. Once again, rather than getting caught up in the detail, our aim is for you to understand the big picture concept first.

Let's look at each column in the table to make sure you understand this important concept.

Year: This is the number of years since the property was purchased.

Property Value: The property's value at the beginning of the year, having increased in value by 8%.

Debt: The total debt at the start of each year, including the debt used to pay their holding costs and compounding interest.

Equity: The property value less the debt.

Holding Cost: This is the cost of owning or holding on to the property, based on 2% of the property's value. This will be Liz and Gavin's cash flow shortfall, being the excess of the interest on their mortgage plus the property's running costs after taking into account the rent.

Interest on Holding Cost: Their annual interest bill for the extra money they borrow from their buffer to service their debts.

Increase in Debt: This is the extra borrowings used for the holding costs plus the capitalised interest on this loan (they take this from their buffer).

Year	Property Value	Debt	Equity	Holding Cost 2%	Interest on Holding Cost	Increase in Debt
Now	500,000	400,000	100,000	11,000	550	11,550
1	540,000	411,550	128,450	11,880	594	12,474
2	583,200	424,024	159,176	12,830	642	13,472
3	629,856	437,496	192,360	13,857	693	14,550
4	680,244	452,046	228,199	14,965	748	15,714
5	734,664	467,759	266,905	16,163	808	16,971
6	793,437	484,730	308,707	17,456	873	18,328
7	856,912	503,058	353,854	18,852	943	19,795
8	925,465	522,853	402,612	20,360	1,018	21,378
9	999,502	544,231	455,271	21,989	1,099	23,089
10	$1,079,462	$567,320	$512,143			
			Total	$159,352	$7,968	$167,320

NOW HERE'S THE IMPORTANT POINT

Despite their debt increasing over the 10 years because they've borrowed the cash flow shortfall each year, then paid interest on this extra borrowing, and in subsequent years paid interest on their interest; Liz and Gavin's equity (*what they own*) has increased much more than their debt (*what they owe*).

Their debt has increased by more than $167,320 over the 10 years, yet their equity has increased by almost $580,000 (their investment property will be worth $1,080,000 with a loan of $512,000).

Best of all, they have achieved this without using any personal income; in other words their property was funding itself. This gives them a safety net because they don't have to rely on their salaries to pay for the holding costs of their property.

This is the way sophisticated investors not only build their property portfolios, but also "buy time" to secure their property investment businesses. And remember the value of their home was also likely to have doubled over this period.

Now I know some readers will be a little concerned about the accuracy of the details in this model. What if the property doesn't increase in value by 8% each year? What if interest rates skyrocket? What if the property is vacant or needs repairs? What if, what if, what if?

Again, in today's more challenging finance climate of responsible lending, Liz and Gavin will have to prove they can service their loans to the bank. However, what I'm suggesting is that you don't focus on the details right now, instead make sure that you understand the big picture.

Once you understand the power of using financial buffers to buy yourself time, and your equity to self-fund your property portfolio, you will have discovered an advanced strategy that very few property investors ever learn. There will be plenty of time for you to work out the details that suit your own personal and financial circumstances and risk profile as you go.

As you work through this book you'll come to realise that property investment is a game of finance with some houses thrown in the middle so I'm going to repeat myself to ensure you understand these concepts.

Liz and Gavin have set up a loan facility against their existing properties for more than they need to enable them to purchase their second investment property. They have enough money to pay for a 20% deposit, all the purchase costs and they have money set aside in a "sinking fund" to cover their interest shortfall for a number of years until the rental income on their property increases so that it becomes cash flow neutral or cash flow positive.

Remember, they don't pay interest on this part of the loan until they "draw down" the funds so having this "safety net" doesn't come at an excessive cost.

INSIDER TIP

Debt can be the same as capital. Debt on their first two properties can be used as capital or a deposit for their third property.

As they build their Cash Machine of investment properties Liz and Gavin keep their jobs in order to service their loans and they invest in property in their spare time. They also educate themselves, listen to Podcasts and use their conservative strategies to buy further investment properties.

They only buy the next property when they have sufficient equity in their existing properties to borrow 100% of the cost of the new property plus money set aside to cover their interest and expenses shortfall for the next five years.

How many properties can they end up buying? Well that depends on the equity they achieve from capital growth and their ability to service their loans, but many strategic investors I've come across have amassed multi-million dollar property portfolios of six or seven properties.

The key here is that strategic investors use debt as a risk management tool. They recognise that having debt is not risky, not being able to have more is. So they set up financial buffers to buy themselves time to ride the ups and downs of the property market and the economic cycle. Having a financial buffer in place to handle unforeseen changes, a rainy day or just to cover your interest rate shortfall buys you time to work through the ups and downs of the property cycle.

Establishing a line of credit or an offset account linked to your loan is one of the best ways to maintain a cash buffer, as it has the added benefit of helping to reduce the amount of interest applied to your loan.

It's like having a big credit card sitting in your drawer.

DO YOU HAVE THE COURAGE TO BE RICH?

The first book I remember buying about real estate and getting rich was called *The Courage to be Rich* by Mark Haroldson. When I discovered it I didn't really understand the meaning of the title, because I knew I was poor and wanted to be rich and didn't think I needed any courage to do so. I just knew what I wanted.

Many years later I came to fully appreciate what the author was getting at, which is why I've never forgotten his book.

To be rich means you have to be different from the rest, and that takes courage. Look at it this way — if you do what everybody else does, you can expect to get the same results that everybody else gets. At best you can be average.

Of 100 people who start equal at birth and all have similar dreams, goals and aspirations, statistics show that at the age of 65, one will be rich, four financially independent, five will still be working and 54 will be broke. And the gap between the rich and the poor in this world is only getting bigger.

So if they all start out the same, why do so many fail?

George Bernard Shaw once said, "People are always blaming their circumstances for what they are. I don't believe in circumstance. The people who get on in this world are the people who get up and look for circumstances they want; if they can't find them they make them".

Unfortunately most of us live in our comfort zones, but the worst part of that is, we do the same as everybody else, and therefore we get the same results as everybody else.

INSIDER TIP
To be successful, find out what 95% of people are doing and do something different!

To be truly successful find out what the 5% of people who are successful are doing and follow their lead.

Do you really want to be average? That's not what this book is about.

You know the definition of average, don't you? It's to be *"bottom of the top and top of the bottom"*. That's not what you want for yourself is it?

THE SINGLE GREATEST TRAIT OF SUCCESSFUL INVESTORS

If you cornered me and asked me to come up with one single trait that I have found in common amongst the successful investors I've come across... what would that be?

Obviously, there are a number of important factors underpinning success, but after recently speaking with Robert I've come to the conclusion that there really is one critical attribute that stands above virtually everything else when it comes to creating success in your investing, in wealth creation and in fact in all areas of your life.

You see... Robert came up to me after attending one of my seminars and thanked me. He said he learned a lot and was inspired.

He then shared with me that he'd been to almost all of the seminars that I'd conducted in Sydney over the past 10 years. When I asked him how many properties he owned he told me he was still getting ready to buy his first investment. He was waiting for everything to be "*just right*".

I couldn't help but explain he'd be much wealthier today if he had bought almost any property when he first considered investing 10 years ago, even if he had made a terrible mistake in his property selection. Sydney property values had virtually doubled in the previous seven years!

So what is this characteristic all successful investors share?

It's that they make decisions and take appropriate action.

In his classic book *Think and Grow Rich*, Napoleon Hill outlined 17 principles that he found to be responsible for the success of the world's top business leaders of his day. Way back in the 1930s Hill discovered that all of the most successful people had the habit of making swift and committed decisions.

This principle, which is just as relevant today as it was almost a century ago, holds the key to determining the level of success you will achieve.

I've found successful investors gather the necessary information quickly, make an informed decision and then take appropriate action. They are able to see the big picture and don't get caught up in the detail.

And even when they don't have all the information they need, they believe it is better to make a decision with some information, than to not make a decision at all. They then take action and gather the balance of the information as they move on.

Of course, they don't always make the right choices. However, over time, the number of correct decisions they make far outweigh the incorrect ones and this propel them to investment success.

It should come as no surprise that others who procrastinate and avoid taking action rarely achieve much success in their lives.

I guess you could say that great investing is about taking action, while average investing is about reacting to the media, the marketplace and the world in general.

So why is it that taking action is so daunting for many people?

One of the big things that hold back so many potential investors is fear, especially fear of making an incorrect decision or fear of failure.

The problem is that as human beings we like to feel in control. We like to have choices. However, when you take action you've made a commitment towards one choice, thereby eliminating a number of other choices that you could have made. So subconsciously we procrastinate, thinking it has left us with options.

The trouble is, we've really made a decision to not make a decision. And that decision has its own consequences.

Do you find it easy to make decisions? Currently the world is riddled with uncertainty and unpredictability. This makes it difficult to be sure of what actions we should take and leads to procrastination.

However, if your life isn't where you want it to be right now, it's likely that you are not making the right decisions or taking the appropriate actions to move forward.

HOW DO SUCCESSFUL INVESTORS MANAGE TO TAKE DECISIVE ACTION?

The fact is that successful investors are faced with just as much uncertainty in their lives as the rest of us, however they manage to take action because they have focus. They have clarity about where they want to be.

Successful investors follow a plan. They have a property strategy, a finance strategy and a tax and asset protection strategy, a rental growth strategy and a living off their property investment strategy.

Every time they have to make an investment decision, they evaluate their actions and the potential consequences in light of their plan and their goals. If the action will move them closer to their goals, they go for it. This makes their investing more predictable, their decisions less emotional and their results more consistent.

It was no coincidence that when I became clear in my goals I began associating with other successful investors who were already very clear in every aspect of their property investing. I don't know who said it... but "to become successful hang around successful people".

The interesting thing is that when you start associating with successful people, you begin to change without knowing it — you act, talk, think and dress like them. You begin to see things in a positive new way.

SIX MORE MASTER SKILLS OF SUCCESSFUL PROPERTY INVESTORS

Apart from the ability to take decisive action I've found that successful investors have mastered six other skills that make it easier and faster for them to achieve financial prosperity. Let's examine these:

1. Creating and controlling capital

Successful investors understand the importance of building a substantial asset base, while the majority of investors chase cash flow. Successful investors know how to create and add value to their properties using techniques like renovations and development. They also add value through their expertise or through smart negotiations and buying well. And it's no coincidence that they control as big an asset base as they safely can by leveraging and borrowing against appreciating assets.

2. Transforming capital into passive residual income

Successful investors grow money trees and recognise that cash flow is the fruit. This means that once they have built a substantial asset base, they transition into the cash flow stage of their investment life by lowering their loan to value ratios and then borrowing against and living off their equity.

Strategic investors follow these four rules of capital.

1. *They concentrate it* — rather than diversifying, they focus their energy and efforts on their area of expertise.

2. *They don't risk it* — once they've built a substantial capital base the wealthy invest rather than speculate. They are prepared to forgo a "potential" future profit so as to not risk their current assets.

3. *They protect it* — by owning their assets in the correct structures to safeguard their capital and by having financial buffers in place.

4. *They value it* — professional investors don't eat away their capital. Instead they convert their capital into cash flow and live off the fruits of their money tree.

3. They are financially fluent

Smart investors recognise it's not how much money they make that matters, it's how hard their money works for them and how much they keep that counts. So they learn how the finance, tax and legal systems work and how they favour investors who treat their properties like a business.

They understand the language of accounting and know how to read balance sheets and income statements, understand how to calculate the Internal Rate of Return on their investments and how to assess their different investment options.

4. They understand the importance of building a great team around them

Savvy investors know they can't do it alone; so they recruit, direct and refine a team of finance, tax, legal and property professionals. They know that if they're the smartest person in their team they're in trouble.

As CEO of their property investment business, the wealthy don't abdicate control of their money to others. Instead they set up systems to evaluate the performance of their investments and their advisers.

5. They understand the true importance of money

They recognise that to be truly prosperous, they need a lot more than money – the time to enjoy it, the relationships to share it with, the sense of purpose and passion with which to direct it. And they understand the importance of contribution to the community, which brings meaning to their lives.

On the other hand, I've found that most people who don't have money spend so much time struggling to make money that they lose out on the quality of life they deserve. It's only when you have enough money that you can go about creating real wealth.

6. They have the capacity for growth

Great investors are usually voracious learners. They know the fastest way to wealth is through consistently investing in their personal development. They read books, listen to Podcasts and cultivate relationships with mentors who can advise and guide them. They also network with other positive wealth builders with whom they can mastermind and bounce ideas off. It is no surprise that the more they grow, the more their wealth grows.

SUCCESS IS A CHOICE

The reason I'm droning on about all this is because over the years I've realised the most important factor in success in property investing (as it is in about everything else in life) is **mindset** – the way you think.

Sure, knowledge is important, as is having a proven property investment system and the right network of people around you, but 80% or more of successful property investing is mindset.

I have found that income seldom will exceed your own personal development. Once in a while income takes a lucky jump, but unless you grow beyond where it is, your income will go back to where you are.

I genuinely believe that if you took all the money in the world and divided it among everyone equally; it would soon be back in the same pockets.

But here's the good news: You can have more than you've got because you can become more than you are.

It's no coincidence that the other side of the coin reads: Unless you change how you are, you will always have what you've got. In order to have more, you need to become more.

I see many beginner investors complain about the market, life, the banks and how hard it all is.

The point I'm trying to make is that unless YOU change, IT won't change. Amazingly, however, when we throw out our blame list and start becoming more ourselves — the difference is everything else will begin to change around us.

This means that it doesn't really matter where you are today, you can be a success at whatever you want as long as you have a purpose in life and a plan to get there. Decide in how many years you want to be financially independent, be realistic and set milestones along the way.

If you really want to become financially independent you need to set goals, have a strategy to achieve them and then take action.

INSIDER TIP

To be successful, you need goals and to have a plan of where you are going. If you don't, how will you know when you get there?

IF YOU CAN SEE WHERE YOU'RE GOING, YOU CAN GET THERE

Many years ago I went to a seminar run by Anthony Robbins, highly regarded as the world's peak performance coach. I knew that part of the seminar involved a fire walk, where the participants took off their shoes and walked three meters across smouldering red-hot coals.

I had no intention of doing the fire walk (I'm not stupid!) I was going to leave this up to the rest of the fanatics. I thought I'd just learn the lessons I could learn on the night and walk away a little smarter.

In the end I did the fire walk, and I'm pleased and proud that I did.

What that evening showed me was that if you focus on the burning hot coals under your feet, all you get is pain. But if you can focus on the cool grass ahead, with positive thoughts in your mind, you can get through anything.

It also reinforced in me how important a positive mental attitude is. That is, if you put your mind to anything, you can achieve it provided you have a specific goal in mind.

If you think of the negatives, you will achieve those too, because you will be drawn towards achieving whatever you are focused on.

What are you going to be focused on? What is your idea of success?

This book is about property, but as we've already discussed, it's really about finding the courage to act and to develop a long-term plan that will allow you to achieve all your goals.

Before you can take a journey you need to know where you want to go, so take the time to think about your aims and to set some clear objectives. In the following sections we're going to start talking about detailed strategies and choices available to investors, so it's important that you have a clear idea of your objectives before you start so you can process and interpret our discussions.

Take the time to create some goals now and remember to put your goal list where you can see it and readily review your goals.

What kind of a life do you want to create? It's your choice!

PART II

WHAT'S AHEAD FOR PROPERTY?

IT IS NOT BECAUSE THINGS ARE DIFFICULT THAT
WE DO NOT DARE, IT IS BECAUSE WE DO NOT
DARE THAT THINGS ARE DIFFICULT.
— *SENECA (ROMAN PHILOSOPHER)*

WHY OUR PROPERTY MARKETS ARE GUARANTEED TO KEEP GROWING

While in the short term many factors like the availability of finance, interest rates, supply and demand and market confidence affect property prices, in the long term prices are really driven by two main factors:

1. **Household formation** – in other words the demand for more dwellings. But this alone isn't enough. It must be accompanied by...

2. **Increasing wealth** – the ability to pay more for property.

In other words, demographics – how many of us there are, how much we earn, how we want to live, where we live and what we can afford will remain one of the biggest drivers of our property markets in the future.

But, as always, the performance of our various property submarkets will be fragmented. As more people choose to live close to high paying employment opportunities, which will in general be in the service sector, demand for housing in inner and middle ring suburbs of our big capital cities will increase, placing pressure on property prices in these locations.

And this will continue to be so particularly for Melbourne and Sydney, our two super star cities, and Brisbane – our New World city.

WHAT'S HAPPENING TO AUSTRALIA'S POPULATION?

In mid-2024, Australia's population was estimated to have topped 27.3 million people.

The Australian Bureau of Statistics has projected that we have:

- one birth every one minute and 42 seconds
- one death every two minutes and 52 seconds
- one person arriving to live in Australia every 42 seconds,
- one Australian resident leaving Australia to live overseas every two minutes and 37 seconds, leading to...
- an overall total population increase of one person every 47 seconds.

So by the time you've finished reading this chapter, Australia's population will hold have increased by another three or four people.

While Sydney is Australia's largest city, and Melbourne's population fell during the COVID-19 lockdowns, Melbourne is tipped to overtake Sydney to become Australia's biggest city, according to the federal government's Centre for Population projections.

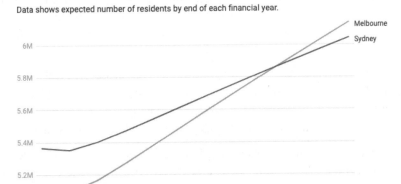

Forecast population change in Melbourne and Sydney

Data shows expected number of residents by end of each financial year.

Chart: ABC News · Source: Centre for Population, 2021 · Get the data · Created with Datawrapper

THE GROWTH OF SOUTH EAST QUEENSLAND

Queensland's status as Australia's population magnet has been strengthened by the COVID-19 pandemic, with annual net interstate migration for the Sunshine State during 2021 at its highest level in almost 20 years.

And it's likely that Queensland's job creation and strong economy, underpinned by infrastructure spending for the 2032 Olympics, will continue to be a lure for interstate and overseas migrants.

There is no doubt Brisbane, and in fact most of South East Queensland, is an amazing place to live, it's got it all — the lifestyle, the weather, the list goes on. But what has really changed over the last few years is more and more jobs are being created in the Sunshine State and this creates opportunity with many more people willing to make the move to live there.

WHAT'S AHEAD FOR PROPERTY OVER THE NEXT FEW DECADES?

Being a safe, stable, resources-rich and attractive destination, there's no shortage of people wanting to migrate Down Under, and with our borders once again open forecasters expect net overseas migration into Australia to remain very strong over the coming decades.

It has taken over 200 years to reach a population of around 25.5 million people and now Australia has a "business plan" to squeeze an extra 12 million people into the country by mid century. It will be like adding another Sydney, Melbourne and part of Brisbane to our population and most of these, around 7 million, are likely to come from overseas. In other words...we are going to have a People Boom.

And as our population grows, and it surely will, this will place an increasing demand on our infrastructure and maybe we won't be able to keep up. Of course, it's much more than just being stuck in the traffic or wedged in overcrowded public transport just to get where you need to get to. With this large number of new people coming to our country we're going to need significantly more infrastructure — roads, schools, utilities, social infrastructure.

To meet this demand, a high level of housing construction in our major cities will need to occur. It's been suggested we'll need to build one new dwelling for every three existing dwellings and with growing community resistance to more development, building enough housing to meet a growing population will continue to be a major challenge for all levels of government.

Today close to 90 per cent of immigrants initially head to our capital cities and mostly they stay in the big cities once they've arrived, and this unlikely to change.

But here's a sting in the tail... in line with this surging population, the number of vehicles we own is on the rise in Australia. It is currently 776 vehicles per 1,000 people. A decade ago it was 723 and just 644 in 1998.

It is no surprise that traffic congestion has become much worse. There are just over 20 million registered vehicles in Australia, which is up more than 25% on ten years ago, yet our infrastructure capacity hasn't increased anything like that volume over that decade.

So, when you hear all the positives about population growth, remember every 1,000 additional people means 776 more cars on the road and our freeways will become more like parking lots.

As our roads get more clogged, proximity to infrastructure including public transport, jobs shopping, schools and parks will become more important.

Maybe driverless cars, Uber and car sharing will become a trend, but for mine, people are going to have to compromise on the housing as they'll want to live closer to where they work and end up trading space (a big front and back yard) for place (proximity to work, lifestyle and amenities). This is a theme I'll keep repeating in this book.

On the positive side, in general immigrants are young so they reduce the dependency ratio, at least in the short term, and slow the aging of the population, they mostly work, and therefore they add to demand, and pay plenty of tax over their working lifetimes.

Clearly this significant growth will create some amazing opportunities for property investor.

WHAT WILL FUTURE HOMES LOOK LIKE?

Prior to COVID-19, the average Australian was prepared to trade space (a big front and backyard) for place — being close to the CBD and work, however the pandemic restrictions have significantly changed home ownership goals and what Australians want most in their next home.

Moving forward more Australians will continue working from home, at least part time, and the need to be able to juggle work, school and family commitments under one roof means spacious living is now the top priority. A separate study or zoom room is now a must for many, while others have prioritised outdoor features like a backyard, or a garage big enough to convert to a home gym.

One of the largest growing housing sector in the coming decade is likely to be first home buyers, in part driven by our high overseas migration, as the average age of a new overseas migrant is 29 years.

At the same time, Baby Boomers, who have been driving our housing requirements for the last few decades are now starting to retire. Many will be keen to remain in their family homes but if they do move they'll want to stay in their local areas, and move into smaller homes, townhouses or large apartments. Most will not be interested in trading in their detached home for a squashy mid to-high rise apartment.

My conclusion is that over the next decade more housing that fits between traditional detached homes and a small apartment (near the CBD in a large, soulless complex) will be needed.

Town planners call this the "missing middle". We'll need more homes on compact blocks of land in our middle ring suburbs such as townhouses which will accommodate our downsizers but leave room for kids and grandchildren to return.

One thing I know many of those living in Melbourne (which was locked down for over 260 cumulative days) learned was the importance of their "third place". If our first place is home and our second place is work or the office, it has been the ability to go to a third place that was taken away from many of us during the lockdowns. It may be a favourite café, a gym or a place of worship and even local shops and pubs.

I believe being in the right neighbourhood will be a major requirement for home buyers moving forward.

It seems that in our new "Covid Normal" world, people love the thought that most of the things needed for a good life are within a 20-minute public transport trip, bike ride or walk from home. Things such as shopping, business services, education, community facilities, recreational and sporting resources, and some jobs.

In urban planning circles, it's a concept known as the 20-minute neighbourhood. Many inner suburbs of Australia's capital cities and parts of their middle suburbs already meet a 20-minute neighbourhood test. However very few of the outer suburbs would do so.

It's about more than walkability. For outer suburbs to become 20-minute neighbourhoods two key requirements must be met.

1. Local development densities need to be increased, to say around 25–30 dwellings per hectare, which will better support local activity and services provision. An introduction of a mix of uses into these neighbourhoods. This would bring more jobs and services close to where people live. They would also have a range of housing to support a mix of household types, income levels and age groups. This combination is often known as density plus diversity.

2. Local public transport service levels need to be greatly improved.

WHAT DOES ALL THIS MEAN FOR PROPERTY INVESTORS?

We know that location will do 80% of the heavy lifting in your property's performance and that some locations outperform others by 50% to 100% over a decade with regard to capital growth.

How do we identify these locations? What makes some locations more desirable than others?

A lot has to do with the demographics – locations that are gentrifying and also locations that are lifestyle locations and destination locations that aspirational and affluent people want to live in will outperform.

It's well known that the rich do not like to travel and they are prepared to and can afford to pay for the privilege of living in lifestyle suburbs and locations within a 20 minute neighbourhood. So lifestyle and destination suburbs where there are a wide range of amenities with 20 minutes walk or drive are likely to outperform in the future.

At the same time many of these suburbs will be undergoing gentrification – these will be suburbs where incomes are growing, which therefore increase people's ability to afford, and pay higher prices, for property.

The key criteria for a 'good' neighbourhood

Neighbourhood has always been a key factor to consider when buying an investment property, and now it's even more important. Here is a list of 7 primary neighbourhood factors which have the potential to drive up property prices:

1. **Close proximity to public transport.** Neighbourhoods with properties that are within walking distance to public transport, such as the train, bus, ferry or light rail, are popular with buyers and therefore are likely to add value over the longer term.

2. **Close proximity to schools.** Some buyers will pay a premium to be in the catchment area for particular schools and as such, high demand generally means higher property price points.

3. **Accessible amenities.** As we have previously discussed, a neighbourhood with all the local

amenities you could want — parks, shops, restaurants, cafés, gyms, the beach etc. — would fetch a premium price for its local properties.

4. **A low crime rate.** It goes without saying that a property in a neighbourhood with a low crime rate will be more valuable than one with a high crime rate.

5. **It's well maintained.** Neighbourhoods and homes which are well maintained and clean indicate a level of community care which can help add value to properties in the local area.

6. **Planned upgrades which are beneficial.** Neighbourhoods with planned upgrades could be beneficial or detrimental to property prices in the area. For example, improved public transport and any plans to make the neighbourhood more visually attractive (improvement to the appearance of buildings or footpaths for example) could increase property prices.

7. **Any historic charm.** Historic charm brings unique character to a neighbourhood that is often in demand by buyers and in the long term buyer demand for this type of area has the potential to translate to higher property prices going forward.

AND HERE'S WHAT THIS MEANS...

There is no doubt that our population growth will bring with it significant, social, infrastructure and environmental impacts. In Australia at present, 87% of us live in urban areas; with an obviously emerging trend toward smaller dwellings and inner-city lifestyles more of us are going to be concentrated around our major capital cities.

With more and more of us wanting to live in the same five or six capital cities, and even in the same suburbs of those capital cities, our old friend — the supply and demand ratio — will keep pushing up the value of well-located inner suburban properties.

Sure these properties will be unaffordable for some, who'll remain tenants, but others will be able to afford these higher priced properties, as I don't think that anyone would argue that as a nation Australia will become wealthier over the next few decades.

Australia is well positioned to benefit from the growth of Asia, which represents 50% of the world's population. Our economy will be driven by a rapidly expanding services sector.

Interestingly, service related industries like finance, engineering, education and tourism already employ nine out of 10 people and account for 75% of Australia's GDP.

As a property investor this is the industry sector you need to know about, because this is where employment opportunities will lie for our future generations and the many new immigrants who will seek accommodation close to their workplaces.

Historically speaking property prices have always increased more in urban areas close to Australia's major CBD centres. The reasons are obvious — employment, amenities and infrastructure, all more widely and readily available in and around the "big smoke".

Given that most service industries are city-centric and regional unemployment levels are on the rise, it's fair to assume that the majority of future economic and jobs growth (and in turn wages growth) will be localised to pockets of inner Sydney, Melbourne, Brisbane and Perth over the coming years.

Sought after postcodes near our big cities is where we can anticipate a spike in accommodation demand, with people wanting convenient access to their high paying, city-based jobs.

What's more, modern day YUPPIES (remember them from the '80s? – Young Upwardly Mobile Professionals) are willing to, and will be able to afford to pay a premium for housing in higher priced, inner urban locations to avoid a hellish outer suburban commute each day.

Over the COVID-19 pandemic, apartment living fell out of favour, but moving forward affordability constraints will mean more Australians will embrace apartment living, and as competition for inner urban dwellings becomes increasingly fierce these more affordable, higher density living options will likely gain increased favour with younger generations of homeowners and tenants.

This means we can expect the already considerable price gap between popular inner and middle ring suburbs and the outlying regions to widen further, which makes an investment in quality "family friendly" apartments (not the Lego Land high rise apartment towers built out of paper mache) or townhouses in areas popular with tenants and homebuyers working in the service industries a sound prospect.

While there will be ups and downs and lots of problems ahead, we are indeed the lucky country and our economy will remain the envy of the developed world. Needless to say a strong economy is good for our property markets.

While nothing in life is guaranteed, there are many rational, logical and understandable reasons to believe that property values will appreciate over time.

So, if like me, you are confident that Australia has a prosperous future, and you agree that our population is going to keep increasing and that most of us are going to want to live in much the same parts of our lucky country, you can understand why I see a strong long-term future for our capital city property markets.

INVESTING FOR CAPITAL GROWTH, NOT CASH FLOW

Of course, every property investor is looking for the secret to success, aren't they?

Some spend years searching for a mythical investment strategy that will be their path to untold riches. Alas, while they are on their unhelpful hunt, they miss golden opportunities that could have helped them achieve their financial goals and dreams much earlier. And one of the most common mistakes that novice investors make is being fixated on cash flow instead of on capital growth, which is where the secret really lies.

I know some so-called "experts" suggest you should invest in property to achieve positive cash flow (rental returns that are higher than your mortgage repayments and expenses leaving money in your pocket each month). Then others suggest you should invest for capital growth (an increase in the value of your property).

But there is a third element to investment that many commentators forget to mention and that is risk. Considering cash flow, capital growth and risk, when investing in residential property you can only typically have two out of the three.

If you want a property investment that is low-risk and has a high cash flow you will have to forgo high capital growth. If you are looking for a low-risk investment that has strong capital growth, you will usually have to forgo high rental returns (cash flow).

There's no doubt in my mind that if I had to choose between cash flow and capital growth, I would invest for capital growth every time. To prove my point, let's take a look at some capital growth facts.

1. It's the key to duplication

The thing is most people's incomes mean they only have the capacity to invest in one property at a time. Clearly you can't invest in property without a deposit and it's always been hard to save one of those. The key to growing your portfolio is duplication, which necessitates more deposits.

It's highly unlikely that many people can save multiple deposits over their lifetimes. But what they can do is use the capital growth (or equity) in their properties instead. If they'd invested in cash flow properties, while they might have solid rent coming in, they generally won't do anything to help you with a deposit for your next property.

2. A question of debt

How do you feel about carrying debt? Some people can't sleep at night for fear of a market crash or interest rate rises. But, as I've explained, "good debt" like mortgages on investment properties, can provide you with leverage to magnify your gains.

Yet in order for this to work, you need to have gained to start off with, which isn't necessarily the case with cash flow properties. I've seen more than my fair share of investors whose borrowing capacity has been limited by owning low capital growth assets, which prevent them from borrowing to buy better-performing properties.

And of course, in today's relatively low-interest-rate environment, good debt is really an asset because you can borrow funds at around 4–5% while a well-located property that you will buy with that debt will increase in value at twice that rate.

And it's likely that your cash flow shortfall will be minimal in this low-interest-rate environment.

3. Less than ideal liquidity

It should come as no surprise that cash flow properties have less than ideal liquidity. What I mean by that is they can be more difficult to sell if your circumstances change. Plus, you'll likely walk away with very little additional proceeds from the sale because it hasn't increased in price overly much. On the other hand, an investment-grade capital growth property will be more attractive to potential buyers and you're likely to walk away with much more money in your back pocket after the sale.

4. Equity means choices

If you think about it, if you buy a property that doesn't grow in value you have to hope that the rent continues to cover the costs of ownership. But the fact is that it's unlikely that you'll get rental growth in a location where capital growth is minimal. But if you buy an investment property that goes up in value, you have a number of options that increase over time. If you want to, you could use the equity to buy another property and maybe refinance in order to free up cash flow for other investments. And it's likely the rent you receive will also keep increasing.

THE BEST OF BOTH WORLDS

Of course, in an ideal world we'd all like to buy properties that have high growth, strong cash flow and low risk, and while this combination is possible, it's far from the norm. I manage to achieve all of these by purchasing properties in high growth areas and then adding value by renovating them or redeveloping them into townhouses. The extra rent and the taxation benefit I achieve give me high-growth properties with high yields.

THE POWER OF CAPITAL GROWTH

If you have any doubt about the importance of capital growth, the calculations in the table we are about to discuss may change your mind.

Over the long term, "average" property investments in our four big capital cities tend to return around 7% capital growth (averaged over the last 40 years) and 4% rental yield. The table would be turned the other way in many regional areas that may only achieve 5% capital growth, but a higher rental yield of say 7%.

The argument then continues; if you're going to achieve 11 or 12% per annum from your property why not go for the high rental returns? I guess that's why many Beginner Investors make the mistake of viewing their property investments as income-driven rather than striving for capital growth.

The problem with this argument is that while the first part is generally correct – properties with high growth will give a low return and vice versa – the second part is clearly wrong. The two types of investments do NOT give similar results over time.

This is easy to explain with the following example.

Imagine you bought a property worth $500,000 in a poor growth area delivering 5% capital growth and 7% rental return. The calculations in the table below illustrate that in 20 years your property would be worth around **$1.3 million**.

If you bought a different property for $500,000 in a higher capital growth area, showing 7% per annum capital growth and 4% rental return, this property would be worth over **$2.3 million** at the end of the same period. That is a massive difference in the final value of your investment property – **over $1 million more**.

In the meantime the rentals on this property would also grow substantially, in line with its capital growth, and they'd slowly catch up to the rentals you'd achieve on the first (high return) property.

Capital growth vs rental income on a $500,000 purchase			
7% capital growth	4% rental return on property value	5% capital growth	7% rental return on property value
Year 1	$535,000	$21,600	$525,000	$36,750
Year 5	$701,276	$29,387	$638,141	$44,670
Year 10	$983,576	$43,178	$814,447	$57,011
Year 15	$1,379,516	$63,443	$1,039,464	$72,762
Year 20	$1,934,842	$93,219	$1,326,649	$92,865

Let's look at the same information graphically – using the concept of compounding you can see how different levels of capital growth affect the value of your asset base over time.

I'm trying to show you that if you could outperform the averages – which you will after learning the lessons in this book – and find a property that goes up by say 10% annum (averaged out over a property cycle) over the next 20 years you would make a further $1.5 million in equity.

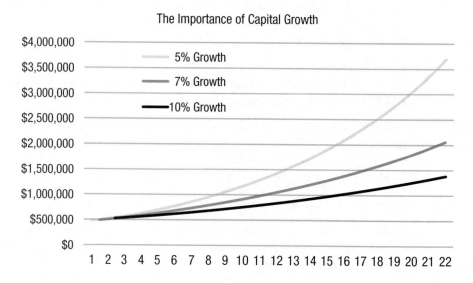

The Importance of Capital Growth

The real bonus for the investor who bought the high-growth property is that they would be able to access the extra equity and borrow against it to invest in more assets. It's very hard to do this with properties that have high rental returns but poorer capital growth.

The few dollars a week you get in positive cash flow is not really going to make much difference to your lifestyle or your ability to service other more desirable properties. Wealth from real estate is not derived from income, because residential properties are not high-yielding investments. Real wealth is achieved through long-term capital appreciation and the ability to refinance to buy further properties.

Another problem with investing for cash flow is that you lose too much of your income though paying income tax. I'll show you a table that demonstrates this clearly in the section on tax.

INSIDER TIP

Well-located residential property is inherently a low-risk, high-growth investment. This means it has low rental returns. Looking for strong cash flow from residential property investments is attempting to make a property investment something it is not meant to be. If you want high yields, look at other types of investments, such as property trusts, managed funds or shares.

ALWAYS BUY AND SELDOM SELL

Over the years I have met many investors who were tempted to sell their properties. They seem to do this for one of two reasons.

1. Beginner investors often buy near the peak of the cycle and then find that over the next couple of years the property market is flat and there is little or no capital growth. They are concerned that their investments aren't going up in value and choose to sell. These investors usually compound the error by selling just before the property market starts rising again and lose out on the potential growth.

2. Other investors sell their properties because their property has gone up in value and they want to take advantage of that growth and access their profits.

The difference between my strategy and this approach is that most people use finance to buy property. I am the opposite – I use properties to obtain finance. After all, that's really what I'm after – MONEY. I use the finance to buy further properties or as cash flow to live the lifestyle I want.

As opposed to most other assets, the great thing about property is that you don't have to sell it to access your increased equity when the property goes up in value. You just borrow against your increased equity.

INSIDER TIP

The difference between my strategy and that of the average property investor is that most people use finance to buy property. I am the opposite – I use properties to obtain finance.

Let's imagine you buy a property for $500,000 and it goes up to $600,000. Sure you could sell it. But you wouldn't keep the extra $100,000 after agent's commissions and solicitor's fees. You would probably have more like $90,000 and you would pay capital gains tax on a portion of that, which may only leave around $60,000.

Why would you sell the property for $60,000? What could you do with $60,000?

Think about it. That property which is worth $500,000 on average will increase in value by 7% a year, so next year it will go up $35,000 in value and the year after it could go up another $37,450 or so. The next year it will go up in value again, but this time a bit more because of compounding.

What that means is that over the next three years, depending on the state of the property cycle, your property could have gone up in value by approximately $100,000 and you'd have forgone this for a quick short-term profit of $60,000 or so.

The problem is many investors take a short-term approach to real estate which is really a long-term investment.

They try and make a quick profit such as buying cheaply, or looking for the next hot spot, which is a short-term approach rather than taking the long-term approach of owning the best asset they can which will give them long-term compounding growth and in time produce substantial wealth.

And these long-term profits are tax-free unless you sell the property. Yet you can still access these funds by borrowing against the increased value of your property and use the money as a deposit to buy more property. This is the process which I have called pyramiding.

Of course all this works because of the principle of compounding, but investing in property offers a special type of compounding — the capital growth (increase in value of your property) that you achieve is not taxed, which means you are left with a larger asset on which to base your compounding for the next year. I'll explain this in more detail with some numbers and charts in the tax section of this book.

A POINT OF CLARIFICATION ABOUT MY BUY AND SELDOM SELL STRATEGY

Here's an important point — what I've been trying to explain is that you create wealth through property by holding it in the long term and allowing compounding of capital growth to grow your asset base, not by trading it for short-term profits.

But I'm not suggesting that you should never sell property.

In fact that's one of the big mistakes I see investors make — not selling an underperforming property, holding on and hoping it will eventually increase in value. That's a *buy and hope* strategy, not a *buy and hold* strategy.

The fact is — some properties will always outperform the averages, while others will underperform. As I'll explain in more detail later on, when you conduct your annual review of your portfolio, if you find yourself stuck with an underperforming property, sometimes it's appropriate to sell it and replace it with a superior property, even if you crystallise a loss or have to pay some capital gains tax.

CAPITAL GROWTH BEATS CASH FLOW IN THE LONG RUN

I know I've gone on and on about capital growth, but this concept is so important, I still feel I have to make my point yet again.

I can understand why beginner investors would be keen to buy a property with positive cash flow. They tend to be cheaper and it is easy to purchase and support this type of property. While these properties will give you short-term income, which may be attractive, they will never allow you to accumulate the equity necessary to become truly wealthy.

And while the rent may seem relatively high initially, it is the ongoing capital growth of your property which will underpin its long-term rental income, which means that if you buy in low capital growth areas, your rents won't increase that much over the years.

Sure, cash flow is important, but it won't make you rich.

Cash flow will keep you in the game, but capital growth will get you out of the rat race.

Remember as a Level 3 investor your focus should be on safely building your asset base so you can eventually develop the passive income from your assets that will allow you to enjoy the freedom of a Level 4 investor.

One of the main reasons properties increase in value is the scarcity value of the land they sit on, meaning you should buy properties with a **high land to asset ratio** (the land component should make up a substantial portion of the value of the property).

If you think about it, when you by a cash flow type property in a regional area where prices are lower, the land value per square meter tends to be low because there's plenty of land available compared to the level of buyer demand. This means the building accounts for most of the asset's value. In these areas the building may lose value faster than the land can gain value thus hampering long-term capital growth.

Let's compare this with buying high growth property.

When the property price is high, the land value probably is as well. You're likely to have purchased in an area with a limited supply of land relative to buyer demand and your land to asset ratio is likely to be high meaning the land component makes up a higher proportion of the property's overall value, giving the asset strong capital growth potential. In general, this makes this type of property, typically negatively geared, a lower risk than positively geared property over the long-term.

On the other hand, properties with positive cash flow could be seen as more of a liability as the years go by and capital growth fails to occur. They are dependent on achieving high rentals and you may need to undertake regular and significant renovations to attract suitable tenants and to maintain an acceptable income.

In the current property markets, the low interest rates mean that the cash flow shortfall for buying high growth properties is the smallest I have seen for decades, and anyway it is very difficult to find properties with strong positive cash flow even in regional Australia.

I'll explain my property investment strategy in more detail shortly, but in essence there are four stages:

1. **The Education Stage** – that's what you're doing now.

2. **The Accumulation Stage** — build your asset base (net worth) through capital growth of well-located properties. You can speed up your wealth accumulation through leverage, compounding time and "manufacturing" capital growth through renovations or development

3. **Transition Stage** — once you have a sufficiently large asset base, slowly lower your loan to value ratios so you can move on to the...

4. **Lifestyle Phase** — This phase is all about enjoying your life living off the cash machine you have produced in the first three phases.

What you may not realise is that when you retire, the majority of your asset base won't be money you've saved, or rent you've earned, but it will comprise the tax free capital growth you will have achieved from your property investments.

The challenge with investing for capital growth is finding the courage to take on considerable debt to allow you to profit through leverage. If you find this confronting, the next chapter will give you confidence. We will examine some very good reasons why you can fully expect to always see growth in any 10-year timeframe. No incurable optimism will be required!

A LOT CAN HAPPEN IN 10 YEARS

Thinking back to when I wrote the first edition of this book in 2006 — it was a time when after a number of strong years property prices seemed too expensive and many property commentators suggested property investment had had its day. How could I have been so audacious as to write about the coming property boom?

Well, my predictions were correct and most investors who bought a property then would have experienced significant capital growth. In fact, I know of many who used their increased equity to buy further properties and who have since grown a multi-million dollar property portfolio in their spare time. (Now that's a good name for a book isn't it?)

Have you ever driven past a house that's up for sale and thought: "Gee, I wish I bought that when it was for sale 10 years ago at half the price?"

If you had known for certain that the price of a property could have doubled in the next 10 years, what lengths would you have gone to in order to get finance and buy more property in 2010?

However, looking back we've had some turbulent times since then with periods of high interest rates and more recently low interest rates. We had just come out of the worst world economic downturn since the great depression (the GFC of 2008-9.) We've had a mining boom and commodities bust, governments of both major persuasions and more prime ministers than I can remember. We've gone to war and been plagued by terrorists. And in 2017-19 we'd had the worst property downturn in modern history in Sydney (where median house prices fell 15%) and Melbourne (where prices fell 11%).

Yet the value of well-located properties in our major capital cities doubled in value in the last decade and that's likely to happen again.

Today, as the world works its way through the economic challenges caused by the lockdown due to the Coronavirus pandemic, many people again doubt the long-term future of our property markets.

I've already laid out the reasons for my long-term confidence in property and in this and the next chapter I'll get into more detail and explain how the study of future housing supply and demand and the study of the changing nature of Australia's population — "demographics" will hold the key to the future of Australian real estate.

You'll soon realise that I see demographics — how and where will people want to live — as having a bigger influence on our property markets over the medium to long term, than changes in consumer sentiment, fluctuations in interest rates or government regulation.

As I explained in a previous chapter, our government will continue to purposefully "import" more people to help boost our economy, fill many job vacancies and pay tax. The current day immigrant is chosen with different criteria to the past; they are required to bring a baseline of skills, money and employability. It has been shown that two-thirds of these arrivals will buy a home within a few years of arriving in Australia.

WHERE ARE ALL THESE PEOPLE GOING TO LIVE?

As always, our capitals are going to attract the lion's share of the population growth, with a disproportionate number coming to NSW and Victoria where jobs growth is greatest.

Over the last decades there has been a steady increase in the proportion of the country's population living in the capital cities and given that the capital city markets tend to enjoy higher wages and have better job opportunities this trend is likely to continue.

While in the short term some better performing regional locations have outperformed the poorer performing capital city suburbs, the trend is clear — population growth and capital growth in property values in our main capital cities will eclipse growth in regional Australia in the long-term. That's why I avoid regional locations despite the fact that properties are cheaper there, and some may even return a modest positive cash flow.

I've always avoided investing in regional towns because of their heavy reliance on a small number of industries to sustain their local economy and population. Remember, when those industries take a battering, it's not long before local house prices start to go down in value. Instead, I look to invest in areas where property values will be driven by a large and growing population base, a diverse economy and the scarcity of supply of well-located properties and where high income earners like to live.

Remember, when you retire your income will be dependent upon the income of your tenants and their ability to keep paying you higher rents over time. It is unlikely that incomes in regional towns will keep pace with income growth of the skilled labour force in our capital cities. After all, that's where the high paying jobs are.

And the fact that we all want to live in the same cities, and in general in many of the same suburbs, will underpin the capital growth of properties in these locations.

While many of our new dwellings will be built in the outer suburbs, most of the new high paying jobs will be created in the more skilled service sectors close to our CBDs. So there is a mismatch of where people will be living and where their jobs will be. Add to this all those extra cars on the road and it's hard to imagine the travel required to get to work. This means more of the young people in higher paying jobs (often in the knowledge and service industries) will be prepared to and be able to afford to pay a premium to live close to their work in the inner and middle ring suburbs of our big capital cities. And many will trade back yards for balconies for the convenience and lifestyle.

It is critical to understand these changing trends, because to become a successful property investor it will be important to own the types of property that will be in continuous strong demand by tenants and owner-occupiers.

THERE WILL ALWAYS BE SOMEONE TELLING YOU NOT TO INVEST

Despite all the positives that investing in property can offer, over the years there has always been somebody telling us why property investment should be avoided.

Just look back to 2008 when we were working our way out of the Global Financial Crisis, a number of analysts suggested that property values would not increase in Australia for another decade. Well, they've been proven wrong, as many property owners have enjoyed substantial growth in the value of their properties for a number of years.

Remember all those warnings of falling off a "fiscal cliff" during the Covid pandemic and warnings of real estate Armageddon? Yet the value of all the residential real estate in Australia increased by around $2 trillion in 2021 alone.

At times these destructive arguments seemed to make sense, but history has proven them wrong. The average price of a home in the major capitals of Australia has just kept going up and up.

What did your parents pay for their house? Who would not want to buy their parents' home at the price they paid for it?

In 1978, my parents paid $25,000 for their house and took a 30-year loan from the bank to pay it off. About 30 years ago my mother sold that house for more than $600,000 and she had done little to improve its value. Today it would be worth more than $2.5 million.

Yet over those years there have always been plenty of ready excuses on offer to put off investing in property. The only thing you should learn from history is that we don't learn from history. Every year there are forecasts of doom and gloom, and we don't learn the property values are very resilient.

Let's have a look at a few of the excuses I could have used not to invest over the past 40 years or so:

- In the early- to mid-60s we had just emerged from a major credit squeeze and finance had dried up.
- In the late-60s we had the nickel share boom and property was proclaimed an inferior investment.

- In the mid-70s we had a recession.

- In the late-70s we had rising inflation and the OPEC Oil crisis.

- In 1983 there was a recession with high interest rates and peaking inflation. A few years later commentators said property prices were too high and would take years to recover.

- In 1985 the government changed the tax laws pertaining to property with the quarantining of the tax benefits of negative gearing and the introduction of the capital gains tax. Commentators explained how this was going to be the end of property investment as we knew it.

- In 1987 there was the fear of a "1930s-type depression" after the stock market crash.

- By 1989–90, interest rates and inflation were again too high and led to the famous "recession we had to have" — a heaven-sent excuse for procrastinators to stay out of a property market awash with bargains! I still remember in the late '80s the cry was "Our children will never be able to afford to enter the property market" or "Prices will never go any higher, don't invest in property".

- In 1991 Australian unemployment was 11.3% and people were selling their houses at bargain basement prices, as most people felt property values would only fall further.

- The mounting foreign debt and current account deficit of 1993–94 was enough to scare people off buying property.

- The "world economic slowdown" and the "Asian currency crisis" were good excuses not to buy property in the mid-1990s.

- In the mid-90s we were told inflation was low so property prices would stop rising.

- Rising oil prices, September 11 and an oversupply of investment property in the inner-city areas could have been great excuses not to invest in property over the last decade.

- In 2001 we had a recession and the introduction of GST, which was predicted to put a damper on property values.

- The property slump of 2004–06 was accompanied by much negative press and at times seemingly experienced property commentators were suggesting that property values wouldn't increase again until 2010. Then there was further confusion about land tax, vendor's tax and interest rate increases.

- Despite many forecasters predicting a property crash in 2008/09, the major property markets around Australia, other than the specialised Gold Coast market, have had a soft landing.

- In 2011 and 2012 many thought the world's financial markets could collapse due to the economic troubles in Europe and the USA.

- In 2016 the world's economy was faltering in part due to China's slowing economy and falling commodity prices.

- In 2018-19 property values in Sydney and Melbourne had their biggest fall in modern history slipping 15% and 11% after growing 70% and 50% respectively over the previous five years.

- In 2020 and 2021 the concerns about Covid, rising unemployment and a fiscal cliff stopped many prospective property buyers, but look how wrong they were.

- In 2023 there were concerns about a fixed mortgage rate cliff and an unemployment cliff that would topple our housing markets, but that didn't occur.

Through these times the value of well-located capital city residential properties has increased consistently, at around 7% per annum.

The first investment property I bought for $18,000 would be worth over $1,800,000 today if I hadn't pulled it down to build two townhouses on the land. Over the years the rent from my properties has helped pay their mortgages and the capital growth has allowed me to borrow against their increased value and pyramid myself into other property investments. In fact I've built a very substantial multi-million dollar property portfolio starting with my initial $2,000 deposit. And I haven't really put any of my own money into my portfolio since. It's all come from compounding capital growth.

10 YEARS AT A TIME

Moving into the next stage of the economic cycle I see future capital growth a little more subdued over the next few years, but I believe the next 10 years are going to be just as good as the last decade has been, and the one before that too!

If you think about it, a lot has happened in most Australian property markets in the past decade. If you visited any of our capital cities 10 years ago, and came back today, you would scarcely recognise the skyline and the impact of the high-rise buildings and city apartment developments. In Melbourne there is Docklands, in Perth, the Golden Mile on the drive in from the airport as well as the new high-rise apartments, and the Sydney and Brisbane landscapes are now peppered with inner-city apartments. As well as this many of the old houses in our suburban streets have made way for modern townhouses and apartments.

What will our major cities look like in a decade from now?

This is an important question because if you want to you own a top-performing investment property, you'll need one that will be in continuous strong demand by both owner-occupiers and tenants. It's through analysing demographics, that we'll come to understand what the future of the property markets hold for us.

WHAT CAN WE EXPECT TO HAPPEN IN THE NEXT 10 YEARS?

A lot will happen over the next decade but before I give you my thoughts it's important to understand the difference between forecasts and expectations:

- I expect there to be another recession in the next decade. But I don't know when it will come.

- I expect the property market to boom and then prices will tumble again. But I don't know when.

- I expect that some investments I will make won't do well. But I don't know which ones they will be.

- I expect interest rates to remain high for longer than we hoped and then fall, but I don't know when.

- I expect that some investments I make won't do well. But I don't know which ones they will be.

- And I expect another world financial crisis. But I have no idea when it will come.

Now these are not contradictions or a form of cop out.

As I said...there's a big difference between an expectation and a forecast.

An *expectation* is the anticipation of how things are likely to play out in the future based on my perspective of how things worked in the past.

A *forecast* is putting a time frame to that expectation.

Of course, in an ideal world we would be able to forecast what's ahead for our property markets with a level of accuracy. But we can't, because there are just too many moving parts.

Sure, there are all those statistics that are easy to quantify, but what is hard to identify is exactly when and how millions of strangers will act in response to the prevailing economic and political environment.

Then there will always be those X factors that crop up. Those unforeseen events that comes out of the blue, which could be local or overseas that undo all the forecasts we made.

So what should you do about this? I've found the most practical approach is to have expectations of what could happen without specific forecasts.

That's because when you expect something to happen at some stage in the future, you're not surprised when it happens.

Expecting the worst while preparing for the best forces you to invest with room for error, and psychologically prepares you for the inevitable disappointments.

This is exactly how I planned for the property downturn in 2020 as well as the uncertainties of the effects of the Covid pandemic.

I didn't know when these problems would come, how long they would last or how they would affect the value of my property portfolio or the cash flow of my business. But I knew a downturn would come once again, and I was prepared for it with cash flow buffers to see me through the difficult times.

What I'm trying to explain it that there's a huge difference between, "I expect another next property downturn sometime in the next decade" and "I expect the next property downturn in the second half of 2026."

One of the big differences is how I invest.

If I expect the property **upturn** we've been experiencing will be followed by another property downturn, then I won't be surprised when it comes. But since I don't know when this will happen, I won't make the focus of my property investing trying to time the property cycle.

That's because trying to time the property cycle or looking for the next "hot spot" are two of the reason many property investors fail.

On the other hand, strategic investors maximise their profits during property booms and minimise their downside during busts by investing in assets that have *"always"* worked, rather than looking for the next hot spot or for the type of property strategy that works *"now"*. They own investment grade assets in investment grade inner and middle ring suburbs of Australia's three big capital cities. The type of property that keep growing in value over time without fluctuating wildly in price when the property cycle slows down.

BUT WHAT'S AHEAD FOR PROPERTY?

Having said that, if you're like most readers of this book, you'd still like to know what's ahead. I know some people suggest that if you want to know what lies ahead, start by looking at the clues behind you, but in my mind this new decade will be very different to the last decade. Let's start with...

What will stay the same over the next decade:

1. *Australia's population will keep growing* and we will be adding about 1 million people every three years, with immigration continuing to account for a significant portion of this increase as we keep importing skilled migrants to replace our retiring Baby Boomers in the workforce.

Australia's population is likely to hit 30 million people in the early 2030's. That's over 2.5 million people coming to Australia looking for a home, and population growth will remain concentrated in our three capital cities. Despite government attempts to increase population growth in our regional centres, young people will keep leaving regional Australia to move to the big smoke and migrants will only stay there for the length required by their Visa before they move to the capital cities.

Over 80% of Australians still dwell in detached homes, mostly in the sprawling suburbs that make our cities among the largest in the world by land area.

2. *More congestion on our roads.* Our love affair with cars will continue, with half of all households having access to two or more cars.

While it has been shown overseas that cities can be liveable despite having very large populations of many millions, the infrastructure and in particular public transport needs to be able to accommodate the population. Unfortunately, Australia's infrastructure growth has not kept pace with our rising population meaning roads will become more clogged and accommodation in proximity to public transport will become more sought after and relatively more valuable. After a long period of low wages growth, the average Aussie will earn more this decade.

3. *Property prices will continue to increase...*just as they have since Federation, but some areas will increase in value more than others. Property values in the inner and middle ring suburbs in our large capital cities, where the locals will be relatively wealthier and have more disposal income, will increase proportionally more than the outer suburbs. Over the forthcoming decade the poor will live further out than ever because the rich do not like commuting and will continue to live in our leafy more established suburbs close to amenities and public transport.

4. *The property cycle will continue.* The long-term upward trend will be driven by owner occupiers, while the cyclical ups and downs will be more influenced by investors falling prey to fear and greed.

5. *Australians will continue to aspire to home ownership*, which will continue to underpin our property markets. A large percentage of the hundreds of thousands of migrants coming to Australia will also aspire to home ownership, in fact that's of the many reasons they have come to Australia. However, over the coming decade more of us will move to medium and high density living – apartments and townhouses.

6. Ordinary Australians will continue to try and *secure their financial future* through property investment.

7. The *property pessimists* will still be out there telling us not to invest because our property markets are going to crash. And *property spruikers* and get rich quick artists will still be there taking money from naïve property investors looking for a shortcut to get rich quickly in real estate.

8. We will be living in the best country in the world at the best time in history.

NOW LET'S LOOK AT WHAT WILL BE DIFFERENT OVER THE NEXT DECADE.

1. Interest rates will slowly fall over the next couple of years as inflation comes under control, but will remain higher than they were over the last decade.

2. After a long period of low wages growth, the average Aussie will earn more this decade.

However certain demographics will have higher wages growth than average because of their skilled jobs or they may have multiple sources of income, and these people will be able to afford to pay more for their homes or for prime investment properties. The result will mean the rich will keep getting richer and one way they will do this is by owning the right type of properties.

Fact is: while there has been very little real change in household income over the past ten years, there has been an increasing share of wealth held by the top 10% of wealthy households because they own real estate and have superannuation; a contraction in the size of the "middle class" and a large increase in the number of Australians in struggle street.

3. Millennials will move out of apartments into family-sized houses. As Australia's largest generation reaches the family formation stage of their life they will continue to leave their hipster neighbourhoods in the capital cities, searching for family-sized homes in the suburbs.

4. We will need to build over 1.2 million new dwellings over the next five years to house our growing population, but we will fall short of this target, meaning there will be a shortfall of well-located desirable accommodation.

5. *Lower levels of home ownership.* Difficulty saving a deposit will mean that there will be lower levels of home ownership for those in the typical first home buyer age group; and possibly even falling levels of home ownership rates for those in their 40s and even 50s.

While around 30% of Australian households tend to rent their accommodation, I wouldn't be surprised to find that two out of five households could opt to rent over the next decade.

6. While during Covid, household size was shrinking, it's likely this trend will revert to the pre-Covid trend where, *household size was increasing* and over the next decade we're likely to see more multi-generational clans living together as continued multiculturalism, rising house prices and an ageing population lead to an increase in the number of households that see children, parents and grandparents all living under the one roof.

Plus, the mix from overseas has changed, with more migrants now coming from those countries with large family units.

However, falling birth rates mean that the proportion of younger age groups in the population will continue to shrink in the coming decade, while the share of older groups will rise rapidly.

7. At the other extreme there will be an *increase in those living as a couple or alone* as more of us live longer and live alone longer, especially women over 60 years, and sadly, most will have limited financial means.

8. The cherished *dream of owning a quarter acre block* with enough space for a game of backyard cricket will be nearly gone with more of us trading backyards for balconies and courtyards, while new land releases will be of much smaller sized blocks of land.

9. *30–40% of the jobs we know could disappear* in the next decade and there will be a casualisation of the workforce. Many local jobs will disappear offshore while others will be replaced by artificial intelligence. Now I'm not suggesting that this will lead to mass unemployment, it will lead to redeployment as a range of new occupations, that we haven't even thought of yet will come to light.

I see the trend of working from home, at least for a few days a week, continuing and at the same time more of us will be working a range of casual or part-time jobs and as part of this trend, more oldies will be working than in previous generations. They will be doing so because they have to financially, rather than because they want something to do.

10. *Most Baby Boomers will have retired* in the next 10 years and Gen Xers will be coming up to retirement age. I'll discuss these and more demographic changes in the next chapter.

11. We will be inundated with new technology we haven't even dreamed of yet. At the same time, it's likely we'll become a cashless society and even credit cards could disappear in the next 10 years.

As always, over the next decade, our property markets will be driven by the growth in our population as we need one new dwelling for about every 2.5 people added to this country. And the types of dwellings we are going to want to live in will be dictated by our changing demographics. The increasing wealth of our nation together with the changes in our population (migration and immigration) will drive demand for housing over the next decade. Trends in these two areas help explain, and help us predict, house price growth for each state.

Typically, Australians move from one state to another when they think that a particular state has better job prospects and living standards and cheaper housing, so interstate migration is driven by the affordability of housing close to good jobs and the relative strength of the different state economies. Overseas immigrants are attracted to Australia when employment growth is high and they like our relatively stable political environment, our security and predictable tax system.

And remember... migrants don't bring houses with them when they come here, meaning that the demand for new housing caused by these population movements will cause property prices to rise some 12 to 15 months after waves of migration happen as the newcomers push up property values. The majority of our population growth in the future is expected to occur in our capital cities resulting in further concentration of Australia's population within those cities.

All this becomes a lot more fascinating when you consider the economic impact this will have on the property market.

For every 10,000 people who move into a region, it not only creates tremendous job growth, but it creates the requirement for around 3,000 new suburban homes or up to 5,000 new apartments. These 10,000 people will probably spend $100 million in retail stores each year and $50 million in supermarkets.

More people means more infrastructure and the impact on the construction sector over the next 10 years alone should give you confidence to invest now for the great boom ahead.

WHAT'S THIS GOT TO DO WITH PROPERTY?

Throughout this book I use the premise that property values are going to increase in the future and that they are likely to do so at an average of around 7% per annum. This growth won't happen year after year, but over a full property cycle the price growth of well-located properties should average out at 8% per annum.

Why do I think this type of growth will continue to occur?

Well, a simple answer could be that the best predictor of the future is past performance, but the reasoning behind my predictions of continued strong growth is much more than that. It is based on the scarcity of well-located land and the strong demand for properties created for certain types of households by our increasing population and our changing demographics – our requirement for more modern, secure, medium-density dwellings near our major capital cities.

I've already explained this, but the point is so important it's worth repeating... in the long term our property values are driven by the *wealth of our nation* and *population growth*. For property values to increase significantly, you need both of these influences working simultaneously.

Just look at Japan – it has an ageing nation, but with no population growth and property values are floundering.

On the other hand look at Cairo in Egypt. It has strong population growth with a population almost the size of Australia living in one city with a shortage of housing. But the people there are poor and can't afford housing, so property values are not increasing.

However, in Australia we have the ideal combination of a rising population which, in general, is becoming wealthier and can afford housing. More than this they want to live in the same four or five capital cities and often in the same suburbs in these cities – suburbs close to all the amenities and infrastructure. This is a potent mix that keeps pushing up property values.

WHAT WILL THIS DO TO PROPERTY VALUES?

If the trends that have affected property prices in the past continue, and there is no reason to think they won't, then the future price of the average house in any of our capital cities will be much, much higher than you think.

Analysing four decades of data property as reported by the REIA and the ABS the median house nationally has risen by over 540% – an annual growth rate of 7.62% at this varied state by state:

Over the last 40 years:

- Melbourne had the highest average annual price growth for houses at 8.12%

- Sydney experienced 7.98% average annual house price growth

- Canberra enjoyed 7.9% average annual house price growth

- Brisbane experienced 7.51% average annual house price growth

- Adelaide achieved 6.94% average annual house price growth

- Perth experienced 6.26% average annual house price growth

- There were no 40-year figures for Hobart and Darwin but their 30-year average annual house price growth was 7.29% and 5.48% respectively.

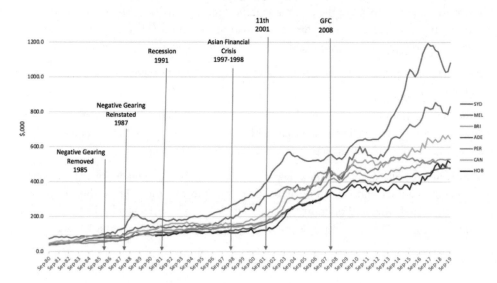

Median House Price by City – Since March 1980

Digging further into this research which spanned over 42 years I found the following trends:

- Our strong housing markets have boosted our household wealth as so many Australians have the bulk of their wealth tied up in their homes.

- The average mortgage size has increased at roughly the same pace as housing values but with mortgage rates being at such a low levels, home loan serviceability measures have improved over the past decade, despite substantial rises in housing values.

- However households need longer to save for a deposit and more first home buyers are seeking help from the bank of mum and dad.

- First home buyers are a smaller proportion of buyers today. They accounted for 22% of all property transactions in 2000, but now account for less than 17% of the housing demand.

- As our population grew, the urban form of our cities has densified — trading backyards for balconies and courtyards.

Now here's the interesting bit... If property prices were to rise in the future at the same rate as the past twenty-five years, Australia's median house value would reach $2.9 million by 2043.

Extrapolating past growth forward for the next 25 years here's what median house prices could look like:

- Sydney $6.3 million
- Melbourne $5.8 million
- Canberra $2.9 million
- Perth $2.5 million
- Hobart $2.4 million
- Brisbane $2.3 million
- Adelaide $1.9 million
- National $2.928,009

Source: Aussie Home Loan based on CoreLogic data Median values have been extrapolated based on applying the annual compounding growth in median values over the past twenty-five years to current median house values.

You're probably saying to yourself "That's not right Michael — the median price for a home in Sydney won't be close to $6 million dollars in 25 years!"

When I bought my first investment property in 1972 it cost me $18,000. In fact the median price for a house in Melbourne was $12,000 then. And I remember my first rental cheque was $12 per week and I was really excited, but to put that in perspective the average wage at the time was $55 per week and the most popular family car at that time was the Holden Kingswood and you could drive that out of the showroom for $2,000.

Over the next 30 years the median house price increased 15 times, as did the average rent and interestingly the Kingswood is long gone, but its replacement Holden Commodore cost around $30,000 thirty years later, also increasing in price about 15 times.

What this means is that to become financially independent you are going to need to own a multi-million dollar property portfolio. While you could buy yourself a top investment property for $650,000 today, in 25 years from now this may not buy you a double garage.

THE IMPORTANCE OF MARKET EXPOSURE

When we look back at history, property values have not risen continuously or consistently – they don't go up in a straight line. There will be times of no growth and even some periods of falling prices, as well as times of extreme growth and we can expect this cycle to continue. However, for investors, the important thing is that over the long term the market will continue to rise, driven by population growth and the increasing wealth of the nation.

There will be no other alternative, simply because we will need a massive number of new homes to house millions of new people over the next 10 years. As new properties come on the market the cost of producing them keeps increasing. Land costs more, infrastructure costs are increasing, building costs have escalated, town planning regulations cause delays and putting this together means the cost of housing is increasing dramatically.

INSIDER TIP

Over the next 10 years properties will go up in value by billions of dollars and it won't matter who owns them. Wouldn't it be great if it were you?

While the quality of the assets you invest in will be critical, to eventually build your cash machine investing over long periods of time will be an even more important factor. Sure, it would be great to find the next hot spot and make a one-time 50% return on an investment. But making a 7% return each year for 40 years is a far better outcome, as it multiplies your initial investment by a factor of 15!

You see... even moderate returns over long periods generate massive wealth.

As we go forward exploring the concepts in this book, I am going to suggest ways you can be part of this huge growth in the property market and showing how you can take advantage of opportunities that will arise from the great property boom ahead, while hopefully escaping some of the traps. This will allow you to grow your own multi-million dollar property portfolio. In the next chapter I will begin by taking a closer look at the study of demographics and what it can tell us about specific trends in the property markets of the future.

WATCHING PEOPLE PATTERNS: THE STUDY OF DEMOGRAPHICS

Demographics will determine our property destiny because ultimately the number of homes in Australia will be determined by the number of people in Australia, how they want to live and where they want to live.

To be a successful property investor you must own the type of property that will be in continuous strong demand by both owner-occupiers and tenants, so it should hardly be a radical idea that one of the keys underpinning the strength of our property markets will be people and their changing lifestyles and housing demands and preferences. All major property booms in Australia have had migration and immigration patterns (the influx of people) as one of their driving factors. This dates back to the Gold Rush of the 1800s.

That's why I'd encourage you to become a student of demographics, which is the study of the characteristics of human populations and population segments. This will allow you to look past the cold, scientific number crunching and consider the trends occurring in each generational group and their changing needs.

As you do, you'll realise that each generation typically has a similar set of values, fusing an otherwise disparate group of people.

WHAT CREATES THESE VALUES?

Childhood experiences, the fact that they all confront similar situations at similar stages in their lives and the influence of the generations that came before them.

For example, the generation born in the 1930s and early 1940s, are now aged 80-plus, are very different from their children, the Baby Boomers.

This "frugal generation" switch off lights when leaving rooms; only replace their clothes and their cars when they're worn out and they are uncomfortable with debt. They borrowed to buy their homes, and then struggled to pay off their mortgages as soon as they could. Despite this background, and much to the surprise of their children, they seem to have enjoyed far greater happiness in their lives and their marriages than any of the generations that have followed.

Contrast this to their children, the Baby Boomers. This generation has been very different to their parents — being anything but frugal. They invented the concept of "hippies" and grew their hair and protested. They first wore denim (now everyone does) and eventually grew up to be "dinks" then "yuppies".

They've often been called the "spoilt generation" and passionately embraced corporatism and a "greed is good" mentality in the 1980s. Now they're in their 60s or 70s, about half of them have been divorced and some are looking for more out of life.

The Baby Boomer's children, Generation X and Generation Y (also called Millennials), are now exerting a huge influence on housing markets through their attitudes, lifestyles and housing preferences.

There will be a fundamental shift in our social composition as Australia's population ages and a significant change of housing requirements will be the result. So let's take a closer look at...

DEMOGRAPHIC CHANGES

As I've already mentioned, understanding Australia's lifestyle and demographic shifts will provide you with major insights when choosing your investments as these trends aren't going to change overnight, or even in the medium term.

Firstly, here are some interesting demographics trends as well as the implications for these changes.

1. Our population is ageing.

Our Baby Boomers are becoming empty nesters and as a result, their lifestyles are changing. Many are ready to retire from work and travel more. ABS population projections tell us the population of Australians aged 55 years and over will increase from 5.1 million to 7.9 million between 2011 and 2031 — a 55% increase.

2. Our population is changing.

While families continue to make up 70% of households, these have shrunk from on average 4.5 people in 1911 to 2.6 at the 2016 census as the proportion of lone-person households, couple only and single parent plus dependent children households are on the increase. Theoretically this means there should be less demand for sprawling properties, yet today the average home is bigger, better and more lavishly equipped than before, with an average of 186 sq m of inside area, making Australian houses second in size only to those of Americans.

3. Our population is growing.

Australia has a business plan to increase its population to 40 million by the middle of the century. Clearly the demand for property will be enormous and medium and high-density housing will be easier to supply to service this population growth — in fact, building approvals for higher density housing outnumber those for detached houses in the Sydney and Melbourne property markets.

4. We're becoming more diverse.

Around 30% of Australians were born overseas and we will continue to become more diverse every year.

The face of the nation is changing as a new wave of nationalities call Australia home.

Demographer Simon Kuestenmacher explains that in the decades after WWII, migrants from Greece and Italy shaped the nation. Upon arrival, they convinced Australians to take up Mediterranean cuisine, supplement tea with coffee and potatoes for pasta.

We even started to build houses based on the Mediterranean rather than English design principles. Australians have always picked up the best practices and habits of newly arrived migrants.

5. First home buyers will continue to struggle.

With housing affordability, in particular in our capital cities, among the most expensive in the world, the property market is becoming less accessible for first time homebuyers. First time home buyers are willing to compromise their housing preferences just to get into the market with many moving to apartments, while others becoming renting investors (I'll explain this in a moment).

6. Our preferences are changing.

The backyard has become a victim of the modern, cosmopolitan lifestyle embraced by a nation of city dwellers. Millennials have has different preferences to the generations before them with many wanting to live in the inner city to be closer to work, social life and attractions. They are uber busy, and as much as the idea appeals, they just don't have the time to look after a garden, meaning townhouses and "family-friendly" apartments are much more convenient for their lifestyle.

Today typically both partners work as compared to the 1980s and '90s, so for them to sacrifice a large backyard and living closer to work buys them a couple of hours commuting time a week.

7. Our overall level of home ownership is decreasing.

The rate of home ownership has fallen from 72% in 2001 to around 66% today.

This decline is in part due to younger Australians finding it more difficult to become owner-occupiers. It is also due to growing numbers of Australians dropping out of home ownership because of lifestyle choices.

And these trends are likely to continue.

THESE TRENDS HAVE SOME SURPRISING IMPLICATIONS

These factors all add up and their combined pressure is sure to result in a change to the type of property that will be in continuous strong demand in the future.

In the 1970s and '80s, the family home on a quarter acre of land in the middle and outer suburbs was our "castle" and apartments (or "flats" as they were called then) were for those who couldn't afford to buy a home. Now and in the future, the market is increasingly looking for smaller, more affordable accommodation in premium locations. There will be an increasing demand for medium-density developments – townhouses or apartment buildings, which offer privacy, security, low maintenance, convenient access to community facilities, attractive design and good facilities such as car parking and recreational areas.

The demand for this type of property will occur in most suburbs, not just close to or in the CBD. At the same time we've seen a falling demand for the traditional three-bedroom, two-bathroom house on a standard block.

Unfortunately many councils are increasingly coming under pressure from action groups to stem the tide of these higher density developments – especially in quality areas. This restriction on supply can only add pressure to the developing demand and result in consistent price growth for this type of property in the foreseeable future.

DIGGING DEEPER INTO DEMOGRAPHICS

Demographic theory is a bit like astrology which ascribes behaviours and traits to people born in particular months. Generational theory does the same for people born across a decade or more.

Clearly the idea that a group might think and act alike is abhorrent to most of us who would like to think we are unique, special and different to everyone else. However, I've found that segments of our population do think and act sufficiently alike and a lot has to do with their childhood. Boomers were raised by frugal parents. Millennials were raised in prosperous households with smaller families where both parents worked.

Now each Australian demographic group is currently reaching a significant milestone.

Gen Y hit their mid-30s, Gen X hit mid-life at 50 and the Baby Boomers approach the 70-year milestone. Each of these generations is living younger than their years would suggest, so let's look at the different needs of the various demographic groups.

BABY BOOMERS

With the end of World War II in 1945 Australia's servicemen and women returned and family life resumed after an interruption of almost six years of wartime conflict. Nine months later saw the start of a population revolution as childbirth rates soared — more than four million Australians were born between 1946–1964.

People born during this period became known as Baby Boomers. Combined with an increase in European migration to Australia, the Boomers changed Australia (and the world) in the second half of the 20th century.

The Baby Boomer generation has always distorted the market — demographer Bernard Salt describes it like a tennis ball through a garden hose. In fact some studies suggest that this demographic group, by its very existence alone, generated about a third of the house price growth over the past 40 years.

This population swell had a huge economic and cultural impact on Australia. Whatever was required by their parents' generation had to be geared up by a factor of at least 50% for the Baby Boomers. In other words, we had to quickly produce new schools, new shopping centres and new houses.

This didn't happen for the succeeding generation, because even though there are more Generation Xers than Baby Boomers, the difference in generational numbers is only about 10%.

Economically, Baby Boomers represent an even bigger future challenge. As they grow older this group will distort Australia's non-working population, just as they increased its working population throughout the 1960s and 1970s. An older non-working population will put a greater strain on Australia's hospitals, aged-care services and pensions with some commentators predicting a financial crisis.

The 5.1 million Baby Boomers in Australia, around 20% of them have a university degree and they account for 20% of the country's population as well as around 20% of our workforce, but as they retire they are likely to only make up 5% of the workforce in 2028.

Think about it — the changing lifestyle of retiring Boomers will create a demand for somewhere between 75,000 and 100,000 households each year. It's suggested that in 10 years' time, as 150,000 Baby Boomers reach retirement age each year, this could account for over 50% of our property market.

While some Boomers are moving to new inner-city apartments, studies show that most are ageing in place. They would rather go down the road and meet their friends for a coffee and stay with the same doctor and hairdresser.

What this means is that well-positioned, modern and secure apartments or townhouses in our middle ring suburbs and near good shopping strips are likely to be the increasingly preferred style of accommodation in the decades to come.

So if you want to own a property that will be in continuous strong demand over the next 20 years or so, keep the needs of the Baby Boomers in mind.

But gone will be the oft promoted image of Australian retirement as a happy couple walking along a beach at dawn or dusk. It will be replaced by the reality of weathered hands still working as many Baby Boomers will not have enough savings or superannuation to see them through their golden years.

Moving forward this means the pension and health care system just won't be able to cope with the avalanche of Baby Boomers careening into retirement. As life expectancy increases it will be necessary to push out the "official" retirement age and when the pension or health care benefits kick in. Across the world the average age of retirement generally starts at 65 but already many countries, including Australia, are pushing this to 67 or 68.

Leading demographer Simon Kuestenmacher believes Baby Boomers are redefining retirement. He sees four major tribes of Boomers moving into retirement:

The Lifestylists — aged between 55-64 years who preparing for retirement. They will slide into retirement, rather than jumping into it all at once, by continuing to work part time for some years.

The Active Retirees — aged between 65-74 who are still somewhat linked to work. They want to stay active and remain in their family home as long as possible. They will only move house when they are forced to.

The Downsizers — generally aged between 75-84. At this stage, they are slowly starting to prepare for old age. Physical problems will force this group to slowly start changing their housing needs

Old Age — 85 or older and likely to be experiencing quite a few physical ailments. However, they still want to live as independently and as healthily as possible.

As I see it, single household Baby Boomers are becoming a force to be reckoned with in our property markets. They're single, they're independent and know what they want and they probably have pets. This means an increasing demand for smaller houses, townhouses and pet-friendly apartments.

While some are choosing this lifestyle, others do not live alone by choice. They have been forced to by divorce or the death of a partner.

These single Boomers underpin a huge demand for housing, so as a property investor it is interesting to understand the type of property that would attract this demographic. Unlike the young singles, who are more likely to live in an inner city or near city high-rise apartment, these

Boomers are more likely to prefer a smaller dwelling or a unit in the middle suburbs.

Remember, these single Baby Boomers are not hermits. Many have a relationship, but they just don't want to live with another person, particularly if they are recently divorced. Instead they prefer living with animals who require less emotional and physical "maintenance".

I have always been "pet friendly" as a landlord and it has repaid me well. I can think of a number of my long-term tenants who fall into the Mingle category.

In particular Rosemary who has lived with her dog in one of our investment properties, a single-storey unit in the bay side suburb of Brighton for over sixteen years. She treats our property like her own and watches over our other tenants and the common areas like a mother hen. She's been a great tenant who, interestingly, didn't tell us about her dog when she first applied to rent the property – but I'd choose a single Boomer with a pet as a tenant any day.

HOUSING AND GEN-X

The housing preferences of Gen-Xers (born in 1965 and 1980) are just as significant as those of their Boomer parents. Around 4.8 million Gen Xers make up around 19% of our population and 31% of our workforce and most are in their peak earning years. Around 25% of Gen X have a university degree and it is estimated that in a 2028 they will account for 25% of our workforce.

In general Gen-Xers prefer living in the inner suburbs close to work, shops and entertainment and are less attracted to car-based transport. They think and act differently to their parents. They're smart, financially literate and comfortable with technology. They are the first generation to be childless throughout their 20s. Being unmarried and often still studying for their second degree, they prefer to live in proximity to cafés, bars, restaurants and nightclubs.

Younger people drive urban regeneration and Gen-Xers are keenly renovating old houses and demanding better retail goods and services such as cafés, restaurants and delicatessens.

GENERATION Y — NOW CALLED MILLENNIALS

This generation includes those born between early 1980s to 1995. There are around 5.5 million of them making up 22% of our population and 35% of our workforce. More of this demographic are completing tertiary and postgraduate studies (one in three have a university degree), delaying marriage and children. In 2028 they will make up 32% of our workforce.

This generation is prioritising their friendship networks over the nuclear family and, according to demographer Bernard Salt, many prefer to spend their hard-earned cash on smashed avo and soy lattes rather than saving for a house deposit.

Gen Y is often described as a 'generation of renters'. They're living in their favourite lifestyle suburbs — which are often locations that are too expensive for them to buy in, or they're remaining at home with their parents which is more appealing than doing what their parents did — scrimping, saving, buying a small first house on the outskirts and commuting to work.

But they aren't giving up on property as research by Domain shows 16% of Gen Ys already own two or more properties compared to only 17% of Gen X and Baby Boomers. They are what I call renting investors who realise that once you're in the market, it becomes much easier to buy other properties down the track — either more investments or the dream family home.

Many Generation Ys will turn 40 over the next decade and their preferences will be a major driver of our property markets next decade.

GENERATION Z

The 4.3 million people in this demographic were born between 1995 and 2010 and make up 19% of our population.

They're not really a force in our housing markets yet, making up around 14% of our workforce, but they will be a major influence in the future as it's projected they'll make up one third of our workforce by the end of this new decade.

THE TYPICAL LIFE CYCLE AND THE HOUSING MARKET

Sure, some behaviours, values, and preferences differ markedly between the generations. On the other hand, some things stay mostly the same. For example, every generation goes through predictable life stages at roughly the same time and moves home at roughly the same stages in their lives and these shape our housing markets.

Our census shows us that about 17 per cent of all people living in Australia (about 4.3 million of us) move house in any given year.

Demographer Simon Kuestnmacher has summarised it as follows:

"The younger your kids, the more likely you are to have moved home in the last year. Young parents look for larger dwellings as their kids get older. At age 14, kids arrive at the most stable phase of their youth, as only 13 per cent will have moved in the last year. Parents try to provide stability to kids in their most unstable developmental phase.

Starting at age 18 the most mobile phase of the lifecycle kicks in and peaks at age 23, when 37 per cent of Australians will have moved within the last year.

Young adults move around a lot before they enter the family-formation stage and look to settle down. They leave the parental home for their tertiary studies, move into a series of shabby share houses, and eventually progress into their first apartment with partners.

Once Australians enter permanent relationships, moving becomes a less frequent activity and the dream of home ownership emerges.

The older we get, the more likely we are to stay at one place. At age 77 only 5 per cent of Australians will have moved within the last year. Starting at 77, we tend to move more frequently again. That's when downsizing starts."

As we move through the life-cycle, we are also more likely to become homeowners.

Millennials, of course, delayed home ownership quite a bit. This was partly because they partnered up later in life, delayed first child birth, and partly because housing is becoming more unaffordable every year. That said, many are now in the family formation stage of their lives and keen to move out of the apartment into town houses or homes.

THE TYPICAL LIFE CYCLE AND THE HOUSING MARKET

Sure, some behaviours, values and preferences differ markedly between the generations. On the other hand, some things stay mostly same. For example, every generation goes through predictable life stages at roughly the same time and moves home at roughly the same stages in their lives and these shape our housing markets.

Our census shows us that about 17 per cent of all people living in Australia (about 4.3 million of us) move house in any given year.

Demographer Simon Kuestnmacher has summarised it as follows:

"The younger your kids, the more likely you are to have moved home in the last year. Young parents look for larger dwellings as their kids get older. At age 14, kids arrive at the most stable phase of their youth, as only 13 per cent will have moved in the last year. Parents try to provide stability to kids in their most unstable developmental phase.

"Starting at age 18, the most mobile phase of the life-cycle kicks in and peaks at age 23, when 37 per cent of Australians will have moved within the last year.

"Young adults move around a lot before they enter the family-formation stage and look to settle down. They leave the parental home for their tertiary studies, move into a series of shabby share houses, and eventually progress into their first apartment with partners.

"Once Australians enter permanent relationships, moving becomes a less frequent activity and the dream of home ownership emerges.

"The older we get, the more likely we are to stay at one place. At age 77 only 5 per cent of

Australians will have moved within the last year. Starting at 77, we tend to move more frequently again. That's when downsizing starts."

As we move through the life-cycle, we are also more likely to become homeowners.

Millennials, of course, delayed home ownership quite a bit. This was partly because they partnered up later in life, delayed first child birth, and partly because housing is becoming more unaffordable every year. That said, many are now in the family formation stage of their lives and keen to move out of the apartment into town houses or homes.

DIFFERENT STROKES FOR DIFFERENT FOLKS

What I've tried to explain is that the different tribes (demographic groups) have different ways of living and different housing needs.

The Baby Boomers' parents typically lived in small homes in what are now our inner ring suburbs. Today few still live independently — many are in nursing homes.

Middle suburbia, the three-bedroom home on a quarter-acre block was developed in the 1950s and 1960s to house the Baby Boomers while some built a McMansion — very large houses on the edge of town in tree-change type locations.

Gen Xers moved back to the inner suburbs in the 1970s and '80s gentrifying them and then the age of apartments kicked off from the middle of the 1990s — first in Sydney, then in Melbourne around a decade later and then this trend grew in Brisbane and Perth. Some call this the Manhattanisation of our capital cities.

At the same time, multiculturalism and technological advancements are among the social changes that will lead to the development of a new set of demographic "tribes" over the next decade. According to leading demographer Bernard Salt, these will include:

- *Social singles* — In the fastest growing trend, it is predicted by 2030 more than 26% of Australians will be living in single person households.

- *Multigenerational clans* — Continued multiculturalism and changing age demographics within the Australian population are tipped to increase the number of households that see children, parents and grandparents living under the one roof. At present almost one in five (18%) of Australia's households hold two generations and 9% hold three generations. These figures are expected to rise to 24% and 13% respectively within the next decade. Yet it seems that less than 5% of Australia's existing housing stock successfully caters to this multi-generational market.

- *Homework tribes* — It is possible that one in three people be employed on a freelance basis by 2030. This trend emphasises the need for at home workspaces as well as more spaces for communal work.

- *Peter Pans* — these are the Baby Boomers, and as mentioned above they will not be looking for sea change, tree change or retirement villages, but will want to spend their golden years in the same locations, enabling them to continue enjoying their lives close to their families, friends and familiar surroundings.

PART III

CHOOSING WHEN, WHERE AND WHAT TO BUY

SUCCESS DEPENDS ON PREVIOUS PREPARATION,
AND WITHOUT SUCH PREPARATION
THERE IS SURE TO BE FAILURE.
– *CONFUCIUS*

MY STRATEGIC APPROACH TO PROPERTY INVESTMENT

I have been educating investors on wealth creation through property for well over 20 years and I often ask them what they feel is the most important factor in selecting a top-performing investment property: What you buy or where you buy or when you buy?

By "**what you buy**" I mean buying a new property instead of an established property. Do you buy a house or do you buy a townhouse or an apartment?

When I ask "**where you buy**" I'm talking about the old concept of location, location, location.

And when I mention "**when you buy**" I'm talking about your timing in the property cycle.

In the good old days when I conducted seminars very few people raise their hand for "what you buy". A few more admit to "when you buy". By far the bulk of attendees at every seminar believe that location is the most critical factor in choosing a top performing property investment.

Before I told them my thoughts I always teased the audience by suggesting it is possible to get all three right and shortly I'll explain my thoughts on each of these factors. But if I had to choose just one, I would choose location — **where you buy** — over the others, every time. However, you can't just buy any property in a good location and hope it becomes a great investment.

You see... when you decide to buy a property there are three major variables.

1. **Your budget** – this will be determined by your lender and will be a major influence on the next two factors.

2. **Location** – you can't compromise on this.

3. **The type of property** you buy – you must buy the best property your budget allows in the best location you can afford. Depending on your budget it could be a house, townhouse or apartment. I'd rather buy an apartment in a great location if that's all my budget allows rather than a house with land in a location with less capital growth. You'll understand why as I explain more...

HOW TO MAKE SURE YOU BUY THE RIGHT PROPERTY

While at any time there are hundreds of thousands of properties for sale, not all will make good investments. In fact, most won't — in my mind less than 4% of the properties currently available for sale are "investment grade". To ensure I buy a property that will outperform the market averages I use a **Top Down Property Selection Approach**.

This is the property investment system that I've fine-tuned over five decades and has helped me and many of my clients build very substantial property portfolios.

1. It starts with buying at the **right stage of the economic cycle**. I look at the big picture — how the economy is performing and where we are in the economic and property cycle.

Currently the world has its share of economic problems and while Australia's economy is not growing at the rate many would like, it's still the envy of most developed nations.

2. Then I look for the **right state in which to invest** — one that is in the right stage of its own property cycle.

Each state in Australia has its own property cycle, and while not trying to time the cycle, I don't want to buy right near the peak and then wait a couple of years for capital growth to return.

3. Then within that state, I look for the **right suburb in the capital city**.

I only invest in capital cities because that's where the bulk of our economic and population growth occurs and where there are multiple pillars underpinning the economy and multiple growth drivers pushing up property values.

I steer clear of regional towns, tourist destinations and our smaller capital cities where property values tend to be more volatile.

Then within the capital city I look for a location that has a long history of outperforming the averages with regards to capital growth, and one that is likely to continue to do so because of the demographics of the people who live there. By now you now that demographics is one of the biggest factors determining capital growth and I've found some suburbs have 50 to 100% more capital growth than others over a 10-year period. Obviously those are the suburbs I target.

This is different to the speculative approach some investors adopt looking for the next "hot spot". They say things like, "Oh, this suburb hasn't had much capital growth — maybe it's time has come," or, "That's a brand-new suburb. They're getting a train line down there so it must grow in value."

Instead I look for suburbs that are gentrifying or locations where wages growth out performs the averages. These tend to be suburbs close to the CBD where the inhabitants work in service industries where wages are rising substantially.

This means I avoid the blue-collar areas (where wages are usually capped to the CPI and may suffer if unemployment creeps up) and first home buyer suburbs which tend to be more interest rate sensitive.

Some of the other factors I look for in selecting an investment grade location include:

- Economic growth which will lead to jobs growth and in turn population growth.

- A suburb that has

    o   Market depth — a substantial turnover of properties with a large pool of affluent buyers willing to purchase there.

    o   Low "days on market" — this is a factor of supply and demand and means dwellings sell relatively quickly.

    o   A high proportion of owner occupiers — they are a steadying force in a local property market. You see… investors create property booms, but when the market turns investors often have to sell up. On the other hand, owner occupiers would rather eat dog food than sell up their houses.

    o   A low vacancy rate — another measure of supply and demand of property, but this time for tenants.

    o   Convenience, infrastructure, and good public transport — these are all important factors for owner occupiers.

In a moment I'll explain a bit more about finding the right suburb.

4. Once my research shows me the suburb to explore, we then look for the **right location** within that suburb.

Some liveable streets will always outperform others, and in those streets some properties will always be more desirable than others and outperform as investments. As most suburbs tend the have three or four separate districts with different attributes and different price points, it's important to have on the ground knowledge to differentiate them. Think about the suburb where you live — there would be areas you'd happily live in and areas you would avoid, like on main roads or too close to shops, schools or commercial areas.

I even drill down to different sides of the street. There are some streets in Sydney where a house on the north side would get magnificent views of the water and the Sydney Harbour Bridge and a house on the south side gets magnificent views of the house on the north side which has views of the water and the Sydney Harbour Bridge. Prices in the same street can vary by up to 30%.

5. Then within that location we look for the **right property**, using my 6 Stranded Strategic Approach I'll explain in a minute. And finally, I look for…

6. The **right price**. I'm not looking for a "cheap" property (there will always be cheap properties in secondary locations). I'm looking for the right property at a fair price.

I choose my properties in that order, using a top-down approach, leads many people to ask why price is at the bottom of the list since they've heard that you make your money when you buy your property.

While that is correct, it's not because you pay a cheap price or because you get a bargain. You make your money when you buy because you purchase the right property — one that will be in continual strong demand by both owner-occupiers (who push up property values) and tenants (who help you pay off your mortgage).

If you think about it the value of your property only really matters three times. The day you buy your property, the day you refinance it, and the day you sell.

I've seen many investors buy a secondary property cheaply thinking they bought a bargain until they try to refinance it a few years later and find they didn't get the capital growth they hoped for. A cheap property today will most likely be a cheap property tomorrow.

In summary, the location of your property will contribute the bulk of the growth of your property and owning the right property in that location will contribute 20% of its performance.

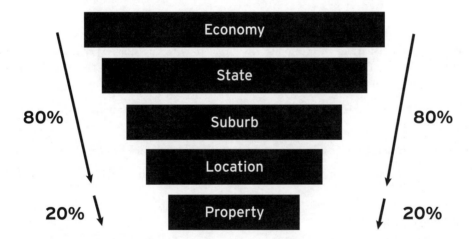

FINDING THE RIGHT SUBURB

Fact is, not all land is created equal. Some suburbs will always be more popular than others, some areas will have more scarcity than others and over time some land will increase in value more than others.

It's no coincidence that things like the socioeconomic level of the people who live or work in a particular neighbourhood, its proximity to public transportation, crime rates, the closeness to prestigious universities and medical facilities, traffic congestion, zoning restrictions, the quality of schools make some locations more desirable.

Of course, these are the areas property investors should target, as that's where they'll get above average capital growth.

There are basically four types of locations where you could buy properties and as you'll see a lot has to do with the demographics of those who want to and can afford to live in these suburbs.

1. Discretionary Locations

These are the most expensive locations in our capital cities — the "established money" locations where most of the residents have lived for a long time and where many residents have paid off their home loans years ago.

In general, these locations are the established inner-ring suburbs of our capital cities or suburbs close to water. Think of Toorak, Brighton or Kew in Victoria, Teneriffe or New Farm in Brisbane, and Darling Point or Bellevue Hill in Sydney.

Over the long term this sector of the housing market outperforms the other segments, in part because of its scarcity, but in particular because, as we know, the rich are getting richer than the average Australian and they can afford to and are prepared to pay a premium to live in these prime locations.

Interestingly over the property cycle values in these suburbs are often more volatile. During property booms and periods of economic growth such as we are now experiencing, wealthy Australians have the financial capacity to indulge their emotional wants and buy the most expensive properties they can.

Then during the inevitable economic downturns activity in these locations tends to quieten down.

However, over the long term, this segment of the market outperforms the other sectors.

Of course, not everyone can afford to buy at this end of the market, so strategic investors often look to invest in...

2. Aspirational Locations

These are the upper-middle-class areas and gentrifying locations of our big cities. Suburbs like Bentleigh or Elwood in Melbourne; Paddington, Mosman, Randwick or Newton in Sydney, and Camp Hill or Grange in Brisbane.

These are the suburbs where many affluent millennials are aspiring to move as they enter the family formation stage of their lives. When this wealthier demographic moves into a suburb they tend to push up property values.

As you wander through these suburbs you'll see a changing neighbourhood with new developments and infrastructure improving the quality of services for the residents as well as driving economic and jobs growth. These developments also create a ripple effect producing economic, social and cultural change.

Interestingly there are several different types of aspirational suburbs:

- Lifestyle suburbs – where people love to hang out and be seen.

- Beach, water and sand belt suburbs – for those looking for a particular type of lifestyle.

- Knowledge centres – suburbs where highly paid knowledge workers like to congregate.

- School zone suburbs – where young families will pay a premium.

- Tree change and green change suburbs became more popular during Covid.

- Cultural suburbs – many immigrants like living in the same suburb as others from their homeland for cultural reasons.

3. Affordable Locations

This is where most homeowners and many investors look because that's where they can afford to buy. However, sometimes investors buy in these suburbs because they are "advised" to buy at the cheaper end of the market.

There is no doubt some affordable areas make good investment locations, especially those that benefit from the ripple effect from adjoining aspirational suburbs and eventually become aspirational suburbs themselves.

On the other hand, most locations at the affordable end of the property market underperform with regards to capital growth and rental growth because many of the owners are young families who have stretched themselves to their financial limits and are often only a week or two weeks away from broke.

Similarly, the tenants who rent in these locations live there because that's all they can afford and are unlikely to be able to pay you increasing rents over time since they are also only one or two weeks away from being broke.

As an investor I would steer clear of these affordable locations – most of these will never gentrify in your lifetime and they will underperform with regards to rental growth and capital growth. Remember... your rental increases are your future income and in these locations the future income growth of the residents will not be as high as in the more affluent locations meaning your rental growth will not be as high.

Often owning properties in these locations will be more trouble than they're worth.

4. Last Choice Locations

In every city, there are suburbs where people live because they really have no choice. No one wakes up in the morning wanting to live in these suburbs, but social circumstances force them to. Of course, investors should steer clear of these locations.

But there's more...

Just like not all properties locations are the same, not all properties within each location of the same. Even in the best suburbs, there are some properties I would avoid – they just don't make good investments and others I would be keen to have in my portfolio.

- **A-grade homes and "investment grade" properties** are the type of assets you want to own, and the type of properties, where great tenants want to live, not because they need to, but because they want to and are prepared to pay extra to live there. Think of family-friendly apartments in the great neighbourhoods of Bondi in Sydney or Elwood or Fitzroy in Melbourne.

- **B-grade properties** still have a lot going for them, and during hot property markets like we are currently experiencing they still perform well, but their second location within their suburb or the less than perfect attributes of these properties means they will slump more in downtimes when buyers and tenants are more choosey.

- **C-grade properties** are to be avoided unless they're in a great neighbourhood and your intention is to demolish the property and replace it with something more appropriate for the location.

To ensure I buy the "right property" in that location, one that outperforms the market I use my **6 Stranded Strategic Approach**, which means that I would only buy a property:

1. **That appeals to owner occupiers.** Not that I plan to sell my property, but because owner occupiers will buy similar properties pushing up local real estate values. This will be particularly important in the future as the percentage of investors in the market is likely to diminish.

2. **Below intrinsic value** – that's why I would avoid new and off-the-plan properties which come at a premium price.

3. **With a high land to asset ratio** – that doesn't necessarily mean a large block of land, but one where the land component makes up a significant part of the asset value.

4. In an area that has a long history of strong capital growth and that will **continue to outperform the averages** because of the demographics in the area as mentioned above.

5. **With a twist** – something unique, or special, different or scarce about the property, and finally;

6. Where I can manufacture capital growth through refurbishment, renovations or redevelopment rather than waiting for the market to deliver me capital growth.

While most investors read a book or two, do a little research and then buy one of the first properties they come across, strategic investors are smarter than that. They follow a system that is rooted in the real world and has stood the test of time in changing markets.

By following my 6 Stranded Strategic Approach I minimise my risks and maximise my upside as each strand represents a way of making money from property and combining all five is a powerful way of putting the odds in my favour. If one strand lets me down, I have three or four others supporting my property's performance.

Location:

- Correct state, right time in cycle
- Economic growth – wages growth population growth
- Capital City
- Suburbs with future capital gains potential – best neighbourhood
- Infrastructure
- % owner occupiers
- Supply and demand, market depth, days on market, low vacancy rate
- Affluent demographic
- Convenience, Walk Score, public transport, amenity, community

Property:

- Owner occupier appeal
- Below Intrinsic Value
- Scarcity
- Land to asset ratio
- Twist
- Add Value
- Layout
- Low maintenance and outgoings

CAPITAL GROWTH FIRST, THE CASH FLOW

Just to make things clear... the crux of my successful property investment strategy is that residential real estate is a high growth, low yield investment.

Let me explain what I mean.

Property investors make their money in four ways:

1. *Capital growth* — as the property appreciates in value over time.

2. *Rental returns* — the cash flow you get from your tenant.

3. *Accelerated or forced growth* — this is capital growth you manufacture by adding value through renovations or development, and

4. *Tax benefits* — like negative gearing or depreciation allowances.

I have found that of all of these, capital growth is the most important. I know not everyone agrees with my strategy. In fact when it comes to property investment you'll often hear two somewhat conflicting philosophies being bandied around.

While successful investors invest for capital growth the other school are the "cash flow" followers who suggest you should invest in property that has the capacity to generate high rental returns in an attempt to achieve positive cash flow. In other words, they want rental returns that are higher than their outgoings (including the mortgage payments), leaving money in their pocket each month. In my mind, this just doesn't work in today's financial era.

Sure we would all like to buy properties that have both great capital growth and high rental yields, but if you purchase an investment grade property, that's just not the way it works. As

I've explained, in order to achieve financial freedom you're going to need to build a substantial asset base. To build your asset base, and in turn your net worth, you need to buy high growth investment properties.

This is because capital growth builds your equity much faster than loan repayments and rental income will.

But here's the trick...

You can never turn a cash flow positive property into a high growth property, because of its geographical location. But you can achieve both high returns (cash flow), as well as capital growth by renovating or developing your high growth properties. This will bring you a higher rent and extra depreciation allowances, which convert high growth, relatively low cash flow properties into high growth, strong cash flow properties.

This means that you can get the best of both worlds.

TWO-THIRDS OF THE MARKET ARE HOMEOWNERS

It's interesting that while owner occupiers are one of the most significant influences on property, they are commonly overlooked by property investors. Yet you've probably noticed I've emphasised focussing your research on those often overlooked home owners.

Think about it...with almost 70% of all homes in Australia owned by owner occupiers, this underpins the steady long term growth of property values. On the other hand investors, who comprise just 30% of the market, create our property booms (often driven by Fear Of Missing Out or greed) and our property downturns (when they exit the market by sitting on the sidelines or selling up) creating volatility.

So as you can see owner occupiers outnumber investors two to one, which is why I always recommend buying the type of property that will appeal to owner occupiers.

You see...in my mind an investment grade property must have owner occupier appeal. And I want it to be attractive to affluent owner occupiers who will have the money to and be prepared to pay a great price to own this type of property which would be located in an aspirational or gentrifying suburb.

Now this is different to what most investors look for, isn't it?

They wonder who the tenant will be, how much rent will they get and what tax benefits will be available; and then end up buying in one of those Lego Land high rise apartment towers and wonder why their investment under performs.

On the other hand, owning a property with an element of scarcity which is located close to amenities, jobs, transport, lifestyle features and cultural, social aspects like cafés, bars and arts precincts will always attract home buyers. But these are features that appeal to tenants, too. And if you buy a property that ticks all these boxes, you know you're investing in a dwelling with broad, lasting appeal.

BUYING RIGHT OR BUYING WELL

In my mind there is a big difference between buying right and buying well. Some investors take far too long researching the market and never make a move because they are looking to "buy well". Their sole focus is to buy a bargain and pay under market.

Buying right on the other hand, is not purely influenced by price; rather the emphasis is on the quality of the property you end up with. Here your focus is on buying top quality asset that will outperform the averages.

Let's consider two scenarios to illustrate how **buying well** compares to **buying right**.

John buys an investment property in a poor location, an area where there is no strong demand from owner buyers and purchases a $500,000 property $30,000 below what he considers market value to be — only paying $470,000 for his investment. Now remember this property is in a secondary location so it only achieves capital growth of about 4% per annum.

In our second example, Julie buys an investment property in an area where properties increase in value at about 8% per annum. Because this is a highly sought-after area there is plenty of competition from purchasers and she has to pay $530,000 for her property, which is $30,000 above what she believed would be a fair market value.

John can buy his property a bit below the market value because it is in an area where there is little demand. While John may get an immediate gain of $30,000 as well as an interest savings because he borrowed less to pay for his property, in the long run he will be worse off than Julie who paid more for her better asset. This is because Julie's property will grow in value by around 8% per annum, while John's property will increase in value by only about 4% each year.

In fact, Julie who bought "right" is better off by over $125,000 after only five years and is $350,000 wealthier than John after ten years because of the increased capital growth of her property. And because of the solid capital growth of her property, Julie will continue to enjoy more capital growth in the value of her investment property and stronger rental growth than John who tried so hard to buy well in the beginning.

	Today	Capital Growth	Value in 5 years	Value in 10 years
John	$470,000	4% per annum	$608,000	$740,000
Julie	$530,000	8% per annum	$735,000	$1,080,000

While it is true that **the profit is in the buying,** this doesn't always mean buying cheap — it means buying right. As you can tell from the above example, the long-term capital growth prospects for the property are far more important. So next time you are looking to buy an investment property think about the potential long-term growth of the asset (and the ability to boost this through renovations) and not just the short-term gain you may achieve by buying under market.

Buy the right property in the right location so that you achieve short, medium and long-term profits through strong rental returns and more importantly capital growth. If you are in the property market for the long term — and you should be as property is really a long-term, high-growth and relatively low-yield investment – then you should focus on factors that are going to influence your property's value in the long term.

Focusing your efforts on the initial price or getting the property at a certain discount to the asking price or to its market value is only going to influence your short-term profits. On the other hand, buying the right property will really pay off and leave you laughing all the way to the bank for the long term.

THE OPPORTUNITY COST OF NOT INVESTING

To consider the concept of the "*opportunity cost*" for people who have the available equity in their homes or investments properties but don't use it to buy further properties, let's take the example of two other investors, Jill and Brian.

Imagine Jill bought her investment property a few years ago, while Brian procrastinated and didn't do anything until three years later when all the papers were full of the news about how well the property markets had performed and the price of properties had risen considerably.

Here are some basic assumptions we will use:

If you think about it, Jill would have had to borrow 100% of her funds to purchase her investment — firstly the 20% deposit (which may be borrowed using the equity she has in her home) and then the balance of the purchase price.

I am going to make some further assumptions for this exercise...

Firstly, Jill has read this book and bought a well-located investment property for $500,000 at the right time of the property cycle and the property increased in value by 10% per annum. Also that she paid interest on 100% of the value of the property — her deposit plus the balance of the purchase cost at 5% per annum. I have also assumed that she received rent at 3.5% of the property's value (so this increased every year) and that her property outgoings (rates, taxes, insurance, managing agent's commission etc.) amount to 2% of the property's value.

Then I have assumed Brian buys a similar property three years later — at today's market value.

Sure I've made a lot of assumptions here, but what I'm really trying to show is the big picture view of what happens if you delay purchasing an investment property. So let's look at the following table:

Jill bought a $500,000 property three years ago

	Growth	Year End Value	Rent p.a.	Interest p.a.	Outgoings	Cashflow
End of year 1	$50,000	$550,000	$19,250	$25,000	$10,000	-$15,750
End of year 2	$55,000	$605,000	$21,175	$25,000	$11,000	-$14,825
End of year 3	$60,500	$665,000	$23,275	$25,000	$12,100	-$13,825

A couple of things are obvious from these figures:

1. Buying well-located properties that increase in value means that while you get strong capital growth, you tend to be cash flow negative (especially when you borrow 100% of the money as has happened here).

2. Over the first three years Jill made a respectable capital gain — her property increased in value by over to $160,000. At the same time because the rent didn't cover her outgoings (interest plus holding costs) she had negative cash flow of almost $45,000. Even so, Jill has made around $120,000 in the first three years of owning her investment (the increase in value minus her holding costs). She could now use this extra equity as a deposit to purchase another property.

By delaying his purchase decision for three years Brian:

*   Has lost the opportunity to make the $120,000 that Jill made — that's about $770 per week. As Jill's profit is not taxed Brian would have had to earn well over $1,000 extra each week to be in the same position.

*   He now has to pay a higher price to enter the market — probably $160,000 more which means he needs a larger deposit, will pay more stamp duty and higher interest.

*   Brian can't buy a second property like Jill can and pyramid his investment income.

REGULARLY REVIEW YOUR PROPERTY PORTFOLIO

When I ask investors how their properties are performing they usually have no idea. They've just closed their eyes, crossed their fingers and hoped for the best. It makes no sense to invest in a property and then not review its performance every year or so. Strategic investors regularly review their investment portfolio's performance.

Interestingly every year I like to ask myself a couple of questions about each of my investment properties:

*   How has this property performed over the last few years?

*   Knowing what I know now would I buy this particular property again?

*   Is this property likely to outperform the averages over the next decade?

*   Is there anything I could or should do to improve this property and generate a better return on investment for me?

Logically, if a property has not performed well over a three- or four-year period, it's possibly a dud investment. The answers to these questions help ensure that I only retain top performing properties in my portfolio and that my money is working hard for me.

This means that if your property isn't giving you the return you feel it should, then it might be time to make a change either through renovations, by changing property managers or by selling up and buying a better performing investment property.

I know the current market is flat and you may not get the optimal price today, but don't wait until the market picks up because the gap between your underperforming property and better performing investments will only widen as the market improves and it will become harder and more expensive to buy the type of property you'd like to own.

Essentially the sooner you can identify and offload an underperforming property, the better. Sure you may crystallise a loss, or have to pay some capital gains tax on the sale and then pay stamp duty on your next purchase.

I understand this may mean that you'll take two steps back to move three steps forward; but if you treat your property investments like a business, and that's what all strategic investors do, you'll recognise that it's not how much money you make that matters; it's how hard your money works for you and how much you keep that counts.

If you treat your real estate investment like a business, then you should consider your properties as employees.

What would you do if one of your employees consistently came to work late, played on Twitter and Facebook all day, took a long lunch and didn't pay enough attention to your customers or clients?

You would probably do a performance review (essentially those questions I suggested you ask about your properties are a performance review) and then you are likely to sack them. You may even have to pay a redundancy package to let them go, but it would be worth it because you would be able to employ a more efficient replacement.

It's really the same with your properties – If due to your financial capacity you can only afford to employ (own) three or four properties, they'll need to be the best three or four you can employ (own); and if one is underperforming over the long term be prepared to pay that redundancy package (selling and purchasing costs as well as possible capital gains tax) to enable you to buy a better property.

With that introduction, in the next few chapters I am going to cover the when, where and what of property investing in considerable detail, to help you make good property buying decisions.

THE CROWD IS ALWAYS LATE

UNDERSTANDING TIMING

Often at a football match, a concert or any big event, you'll see one or two people in the crowd get up and head for the exit a minute or two before the end. You might have done this a few times yourself — I know I have.

And because of this head start, I've ended up at home half an hour earlier than I would have if I'd waited a few moments longer to leave. Those few minutes have put me in the car park ahead of the crowd, so instead of having to work my way through a traffic jam, I've whizzed home quickly on uncluttered roads.

I have done this hundreds of times and saved countless hours, which I've put to better use. Whenever I have to drive into the main Melbourne CBD, I try to avoid the peak hour traffic, and find I can make the journey in half the time that it would take if I left when the main crowd is going to work.

As a general rule, I always try to be a few minutes ahead of the crowd or, if I can't, a long way behind it.

TIMING IS IMPORTANT IN PROPERTY INVESTMENT

Often at a football match, a concert or any big event, you'll see one or two people in the crowd get up and head for the exit a minute or two before the end. You might have done this a few times yourself — I know I have.

And because of this head start, I've ended up at home half an hour earlier than I would have if I'd waited a few moments longer to leave. Those few minutes have put me in the car park ahead of the crowd, so instead of having to work my way through a traffic jam, I've whizzed home quickly on uncluttered roads.

I have done this hundreds of times and saved countless hours, which I've put to better use. Whenever I have to drive into the main Melbourne CBD, I try to avoid the peak hour traffic, and find I can make the journey in half the time that it would take if I left when the main crowd is going to work.

As a general rule, I always try to be a few minutes ahead of the crowd or, if I can't, a long way behind it.

INSIDER TIP

The sooner you live through an investment cycle and see the recurring nature of booms and busts in property and other investments, the sooner you will become a better investor and understand the importance of timing.

TIMING CAN MAKE OR BREAK INVESTMENTS

As most property investors purchase property to hold for the long term, they have been led to believe timing of your property purchase does not really matter. Sure **"time in"** the market (holding your property for a long time) will make up for poor **"timing"** of your purchase, because the property market is forgiving, but why not aim for good timing?

I have seen poor timing of property purchases force investors to sell their properties. This tends to happen when investors buy property near the end of a boom using a negative gearing strategy. They soon feel the strain of the monthly shortfall between rental income and their mortgages. This, combined with the bad press property receives at the depth of the property cycle, and the fact that the value of their properties are not increasing, rapidly makes them doubt their investment decisions.

Some of these investors have taken on more debt than they can safely handle, encouraged by booming prices at the time of their purchase, and have failed to keep their borrowings to a manageable level or don't have a financial buffer in place. Then, as interest rates rise (which tends to happen at the end of a property boom), they have difficulty coping and start to panic.

Sadly, many investors in this situation lose confidence with the worst possible timing. In general they're too impatient to see the fruits of their investments and this causes them to sell before they've held the property long enough to benefit from serious capital growth.

It can take seven to ten years for a market to turn a complete cycle and if you purchase at the worst time, it may take a number of years before your property even starts to increase in value and sometimes it even falls in value.

Let's take a look at a real-life example. The following are situations that faced friends of mine. While this happened quite some years ago, the lessons are still relevant today. Both friends were professionals who upgraded their family homes, but that's where similarities ended. While both stories relate to my friends' homes and not to investment property, the lessons are there to be learned. Their views were so different that you could almost be forgiven for wondering if they were talking about the same thing!

Danny's story

Danny, a solicitor, was a partner in a large city law firm. In the late 1980s his practice was booming and many of his clients were making fortunes out of property development and speculating. Danny was doing very well from all his legal work and he'd even made a tidy sum by being a silent partner in a few small development projects.

In late 1988 he and his wife Judy felt that they'd like to upgrade their home. They'd bought their original family home about seven years earlier and in the meantime property values had risen considerably and they'd built up quite some equity.

So they went shopping. They fell in love with the very first house that they inspected in a prestige Melbourne suburb. It was architect-designed, had a swimming pool (ideal for their two boys) and had been featured in Vogue magazine. In fact, the very issue featuring the house was opened at the appropriate page and left draped on the coffee table during inspection times before the auction.

At the auction they had a long bidding war with a couple of other keen purchasers and eventually bought the house for $930,000. This was $80,000 more than the limit they'd set themselves (and remember this was around 30 years ago)! Nonetheless, they had their dream home and were comforted by the fact that so many others were willing to bid almost as much.

And they lived happily… for a while anyway.

Danny and his family loved the new house and enjoyed the pool and the nearby park where they'd walk the dog. But when the recession hit in the early 1990s, property prices started to drop and solicitors' incomes began to decline. Danny started to have a little difficulty meeting his mortgage repayments. He considered selling the house, but when agents advised him that he'd probably only get around $800,000 for it, he just kept making the monthly mortgage payments to the bank.

In 1993 when interest rates dropped from the highs of the late 1980s Danny refinanced. His plan was to keep up the mortgage payments until the value of his house returned to its previous level and then decide whether to sell.

In 1996, when his three-year mortgage term expired, he once again looked at selling up, but the best price he could achieve at auction was $650,000. He couldn't accept this — it was a loss of over $300,000 in capital value (considering the initial purchase price and purchasing costs) and his six years of mortgage payments would have all gone down the drain.

Danny kept his house on the market for over a year with various agents, but didn't get any offers that he would accept.

When I spoke to him in late 1998, he had just sold his house for a price close to $700,000 and was moving into a rented property with his family. He explained that he'd lost over $250,000 in capital over the 10 years that he had owned his house, as well as all the mortgage payments and all the rates and taxes.

He was sure that property was a bad investment and felt that he would be better off renting a house for the rest of his life and leaving all the troubles of property ownership to his landlord.

Contrast this to the story I heard from Michael, a successful ear nose and throat specialist, only a few days after Danny had cried on my shoulder. He'd also bought his family home in the same suburb, but he bought his in 1993, about four years after Danny.

What a difference a little timing can make!

Michael's story

I was visiting my friend Michael because I had an ear infection and as usual the topic of conversation turned to real estate investment since he knew my interest in the subject. Michael explained to me that he was keen to buy some more property investments as he was buoyed by the huge capital gain he'd made from the family home he had bought.

He reminded me that he'd bought the property in the middle of "the recession we had to have", when real estate prices were low and nobody was keen to buy luxury houses.

He had to spend about $100,000 improving the house, which was now worth about $2 million. Almost double what he paid for it five years earlier!

He told me that agents regularly approached him with buyers keen to purchase, and how pleased he was that he'd had the courage to buy when no one else was interested in luxury property. He admitted that today he couldn't afford to buy into the luxury suburb in which he lived if he hadn't taken those brave steps to go against the crowd a few years earlier.

So here we have two tales in which the outcomes couldn't have been further apart. Yet there were a lot of parallels in these stories. They both bought similarly priced homes in the same Melbourne suburb — a top location. Yet Danny lost hundreds of thousands of dollars and Michael made close to one million! And what was the difference?

In reality Danny made two mistakes — **timing and paying way too much!**

He bought his house at the top of the property cycle, when prices were at their peak. In retrospect, he overpaid for his house at the time and it took more than seven years for the market to complete a cycle and for its value to return to the historically high levels of the late 1980s. He also bought a home in a prestige suburb and I've found the top end of the market is more volatile than the middle price ranges, with wealthy people overpaying for their "trophy home" during times when business and the economy is good, and being more circumspect during difficult times.

On the other hand, Michael had bought his house after property prices had dropped during the depths of a recession. Since then others have seen the intrinsic value of similar undervalued houses and pushed up property prices allowing Michael to sit on (or sleep in) a huge unrealised capital gain.

UNDERSTANDING THE PROPERTY CYCLE

In a free market economy prices will tend to drop when supply is plentiful and demand is low. In other words, when there is more than enough of something, it's said to be a "buyer's market" because sellers must compete, typically by lowering their prices, to attract a buyer. Conversely, when supply is low and demand is high, prices will tend to rise as buyers bid up prices to compete for the limited supply. This is called a "seller's market".

Over the long term, income growth and household formation determine the path of our property markets because they determine demand and the ability to pay. Home prices rise in line with the rise in disposable household incomes in the long term, but the level of construction amongst other things, determines the level of supply available for these newly formed households.

The property cycle describes the ups and downs around the relatively stable long-term upwards trend. This is because in the short term, property values and new construction get ahead of themselves and rise above their historic trends during the upturn phase of the cycle and the opposite is the case in the downturn. The good news is that eventually the excesses of the cycle, both at the peak and the trough tend to be self-correcting.

A simplistic version of the cycle goes something like this...

As populations grow, boosted by immigration, there is an increased demand for property and this causes an increase in values. Home buyers often get in early in the cycle and then investors become attracted to property later in the cycle as they see property values rise. By the time the main crowd starts buying property, a significant hike in prices will have already occurred. Over time higher property prices lead to a lack of affordability and property price growth stalls.

INSIDER TIP

The property market moves in cycles and despite what many will tell you, real estate values can and do fall. Then, in other years, values may rise substantially.

Understanding these principles doesn't make the real estate cycle is easy to read. The various phases are not clearly defined and the length of each cycle and its various stages varies from cycle to cycle, but the following graph shows what could happen over two property cycles. The thick black line shows how "on average" property values increase over time, because well-located capital city properties tend to double in value every 10 years or so. But the curved grey line shows that at times the value of properties in a region remains flat for a number of years (or even drops in value) – this is the slump stage of the property cycle.

Then there is an upturn phase where property values increase slowly but steadily. And finally the shortest phase of the property cycle is the boom stage when property values overshoot their natural levels.

The Property Cycle

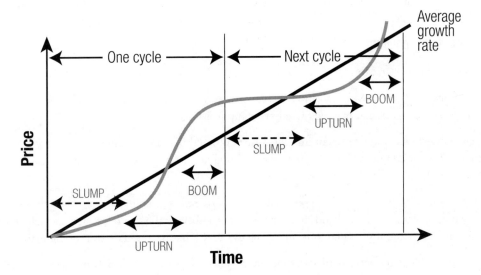

As you can see, at various stages in the cycle property values **exceed** the underlying long-term trend (such as in boom times) and at other stages they **fall short** of the long-term underlying value, such as during property slumps.

The length of each property cycle varies and is not always seven to 10 years as is often suggested. This is because cycles don't occur simply because a certain number of years have passed; they occur because of a combination of macro and micro economic factors and the interplay of several social and political issues.

Keeping an eye on certain key indicators is the way I try to predict how the market is likely to behave in the future.

DRIVERS OF THE PROPERTY CYCLE

1. Demographic demand

As I've already explained the demand for residential real estate is determined by how many new households are being formed and how and where we want to live. As our population expands, housing supply fails to keep up with demand pushing up rents and home prices and this encourages new construction. Obviously our ability to pay more (which is linked to employment, wages growth, the strength of the economy and inflation) also plays a significant role.

The property cycle is partly created by the lag as new construction fails to respond in a timely way to our housing needs. However, once a boom is underway, construction generally overshoots demand, creating an excess in supply which contributes to the next downturn.

2. Human psychology

Market confidence and our attitude towards property fluctuate over the course of the cycle.

Put simply, our home buying and investment decisions are driven by emotion and people often suffer lapses of logic when making these important decisions.

We tend to extrapolate the present into the future. When things are booming we think the good times will never end and when the market mood is glum, we have difficulty seeing the light at the end of the tunnel.

Think about it... when the media reports falling property prices or an impending housing crash, many investors become scared and sit on the sidelines, believing the end of property is nigh and things will never improve, when in reality much of the risk has been removed from the market.

Conversely, when property markets are booming and stories of investors making large gains overnight abound, people want to jump on the bandwagon and cash in – often at a time when the market is near its peak.

Other emotional traps include becoming overconfident, wishful thinking and ignoring information that conflicts with your current views. In other words, many investors create their own "reality".

Can you see how this type of activity, influenced by investor psychology, drives booms and busts? How the dominant investor mentality of the time helps drive the property cycle? Simply, when home buyers and investors put on the brakes, housing values tend to stagnate or fall due to lack of demand. And when they jump back into the market, demand rises and up go prices. In my experience investors have been a large driving factor of all property booms.

Obviously one or two misguided investors won't be able to influence property prices, but investor sentiment is contagious. People tend to want to do what others are doing – they "follow the crowd" because going against popular opinion is seen as risky. "What if you make a mistake? What if the others are right and you are wrong?"

3. Availability of Credit

In the short term the property cycle is extremely sensitive to changes in the availability of funding. Easy credit and low interest rates stimulate both purchasing of established homes plus the construction of new dwellings.

As the cycle progresses, banks tend to relax their lending criteria, allowing more people to buy properties with lower deposits and lower loan servicing criteria. Near the peak of each boom new lenders appear with new financial instruments that add fuel to the fire and allow borrowers who overextend themselves and take on loans they'll have difficulty repaying.

Then as the boom rolls on our regulators decide to slow the market down and either raise interest rates or make it harder to get finance as they have with the credit squeeze that commenced in 2014 with APRA's intervention which eventually stopped the last property boom in Sydney and Melbourne in 2017.

Then of course easy credit and cheap money at a time of pent up demand following this period of credit tightening drove the property boom of 2020–21.

Thus in both good and bad times, the behaviour of lenders amplifies the property cycle. As I said – property investment is a game of finance with some houses thrown in the middle.

4. Government policies

Both Federal and State governments have over the years bolstered the property market by offering incentives to buyers including First Home Owners' Grants and stamp duty incentives. They see it as a quick way of stimulating the building industry and the economy in general, however when housing is buoyed up by governments, participants take on more risk.

5. The Global Economy

While the property cycle is a national phenomenon, our economy, financial markets and market sentiment are very dependent on what's happening in the global economy.

THE FOUR PHASES OF THE PROPERTY CYCLE

History has shown that the property cycle consistently passes **through four phases** as depicted in the diagram below. Let's have a look at these in more detail:

The boom phase

This tends to be the shortest phase of the cycle. While the boom often begins slowly as home owners, and to a much lesser degree, investors recognise that property values are rising it frequently peaks with property values increasing by up to 20% per annum. Remember Sydney in 2015-17?

Each property boom brings a whole new generation of investors coming into the market, driven by property seminars, the press, TV shows and the like. Greed starts to kick in and much speculation occurs at this stage of the cycle. Often potential investors who can't really afford to buy property extend themselves and speculate. Some even buy "off the plan" hoping to sell at a profit, expecting prices to keep rising.

At this stage of the cycle banks often encourage investors with easy credit, sometimes lending them 80, 90 or even 100% of the cost of their investment properties, causing some to over-commit themselves financially.

Fear also drives property booms as would be home owners and investors see property prices going up all around them. They are worried they may miss out on the profits the boom has delivered to others. You'll often find them willing to negotiate to buy at considerably above the asking price at a time when sellers keep racking up their expectations as they notice the high prices achieved for neighbouring properties.

In general, booms are stopped when the Reserve Bank (RBA) increases interest rates to slow down the economy, and in the past it's been quite effective at doing this. More recently (in 2014-18) the Australian Prudential Regulation Authority (APRA) has made the banks tighten their lending criteria to investors to deliberately slow a market that it judged to be overheated.

Each peak is accompanied by a chorus of voices who deny the top is anywhere in sight and it's impossible to predict with any accuracy the moment when the cycle turns, however a peaking market is likely to have several of the following characteristics:

- *Property values have risen strongly* for a number of quarters.
- *Auction clearance rates* are at high levels indicating a strong sellers' market.
- *High levels of credit growth* have occurred because consumers are borrowing more.
- *Banks' lending criteria have loosened* and there are lending instruments. In the last big boom, no-doc and low-doc loans proliferated allowing almost anyone to get a loan to buy property.
- Builders and developers become over-confident and a high level of construction leads to an *oversupply of properties* and *higher vacancy rates.*
- *Housing affordability* becomes stretched.
- *Speculation* is rife with a new generation of investors getting involved in property hoping to "get rich quick".
- The RBA tries to dampen speculation by *raising interest rates.*
- A *credit crunch* occurs and banks tighten their lending criteria.

The downturn phase

Booms are always followed by a downturn or slump phase that is often characterised by an oversupply of properties due to the over-exuberant activity of builders and developers during the preceding boom. This causes increasing vacancy rates and **decreasing investment returns**.

Property prices stop growing and sometimes drop by around 5-10% but in the most recent downturn of 2017-19, the value of some properties in Sydney slumped up to 15%, and Melbourne properties fell in value 11-12%. This phase lasts a number of years, but prolonged booms are usually followed by a longer and deeper slump phase with a greater likelihood of prices falling further.

During the slump, property is out of favour in the media and investors often struggle with decreased cash flows, higher interest rates and stalling values. This is the time many consider selling their properties. However, when they do this in a falling market with few willing buyers, they exacerbate their problems and crystallise the loss in value of their properties.

Near the end of this phase of the cycle interest rates slowly drop as the RBA tries to stimulate consumer confidence and the economy, because the prevailing sentiment is often fear and desperation. Around this time the banks becoming more "investor friendly" and start loosening their lending criteria.

The stabilisation phase

Eventually the market moves on. Falling interest rates, rising rents and pent up demand during the slump phase set the stage for the next property upturn. But prices don't suddenly start escalating wildly. The downturn is usually followed by a period of time when buyers tentatively move back into the market soaking up the properties for sale, but as the number of buyers and sellers is in rough equilibrium, property prices remain flat or only move up slowly. This is a time of **great opportunity**, yet it is not easily recognised by most investors, despite it still being a buyer's market.

In the most recent property cycle this stage was extremely short as the markets in Melbourne and Sydney surged in the second half of 2019.

The upturn phase

In time the cycle moves on and eventually we move into the upturn phase when vacancy rates slowly fall, rents start to rise and property values begin to increase.

At this stage of the cycle property is generally affordable, returns from property investments are attractive and home buyers and smart investors begin to enter the market. This is obviously a great time to buy property and while professional investors take advantage of the opportunities in the upturn phase, many beginner investors take longer to be convinced that property is a good investment.

However, this is a time of great opportunity to get set for the property boom that will eventually follow. This is also when many builders and developers begin work on new development projects, aiming to have them completed by the late upturn or boom phases of the cycle.

At the beginning of the upturn phase of the property cycle interest rates are usually low and it is easier to get finance. As the upturn phase rolls on (remember this stage could last three or four years) more investors and first-home buyers enter the market as conditions seem more favourable. They see property values increase and are concerned that they may miss out if they don't buy a property.

While property values increase, they tend to do so much more gently than the "heady" price rises of the boom phase, which is just around the corner. At the end of the upturn phase real estate prices will have risen substantially and property starts to become less affordable to many Australians.

HOW IMPORTANT IS TIMING THE PROPERTY MARKETS?

Now that you think you understand how important timing is to property investment, *forget everything I just taught you.*

Well not really... let me just put a different spin on it.

While timing is important, I've found it to be one of the most misunderstood concepts with regard to investing. The truth is successful investors know how to create wealth at any point in a cycle.

Of course timing matters, but strategic investors find that timing isn't really that important.

INSIDER TIP

Now that you think you understand how important timing is to property investment, forget everything I just taught you. Strategic investors find that timing isn't really that important.

Have you noticed how some investors seem to do well in good times and do even better in bad times? Market timing isn't really important to them? On the other hand, others do poorly in good times and even worse in bad times? Market timing seems to have very little effect on them as well. Interesting, isn't it?

What is it that differentiates that small group of successful investors from the crowd?

The fact that successful investors manage to make money while unsuccessful investors lose money at the same stage of the property cycle suggests that's it's not our external world that determines whether we make or lose money, it's something inside us.

Many would argue that it's about knowledge, but I don't think that's quite right. Sure successful investors have a level of knowledge and financial fluency that the average investor lacks — yet knowledge alone doesn't make them successful investors. What allows some people to become super successful investors is their mindset — the way they think about money and wealth.

There will always be someone who'll have more knowledge and research data than you and some developers or architects will know more about town planning, development or construction than you ever will. Yet knowledge alone doesn't make them successful investors.

SO WHEN IS IT THE RIGHT TIME?

The right time to buy isn't necessarily when the newspaper headlines say so. There's an old Chinese saying: *When is the best time to plant a tree? Twenty years ago. When is the second best time? Now!*

While some investors are getting in the game taking advantage of some of the best buying conditions property investors have experienced in their lifetime, others are waiting for the perfect timing.

Only a few weeks ago I spoke with David who has been waiting for more than 10 years for the timing to be "just right" to start investing in property.

The timing will never be "just right". There will always be challenges, situations, circumstances, obstacles, fears, doubts and things that you are going to have to overcome. The timing is never going to be perfect.

Ten years ago David saw some obstacles and didn't get into property investment. If he had, chances are that wherever he bought his property it would have doubled in value by now, even if he had made a mistake and paid a bit too much or bought in the wrong street. Wealth is attracted to people who are decisive and committed. If you are waiting for the timing to be perfect – the timing will never be perfect to you.

Currently property investors are being offered a unique window of opportunity as our property markets enter a quieter phase of the property cycle.

Sure there are economic challenges out there, but testing times creates great opportunities. Walt Disney started the company that became Disney just at the start of the Great Depression. Bill Gates began Microsoft's march to world domination in a recession. Jeff Bezos launched Amazon in 1994 during a recession.

The list is long of wealthy Australian property investors who sowed the seeds of their portfolio in the early '90s property slump, with "remarkably poor timing". And there are many others who started building what are now very substantial property portfolios in the downturn of 2004 -2006, while others did so during the slump of the Global Financial Crisis in 2008-9.

These successful investors were busy doing while others were pondering. While the timing might seem unfavourable to some property investors right now, others are going to do very well over the next few years. That's the way it always has been.

I'm certain that in ten years' time, there will be a group of successful property investors who will tell stories of buying properties when everyone advised them not to, when everything seemed difficult, when banks made access to credit more difficult, when the media was very negative – right now.

WHY THE DIFFERENCES IN EACH STATE?

It's not enough to understand how the overall property cycle works – you also need to be aware that different states in Australia are often at different stages in their own cycle. And within each state there are various property markets, defined by geography, price point and type of property – sometimes each at different stages of their own cycle.

Let's revisit the Australian property in 2013 to 2017 when our markets were a two-horse race with double digit capital growth in Sydney and Melbourne, slow capital growth in Brisbane, Adelaide and Tasmania, and falling property values in Perth and Darwin.

Yet all these markets were affected by the same low interest rate environment as well as the same federal government and tax laws.

There's nothing new about different states being at different stages of the property cycle. It happens all the time. It was much the same in 2006–2007. While Melbourne, Brisbane, Adelaide and Canberra property prices boomed (in some suburbs prices rose by well over 20%); Sydney property values remained flat and Perth property values fell in 2007.

The reason for this lies in local economic and jobs growth, local supply and demand factors and local consumer confidence to buy or upgrade their homes.

Here's another factor contributing to the property cycle…

PROPERTY DEVELOPERS DON'T HELP

During booms a number of things happen. One of the key activities is that the rate of new property construction increases.

The reason this happens is that property developers are constantly monitoring the investment equation. They're looking at land costs, calculating that if they bought land for $X, spent $Y on construction and other costs and sold for $Z on completion, they'd make a profit.

When values are rising strongly, potential profit margins are significantly improved and more developers commit to projects. Nobody tells builders, developers or speculators when to stop. They keep building as values are rising to take advantage of the strong market.

Then, at some point in time, there will be more dwellings built and placed on the market than there are people to occupy them, and then the market stalls. How can values rise any further when there's a surplus of properties and not enough people in the market wanting to buy or rent them? Values tend to level off and in some areas they will even fall.

At this stage the rate of new construction will decline, but this can take time as it's not easy to stop when you're in the middle of a project. So the construction level continues to overshoot for some time. Over time, the population continues to increase, and those reaching household formation age continue to enter the market and slowly the surplus is taken up.

The supply and demand see-saw will go on forever. Currently there is an oversupply of inner CBD apartments looming, especially in Melbourne and Brisbane, and some middle ring Sydney suburbs. It's likely many investors who bought into these large buildings will need to wait a decade or more before they see any capital growth.

INSIDER TIP

Supply and demand determine whether property values rise or fall, and this overshadows interest rates, tax changes, budgets, elections, and other factors.

SO WHERE ARE WE IN THE PROPERTY CYCLE?

Of course **there is not just one property cycle**. In Australia there are different property markets each moving in their own cycle.

Within each capital city there are minor cycles with some suburbs outperforming others, usually related to that important factor we have been discussing – **supply and demand**.

As the graph below shows how property prices increase over time. It also shows the "**real property cycle**" and what I call the "**perceived property cycle**". This illustrates the lag between what's actually happening in the market and what the average investor perceives to be happening.

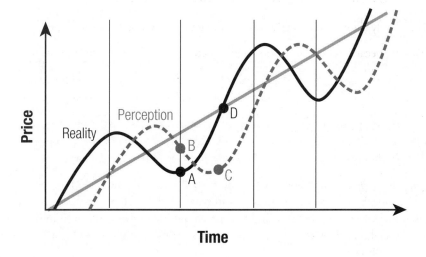

As we discussed earlier, **the crowd is always late, as it follows the perceived cycle**.

To illustrate this point, just look back to early 2020, at the beginning of the Covid pandemic. Our markets were taking a breather and the Melbourne and Sydney property markets were heading towards point **A**; yet the perception of the general public was that the markets had a long way to fall and many considered selling their properties. They thought we were at point **B**.

The general public did not get back into buying property, particularly investment properties, until it "felt" the market was strong and rising again late in 2020 and early in 2021. The general public buys property on gut feel, on emotion. And where do they get their gut feel from? Usually it's from the popular press and the media.

So they didn't re-enter the market until they heard that auction clearance rates were increasing, that property prices were rising and that everyone else was buying property. They didn't re-enter the property market until point **C** in the graph above. What has really happened is that in the meantime strategic investors, who don't buy on gut feel, but on considered research, had pushed prices up to point **D**.

You'll hear lots of people recommend buying real estate and holding it as a long-term investment, suggesting that time will make up for the ups and downs of property values that occur over a cycle. While this is true, you'll recall from the stories of Danny and Michael from the previous chapter, you can make much greater profits if you carefully time your property purchases.

You'd think that people would learn from history, but this appears not to be the case. Human nature drives us to do what everyone else is doing when everyone else is doing it. Buying property when no-one else is buying requires confidence, but it may be easier if you remember that only 1% of investors achieve financial success. Do you really want to be part of the crowd that doesn't?

WHAT ABOUT FINDING THE NEXT PROPERTY HOTSPOT?

Now is probably a good time to give you my thoughts on finding the next property "hotspot".

Over the last decade a number of hot spotting courses and websites have sprung up with the promise of helping you time your entry into specific segments of the property market before the next wave of growth occurs.

I understand why naïve investors so desperately try to time the market, but while they think they're investing in property, in reality they're speculating.

By definition, speculation is *"the practice of engaging in risky financial transactions in an attempt to profit from short or medium term fluctuations in the market value rather than attempting to profit from the underlying financial attributes embodied in the instrument."*

Yet so often I hear people who think that they are investing say things like: "I know this area has had poor capital growth in the past, but it's about to take off," or "I've bought a report — I know this is the next hotspot."

Of course I understand why, in an attempt to outperform the market, they wonder where the next hotspot is going to be. But when they ask my opinion they're usually disappointed that firstly I don't know, and secondly that I don't really care.

You see... I'm not in the business of speculating. Instead, I make my investment decisions based on proven long-term performance, rather than short-term speculation. To me seeking out the "next big boom" location is speculation and if you look at the track record of people chasing the next trend it's been pretty poor.

On the other hand, to "invest" in property requires the intention of generating long-term capital growth that tracks above average, long-term price growth for the area.

NOW, HERE'S WHAT I FIND INTERESTING

Many of the hotspots predicted by some of Australia's property analysts turned out to be correct. Some of the regional areas and mining towns boomed, at least for a while as investors chased up prices, but unless they got the timing right, chasing the next hotspot turned out disastrous for most investors.

After the initial price growth, often driven by a flood of investors in these small markets, prices stalled and often dropped substantially, leaving many with properties worth considerably less than they paid and with less rental income than they expected. They are now unable to sell their properties as buyers have abandoned these markets, which have little depth from local demand.

If you're into investing in short-term trends, being right isn't what's important; it's being right at the right time that counts. Very few can do that, so the history of investors trying to find the next boomtown is littered with people who get the story right and the outcome wrong.

Instead, I buy in areas that have a proven long-term history of outperforming the average capital growth and that are likely to continue to outperform, because of the demographics of the people living in the area. Hot spotting is virtually the opposite of this sensible, not-so-sexy, tried and tested system for successfully building a property portfolio.

After the initial price growth, often driven by a flood of investors in these small markets, prices stalled and often dropped substantially, leaving many with properties worth considerably less than they paid and with less rental income than they expected. They are now unable to sell their properties as buyers have abandoned these markets, which have little depth from local demand.

WHAT WORKS NOW VS. WHAT HAS ALWAYS WORKED

Now that we've just experienced one of the biggest property booms in history, when the value of almost every property increased significantly, if history repeats itself, and it surely will, some investors will find they got it wrong. They bought the type of investment that "works now" while sophisticated investors will only put their money into "what's always worked".

Yes, some regional locations outperformed the big capital cities. And some speculators appeared to make money out of the "next fad" touted at the get rich quick seminars. But I've found that, in general, this year's new *hot spot* becomes a future *not stop*. Meaning most property investors will never develop the financial independence they deserve.

In my mind property is a long-term investment and therefore my strategy doesn't change because of short term changes in the economy or the markets. I'd only invest in the type of property that has always been a good investment, rather than one that "works now".

I know that location will do the bulk of the heavy lifting in my property's performance, so I would only invest in high growth suburbs in our big three capital cities, knowing that their economic fundamentals, population growth and gentrification will underpin my property's performance.

Then, as I've already explained I would only buy an investment grade property — one that would be in strong long-term demand by affluent owner occupiers and one with a high land to asset ratio.

SUMMARY

Timing is important in the investing game and if you want results that stand out from the crowd, you need to beat the crowd. Luckily, history tells us that markets move in repeating cycles that can be predicted by monitoring prevailing conditions.

The investment clock is a key concept that we'll discuss more in the next chapter as we begin to delve into the indicators that allow us to read and predict the market and we'll look at the all-important concept of counter-cyclical investing. Hang on!

COUNTER-CYCLICAL INVESTING

Now that you understand that property markets move in a cyclical manner, the problem facing most investors is that, as humans, we tend to think in a linear way, and project our expectations into our investing. This can cause us to misunderstand the reality and the risks involved in markets.

THE REALITY IS OFTEN THE OPPOSITE OF WHAT YOU SEE

I already told you that most investors have a tendency to perceive risks as being at their lowest during boom times, when prices have almost peaked. That's because the media is full of stories about amazing profits, television shows on property abound and friends and family are all a buzz with tales of great gains that have been made.

Of course, when prices have almost peaked and are breaking new highs there's a very good chance that they're going to flatten out or drop back a little sooner rather than later.

Similarly, many investors believe the risks are highest when the markets are down and prices have dropped. The media reports the doom and gloom stories of people losing money and these will often sap investors' confidence. Of course, the reality is that lows are often the best time to snap up bargains while prices are cheap. Historically, it's also a lot more likely that prices will rebound and grow from low points — just look what happened to our property markets in mid 2019 when the media was full of negative sentiment.

Our property markets are fundamentally driven by human emotion — in particular fear and greed and that's why the cycle will always be with us.

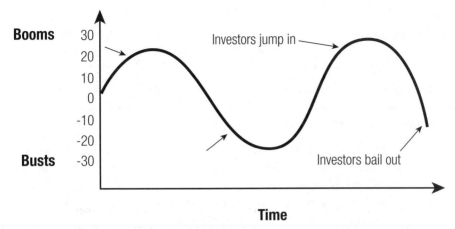

During property booms, the price of houses soars, but obviously this can't go on forever. Properties can't keep selling for more than they are fundamentally worth (above what I call "instrinsic value") and eventually values fall, until money once again becomes easier and cheaper to borrow (as interest rates fall), enticing players back into the game. The cycle eventually moves into its recovery phase and in time this leads into the next boom and the cycle repeats itself.

Boom follows bust which follows the previous boom. Get the picture?

Understanding this recurring relationship between the different stages in the property cycle is critical if you want to maximise the return on your investment dollar, with the minimum of risk.

If you know where things are heading in the property cycle and you buy property before the crowd does, and before prices start to rise, you're likely to make big profits.

This type of investing is called **counter-cyclical investing**. To sum up this philosophy, you simply see what the majority of people are thinking and then consider the opposite as to where the truth may be found.

This system of investing is certainly not foolproof, but it has served me and many other professional investors well over the years. When I wrote the last edition of this book in 2018 I said, "While we may be in the winter of our property markets at present, but for over 6,000 years spring has followed winter, so I'm willing to put my money on the fact that this will happen again." And I'm pleased, but not surprised, to say I was correct.

And interestingly, I could say exactly the same about the current property markets.

Of course, it is difficult for beginners to have confidence in their decisions to invest in property when the press keeps talking the property market down. Obviously most people would rather not put themselves in what they feel is a high-risk position. It's much easier to be doing what everyone else is doing. So the crowd always tends to wait until they think it is safe, based on popular opinion and on what the majority is doing. This is the way most people think before they invest in property or in shares.

INSIDER TIP

See what the majority of people are doing or thinking and consider whether the opposite is true. Waiting until the "crowd" feels comfortable means missing out on the big money!

The crowd misses out on making the big money and, what's more, the crowd will always be late because that's how human beings are. They want to be safe. This phenomenon is known as "herd mentality" or "market sentiment".

Leading articles in investment or business magazines or websites are often good barometers of market sentiment. This is because it's the job of the media to report what people are interested in and what they're talking about. While the ideas that appear on the front pages of the Sunday papers may be wrong, they're still worth reading as they're good indicators of the general market sentiment, which can help us gauge when a change might occur.

Now just to make things clear... this doesn't negate what I just said about hot spotting and any purchase must fit in with my 6 Stranded Strategic Approach – you can't just find a market that's been flat for a while and invest there hoping for the best. Of course that's what many investors do and then say "this property thing doesn't work!"

To help you better understand the cyclical nature of property values, it's also important to take a closer look at the concept that is called the "economic clock" which tells us how general economic cycles (as opposed to property cycles) work.

The notion was first described in the *London Times* at the beginning of last century yet it's still relevant today. While it's not a good tool for predicting the timing of economic trends with any accuracy, it has proven accurate in reflecting the market forces that drive the various investment cycles and the order in which they occur.

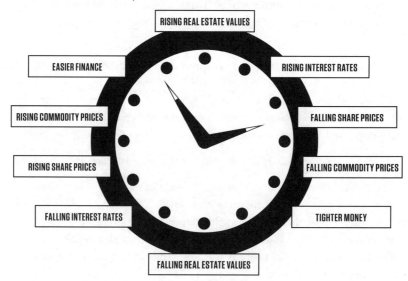

Twelve o'clock is the economic **boom** when a rapid increase in the demand for real estate results in property prices rising. As borrowing primarily funds property purchases, this increased demand for finance causes interest rates to rise. As interest rates rise, companies find it harder to make profits. This, together with the fact that the booming property market and fixed-interest investments seem more attractive, causes share prices to fall or at least stagnate.

As property prices tend to boom at these times, and because interest rates rise, the rapid growth of the property market cannot be sustained for more than a few years. This means property prices stagnate for a few years and sometimes fall.

At about **three o'clock** in the investment clock, the share market is usually doing little and offers few prospects for investors. Interest rates are usually high at this stage of the cycle, making borrowing for property an unattractive option. Other investors just try to battle on, paying more interest on their borrowed funds. High interest rates slow the economy and lead to recessions.

This brings us down to **six o'clock**, in the depths of a recession or downturn. At this point investors are either too scared to, or can't afford to borrow money. As a result, **interest rates slowly start falling**.

Also during these times companies are forced to become leaner and to increase productivity. These measures, and the slowly improving economy, translate into increased company profits and this gradually stimulates **share prices to recover**.

This takes us through to about **nine o'clock**. At this point in the cycle many new investors start to buy shares wanting to get in on the boom. Eventually a point is reached where the company earnings, or net asset backing figures, cannot justify share prices and a sudden correction occurs. With the share market losing its glamour and interest rates being low many investors then **turn to the property market** and real estate prices again start to rise.

And once again we find ourselves at **twelve o'clock**.

WHY DO THE CYCLES KEEP RECURRING?

You may well ask, "If this is so well known, why do property and economic cycles occur in the first place? Why doesn't our market-driven economy find a nice equilibrium?"

With regard to the general economic cycle, the simple answer is that the world economy is a collection of many nations, each at their own individual point in the economic clock. Every nation is made up of millions of people like you and me, each making their own financial decisions in reaction to, or in the expectation of, other people's decisions. The sheer momentum of all these economies means that they always over-swing the mark, and then correct themselves, resulting in cyclical economic movements.

So if economic cycles are well understood and the benefits of being a counter-cyclical investor are evident, why doesn't everyone make a killing? The simple answer is human nature.

As I have already mentioned, two "human" factors drive investment markets like property and shares — **greed** and **fear**. Every 10 years or so a brand new generation of investors enter the market, but haven't had the opportunity of learning the lessons of history, and therefore the cycle goes on.

WHY DO ECONOMISTS GET THEIR PREDICTIONS SO WRONG?

But if our economists are armed with all the research available in today's information age, why can't they agree on where our economy and property markets are heading?

In fact a better question would be — why do so many get it wrong?

The simple answer is that market movements are far from an exact science. As I've tried to explain, it's much more than fundamentals that move markets.

The fundamentals are easy to monitor. Things like population growth, supply and demand, employment levels, interest rates, affordability and inflationary pressures.

However, one overriding factor that the experts have difficulty quantifying is investor sentiment.

We're human so we become overconfident, practice wishful thinking and ignore information that conflicts with our current views. In other words, most investors create their own reality.

Can you see how this type of activity, influenced by investor psychology, drives booms and busts? How the dominant investor mentality of the time helps drive the property cycle?

Simply, when investors put on the brakes, housing values tend to stagnate or fall due to lack of demand. And when they jump back into the market, demand rises and up go prices.

Obviously one or two misguided investors won't be able to influence property prices, but investor sentiment is contagious. People tend to want to do what others are doing — they "follow the crowd" because going against popular opinion is seen as risky.

Shane Oliver, chief economist at AMP capital explains that this "collective behaviour" is magnified by several things including:

1. **Mass communication** enabling the behaviour to become infectious. Now more than ever we are bombarded with messages from the media influencing how we think and feel about things. When we hear that real estate is doomed, all but a handful of sophisticated investors get scared out of the game. And when the media tells us housing markets are booming everyone wants a piece of the action.

2. **Pressure to conform**. If your friends or family are doing it, it must be right. Right? Human nature makes us reluctant to do the opposite of what our peers are doing.

3. **A major precipitating event** can give rise to a general belief that motivates investor behaviour. The Global Financial Crisis that saw waves of investors scared out of the markets. On the other hand the resource boom enticed thousands of investors into west coast housing markets to cash in on the resulting property boom.

4. **A general belief that grows and spreads**. When the belief that property values can only go up spreads through an uneducated new generation of investors they enter the market pushing prices up even further, perpetuating the belief and helping make it a reality! Similarly when the crowd believes the market is going to crash, they steer clear, this gets reported in the media and the negative sentiment feeds on itself.

WHAT CAN AN INVESTOR LEARN FROM THIS?

Probably the most important lesson we can all learn is that our property markets are not only driven by fundamentals, but also by the often irrational and erratic behaviour of an unstable crowd of other investors.

Never get too carried away when the market is booming or too disenchanted during property slumps. Letting your emotions drive your investments is a sure-fire way to disaster.

Here's another eight lessons I've learned about property cycles over the years:

Lesson 1 — Booms don't last forever, neither do busts

Whether it's property, shares or bitcoins - booms just don't last forever. The thing is, booms are just one part of a cycle, so they will always end at some point.

Every boom sets us up for the next downturn, just as every flat period provides opportunities to get set for the next upturn. The trick is to be prepared for the downturn when it comes and be ready to make the most of softer market conditions.

Lesson 2 — Beware of Doomsayers

As long as I have been investing I remember hearing people with excuses why property prices will stop rising, or even worse, why property values will plummet. However, in that time, well located properties have doubled in value every eight to 10 years.

Fear is a very powerful emotion, and one that the media used to grab our attention. Sadly, some people miss out on the opportunity to develop their own financial independence because they listen to the messages of those who want to deflate the financial dreams of their fellow Australians.

Lesson 3 — Follow a Proven Strategy

Smart investors follow a system to take the emotion out of their decisions and ensure they don't speculate. This may be boring, but it's profitable.

Don't change your long-term strategy because of short term factors. Look for what's always worked, rather than what's working now.

Let's be honest, almost anyone could have made money during the recent boom years as the market covered up any mistakes. But as Warren Buffet says: "You only find out who is swimming naked when the tide goes out."

In other words, if you're not following a strategy that works in all market conditions you will be caught naked when the market changes. If you prefer to have consistent profits and reduced risk, follow a proven system.

Make your investing boring, so the rest of your life can be exciting.

Lesson 4 — Get Rich Quick = Get Poor Quick

Real estate is a long-term investment, yet some investors chase the "fast money".

You've probably met people like that — they look for that deal that will make them fabulously rich. When you see them a year later, they're usually no better off financially and still talking about the next deal that will make them rich.

They are often influenced by the latest get-rich-quick artist with a great story about how you can join them and become stupendously wealthy. Their stories can be very compelling, even hard to resist. They often pander to the wishes of people who would like to give up their day job to get involved in property full time, but in reality it takes most people many years to accumulate sufficient assets to do this.

Property investment is as much about investing time as it is money, and you need to be thinking about the next 15 to 20 years to allow your properties to flourish.

Patience is an investment virtue. Warren Buffet said it right when he explained that: "Wealth is the transfer on money from the impatient to the patient."

INVESTOR TIP
Wealth is the transfer on money from the impatient to the patient.

Lesson 5 — Take a long-term perspective

During a market downturn, fear starts to rear its head. People who have made poor investment decisions, or those who bought near the market peak, start to panic.

Let's face it: emotions of any kind are not a good idea when investing.

The secret is to keep your eye on the long-term horizon and not worry about any short-term vagaries of the market, because they will pass.

Lesson 6 — Property investment is a game of finance with some houses thrown in the middle

Strategic investors don't only buy real estate — they buy themselves time by having the correct finance structures in place including cash flow buffers to ride through the cycle.

Lesson 7 — Invest in locations with a future, not a past

Since the bulk of your property's performance will be determined by its location, rather than looking for somewhere cheap to buy, find a location where local economic growth will lead to jobs growth, wages growth and population growth.

A suburb where the local demographic can afford to and will be willing to pay for their properties because they earn high disposable incomes.

You'll find that the rollercoaster ride will not be as dramatic in these well researched locations.

Lesson 8 — Watch out for the X factor.

Economists refer to the "X factor" or "Black Swan event" when an unforeseen event or situation blows all their carefully laid forecasts away. These can be overseas factors such as the Global Financial Crisis, the Corona virus pandemic or geopolitical events, or local factors such as the miracle win of the Morrison government in mid 2019 that turned around investor confidence on its head. X factors can have a positive or negative effect on our property markets and by definition are not predictable.

SUMMARY

Cycles are an inevitable part of any investment market.

Remember that there are local, as well as national, property cycles. Each state is in a different stage of its property cycle and the beginning of a new major property cycle has created some great buying opportunities for smart investors. This is a time to be selective and to think long term. But more about that in the next chapter!

Now that we've talked about cycles and clocks and how timing can make or break an investment, I'm going to go soft on you and seemingly contradict myself a little by saying that your timing doesn't have to be perfect.

While I do advocate the concept of counter-cyclical investing, and it's definitely important that investment timing is considered and sound, absolute precision-perfect timing is not really necessary with property investing.

In other words you don't have to buy at the very lowest of lows or sell at the highest of highs. Remember that the absolute top and the absolute bottom are only two days out of an entire seven to 10-year cycle and you just can't pick them. The financial wizards, the economists, the PhDs usually can't pick them either.

It doesn't matter if the market has bottomed or not because you're not buying the market. You are buying an individual property in the market using my 6 Stranded Strategic Approach that will ensure your investment property will outperform the market.

When I started investing in property more than 40 years ago I knew nothing about property cycles. In fact I knew very little about property at all. If I had waited until the right time of the cycle or the right market sentiment I might never have started at all.

While it's important to know where you are in the cycle, it's also important to get going with your investment program! Up next — Choosing a place to start.

LOCATION, LOCATION, LOCATION

CHOOSING A PLACE TO START

That location is the key ingredient in property investing is one of the oldest clichés in the industry — while it is true that location does most of the heavy lifting of your property's performance, not all properties in the same suburb, or even the same street, will produce similar results.

That's why I stick to my 6 Stranded Strategic Approach to investment which takes into account location plus much more.

One strand is to always buy in an area with a history of strong capital growth and where this will continue in the future and clearly long-term growth varies considerably between locations.

Looking back, even at times during the cycle when the overall property market was flat or falling around Australia there were suburbs where properties held their values well and even increased.

Interesting isn't it?

LET'S LOOK WHAT SORT OF A DIFFERENCE CHOOSING SUCH A LOCATION CAN MAKE

While, on average, capital city properties tend to grow in value by around 7% per annum, it's not too hard to find a suburb that outperform amongst the inner and middle ring suburbs of our major capital cities. If you bought a $500,000 property in a suburb that, on average, grew at 10% per annum over a 10-year period, the value of your property would increase to close to $1.3 million.

Now imagine your research found a suburb that was in greater demand and had an average growth of 12% per annum. Over the same 10-year period the value of your $500,000 property would increase by almost quarter of a million dollars to over $1.5 million.

On the other hand, if you bought in a suburb that grew at only 8% per annum, just above the city's average growth, the value of your $500,000 would be around $1,080,000 in 10 years' time. This means you would **forego over $400,000 in capital growth** and the ability to use this extra equity to fund further property investments.

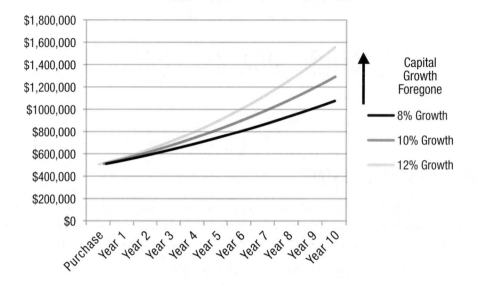

Let's look at this in another way — how long would it take the value of your property to double in value. If it grew in value by 8% it would double in value in around nine years.

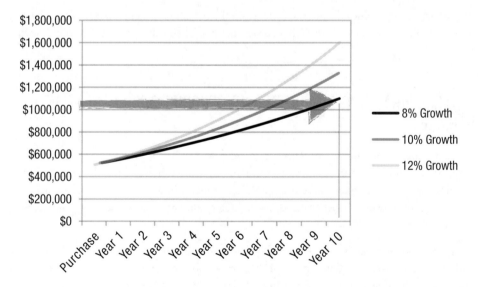

However, a property that has average growth of 10% per annum doubles in value in seven years.

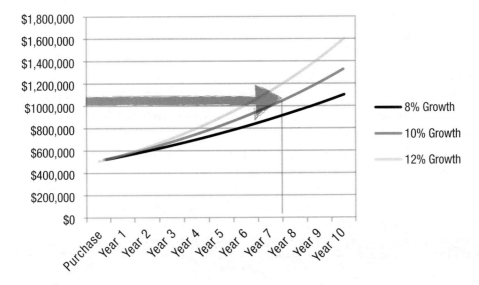

And the better performing property that increases in value at an average of 12% doubles in value in just over five years. This means you can use this extra equity to borrow against and buy further properties, or you can keep it as a financial buffer and borrow against for a rainy day.

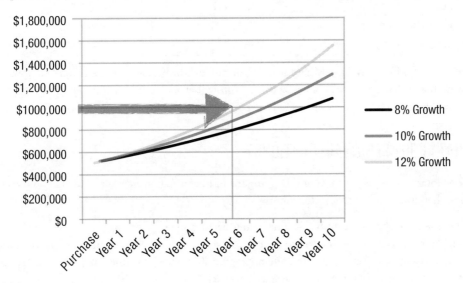

The good news is that is you can speed this process up by adding value and manufacturing capital growth through renovations or redevelopment. But I'm getting ahead of myself. I'll explain this in a future chapter.

Of course in the examples above I'm talking about average growth rates; properties don't go up in value each and every year, but just to make sure you understand what I'm on about, let me explain it a different way.

Imagine you bought a property for $550,000 and it increased in value by an average of 7% per annum. This means it would be worth $1,081,000 in 10 years' time and $2,128,000 in 20 years' time.

But just look the table below to see how much difference it would make if you found an area where properties increased in value just a little bit more — say 8% per annum. This increased rate of growth when compounded would make your property worth $435,000 more in 20 years' time (and that's in today's dollar value). Obviously the story gets better if you select a location with even better capital growth.

PURCHASE A $550,000 PROPERTY		
	10 Years	**20 Years**
7% capital Growth p.a.	$1,081,933	$2,128,326
EXTRA VALUE IF		
1% Better Capital Growth	$105,476	$435,200
2% Better Capital Growth	$220,117	$954,099
3% Better Capital Growth	$344,625	$1,571,799
5% Better Capital Growth	$626,283	$3,177,135

The successful investors I know have made their millions by buying in these better locations. Buying high growth properties allowed them to grow their property portfolio faster because the extra equity in their properties provided the deposit for their next investment.

WHAT ABOUT REGIONAL LOCATIONS?

For as long as I've been investing the argument has been raging: regional Australia vs. capital cities; then inner suburbs vs. outer suburbs.

While there are always exceptions — some better performing regional areas have exhibited more capital growth than some underperforming capital city suburbs and some high growth outer suburbs have grown faster than some demographically challenged inner suburbs — the simple fact is that for strong, stable long-term growth which outperforms the averages, the inner and middle ring suburbs of our capital cities are the place to invest.

NOW THIS WASN'T ALWAYS THE CASE

According to research done by John Lindeman from www.LindemanReports.com.au, around the time of Federation (at the turn of the 20th century) the price of country property was equal to and in some cases greater than the cost of similar properties in the city. But over time this has slowly changed as we have moved from an agrarian society to an industrialised nation.

After the Second World War the arrival of a large number of overseas migrants who preferred to live in cities, in particular Sydney and Melbourne, led to a larger increase in the value of capital city properties over regional properties.

I guess it's much the same today, the vast majority of the hundreds of thousands of migrants who come to Australia each year want to live in our capital cities where the jobs are. And this trend is unlikely to change in the foreseeable future with few significant decentralisation initiatives in the pipeline.

This means investors seeking long-term capital growth should only be investing in our larger capital cities. You will not be able to replace your income with the type of cash flow you get from cheap properties. While regional properties may initially seem cheap, their lower capital growth means in the long run they are expensive because they don't get you to your financial goals.

If you're on a budget, I'd rather you put your money in a "family friendly" apartment in a great capital city location than buy a house in a regional area.

The bottom line is that the most reliable and consistent property markets when it comes to capital growth are found in and around Australia's capital cities. The larger populations in these markets will mean less volatility in prices.

INNER OR OUTER SUBURBS?

I've seen a number of studies showing that (in general) properties closer to the CBD increased in value faster than those further from the CBD. This general trend was confirmed by a paper from the Australian Housing and Urban Research Institute (AHURI), which found that both in percentage terms and in absolute terms over the long haul, suburbs located reasonably close to the CBD, where demand is high, employment is in close proximity, the majority of people want to live and where there is no land available for release, outperformed the outer suburbs.

The paper explained:

"Housing markets, which were once relatively egalitarian cross Australian cities, have become polarised.

"The homes affordable to present (and future) lower moderate income home buyers are now confined to the outer suburbs and will only increase in value at slower rates compared to housing in the more expensive inner and middle suburbs — effectively trapping poorer households on the edges of our cities."

NOW THIS BRINGS UP A WHOLE RAFT OF SOCIAL ARGUMENTS

The process of gentrification and rising prices has locked a generation of younger people out of inner-city housing and it is likely that the gap will only widen over the years.

I'll leave discussion of the remedy for this to the politicians and town planners, but the conclusion for property investors is that if you want to own the type of property that will outperform the averages, the inner and middle ring suburbs are the place to be.

Of course it's the same all over the world. Go to any major city in the world — London, Paris, Vienna, Los Angeles — and you'll find that the wealthy people tend to live within 10 to 15 minutes' drive from the CBD or near the water.

Why is this so? The cynics would say because they can afford to. And in part that's true.

It's also because, in general, the more established suburbs with better infrastructure, shopping and amenities tend to be close to the CBD and the water and that's where the wealthy want to and can afford to live. And they're prepared to pay a premium to live there. Remember how I explained about the "20-minute neighbourhood" in a previous chapter?

Simply put, when there are more willing buyers than dwellings to accommodate them in a location that is made highly desirable by its amenity, market competition puts consistent upward pressure on prices.

Conversely in an area that has an abundance of developable land, new greenbelt housing estates on the outer urban fringes for instance, yet lower buyer demand relative to the excess supply, there is very little force exerted on values.

Another factor that makes properties in these areas poor investments is the low land to total asset ratio. Usually land only makes up around 50% of the value of the property (e.g. the land component is worth only $200,000 of the total house price of $400,000).

In the inner suburbs the proportion of the land value to the total property price is usually considerably higher, and remember it's the land that is scarce and increases in value. Also in the inner and middle suburbs of our major capital cities, there is strong demand from a wider range of owner-occupiers but there is restricted supply. And as most of the land is already built out, there is limited scope to increase the number of dwellings

But as they say in the ads — there's more...

GENTRIFICATION

One of the significant changes in the way we live in Australia over the last few decades is the gentrification of our inner suburbs. This usually happens in those aspirational suburbs I just mentioned.

When I was young housing in the inner suburbs was cheap and home to the working class and migrants being full of single fronted terraces, pubs and factories. But within a few decades, the process of gentrification saw these ugly duckling suburbs transformed into graceful swans as higher income households displaced blue-collar workers; changing the character of these neighbourhoods and resulting in a significant increase in local property values.

What caused this gentrification?

One of the main factors behind this revitalisation was the exodus of manufacturing to the suburbs driven in part by cheaper transport and better roads. At the same time many migrant workers departed to the suburbs to live in detached houses with front and back yards.

Interestingly at much the same time our society started to experience higher education levels which necessitated more people being closer to campuses, that were usually in or near the CBD.

Similarly, the diversity of serviced based jobs located in the CBD, the increasing number of women in the workforce, declining household sizes and lifestyle all made living in those smaller properties near the city more attractive to a larger cohort of potential buyers.

Of course, it should come as no surprise that this increasing demand led to house prices in the inner-ring rising much faster than in the outer suburbs.

Identifying gentrification

Gentrification is a change in the fortunes of a suburb as it is discovered by a higher income demographic which slowly pushes out the lower income residents. These new, more affluent residents invest time and money improving their new neighbourhood, pushing up prices and rents.

As these changes take place the area loses its stigma and more individuals on higher wages move in, putting further upward pressure on values.

Looking back, one of the significant transformations of our inner suburbs was that household incomes grew significantly as residents were better educated and had higher-paying jobs. Two incomes in a household instead of one meant that people had more money to spend on housing – and spend it they did!

Therefore one of the keys to identifying a gentrifying location, one where property values will increase above average, is to find suburbs where incomes are growing, increasing people's ability to afford and pay higher prices for property.

Digging into the Census data shows that while wage growth has been slow over the last few years, there are some suburbs where wages have grown 20-30% more than the State's average. You're likely to find these suburbs are home to a number of other identifying features of gentrification such as top-end cafés or restaurants as well as higher-end stores where the wealthier population can spend their money, because that's what they generally do. Not surprisingly household sizes tend to be smaller in these locations with more interest from empty nesters, young professionals and DINKs (Double Income, No Kids).

The secret to identifying gentrification, therefore, involves researching locations where a number of economic factors are changing at the same time.

To make things clear... just because a suburb has cheap properties doesn't mean it's destined to become the next growth area.

Some suburbs are inexpensive for a reason and won't improve because of various socio-economic factors. There might be too much industry in the area, a lot of social/public housing or possibly a crime, gang or drug problem. Or maybe they are outlying suburbs with poor infrastructure, facilities or public transport.

On the other hand, the type of suburb to look for is one that is relatively cheap today but has the potential for future capital growth. Some of the major drivers of capital growth are:

- Proximity to the city or the water.
- Adjoining a more expensive neighbourhood so it can benefit from the ripple effect.
- Desirable amenities such as good public transport, a large shopping centre, or within the catchment of a highly prized public school.
- Older attractive houses with character features, that are ready to be renovated.
- Areas where governments are investing in local infrastructure or beautification programs.

So what do you look for in a suburb?

Some of the steps you can take to find a suburb that is improving is to go for a drive and a walk. You'll "know it when you see it" because you'll find evidence that people with money are moving in.

- They will be spending large amounts of money renovating or extending their homes.
- There will be white (the new black) SUVs parked in the driveways rather than old Ford Falcons and Holden utes.
- The nature of the shops is changing. The gyms are offering Pilates; the cafés sell cold press coffee, and the deli's serve goat's cheese pizza.

As a property investor, if you can pick an area going through gentrification, one that's shifting from dreary to in demand, you can benefit from its accelerated growth.

And the good news is that you don't have to get your timing perfect — the gentrification process lasts a number of decades.

With our population growing at just around 1.4% per annum, this means that over the next seven years or so our population will grow by over 10%, much of it fuelled by immigration.

However, while many people will be moving to the more affordable outer suburbs of our four big capital cities, most of our economic growth, jobs growth and wages growth will be occurring in and around our CBDs. This will create a discord between where the jobs are and where people are going to be living.

Now fast forward seven years with 10% more people living in our cities and up to 10% more cars on our roads, it's likely that more people are going to be prepared to trade their backyards for balconies and live closer to the CBD with jobs are, where the infrastructure is and where the action is.

This will create a Manhattanisation of our big capital cities – young people won't be able to afford to buy there, so they'll rent where they want to live and, as I've explained in the section on demographics, many will buy an investment property where they can afford to.

INSIDER TIP

To supercharge the capital growth of your property investments, look for a suburb going through gentrification and use the cycle of this suburb to increase the value of your property.

MORE PROOF THAN NOT ALL LAND IS CREATED EQUAL

Back in 1975 you could buy a median price home for $26,000 in the Victorian outer western suburb of Melton, where many young families were flocking to buy new homes on quarter acre blocks.

In that same year the median property price in the less fashionable, industrial inner Melbourne suburb of South Melbourne was $23,750 and for that you'd only get an old single fronted two bedroom home, often with an outside toilet.

And in the adjoining suburb of Middle Park you'd have to pay a little more, $30,550 for a median priced home which would similarly be single fronted, old and on small block of land, but in a more attractive suburb.

Let's look at what happened to property prices in those suburbs over the next 40 years.

MEDIAN PRICE			
	Melton	**South Melbourne**	**Middle Park**
1975	26,000	23,700	30,550
1980	30,000	44,000	61,000
1985	56,900	87,750	127,500
1990	9,500	185,000	255,500
1995	7,500	213,000	314,550
2000	97,000	375,000	604,000
2005	174,000	648,000	917,500
2010	250,000	759,743	1,500,000
2015	$250,000	$1,205,000	$2,243,750

Now in the last few years the ripple effect has meant that the price of a home in Melton has risen strongly on the back of first home buyers moving out there taking advantage of lower interest rates, but the huge price differential still proves the point I'm trying to make.

	Melton	**South Melbourne**	**Middle Park**
2018	$510,000	$1,630,000	$2,895,000

THE FACTS ARE CLEAR

Yet no doubt the argument will continue to rage. Some will persist in recommending investment in the outer suburbs because they're cheaper, more affordable and the yields are a little higher. And all of this is true.

But remember over the longer term, rents tend to grow more substantially in landlocked suburbs where demand is the strongest and capital values increase more.

If you think about it, your future income and prosperity is tied to your tenant's future income growth – their ability to keep paying you higher rents over the years. Your rental increases will be your future income.

Who do you want to have as tenants? Someone who's on a lower wage, who's one or two weeks away from broke and who won't be able to afford rental increases in the future, or affluent tenants who are not renting because they can't afford to buy, but are renting for lifestyle choices or because of the current stage of their life or career?

At the same time your future financial freedom will depend upon the quality of your assets, so even though the outer suburbs may be cheap at the moment they will restrict you from developing substantial wealth in the future. I've said it before... invest for capital growth first then once you have a substantial asset base you can "buy" cash flow down the track through other investment classes.

In my mind, there is no question that the best locations to invest for long term capital growth are the inner suburbs of our major capital cities where the jobs are, where most people want to live, where incomes are generally higher and where there is no land available for release.

Now here's another concept worth knowing about...

THE RIPPLE EFFECT

When a market is running hot, a common trend that occurs is the "ripple effect", where buyer demand and capital growth *ripples* outwards from one suburb to the next.

Simply, as prices increase beyond the reach of buyers in the suburb of their choice, they tend to look for "the next best thing" that falls within their budget — in adjoining, lower-priced suburbs. As more and more buyers start buying in these adjoining suburbs property prices start to rise. This "ripple effect" in capital growth most commonly moves from the inner suburbs outwards, and along or away from the coastline.

For property investors who want to take advantage of these opportunities, the trick is to identify the most desirable emerging markets, sub-markets and properties and get in early. This requires good timing and plenty of research. One method is to measure property values based on median prices between adjoining suburbs. If there is more than 10% variation, it's possible the suburb next door could play catch-up.

Another method is to closely monitor median price trends. Generally, at the start of a property cycle, the inner suburbs will be the first to show signs of growth, which will then ripple outwards. Once the cycle has kicked off, look for properties within your budget as close to the growth areas as possible. A good rule of thumb when buying in capital city suburban markets is to buy within 12–15km of the CBD — growth is virtually assured to ripple this far out during a cycle.

While I like the ripple effect concept, there is no certainty that it will always occur. Growth does not keep moving outwards indefinitely — there are a few factors that can stop growth from rippling further out.

First, a change in the general property market can stop the growth of property values. When the cycle ends, investors who bet on the "next best" outer ring suburb often miss out when the growth ripple doesn't quite make it that far.

Second, geographic factors can prevent a "ripple" from continuing. For example, if the primary driver of the "ripple" is proximity to a trendy suburb or fashionable dining or entertainment precinct, the reliability of capital growth is likely to decline in line with the distance travelled. A safe rule of thumb is: any more than a five to 10-minute drive is too far!

SHOULD I BUY IN THE CBD?

Over the past two decades there has been a boom in city high-rise living, with more young people taking up this style of accommodation that suits their lifestyle.

But CBD apartments don't make good investments and I'd steer clear of this market.

Several studies of the re-sales of inner-city apartments show that many resulted in significant capital losses for investors. These losses also meant that the investor lost out on the potential substantial capital growth they could have had, had they invested in other areas of residential property.

I avoid inner CBD apartments because:

1. With so many high-rise apartment towers of lookalike apartments there is no "scarcity value" which compromises their capital growth.

2. Most new high-rise apartments are **overpriced**, as they have large marketing costs, builder's costs and developer's margins built in to them. They not purchased at a true market price, but at one set by the developers and often accepted by unsuspecting foreign investors.

3. **Investment stock not investment grade** – most CBD apartments are built specifically to sell to investors, and often to overseas investors, so apart from lack of scarcity, they are often poorly built, have inferior floor plans and are likely to become the slums of the future. Imagine the difficulty getting anything resolved in Body Corporate meetings when most of the owners will be overseas residents with different investment goals to you.

4. **Most dwellers in the CBD are tenants** – in general owner-occupiers will look after their buildings better than investors, but only a small percentage of dwellings in the city are owner-occupied (the rest are investor-owned rentals). This compares with well over 70% owner-occupied in the rest of our metropolitan areas.

5. **Investors have no control over the nature and scale of other new major developments**, which could affect the values of their own properties. Today's apparent AAA locations could be downgraded in the years ahead as new centres of activity and popularity replace old ones.

6. **City tenants come from a narrow demographic group**. Typically, they have no children, earn high incomes and gravitate towards an inner-city lifestyle. These types of tenants, who are generally under 30, are often described as "upwardly mobile" in terms of their careers and accommodation and are more likely to be short-term tenants who to move to the latest fashion building when their lease is up. You also will find many overseas students want to live in the CBD. Do you really want nomadic tenants?

7. **The slums of the future.** Over the last few years it has become clear that the standard of construction of many of the high rise inner city apartment towers has been poor. There have been many well publicised cases of structural issues, water and cladding issues that have led

to a lack of confidence. These issues will lead to a flight to quality, meaning well constructed, medium density apartments and townhouses in the inner and middle ring suburbs will continue to be strongly sought after and will keep increasing in value, making them great investment. On the other hand, owners of poorly constructed high rise apartments in the many "me too" buildings built in the last decade or two will find the value of their properties will languish.

BEWARE THE "HOLIDAY HOME" SYNDROME

Many people like the idea of buying a holiday home and think they can get the dual benefit of a rental income and a free holiday.

I would be cautious because many people fall into the trap of buying with their hearts rather than their calculator. They kid themselves and tell their friends and family that they bought a holiday property for financial reasons when, in reality, they fell in love with the idea of owning a holiday home and often paid scant attention to the investment fundamentals.

I'd rather own my investment properties in prime (non-vacation) locations and then stay at the latest and best accommodation in the spots where I want to holiday.

RENTVESTING

There's one last type of property investment I'd like to discuss in this chapter and it's the concept of deciding to rent where you would like to live (but can't afford to buy) and buying an investment property where you can afford one.

Many young people rent in inner-city suburbs of our capital cities because they are lifestyle precincts and within an easy commute to the city. The thing is that while they can afford to rent there, with high entry-level property prices they can't realistically afford to buy there.

So if they want to stay living there but also want to get onto the property ladder, the answer is rentvesting, because it suits the lifestyle of many millennials — allowing them flexibility in where they live, giving them the opportunity to travel and at the same time grow their wealth.

Rentvesting is the one time that low yields work in the investor's favour. City rental markets haven't yet caught up with accelerated prices. For example, the median price for a unit in Sydney is in the high $700,000s, but the yield is only around 3.5%.

With a rentvesting strategy, you would buy in a high capital growth area further from the city, where prices and yields are more in sync.

A yield of 5%, for example, will give you more rental return to cover your mortgage repayments. Then, you would be able to take advantage of the lower asking rents in the city, or, if you prefer, an enviable lifestyle location you wouldn't normally be able to afford to buy.

For a quick rent versus purchase example, let's say you wanted to buy a house in a middle-ring Melbourne suburb, where the average home is $800,000.

Assuming a 20% deposit (which in this case would be $160,000) and a 5% interest rate, the mortgage repayments would be around $880 per week (principal and interest).

On the other hand, the average rent for a house in the same market is only $500. And of course, that scenario assumes you can amass a deposit of that size. A smaller deposit will attract Lenders Mortgage Insurance, which will bump up the repayments further.

But this idea is not just for the financially challenged. Lifestyle seekers can benefit from rentvesting too. Money isn't always the motive behind buying an investment property first, rentvesting also helps those who:

- Need to move around a lot for work.
- Like to travel for lengthy periods.
- Prefer the flexibility of renting (which eliminates buying and selling fees).
- Want to live in upmarket suburbs or near entertainment hubs that are out of their buying budget.

THE PROS AND CONS OF RENTVESTING

Admittedly, there aren't many items in the "cons" list for rentvesting. If done correctly, it's a simple and effective strategy for starting out in property.

Advantages of rentvesting:

1. Rentvesting gets you into property sooner.

2. You can choose a financial structure that allows for a smaller deposit (less than 20%). If properly structured, a smaller deposit for an investment loan is still a feasible tactic as long as the mortgage is offset by the rental income.

3. You can choose an investment property in your budget, without location constraints. Your investment property doesn't have to be in the same neighbourhood as you.

4. You can live in a location you can't afford to buy, and have the flexibility to move or upsize/downsize. The advantage of renting is the flexibility to move without significant expense, which can be beneficial to those who move around for work, or when personal circumstances change.

5. Tax deductions from the investment property help to offset the mortgage repayments.

The disadvantages:

1. You're still renting. This is a sticking point for some people, who can't shake the feeling that rent money is dead money, or who would like the freedom to personalise their own home.

2. You don't have the security of owning your own home. It's not easy being at the mercy of a landlord, and some people grate at the idea that the place they lay their head is not their own.

3. You may have to pay capital gains tax when you sell. Capital gains tax can be a hefty levy if your property has done its job and grown significantly in value.

SURE LOCATION IS IMPORTANT...

But next we'll discuss what causes property values of some locations to outperform over the long term.

BOOM TO BUST: WHAT MAKES PROPERTY PRICES RISE AND FALL

If you've been interested in property for a while, you would have noticed that there will always be somebody telling you it's the wrong time to get into property. I think it's important to understand what's happened to property values in the long-term and focus on that rather than the short-term fluctuations of the property market.

I've already explained how research by Metropole, based on data by the REA Group and the Australian Bureau of Statistics (ABS), shows that Australia's national median house value has risen by an enormous 540.1% over the past 42 years. This is an average annual growth rate of 7.62%.

Which leads to the question...

WHAT CAUSES PROPERTY VALUES TO INCREASE?

By now you understand all about property market cycles and at what stage in the cycle so let's talk about property price rises, and how and why they grow.

I've divided this discussion into:

• The short-term factors which are what most of the media is concerned about and...

• The long-term influences — which is what strategic investors pay attention to.

8 reasons property values increase in the *short* term

1. **Interest rates:** Obviously low interest rates make it easier for buyers to borrow more, as money is cheaper. But interestingly, the converse isn't true. In the past, property values continued rising for some time, despite the RBA raising interest rates

2. **Supply and demand:** Generally, if demand for accommodation outweighs supply, property prices will rise. But if supply outstrips demand, such as when we go too many apartment towers, prices tend to decline.

3. **Availability and cost of land:** The lengthy time taken to release new land supplies and the vast amount of taxes and charges developers must pay to subdivide new estates has positively contributed to house price inflation in Australia.

4. **Access to credit:** Now I'm not talking about interest rates here, but a borrower's actual *access* to credit. Rising interest rates tend to prompt lenders to tighten their lending standards so borrowers can't borrow as much.

When our Banking Regulator APRA was concerned about the rapid growth in lending to property investors which led to steep increases in property prices in 2014, it instructed the banks and other lenders to be more cautious and set stricter criteria for determining whether borrowers could repay their loans if interest rates were to change. This warning had the desired effect and the share of new loans to investors fell from over 40% during 2014–15 to less than 30% the next year.

On the flip side, during the pandemic boom, banks eased lending standards in a move designed to free up credit and revive the economy — and it worked, hence the price surge.

5. **The general economic climate:** Here I'm talking about things like inflation and employment levels. It seems obvious that periods of low inflation and high employment would see an uptick in borrowing as consumers look to spend the extra cash in their back pocket. And as we know, when buyers fight over property purchases, values are only going to go upwards.

6. **Consumer confidence:** Increasing consumer confidence increases consumer spending. The aggregate demand curve shifts to the right, indicating an increase in demand for goods over services. In other words, a robust economic climate and rising property prices cause a "wealth effect" which leads to higher consumer confidence where buyers think it's the opportune time to spend their spare cash on a property.

7. **Government incentives for first-home buyers:** When the government wants to inject more demand into the market it looks to incentives for first-home buyers. Just look how well this worked during the Covid pandemic as first homeowner grants and incentives boosted jobs in the construction industry as well as in many associated retail industries.

   Australia's new Labor government currently has a few schemes in place for first-home buyers: the Help to Buy program (where the government owns a portion of your property and you pay it off down the track), the Home Guarantee Scheme where you can buy with a 5% deposit or regional first home buyer support.

   And what do these incentives do? They broaden the pool of property buyers, flipping the supply/demand balance and putting pressure on property values.

8. **Investor appetite:** Over the long term, property investors make up about 30% of the housing market. When the market conditions are favourable this leads to high investor demand, and we all know what that leads to.

3 REASONS PROPERTY VALUES INCREASE IN THE LONG TERM

1. Demographics

Demographics are the data that describes the composition of a population, such as age, race, gender, income, migration patterns, and population growth. These factors are significant drivers of what types of properties are in demand and how property is priced and that's because the demographics of a population determines not just how many people there are, but how and where they want to live.

And I'm not really talking about population growth – it's actually household formation that is they key here.

And immigration flows into this also. Australia's immigration policy of selecting skilled workers at the family formation stage of their lives is a significant driving factor for our housing markets.

And Covid has caused a structural demographic change that will affect our housing markets moving forward. Not only that but the pandemic-induced work-from-home movement has changed the demographics significantly – now, many workers are able to work from the comfort of their own home and save on commuting, which means they need the extra space. And it has increased shifts to sea- and tree-change.

The pandemic has also made people re-evaluate what they want in a home. Many upsized to a larger property, some moved further away from the city and others relocated entirely to regional areas.

And, as I've already explained, the importance of neighbourhood was reinforced. For many it's all about "living locally" – having the ability to meet most of your everyday needs within a 20-minute walk, cycle or local public transport trip of your home.

2. Future population growth

While our population growth stalled through the Covid pandemic, immigration levels are expected to get back to pre-Covid levels and we'll see population growth of about 1.5% or 400,000 people per year. That's the equivalent of adding a city the size of Canberra every year!

3. The wealth of the nation

If we believe Australia's population is going to keep growing, and it will as our government has a "business plan" to have close to 40,000,000 people in Australia by the middle of the century, and that our wealthy nation is going to remain wealthy, this will then underpin long-term property values.

You see, there is a positive relationship between household income ("real income" after inflation) and housing demand. The truth is household wealth and property price increases go hand-in-hand. And Australians are amongst the wealthiest people in the world and household and individual wealth is a very influential factor for property markets.

In every society, property is generally considered as the major store of wealth, and in Australia gross housing assets account for more than half of total personal wealth.

Owner occupiers and property investors feel wealthier when prices of existing houses rise – this is called the "wealth effect" which leads to an increase in consumption expenditure. As a result, aggregate demand, and thus economic growth, occurs which in turn supports rising housing prices through a self-reinforcing cycle.

The RBA has published a range of research that calculates the benefits of a change in wealth when house prices increase. In simple terms the RBA found that when wealth increases as house prices rise, spending grows and helps the economy and when house prices fall spending growth slows.

And I guess that makes intuitive sense. If a property owner feels the "wealth effect" as their property increases in value, they are inclined to borrow against their wealth and in turn increase their consumption spending. This means rising housing wealth and the associated growth in household consumption feeds through to the other parts of the economy and creates jobs. It increases the level of employment which in turn feeds into better-than-otherwise wage increases.

In my opinion the high house prices in Australia are a reflection of living in the best country in the world with large coastal cities. There are long queues of people wanting to live in this country – you don't see people queuing up 20 years to live in Indonesia.

So rather than wishing for cheaper house prices, as some naysayers are hoping for, we should be looking to improve the financial situation for Australians.

Because when house prices fall it leads to a weaker economy, high unemployment, problems in the banking system and a slumping construction. And who would want that?

Sure, property affordability may improve, but crashing house prices will not build home ownership rates. In fact, on the contrary, a house price crash may lead to even lower home ownership rates if unemployment is higher and banks continue to tighten lending.

HOW TO CHOOSE AN INVESTMENT WHICH OUTPERFORMS THESE MARKET AVERAGES?

The key to achieving above average capital growth is buying the right property at the right price, and most importantly, in the right location. I've already explained the frameworks I use for this – my *Top Down* approach to selecting the right location and my 6 *Stranded Strategic* approach to finding the right property in that location.

There's no doubt there are many economic challenges ahead of us and it's easy to forget that this phase is just part or the normal economic and property cycle. Sure, we're heading into the Winter of the cycle but just like in nature, Spring follows Winter. It has for tens of thousands of years, and I'm prepared to put my money on the fact that it will happen again this time.

So plan for the worst, but expect the best, and invest with a long term perspective.

THE TYPES OF PROPERTY AVAILABLE

So far we've looked at the when and where of residential property, now we'll look at the "what" because not all properties make good long term investments.

There are close to 10.8 million dwellings in Australia and in 2021 almost 600,000 properties changed hands, but not all properties make good investments. In my mind less than 4% of those on the market currently are what I would call "investment grade" so let's look at the different types of property available and why you should consider buying certain types of property and avoid others.

If you hang around property investors long enough, you'll hear someone say: "Land appreciates and buildings depreciate" and this is why many investors believe they should invest in a house on a big block of land, rather than in apartments or townhouses. They incorrectly conclude the more land the better.

All else being equal this makes sense, but as I've explained, not all land is created "equal".

If an investor has $1 million to spend, they could probably only buy an apartment in the inner suburbs of Sydney or Melbourne. They couldn't buy a house on a plot of land in these locations. If they wanted to buy a house and land on their budget they would most likely have to buy 30 to 40 kilometres from the city.

Would you rather have 700 square meters of land 50 kilometres out of the CBD, or 100 square meters three kilometres from the city centre? I'd buy the small block of land sitting under an inner suburban apartment any day.

Rather than looking at the size of the land, I look for the land to asset ratio. I like the land component to be a high proportion of the price I pay for my property.

What I'm trying to explain is while there is no doubt that land is a valuable component in the investment mix, you can't just buy any land. Land only has value because of its scarcity, which is directly tied to its location.

So certain land will increase in value more than other plots of land. That's why I only buy properties in areas that are built out; in the inner and middle ring established suburbs of our capital cities where land is in high demand but short supply. And I avoid buying properties in new suburbs where there is no shortage of land.

There are a number of other reasons I avoid buying houses in the outer suburbs or in new estates. Think about it...

When you buy a new house on a block of land in one of the new outer suburbs, you may be paying $700,000, of which the land — the bit that increases in value — could be worth around $350,000. This is a very low land to asset ratio indeed.

While these might be great places to live and bring up your family, in general capital growth will be subdued in these suburbs. Firstly, new homeowners in these "mortgage belt" suburbs are more interest rate sensitive as they tend to have less disposable income than people who live in more affluent suburbs.

Secondly, there is rarely a scarcity factor about properties in these locations. Many homes look the same and there is always another estate with similar houses and more land just across the road. And of course, scarcity is one of the major reasons properties increase in value.

And as I've already explained, another reason we avoid buying in these areas is demographics. While they make good areas for young families and new home owners, there is not the same demand from a diversity of affluent tenants as there is in the inner and middle ring suburbs.

By the way, the same applies to buying in high-rise apartment buildings. To make a profit the developer wants to get as many apartments on the land as he can — he wants a low land-to-asset ratio. That's the opposite of what you want.

Instead, I would suggest that you buy established "family friendly" apartments (these used to be called flats when I grew up), villa units or townhouses in the inner and middle ring suburbs of our capital cities where land is fully built out and supply of this type of property is scarce, but demand is strong. This will ensure long-term capital growth and a steady stream of potential tenants allowing you to grow your property investment business.

Anyway... let's dig into each of these a little further:

LAND

While it's not a strategy I'd recommend for most investors on two occasions I've invested in raw parcels of land in the outer suburban fringes and added value by subdividing them into small estates of multiple lots and made substantial profits. While this is something large developers do there are inherent problems and risks because:

- You may need to negotiate with councils to get the land re-zoned to allow development.
- It is a capital-intensive investment. There are enormous up-front costs, including developing the infrastructure such as sewerage, drainage and roads, surveying, permits and engineering.
- You receive no income right until the end of the project.

- While subdividing land can be very profitable, especially in a rising market if you've done your research correctly and found a popular growth region, it still remains a highly speculative proposition.

I undertook these projects was I was younger, braver and more naïve, and I made a lot of money from them. But as a general principle I recommend investors should steer clear of buying vacant land. The problem is that it doesn't give you much income because the pesky tenants will always complain about the lack of shelter!

And, since vacant land doesn't generate income, the banks won't lend you as much as they would against an income-producing property. Plus, without rental income, land doesn't have the tax benefits of a rental property, so it actually costs you more to own.

One solution is to buy an old house which is rentable at close to land value and use the concept of...

LAND BANKING

How many times have you driven past a property and said to yourself, "If only I had bought that property when it was for sale five years ago?"

Let's face it, who wouldn't have bought more properties 10 years ago if they had known they would double in value, like many well-located properties have over the last decade?

Fast forward five years from now — would you like to own a development site that cost you much less than the prevailing price? Well that's exactly what I'm doing and so are many of our clients at Metropole — we're Land Banking, which is simply the process of securing future development sites today, at the current price.

Many large property developers buy Greenfield sites, farms or large tracts of land and put them in their "land bank" to ensure they have a sufficient stock of land for future developments. Over time they rezone the land, put in the necessary roads and infrastructure, undertake a subdivision and on-sell the individual lots. While holding a bank or stockpile of land has helped many developers make big profits in a rising market, it has also been the downfall of a number of prominent developers when property values slumped or rising interest rates blew out their holding costs.

But a variant of this strategy is a great approach for smaller developers.

You see... I don't buy vacant blocks of land. I buy old houses close to their "use by date" on well-located blocks of land which have development potential in top suburbs. While the rent I receive partially offsets my holding costs, I add value to my property by obtaining development approval and then over time, proceeding with the development of two, three or four townhouses.

I know many investors who have made small fortunes by land banking because they are able to use a number of different property wealth accelerators that, when combined, generate substantial profits:

1. *Land appreciates* — we've already discussed the concept that it's the land component of your property investment that appreciates, so buying a property close to its land value can be a smart strategy.

2. *Adding Value* — by obtaining development approvals you can add substantial value to a property.

Once you obtain a development approval for subdivision or for building multiple dwellings, apartments or townhouses, you've taken out one element of the development risk — the council approval process. This makes your property more attractive to developers who may be prepared to pay a premium for it and gives you the option of selling for a profit or refinancing your property at its new higher value and continuing with the development process.

3. *Riding the property cycle* — I like securing potential development sites in a "soft" property market. At these times, completing a development may not be particularly financially lucrative, so I can buy these sites at a good price.

As the market moves on, as it always does, if you've chosen he right location, the combination of a stronger market and owning a property with development approval in a prime position allows me to complete my development and make a substantial profit.

This strategy works particularly well in the inner and middle ring suburbs of our capital cities, where there is no vacant land for future development, but there is an increasing demand for new medium-density developments from a whole new demographic of smaller households. This includes Gen Ys starting out in apartments, to Dinks (Dual income no kids); Mingles (Middle-aged singles) and Baby Boomers who are downsizing.

The combination of the current slowing property market, a limited supply of potential development sites and the future demand for more medium density development make a perfect recipe for successful land banking.

Whilst this strategy offers significant rewards, there are a host of traps for the unwary. The biggest one is in relation to what type of development (if any) can fit on the property? There are some properties, in fact many properties that, even if in the right location, don't make good development sites. To use this strategy it's important to understand your local town planning regulations.

Of course I don't sell my development projects on completion — I keep them as long term investments — remember the main aim of the property game is to build your asset base.

HOUSES

When I first started investing I invested in houses, but today the only houses I buy are those for my Land Banking strategy. My long-term residential investments are all medium-density dwellings — apartments or townhouses as these will be the preferred style of accommodation for an increasing percentage of our population. (I also own a substantial commercial property portfolio — but that's another story.)

While medium density is the way to go in Sydney and Melbourne, currently houses make great investments in Brisbane or Adelaide's inner suburbs where you can buy a dwelling on a good-sized block of land for much the same price as an apartment in Sydney.

INSIDER TIP

Some older and run-down properties can be bought close to land value. These are the ones I like best, because I can increase their value dramatically by getting a development approval for multiple units on the land.

TOWNHOUSES AND VILLA UNITS

Townhouses are either single or double story stand-alone dwellings on their own small plots of land. They often share common land or facilities such as driveways with other dwellings in the complex and are the preferred type of housing for a growing segment of our population, making them great investments.

More of us are opting to live in townhouses, which include semi-detached, row and terrace homes.

The increase in townhouse living is partly due to the fact that townhouses provide a family-friendly alternative to a detached house, at a lower entry price. They offer a greater level of privacy than an apartment, with a common driveway often the only shared space. Most importantly, for family-friendly living or perhaps pet lovers, they often have private outdoor space in the form of a courtyard or small garden.

A large proportion of my personal property portfolio are townhouse complexes that I've developed and kept as they provide modern "house style" accommodation on compact blocks of land.

APARTMENTS

For generations backyards, barbecues and big houses have been the norm for Australian homeowners, but that's all changing and now as our lifestyles are changing there is evidence of a growing preference toward apartment-style accommodation in Australia.

Sure this was put on hold for a short time during Covid, but now affordability constraints will mean more of us will be swapping our backyards for balconies, meaning the right type of apartment — good-sized, family friendly apartments, will make great investments. I own a number of blocks of apartments that have proven to be very solid investments because of their prime locations.

What about all those outgoings?

I know some investors dislike apartments because they don't like the idea of paying Body Corporate (or as they are sometimes called Owners' Corporation) fees. But before you jump to the same conclusion, let's look at what they are made up of:

1. **Building insurance** — this is an expense you would have to pay for a standalone house anyway.

2. **A sinking fund** for future maintenance. If you owned a house as an investment it would be a smart idea to put away money every month to pay for the repairs that will eventually be needed to the exterior or for painting or for the gutters that wear out.

3. **Maintenance of common property**. I'm happy for the Body Corporate to look after my investment and keep it maintained and well presented. But I would avoid the large apartment complexes with exorbitant fees related to pools, gyms and lifts.

Clearly if you want a top performing investment property you just can't buy any apartment. All the rules I've already discussed with you regarding timing and location also apply here. In fact, I love investing in established apartments because they have great potential for adding value through refurbishments. They often have more character, higher ceilings and bigger rooms.

I've really explained that you should avoid CBD high-rise apartments and instead look for what I call "boutique developments". The scarcity factor of this type of property contributes to its higher capital growth. Units in boutique developments generally have special attributes that appeal to a wider cross-section of the population. Many are in inner suburbs that feature an appropriate balance of development to green-space, together with schools and neighbourhood amenities — the sorts of things the vast majority of the population want.

Let's face it, as our population grows there's no doubt more of us will need to embrace the apartment culture, but this should not be a real problem, as fortunately our lifestyle preferences are changing.

OLD OR NEW?

Another consideration is the age of the property you buy. As I see it they can fall into three main categories:

1. Established properties

2. New properties

3. Off-the-plan properties

Let's look at each of these in turn.

New properties

New property investments, be they a house or an apartment, are often pitched on the benefits of:

- Wide tenant appeal
- Lower maintenance
- Structural and building warranties to cover defects for the first few years
- Depreciation allowances

All this is true, but usually comes at a cost:

- The price premium you pay for new properties (which includes the developer's margin, selling agents and marketing costs) often means that you've given away the first few years' worth of capital growth to the developer, and it's not his to have.
- There is no opportunity to add value to new properties and, as you know, this is part of my 6 Stranded Strategic Approach to investing.
- More often than not, you'll find new apartments in the centre of the CBD or on main roads – both secondary locations. While new houses tend to be in an outer suburban estate and I've already explained how these locations underperform.
- The value of new properties tends to be the first to fall when the market falters.
- The highly publicised structural issues experienced by some new apartment buildings over the last few years has left most new buildings "tarred with the same brush" and many potential buyers are wary of buying into these buildings, meaning there is a smaller secondary market for your apartment if you wish to sell.
- Similarly, as many investors (mistakenly) buy into new apartment complexes because they receive depreciation allowances on new dwellings, there is a limited pool of buyers if you need to sell your apartment as it will no longer be "new" and therefore won't be eligible for depreciation allowances.

Now, let me explain why I believe established properties are a much better investment prospect for solid, long term wealth creation.

Established properties

Sure established properties may not initially be as attractive, but rather than paying a premium to buy an attractive property with higher rents and depreciation allowances, I'd rather "manufacture" my depreciation allowances and higher rents by purchasing an older property knowing that the right renovation gives me a once off quick boost of capital growth as well as making my property appealing to a wide range of tenants.

It is also easier to buy an established property below its intrinsic value, because rather than dealing with a developer selling off a price list to satisfy his bank's profit margin, I'm dealing with a motivated vendor whose reasons for selling could work to my advantage in the negotiation process.

Also when buying an established property you'll be able to check it's past sales history and long-term capital growth performance, something you can't do with a new property. And you should be able to buy it for a much lower cost per square metre than a new apartment.

Of course older properties can present their own potential issues for investors. They're not as appealing as a new property and may have maintenance issues, but both of these would be resolved by undertaking a renovation.

Needless to say not any old established property will do, it needs to tick all of the other boxes I've shared with you.

Off-the-plan properties

Open any weekend newspaper and you'll see a large number of proposed new apartment projects being marketed before building has even been commenced, which might make you wonder – why on earth would anybody buy a property that hasn't been built yet?

Plenty of people do, you know. It's called buying "off the plan" and many investors are considering buying properties these properties enticed by the advertising hype of stamp duty savings and so called "cheap" prices.

They hope that by getting in today and settling on their apartments in a few years' time that the value of the property will have increased and they will have turned a relatively small deposit into a substantial profit, all while avoiding those nasty holding costs.

Others never intend to settle their purchase, hoping to sell the apartment for a profit on completion.

But does buying "off the plan" make good investment sense?

The answer is usually no.

While a few investors have made money buying off the plan, the landscape is littered with many more who have regretted their purchase.

Frequently they've found that the value of their property on completion is considerably less than they paid. There are many other issues with buying off the plan, but before I explore them let's first understand why projects are marketed this way.

While developers know that they can get a better price for a completed property that buyers can see, touch and feel, lenders who provide construction funding will only do so on the basis that a substantial portion of the units are pre-sold, to ensure the financial viability of the project is underwritten.

Obviously the banks expect the developer to make a reasonable profit margin - and so they should. But this is built into the final price, as is the substantial marketing budget which covers the cost of those full-page ads in the papers and expensive glossy brochures and display suites built for the project. Add to this the generous selling commissions given to project marketers and incentives offered to financial planners, and you can understand why the initial selling cost is inflated.

Remember, there is no such thing as a "free lunch".

If 10 to 15 % of the project's budgeted selling price is spent on marketing and selling costs, then the buyer must pay for this.

As the completion date for many high-rise inner-city projects may be a few years away, the inflated price can be buried in advertising hype such as "buy at today's prices and settle in two years". The developers are counting on the fact that the longer the settlement period, the less chance you have of knowing if the final price will represent good value for money.

Looking back, many investors who purchased "off the plan" over the last decade found that the price they paid was way too high and on completion their properties were valued at considerably less than their purchase price. In fact, many have had to wait for over a decade to get any capital or rental growth.

Here are a few other reasons why I would steer clear of off the plan purchases:

1. *Too many fingers in the pie*

I've seen far too many off-the-plan properties with large commissions built in for middlemen, marketing budgets and sales people, meaning the investor pays well over its true underlying value.

Don't be lulled into a false sense of security just because you've been told a number of presales have already occurred. You're likely to find many are at inflated prices to overseas buyers who are unable to buy established properties, have little knowledge of the local markets and have unique motivations for buying property in Australia, such as a desire to emigrate in the future or place their money in a more stable country.

2. *The banks won't buy it!*

Given that most loan approvals are only current for three months, obtaining a formal pre-approval for an off the plan purchase is a waste of time. The problem is, we currently have four big banks in Australia and they each have a policy restricting their exposure to any one building; most won't lend to more than 15% of the properties in a large complex.

This means that if there are 100 apartments in the building and you are the sixteenth person to approach the bank when the building is completed, they may decline your application and you'll have to go chasing finance elsewhere. And if they do lend for your purchase you may find that because of the inner-city postcode of your new high-rise purchase, they will lend at lower loan to value ratios, meaning you need a bigger deposit.

By the way... some investors who buy off the plan won't be able to settle and will need to sell their property at whatever price they can achieve. Unfortunately when this happens that's what the banks will value your property at the going selling price on completion, not what you paid for it.

Combine this with a lower loan to value ratio and you're likely to need an even bigger deposit than you initially thought.

3. Low land to asset ratio

If you go by the book, you should aim for the highest land to asset ratio possible and to get as much valuable land under your apartment as you can. However, the developer wants the opposite and squeezes as many apartments onto the site as they possibly can.

So essentially, the interests of the developer and you, the investor, are in direct opposition and you'll typically find the land value proportion is less than 10% of the property's value. This means you're mostly paying for the building – the part that depreciates.

4. Investor imbalance

Most off the plan developments are sold to investors which means that you end up with a building occupied by far more tenants than homeowners.

Fact is, owner-occupiers tend to be far more careful when it comes to maintaining the building and enhancing the development's long-term capital value.

By the way... it's not much fun going to a body corporate meeting full of investors who are not keen on spending money (or simply don't have it) to maintain the building.

5. Too many too soon

Currently there is a looming oversupply of new apartments in some of our capital city CBDs. I've seen this before.

It's the usual exuberance from property developers during a property boom. You just have to open Saturday's paper to see the huge number of new development projects coming out of the ground – and there are even more on the drawing board.

This glut of properties driving down prices poses a problem for investors relying on the value of their property to increase by the time it reaches completion.

You'll also be competing with all the other investors who are trying to rent out their new investments.

Both of these issues mean that your investment will lack scarcity value, one of the factors that I look for to help increase the value of my properties.

Even worse, many investors who bought off the plan with a 10% deposit will find that they're going to have to cough up a lot more at settlements.

Another issue is the standard of some of these new buildings, with reports suggesting our CBDs are riddled with poor quality apartments, many with windows that are not openable, nor having particularly good views. And at street level, we will have a situation where there is insufficient open space, wind tunnels and overshadowing effects. And worse still... many are located in secondary locations such as on main roads.

6. *Developer dilemmas*

Did you know that many off the plan projects currently being marketed won't get out of the ground? Sure you'll get your deposit back, but it means you've lost precious time with your money not working in the market.

On the flipside, when the developer completes the project don't be surprised if they have made some amendments to the floor plans or substituted different finishes or fittings. While they have the right to do so in the contract, you'll usually find the changes are in their favour and not yours.

7. *Rental guarantees are not as solid as you might think*

Often developers will offer a rental guarantee to entice investors who might be more focused on their cash flow and worried about vacancies. The problem is, you pay for these rental guarantees in the purchase price, which is another cost that inflates the apartment's already premium price. And once the guarantee expires the rental income reverts back to the going market rate, which is usually lower than that offered in the guarantee.

8. *No Track Record*

Because these properties have not been sold before their price is determined by the developer to cover his costs and his profit margin. The property won't have a proven performance — you really won't know this until a number of resales have occurred in the building.

WHAT LESSONS CAN WE LEARN FROM THIS?

Given that most high-rise projects have a two-year plus construction time frame, it is very difficult to predict what the future will hold, I believe that you should receive a sizeable discount for all of the uncertainty involved with buying off the plan.

There is uncertainty about what the property markets will be like on completion, what the interest rates will be then, whether the standard of finish will be as good as in the display unit or if the developer has cut corners and what will be built alongside, behind, or in front of the project in the future. Let's face it; a great view today may be totally blocked out in two years' time.

To cover all of these uncertainties, surely you should be buying at a substantial discount, but in reality you usually pay a premium, therefore giving the developer your first five or more years' worth of capital growth (and he doesn't deserve it).

INSIDER TIP

I have seen too many investors get burned and lose their money buying off the plan to recommend it as a sensible investment option.

WHICH PROPERTIES TO AVOID

It's probably worth looking at what other types of property not to buy, so let's first explore...

PROPERTIES THE BANKS DON'T LIKE

There are certain properties that the banks don't seem to like and against which they will lend a lower Loan to Value ratio, which means you'll need to fork out a bigger deposit. More importantly, if the banks are wary of them, rather than thinking you know better than the banks, take it as a warning sign and look elsewhere.

In general, the banks restrict lending to properties that appeal to a limited resale or tenant market. By now you know that buying the type of property that appeals to a wide demographic of owner-occupiers is one of my fundamentals. The types of properties I would avoid are...

1. *Serviced apartments.* These are a bit like hotel suites and are popular rentals for business people and holidaymakers for short or extended stays. Investing in a serviced apartment carries a lot more risk than buying an ordinary apartment. You're relying on the operator to get it right and on the tourism and business markets to remain strong to maintain occupancy. These properties have a limited resale market (only investors buy them, cutting out 70% of purchasers) and a limited letting market. In fact you can't re-let them and they often have excessive ongoing management costs. While marketed as residential property, serviced apartments are actually part commercial and part residential. Owners usually hold commercial leases with the operator, another reason the banks won't lend as much for this type of property.

2. *Department of Housing accommodation* – these properties come with certainty of long leases (six to 12 years) and no ongoing maintenance but have a limited resale market and hefty management charges.

3. *Studio apartments and student accommodation* — also have restricted markets because of their size.

4. *Small units* — banks prefer apartments to comprise at least 50 square metres of living space, not including balconies or car parking. However, with our changing lifestyles some will now lend on properties that are 40 square meters.

OTHER PROPERTIES I AVOID

1. *Out of place* — I only buy properties that fit in with the overall character of the neighbourhood. I love terrace houses, but if the property happens to be the only terrace in a street full of bungalows, I'd look elsewhere and buy a property consistent with the streetscape.

2. *The wrong location in the street* — Even the best streets can have sections with an unattractive mix of properties or that are too close to the shops or main road. Choose liveable streets and make sure you buy the right property in the right section of the street.

3. *Encumbrances on Title* — Check the title carefully for easements, covenants or overlays that could restrict your capacity for future extensions or rebuilding.

4. *Other Title troubles* — Banks will restrict their lending for apartments on some older forms of title, such as company-share or stratum titles. This means there will always be a limited resale market for these properties, which are best avoided.

5. *Body Corporation problems* — When buying an apartment carefully peruse the minutes of the last few body corporate meetings. Are there any issues with the building? Are there any excessive expenses planned? Has a sinking fund been set up to handle future repairs or refurbishment?

6. *No car parking* — While absence of parking may save you $30,000 to $50,000 today, it will always limit a property's appeal to tenants, home owners and future investors.

7. *Wrong position in the block* — Avoid apartments in sub-optimal positions in the block. You know what I mean, the ones overlooking the car park or situated near the waste bins.

8. *Avoid main roads* — Sure people live on main roads but it's always harder to sell or lease a property on a busy street. While most properties sell quickly in a hot market, when the market slows secondary properties fall in value first and, if you think about it, homebuyers and tenants will always choose a property in a quiet street over a main road. It's much the same for properties in side streets, which are a bit too close to main roads or noisy neighbours like schools, factories or shops.

9. *Steer clear of secondary locations* — Sometimes you'll see ads for a property that seems cheap, but when you investigate further you realise that these properties are in inferior locations

that don't appeal to owner-occupiers. Avoid these properties, as they'll always be cheap and deliver lower growth in the long run.

10. *Rental guaranteed apartments* — A rental guarantee is where a developer guarantees a purchaser a certain minimum rent for an initial period. As the old saying goes, if it sounds too good to be true it probably is. Rental guarantees are usually a sign of an over-supplied product or area, a weak market, or a property that would otherwise struggle to sell without this incentive. While this type of property panders to those who are worried about vacancies, the cost of the rental guarantee (which is usually inflated to make the return look better than it really is) is added to the purchase price and used by the developer to justify inflated prices. In other words you're paying the developer up front to guarantee the rent for you. And it's not uncommon for the rent to drop when the rental guarantee period expires, leaving you with a hole in your budget.

11. *Holiday homes or apartments* — I'm not saying don't buy yourself a weekend getaway property if you can afford it. What I'm saying is don't pretend you're buying it as an investment, because you're likely to end up with an asset that, on the one hand isn't meeting your lifestyle dreams and on the other, doesn't deliver your financial objectives. Property values in holiday locations are always more volatile — during booms they boom and during busts, boy do they drop in value! Add to that the uncertain and volatile income stream associated with short-term leases, plus the high maintenance and management costs incurred with a high turnover of tenants, and you can see why this type of property does not make a good investment.

In the final chapter of this section we're going to unveil some more rules for selecting properties from among similar alternatives. Keep these in mind when you buy and you'll maximise your chances of property profits.

THE (UNTIL NOW) UNWRITTEN RULES FOR SELECTING PROPERTIES

As a child I used to play Monopoly. Sometimes I won, sometimes I lost. As an adult I've played Monopoly a couple of times with some financially intelligent people and I now realise that, contrary to what I thought as a child, it's not a game of luck. Good players know the right spots on the board to get the best return on their investments. They know how to acquire and control the best "monopolies" in order to collect the highest rents. They've learned to negotiate and find ways to make great deals. They've learned how to take the luck out of Monopoly and consistently win big as a result.

To me, this sounds a whole lot like the real world of investing. You need to learn how to take the luck out of wealth creation and instead develop smart strategies to get ahead. First you need to learn how to play the game, and then you need to know how to win the game. Over the years I've learned that there are a couple of keys to selecting the right properties to buy, and I would like to share these rules with you before you start, rather than you learning them the hard way. This can save you a lifetime of trial, error and expense.

But let me remind you that no one wins Monopoly owning Old Kent Road. Everyone wants the same high-end properties on the Monopoly board and it's much the same in real life. Yet when you think about it, where do most people buy their investment property? Near where they live or near where they want to retire or where they holiday or want to holiday.

These are all emotional reasons and not a good, logical basis for expecting profits. So what rules do you need to know in order to maximise your profits?

I've already described my 6 Stranded Strategic Approach to choosing a top performing investment property, and I've expanded on this explaining the **top down approach** I use.

So now let's take a closer look at 13 of the most important rules you can use to buy the type of property that will outperform the market averages.

1. ONLY BUY WHEN THE PRICE IS RIGHT

You make your profits when buy real estate. You lock it in by purchasing the right property and then maximise your profit by buying at a good price.

Now, this requires some research and legwork on your part. It means not buying just any property and definitely not buying the first property you see. It means looking harder than other buyers, in places other buyers may not think to look, seeing opportunities other buyers don't see and making lower offers than other buyers would dare.

Buying at the right price also means avoiding making emotional decisions. You have to make your buying decisions based on research and with your calculator (or spreadsheet), not your heart.

When I wrote the first edition of this book, as the property markets on the east coast of Australia slumped I emphasised the need for buying properties below the market price. I explained how you should look for a bargain. It's interesting how my strategy changed in just a few short years when I wrote the second edition in 2007. That elusive bargain was no longer to be found as property was being hotly contested by owner-occupiers and investors during a property boom. Now as I write this 17th edition we find the property markets around Australia fragmented — while there are still some hotly contested property markets, many locations have now moved more in favour of buyers.

Now don't get me wrong — I have never suggested you must buy a bargain. Cheap properties today will most likely be cheap properties of the future and not create the capital growth that you require for financial independence.

In a seller's market — where there are more buyers than there are vendors — my recommended strategy is to buy the best property you can afford and don't be scared to pay fair market price, because when you look back in a few months' time you are likely to be comforted by the rising property values.

On the other hand, in a buyer's market — characterised by more sellers than there are potential purchasers — you need a different approach. In these markets there is simply less room for error. If you are going to take the business of building your multi-million dollar property portfolio seriously, you must act like a property professional. No emotion!

What is the right price?

For products that are plentiful, transacted often and largely the same as each other, determining market value is relatively easy. But purchasing property is typically not like buying tomatoes at the grocer. Each property tends to have features that make it unique in the market.

Even two properties side by side on the same street could be valued differently because of their individual attributes. To make things even trickier, property is typically not transacted frequently, so it may be hard to find a recent sale of a property similar to the one you are interested in buying.

We'll take a closer look at valuations later in the book, but for now, in order to understand how you can buy property for the best possible price, you need to understand a little bit about how prices are determined.

Unlike almost all other areas in which we buy goods, in real estate there are no set prices. Buyer and seller must negotiate a price that is acceptable to both of them. While the "asking price" is a rough guide to what the vendor would like to achieve or what the selling agent thinks the seller will get, to an investor the asking price is almost irrelevant.

Vendors are not very good judges of what their homes are worth. It's natural for sellers to want a higher price, thinking that their home is better than everyone else's. They may have over-capitalised their property with expensive renovations or they may just need a higher price to enable them to buy a better home.

Vendors are usually not well-informed about market prices. They value their homes at what they heard their neighbours got for their properties, yet sometimes neighbours say they got more than what they actually did, and sometimes agents mislead sellers about what prices have been achieved by surrounding properties.

How asking prices are set

Usually to gain their business, selling agents give potential vendors an opinion of their property's value based on comparable property sales in the area.

Agents typically give their highest estimates in the hope of securing the vendor's listings, but ultimately the vendor makes the final decisions as to what price a property will be listed for. This is often slightly higher than what the agents suggest, and the agent then waits for buyers to give what is known in the industry as "buyer feedback" or "current market opinion". The agent then slowly conditions his vendor to reduce the asking price to meet the market.

This process used by selling agents to attract vendors by suggesting an inflated sales price is called "buying a listing" in the industry. Sometimes the opposite occurs and the selling agent suggests a selling price below market value.

Why would they do this?

I mainly see this when the estate agency manages the rental property and the owner is overseas or interstate or is elderly and doesn't have a good idea of the market. This also frequently happens when there's an out of area agent selling the property.

To ensure that you don't over pay you simply must know your market — your investment comfort zone.

Who can I ask to find the right price?

The selling agent? A valuer? A buyer's agent? Maybe the bank? Or do you buy one of those online reports?

It probably won't come as a surprise that they are all likely to come up with different "values".

You may have heard of the concept of "fair market value" in property which is defined as "the price a buyer will pay and a seller will accept given that neither the buyer nor the seller is under pressure to close the deal".

Pressure, or motivation comes from life changes such as divorce, a sudden job transfer, difficulty meeting mortgage repayments or a death in the family and these things compel either the buyer or seller to act quickly.

Now when we're talking fair market value, let's get one thing clear — it may not always be "fair" to you.

It may not be what you call "equitable" because fair market value is impartial, it takes no sides and it doesn't care about what you need or what you want. As a buyer you want to buy the property at the best price possible and as a seller you want to achieve the highest price for your home.

So back to my original question — who do you ask for advice?

1. *The real estate agent.* If you ask the selling agent what the property you're considering buying is worth, he is obliged to work for his client — the seller. While he can give you details of comparable sales and an indication of interest in the property from other potential buyers, the selling agent should be trying to maximise the sale price for his vendor.

2. *A valuer.* You could pay $500 or so and get an independent professional valuation, but you'd probably be disappointed.

    I've found that a formal valuation is of limited benefit in setting a realistic market price to purchase a property. Call me cynical, but in the current market when property values are flat and with their professional indemnity insurance is getting more expensive and the little they are paid to conduct a valuation, valuers come down on the conservative side.

3. *The bank.* When you apply for a loan for your new property the bank will determine its value, but again this may not accurately reflect the property's market price.

    Banks tend to value properties at figure that will reflect what they can reasonably expect to recoup if they take possession and on-sell your property if you default on your loan repayments. They either use their own staff or an outside firm of valuers, but these are often driven by valuations without even looking inside the property.

4. *An online report.* A number of property data and research companies provide reports you can buy online to estimate the value of a property. And now most web portals offer this type of report for free.

What's the catch? I've found that they can be 10 to 20% out on the real value of a property. They can be wrong either way — estimating the property is worth considerably more or substantially less than its value.

Think about it — they don't know if the property has had an air conditioner installed or whether it has threadbare carpets or recently polished floor boards. They don't know whether the property has been recently renovated or is in original condition.

In my view, I wouldn't bother with this type of report — they are too misleading.

5. A *buyer's agent* is a good source of independent and unbiased property price advice. If you chose one that works in the geographic patch you are considering, they should have an intimate knowledge of the property market, what is selling and what isn't and the prices that properties are selling for.

To be successful in today's property markets, thorough research and astute property selection is important, as is buying at the right price. Investors can't count on the rising tide of property prices to cover up their buying mistakes.

Clearly the value of a property is a very subjective thing. But this can be to your advantage as a property investor. While a good selling agent may encourage an emotional purchaser to overpay for their dream home, an astute investor may be able to use their negotiating skills to buy a property below its "intrinsic value" from a motivated vendor.

If you are not able to or don't have the time to do the required research yourself, then you need to get a good team on your side to help in your next property purchase or sale. Of course I'm biased — but I'd like you to consider the multi-award winning team at Metropole Property Strategists at www.metropole.com.au who help Australians become financially free through independent and unbiased property advice.

One last point about buying at the right price. I started this section saying you make your money when buying your property and that's true, but it's much more than just buying at the right price which is a one-off win. You make your money when buying because you've bought the right property — one that fits in with all the rules I'm sharing with you. Buying a dud property at a cheap price makes no sense — does it?

2. BUY PROPERTY THAT WILL BE IN CONTINUOUS STRONG DEMAND BY PEOPLE WHO CAN AFFORD TO PAY FOR IT

You need to choose a property that is in a location that will be in continuous strong demand by owners (because they set the market price) as well as tenants. But even in the best locations there will be some properties that don't make good investments, because they don't appeal to a broad range of potential owners or tenants.

The one criterion that makes an individual property more valuable than another is its scarcity value. If it's the right type of property but rare more people will be prepared to pay for it.

This is really just the law of supply and demand. If there is a greater supply of properties than there is demand, such as in the outer suburbs, where there are hundreds of houses that are similar, there is no reason for property values to rise.

On the other hand, if there is more demand than supply, when there are two or three buyers for every property that is for sale, competition pushes up prices.

So this brings us back to the concept of finding a property that will be in continual strong demand.

The two major factors that create this demand are:

1. *Long-term demographic trends*, that is, where and how people want to live, and

2. *Special features* of the particular property that make it desirable, such as proximity to beaches or the water; proximity to popular shopping strips or schools; or special architectural features of the property that make it unique.

On the other side of the supply and demand equation we need to find the type of property that is in restricted supply. Prime real estate will usually be restricted in availability.

Good examples of these are properties near to (but not in) the CBD or near to popular "cappuccino" lifestyle shopping strips, where people tend to congregate on weekends. Proximity to employment hubs, good schools or in school catchment zones also creates demand for properties.

Investing near the beach or with water views is rarely a mistake. It's a classic case of limited supply and constant demand.

If you choose your property correctly, over the long term, the twin pressures of continuing strong demand and restricted supply should provide you with a profitable investment.

Of course there is another component to all of this — your property should be in an area where people can afford to pay for it. Now here's where my strategy differs to many others. Here's what I mean...

3. DON'T LOOK FOR AFFORDABLE PROPERTIES

There's a school of thought that suggests buying affordable property is the way to go for investors. The argument goes — there will always be demand for this type of property, especially by young families.

This has some investors buying houses in the newer or outer fringe suburbs of our capital cities, as they read that these are some of the fastest growing locations in Australia.

I don't look for affordable properties. While I accept that there is substantial population growth in some of these outer suburbs, that doesn't necessarily translate to "capital growth" and it doesn't make houses in these so called "growth corridors" good investments. In fact, one of the factors that limits capital growth in these locations is abundant supply.

Poor planning

While many new outer suburbs have been planned with affordability in mind and therefore may not be expensive in terms of money outlaid to buy a home, they are expensive when it comes to travel costs and the health of the residents.

The problem is flawed planning in some estates has created a dependency on cars as many have bad "walkability" and poor public transport links. There is also a paucity of parks and open spaces in many new housing estates.

In fact, in 2012 a Victorian State Government study showed that some new suburbs in Melbourne (and I can only assume the same applies to some other states) are so poorly designed that residents face an epidemic of chronic diseases such as anxiety, obesity and depression; all factors that may cause these locations to become the slums of the future.

There are other reasons houses in new estates don't make good investments.

Remember residents in these areas tend to have less disposable income than people who live in more affluent suburbs, which means that these regions suffer most in tough times or when interest rates rise.

Also... one of the big factors that enhances capital growth is scarcity, and that's something missing in these suburbs. Many properties look the same, and there's always another estate with more land and similar houses just across the road.

Another reason I would avoid investing in these areas is their demographics, as they don't attract the same demand from a diversity of tenants as the inner and middle ring suburbs do. Then of course there's the low land to asset ratio as I've already explained.

4. LOOK FOR "LIFESTYLE" LOCATIONS

Select your investment properties in suburbs where there is a high demand from "affluent" owner-occupiers and from tenants with high disposable incomes. These tenants will be able to afford rental increases more easily and be less affected by market downturns.

5. SELECT PROPERTIES IN "LIVEABLE" STREETS

Even when you have chosen the right suburb, one with high demand and a history of good capital growth, you can choose the wrong street or district if you're not careful. In every suburb there will be some streets that outperform the others and always attract more tenants and owner-occupiers, causing stronger capital growth.

What constitutes a good street? It mainly comes down to aesthetic appeal and liveability.

More buyers want to purchase in a nice street with a high level of amenity and this increases property values. They look for things such as quiet locations with little through traffic. Tree-lined streets with wide footpaths, pleasant architecture and nice houses are always appealing. They like proximity to, but not being too close to, amenities such as schools, public transport, shopping, parks, cafés and restaurants.

6. SELECT AREAS WHERE LIMITED LAND IS AVAILABLE

If there's limited land available for new development, because the area is already well developed or possibly because of council imposed restrictions on development, you will experience scarcity that increases property values.

7. SELECT PROPERTIES IN SUBURBS WITH A HIGH RENTAL DEMAND

Some areas attract more tenants than others making it easier to lease your property. These are often lifestyle suburbs or close to well-regarded schools or hospitals and universities. You can research how many properties are available for lease in the suburb by doing a search for rentals on realestate.com.au or domain.com.au.

8. CHOOSE SMALLER, LOW-RISE "BOUTIQUE-STYLE" APARTMENT PROJECTS

If you are buying an apartment, select boutique properties, rather than high-rise developments. By this I mean look for blocks with less than 25 or so units.

One of the problems with the large developments is all the competition you have on your doorstep, especially if the property market takes a downturn and you have a whole lot of properties for sale or rent in your building.

The fewer the number of units in your development, the less chance you'll have of there being multiple neighbours or competitors next door, discounting their rental price, which could reduce your own property's rental potential. You'll also have less competition in the event that you need to sell your property. You also have more manageable Owners' Corporation meetings.

And only buy "family friendly", well laid out, larger apartments, rather than a shoe box.

9. CHOOSE PROPERTY WITH OWNER-OCCUPIER APPEAL

In my mind a good investment property has strong owner-occupier appeal.

Now I'm not contradicting myself. I buy the type of investment properties that increase in value more than the average property and as owner-occupiers buy around 70% of the properties in Australia, they are the ones that push up property values.

Also when a valuer comes around to value your property they'll ask themselves: if this borrower defaults and my client (the bank) has to put the property up for a quick sale, will there be a large group of buyers interested in this property. If so he's likely to be more generous in his valuation.

Think about it — if you ever choose to sell your property and it only appeals to investors they will buy your property "using their calculators". You also cut out 70% of property purchasers, owner-occupiers, who buy properties "with their hearts" — with emotion. They may be willing to pay an extra $5,000 to buy a property they want to live in.

10. AVOID SMALL PROPERTIES

Be cautious of purchasing properties that are much less than 50 square meters in size, such as small one-bedroom apartments or bed-sitters. Unless they have an extremely functional floor plan, many of these properties are just too small for today's lifestyles. Also, be aware that some banks will limit their lending for this type of property.

11. LOOK FOR UNIQUE FEATURES THAT TENANTS LOVE

Even though I suggested you buy owner-occupier type properties to have a broader appeal, as an investor you must also keep your potential tenant in mind.

While tenants want similar things to owner-occupiers, they also have some special needs. For example, tenants who share accommodation spend more time in their bedrooms and less time in the living areas, making their bedroom their only private area. It's their quasi-living area where they can obtain privacy and entertain their guests.

Tenants are also concerned about security and the quality of the fixtures and fittings in their properties.

So look for properties that have:

1. Larger than standard bedrooms, as often the size of tenants' bedrooms are more important than the size of the kitchen and living areas.

2. Good security features such as intercom and alarm.

3. High quality internal finishes including granite bench tops, timber floorboards, quality door furniture and European kitchen appliances.

12. GOOD DESIGN IS IMPORTANT

While the size of the property you buy is important, an even more important factor is a good design.

The designs of many apartments I inspect fail to meet the lifestyle requirements of modern households. I've come across two-bedroom apartments that are 70 square meters in size and very liveable because of an efficient open plan design, and I have seen considerably bigger two-bedroom apartments offer less liveable space due to inefficient designs and long wasted hallways.

As a guide to overall sizes of apartments, one-bedroom properties should be no less than 45 to 50 square meters internally plus a usable balcony.

As a general rule, two-bedroom apartments should be no less than 75 (but preferable 80) square meters internally plus at least eight square meters of balcony. Three-bedroom apartments should be no less than 100 square meters internally and once again have a usable balcony.

A well-designed apartment should have rooms no smaller than:

*   Bedrooms: 3 x 3 meters (excluding robes)
*   Living rooms: 4 x 3.5 meters
*   Kitchens: 3.2 x 2.5 meters

Remember someone is going to have to live in these rooms and put in "real" furniture; not the tiny samples they put into display apartments.

Also ensure that there is adequate storage space including linen cupboards, and rooms for mops, brooms and vacuum cleaners.

13. CHECK OUT THE WALK SCORE

When looking at the factors that make up a good location easy access to facilities must be near the top of the list.

Walking distance to transport, shops and the café lifestyle is one the strongest trends attracting buyers and tenants. This is particularly so among the growing demographic of owner-occupiers and tenants who choose to occupy apartments in our inner suburbs.

The good news is that you can find out how "walkable" a location is relatively easily. Walkscore. com, which measures the number of typical consumer destinations within walking distance of a dwelling, with scores ranging from 0 (car dependent) to 100 (most walkable), ranks most properties in Australia.

However, as you would expect, the "walkability index" has a number of shortcomings. Consider the low-scoring regional dweller who enjoys walking their dog on a rural path. Not to mention that what one person considers a "walkable" trip may seem an epic hike to another.

What's interesting about this is that over the past decade, home values in Sydney's walkable neighbourhoods have outperformed the rest of the city and can attract a 20% premium. And it was much the same overseas where studies indicate that properties with above-average levels of walkability command a premium over homes with average levels of walkability.

So when researching your next property purchase consider its proximity to amenities. As our lives become more hectic and our cities become more congested, many of us will be prepared to pay a premium to be close to, but not right next to transport, shops and amenities.

SUMMARY

OK, now we've covered a lot of ground that will help you to focus your energy on your research, and to choose wisely when it comes to where, when and what you might look to invest in.

In the next section we're going to look at understanding all the research data that is available.

INTERPRETING PROPERTY RESEARCH DATA

> "STATISTICS ARE LIKE A BIKINI. WHAT THEY REVEAL
> IS SUGGESTIVE, BUT WHAT THEY CONCEAL IS VITAL."
> – AARON LEVENSTEIN,
> ASSOCIATE PROFESSOR EMERITUS OF BUSINESS, BARUCH COLLEGE.

One of the biggest changes over the time I've been investing in property is the abundant availability of property research data. Today there's a plethora of statistics offered about Australia's property scene – median house prices by the year, the quarter, the month or day, median advertised rents, rental vacancy rates, auction clearance rates, days on market, and the list goes on.

While you'd think this would make research so much simpler, in fact the abundance of confusing and contradictory information often makes it harder.

The first rule about property statistics is that none of the data is perfect. A median price doesn't represent every property in a suburb. Auction clearance rates might represent the health of a particular segment of the market, but they don't tell you why some properties are selling when others aren't. Vacancy rates might be high but still 97% of properties will have a tenant.

That's not to say that studying the data isn't useful, it's just that to get a real understanding of what's going on you need to be "in the market", you need to be doing the kind of research that involves getting out and about to investigate a local market.

That's because property investing is part science and part art. Investors need to complement any applicable data with local area knowledge and expertise, plus experience and perspective in order to make the best-informed choices.

Someone looking at data can make it say almost anything they want; the trick is knowing how to take that information and use it in conjunction with some practical experience in order to accurately make an investment decision. In other words, data and research is a critical step in getting ready to invest, but it is only one of the many important steps.

There is no substitute for practical experience. That's because no two properties are the same –

even two apartments on the same floor in the same building with the same number of rooms may be over ten per cent different in price because of their floor plan and aspect.

This is why the buyers' agents at Metropole are so valuable to our clients — they bring the "art" part of the investment equation to property investors who have done internet and data research to cover the "science" part of the investment. They are ex-selling agents with on-the-ground experience and who understand the local markets and their drivers. They understand why one side of a road or area of a suburb is more valuable than another, or where and why the strongest demand sits in each area.

WHAT TYPE OF DATA IS AVAILABLE?

There are essentially two types of data that I keep track of.

The first provides a macro, big picture view on the state of the world economy, the condition of the Australian economy and the health of the property market, be it at national, state or suburb level. The second is data I use when deciding the value of an individual property I am considering purchasing.

Just to make things more confusing as you start doing your homework you'll find that different research houses report different figures, even on simple, but critical numbers like median house prices.

WHAT IS THE MEDIAN PRICE?

After auction clearance rates, you'll probably find median house prices are the most commonly reported housing statistics, but be careful — observing the change in median property prices may not be as useful as you think. As with any single measure there are some shortcomings that investors need to understand in order not to be misled with what's really happening to house price values.

So here's 5 things you need to understand before you draw any conclusions from the regularly reported changes in median prices:

1. How is the median price calculated?

The median house price is essentially the sale price of the middle home in a list where the sales are arranged in order from lowest to highest price.

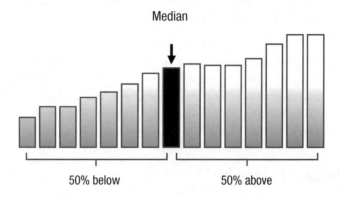

In other words, if fifteen properties were sold and then listed in order from the lowest to highest price achieved, property number seven would be the median price.

Median prices in property are based on the homes that have recently transacted, and are most often divided into units and houses.

2. A change in the median price does not necessarily mean a change in your property's value

While median prices are a useful tool for understanding the price changes of properties that have transacted in a market, a 10% increase does not necessarily mean that your property is worth 10% more. In fact, your property could have dropped in value during this time. What it does reflect, however, is activity in the market.

Look at it this way...

If a number of multi-million-dollar homes came onto the market and all sold the last month this would raise the median price — however the value of your more moderately priced home may not have changed at all.

Similarly, a falling median price in an area could really just indicate that there were more sales occurring at the cheaper end of the market than there are at the expensive end.

Here's another way of looking at it...

Let's assume there were five home sales in your suburb last month as follows: $460,000, $525,000, $550,000, $570,000 and $620,000. In this instance, the median would be $550,000.

Now let's assume that a year later three of these same properties go back onto the market and are resold for exactly the same price as they sold a year earlier (these properties are the ones with a price of $460,000, $525,000 and $620,000).

With these three sales, the median price is now $525,000 — $25,000 less than the median price a year earlier. However, as you can see, each of these houses did not lose any value when they were re-sold. Clearly the sample of sales here is small and not statistically significant. The point I'm trying to make is that to really understand what's been going on you'll need to look deeper into the sales that occurred over the period in question.

Scrutinising the types of properties that sold the previous month compared to the new data can be helpful — you might notice that those selling last month were primarily three-bedroom brick houses, where this month more prestigious homes were selling. This may suggest that the uptick in the median price isn't a sign that your property is increasing in value.

3. Median prices are a more valuable indicator in some areas than others

Changes in median price statistics are more meaningful in determining property price growth in some areas than others. For instance, suburbs where the properties are largely homogenous and therefore of similar pricing are likely to see the median price as a more accurate reflection of true value changes.

And suburbs where many properties transact on a more regular basis will also be more statistically meaningful than in areas where homes are tightly held, sell infrequently and are significantly different from another. Similarly, some suburbs are far too large for the number to be meaningful — with good and bad locations on different sides of a main road that don't perform similarly being lumped together.

Likewise relying on median price changes at a capital city level is too broad and can be misleading.

Medians are also misleading when a suburb has two distinct markets. This is common in bayside suburbs where houses near the beach fall in one price range and are very different to house prices further inland.

Median price changes can also be misleading in many of the new outer suburban areas where the type of property sold a number of years ago, vacant land, has now been replaced by new homes.

And of course gentrification with locals renovating their properties can change the nature or quality of the properties and therefore median house prices.

4. Different data providers measure different statistics

Ever wondered why different data providers' median prices are different? That's because there are three key differences between all the providers.

1. The data they collect,

2. The time frames they report on — daily, monthly or quarterly

3. The accuracy/complexity of the index methodology they rely on.

One way around this shortfall in median property value changes is to use data sets like the Corelogic Hedonic Index which seeks to overcome some of these issues by measuring the attributes of properties that are transacting as part of the analysis.

Understanding factors such as the number of bedrooms and bathrooms, the land area and the geographic context of the property allows for a much more accurate analysis of the true value of movements across specific housing markets.

This method also allows for compositional change in consumer buying patterns when measuring capital gains.

5. Statistics are more reliable if looked at over the long term.

Investors should pay less attention to short term trends and understand that median prices (as with all statistics) are more useful when viewed as a change in trend over a longer time frame and not at over a month-to-month period. This helps you get a better understanding of an area's performance.

Median prices are really best used as an indication of the composition of sales rather than a good indicator of changing property values. That's why I also look at data such as sale

WHAT OTHER DATA CAN YOU USE?

- *Median price growth* — Considering all the biases I've just mentioned, I find it's best to examine the year on year (12 month) change in median prices to get a broader view of where the market is going and to smooth out the anomalies rather than the regularly reported monthly changes.

- *Auction clearance rates* — these are a good barometer of market sentiment and are particularly useful in Melbourne and Sydney, where a higher percentage of properties sell at auction.

- *Comparable sales* — are essentially the sale prices of similar homes in the same locality as the property you are considering and are really the best way of evaluating what price a particular property should be bought for. This is the method valuers use for determining the value of a property. The more recent the sale and the more comparable the properties are, the more accurate the assessment of market value will be.

- *Property market absorption data* — This gives me an idea of market depth and the likely direction of prices. I check for:
  o *Stock on the market* — the number of properties on the market for sale in a suburb,
  o *The number of sales* occurring in a suburb which is a sign of the market "depth" — I like areas where there are always many buyers and sellers transacting,
  o *Vendors Asking price index* — are vendors confident and pushing up their asking prices?

o   *Average days on market* — how long it typically takes to sell a property in a given location once it's been advertised,

o   *Vendor discounting* — the level of discounting required from when a property is originally advertised price gives an indication of the strength and depth of the market.

All these stats give me an indication of how the market is absorbing (buying) newly listed properties and helps me to assess whether prices are more likely to move up, down or sideways in the future.

• *Market segments and market depth* — When researching suburbs most investors focus on the change in property values but leave out an important metric — market depth — how many properties sell each year and at what price point. Just look at the following two tables where property analyst Michael Matusik examines these factors.

TABLE 1: DETACHED HOUSE SALES + MEDIAN PRICE				
Location	Sales	% change	Median $	% change
Adelaide	14,770	-10%	$472,000	2%
Brisbane Region	29,550	-11%	$545,000	0%
Canberra	4,130	-13%	$690,000	1%
Darwin	1,120	-5%	$485,000	-3%
Gold Coast	6,930	-14%	$650,000	0%
Hobart	3,690	-14%	$460,000	8%
Melbourne	46,910	-19%	$714,000	-5%
Perth	23,800	-7%	$475,000	-3%
Sunshine Coast	5,010	-11%	$605,000	0%
Sydney	40,680	-6%	$890,000	-6%

Matusik + Price Finder. Year ending September 2019. % change on year before

TABLE 2: DETACHED HOUSE SALES BY PRICE GROUP				
Location	< $550k	$500k-$750k	$750K-$1m	>$1m
Adelaide	55%	26%	13%	6%
Brisbane Region	41%	31%	18%	10%
Canberra	11%	40%	35%	14%
Darwin	53%	37%	8%	2%
Gold Coast	22%	36%	26%	16%
Hobart	57%	27%	13%	3%
Melbourne	13%	35%	26%	27%
Perth	54%	23%	13%	10%
Sunshine Coast	23%	44%	23%	10%
Sydney	9%	21%	27%	43%

Matusik + Price Finder. Year ending September 2019.

Just look at Hobart, which was the best performing property market for 2017-19. Many more properties sold in Melbourne or Sydney in one month than were purchased in a whole year in Hobart.

In my mind Hobart and most regional towns are too small and don't have enough depth to make them investment grade. Just watch property values boom when they become flavour of the month and then collapse as they fall out of favour. It doesn't take many misinformed investors to move small markets — in both directions.

Sales volumes and especially volumes by price group and product type (house, apartment, townhouse etc.) are key elements to understanding a housing market.

- *Vacancy rates* — Rental vacancy rates measure the proportion of properties available for rent at any given point in time, compared to the total number of rental properties. This gives an indication of the supply and demand ratio of rental accommodation in a suburb and the likelihood of achieving rental increases. There is an oversupply of rental properties once the local vacancy rate gets higher than 2% and rents tend to move upwards when the local vacancy rate falls below 2% (NOT the often quoted 3%).

- *Median rents and comparable rentals* — Median rents provide an indication of what's happening in a particular location, but won't tell you what rent a particular property will fetch. However, it's easy to find comparable asking rents on real estate portals like www.realestate.com.au, www.domain.com.au.

LEADING VERSUS LAGGING INDICATORS

The thing about all of these numbers and percentages is that we are looking at trailing or lagging indicators. Although we can gauge some idea of the current state of the market and possible future trends based on past insight, these statistics fall short of predictive value when compared with what I call leading market indicators, which are more likely to determine the future direction of our property markets.

I know it's often been suggested not to read the papers and not to watch the news because the media loves a sensational story and harps on the negative news and downplays the good news. I've come to recognise that much of what's in the media about the world economy and in fact our local property markets is wrong. I've learned that most forecasts are wrong. Something as complex as the nation's economy has all manner of variables at play, let alone when the vagaries of the whole world are also at work on it.

However, I do still follow a number of economic commentators whose opinions I respect to help me understand the health of the world's economy. Most of them have their commentaries published on my site www.PropertyUpdate.com.au I keep reading widely and use the perspective I've developed from years in the market to filter the information and also present this in my daily blog.

To help me in my background research I also keep track of the following:

1. Economic Indicators

The general state of the economy has an impact on the demand for housing.

A poorly-performing economy will affect the population's prosperity and spending power, including its ability to afford accommodation, buy houses or upgrade their homes.

On the other hand, during periods of economic growth people usually feel wealthy and comfortable buying new houses, upgrading or renovating their existing homes. Economic factors affecting the property cycle include GDP growth, consumer and business confidence, inflation, interest rates and unemployment rates.

2. GDP or Gross Domestic Product

This is the sum of the market value of all goods and services produced in our country and is a good indicator as to the overall health of the economy and our nation's prosperity.

By keeping an eye on forecast growth or contraction for GDP, you should have some insight into where our economy and real estate markets are heading several months in advance. Drilling down further to get estimates on economic growth at the state level, you'll begin to paint a picture of the market's future prospects in your specific region.

3. Employment Growth

A strong economy, employment growth and rising consumer sentiment underpin property prices.

Conversely, when you start to hear about employee redundancies, downsizing or companies moving out of an area, it's likely that bad news for the real estate market will soon follow.

The key when it comes to exploring employment and industry in an area is to look at the quality as well as the quantity. Locations that boast a diverse mix of business and industry will generally be more economically stable and better underpin their property markets.

Similarly, the creation of more professional, white collar employment opportunities in a region will attract a more affluent demographic to the area, who have the financial capacity to drive property prices higher.

4. Consumer confidence

This is also a powerful driver of our real estate markets. When things are going well economically and there is a general feeling of prosperity due to low unemployment and jobs growth, consumer sentiment levels climb.

Likewise, when we're experiencing uncertainty due to concerns about overseas economic problems, our country's financial instability or rising unemployment, our confidence is shaken and consumer sentiment declines.

5. Supply

Supply of property in a residential market means the total stock of dwellings, which exist in that market. The forecast for changes to the number of dwellings is the important factor. This involves quantifying the likely rate of completion of new dwellings, the number of demolitions of existing dwellings, allowing for second or holiday homes that are not primary residences and for any rental vacancy factor. The Housing Industry Association's (HIA) statistics, for example, give us these numbers.

6. Demand

Demand in a property market relates to the number of households that require a roof over their heads, and how that may change over time. Sounds simple, but in fact is quite complex. All of the following points contribute to that demand:

- Number of households
- The shrinking size of those households
- The explosion of single-person households
- High divorce rates
- The immigration cycle
- Interstate migration patterns
- Children living with parents longer than in the past, marrying later, having children later
- The birth rate
- Changes in employment locations and the effect of the information revolution.

All these come together to tell us the rate of new household formations for a given area, and, therefore, the number of dwellings that will be required to house that population.

The impact of household formations — We know that over the past couple of decades the average household has shrunk significantly. You could quite rightly conclude that, even if population did not increase, this change alone has been generating increased demand for housing.

Natural population increases — We also know the approximate rate of new household formation likely to occur from natural population increase. People form new households when they leave their parents' home and this, on average, occurs when the children are in their late teens or early twenties. This can be predicted by looking at the number of people who were born, say, 20 to 25 years ago.

Interstate migration — Interstate migration varies over time and has a lot to do with job opportunities. Remember a few years ago when the resources boom had people flocking to Queensland and Western Australia seeking improved lifestyle, jobs and housing near their employment.

Immigration — In the past, immigration was a political football, but now there is no doubt that the both sides of parliament will encourage more and more people to come to live in Australia, in part to replace the retiring Baby Boomers in our workforce. These people will need more dwellings and this will be one of the big drivers of our next property boom.

7. Building approvals and building activity

To see how the supply of property matches demand.

8. Finance preapprovals

This is an important *leading* indicator — people organise their finance a few months before they end up buying a property, so rising finance figures auger well for real estate.

9. Interest Rates

Which have a major effect on the affordability of property.

10. Inflation

The Reserve Bank likes to keep our annual inflation rate between 2% and 3%. A heated economy leads to inflation and encourages the RBA to increase interest rates thereby dampening demand for goods and services including property.

11. Investor activity

During boom times the effect of investors must be considered, as while normally they can account for around 30% of all property transactions, during property booms this percentage increases significantly.

THE SECRET TO FINDING AREAS THAT WILL OUTPERFORM

While finding an area that will return you solid long-term capital growth is a multi-layered approach, looking for suburbs experiencing strong income growth is the missing ingredient most investors haven't factored in.

Now this is a very different approach to most commentators who are looking for the next "hot spot" and tend to cite factors such as new infrastructure or population growth. But these don't necessarily translate to capital growth. In fact they rarely do!

As I've said, quite often the outer suburbs have plenty of new infrastructure and strong population growth, yet underperform with regard to capital growth.

On the other hand, there are plenty of examples of tightly held inner and middle ring suburbs with minimal new development and therefore minimal population growth, but where house prices are growing strongly due to strong competition for the limited supply of properties from affluent buyers.

The bottom line is that income growth is one of the key drivers of property price growth, because it reflects the ability to increasingly support and maintain house prices and serviceability of the associated mortgages.

So my research begins by looking for the localities that have experienced strong household income growth compared to surrounding regions and to the nation in general.

As I've explained earlier I look for suburbs that are gentrifying and therefore being valued differently by a new and more affluent market segment people such as empty-nesters, young professionals or the ubiquitous DINKs (double income, no kids.)

Where do I find this data? There is a long back series of census data available from the ABS that is also available from SQM Research www.sqmresearch.com.au and more recent updates can be sourced from the ATO.

I've already explained how the Census identified some suburbs where wages grew by double that average rate for the State, implying that some areas accrued a better capacity to take out a mortgage than others.

But, as they say in the commercials, there's more...

You then have to dig deeper and understand why wages were growing and whether this growth is sustainable.

Clearly it didn't last in the mining towns, but wages growth is more likely to continue in the inner and middle ring more established capital city suburbs where many of the residents earn their income in our growing service industries and have multiple streams of income such as wages, property investments and shares.

This is in contrast to many blue collar suburbs where wages growth struggles to keep up with the CPI and where residents are more insecure about their jobs and sensitive interest rate fluctuations.

SOME OF THE BEST SOURCES FOR PROPERTY DATA INCLUDE

Corelogic: www.corelogic.com.au

Rather than reporting median prices, Corelogic reports a hedonic house price index, using a statistical technique known as "regression analysis" to assess the resale value of dwellings using each property's unique individual attributes (e.g. location, land size, number of beds/baths, etc).

SQM Research: www.sqmesearch.com.au

You can get a bundle of free statistical data at this website and good commentary from head economist Louis Christopher. SQM reports Vendor's Asking Prices that measures seller sentiment rather than median prices. You can also use this website to investigate your chosen suburb and drill down to identify vacancy rates, how many properties are for sale, demographics plus a lot more.

On the house: www.OnTheHouse.com.au

A property portal that gives estimates of home values (and this is as inaccurate as all the other free online reports) but offers detailed property data and prices achieved for comparable sold properties.

.id The Population Experts: www.id.com.au

Has a wealth of demographic data by suburb, including a lot of the latest Census data demystified.

McCrindle: www.mccrindle.com.au

Demographer Mark McCrindle has some insightful infographics.

Microburbs: www.microburbs.com.au

Offers free reports including neighbourhood demographics, commute times, schools, crime rates, income levels and much more.

The Australian Bureau of Statistics: www.abs.gov.au

Here you'll find a wealth of statistical data and plenty of graphs and numbers to download.

The Reserve Bank: www.rba.gov.au

Each month the RBA puts out a Chart Pack full of useful graphs and statistics. The problem that many investors will have is interpreting all of this information, so the best resource I know for getting a variety of experts' opinions is:

Michael Yardney's Property Update: www.PropertyUpdate.com.au

Here you can subscribe to my daily blog or weekly newsletter and get opinions and commentary from experts you can trust. Of course I'm biased, but you must really subscribe to this free resource. And while you're at it why not subscribe to my podcast – The Michael Yardney Podcast – on your favourite podcast app.

As you can see there is a mind-boggling amount of data available so it's important not to place too much emphasis on any one measure at the expense of others. And given that property is a long-term investment, don't be overly influenced by shorter-term trends, or a determination to uncover the next "hot-spot", because if you find one you may just get your fingers burned as so many others have when a short-term hot spot reverts to an underperforming also-ran suburb.

SUMMARY

OK, now we've covered a lot of ground that will help you to focus your energy and research, and to choose wisely when it comes to where, when and what you might look to invest in.

In the next chapter we'll look at some of the due diligence you'll need to do once you've found a property.

PROPERTY DUE DILIGENCE

Once you've found a property you're considering buying it's important to you take a businesslike approach and invest the money required for legal advice on the contract, organising a building and pest inspection and, if you're buying an apartment, a strata report.

Now, don't expect a perfect scorecard. Almost every property will have a few issues and this isn't necessarily a reason to walk away. As long as you're aware of any defects and can afford to fix them, it's really not a big deal. You can also use them as a bargaining chip to lower the price.

SOME OF THE THINGS I CHECK ARE:

- *The contract of sale* — ask the agent for a copy and email it straight to your solicitor. Attempting to decipher a property contract without specialist knowledge will make your head spin. Instead get expert advice. Don't be surprised if they ask you to confirm that the boundaries and dimensions of the property are as represented on the tile that forms part of the contract.

- *Building and pest inspections* — This is designed to pick up everything that is "wrong" with the property. On paper, defects can look scarier than they actually are, so meet the inspector onsite to discuss any necessary repairs. Even if a property is new it is still worth doing a building inspection to pick up any shoddy workmanship, inappropriate materials or work done without council approval.

- *Strata report* — If you're looking at buying an apartment, check the body corporate records or get your solicitor to do it for you. In some states, the body corporate is called the owners' corporation. Either way, the building's strata management company will have these records. Check for adequacy of book-keeping; the amount of money in the sinking and administration funds; the historical frequency of special levies; the by-laws; any restrictions on usage of common property; any disputes between residents, any upcoming extra ordinary expenses and any history of structural defects and repairs.

- *What's it worth?* This is toughest question of all, but I've already discussed how I do this.

FINANCIAL DUE DILIGENCE

Yes, even more number crunching. Things to consider are:

- *Does the property suit your budget?* How much deposit is required? What are the additional purchasing costs (usually a minimum of an additional 5% on top of the purchase price), and does your loan cover these? Always allow a contingency as somehow or other, little costs always creep up, things like minor repairs or longer initial vacancy periods.

- *Can you cover the cash flow?* What rent can you expect (don't just believe the selling agent — check it out yourself) and what are your outgoings? Allow for managing agent's commission, insurance, body corporate fees, rates and taxes. Don't be surprised if this eats up around 20% of your annual rent and ensure you can cover the interest shortfall with your personal income cash flow surplus or by having a financial buffer in place.

Even though you are going to have your team around you, as the CEO of your property investment business, it's your responsibility to undertake, or oversee the due diligence process.

Think about it... you would never want your pilot to skip some of the boxes on his checklist, as it would represent too much of a risk. You should take your property investing just as seriously.

SUMMARY

Now that you understand a little about the preliminary homework you'll need to do, in the next section we are going to take the next step and go to market. You will learn some vital strategies for negotiating, dealing with agents, handling auctions and managing your emotions through the roller-coaster that is buying an investment property.

PART IV

AGENTS, ADVICE, AUCTIONS AND NEGOTIATIONS

WHAT WE HAVE TO LEARN TO DO, WE LEARN BY DOING.
— *ARISTOTLE*

TAMING THE TIGER
(DEALING WITH REAL ESTATE AGENTS)

Surveys rating the status and trustworthiness of various professions have never been kind to real estate agents. Now, just for the record many of my team at **Metropole Property Strategists** are estate agents and I have many friends and very good professional colleagues in real estate that I absolutely trust. (OK I'll admit it – I'm also a licensed estate agent but I don't work as an estate agent.)

However, the general perception of agents doesn't surprise me one bit. It is no coincidence that one of the reasons I've been able to establish good relationships with many agents is that I've taken the time to learn their business and I know the tricks of the trade.

Without wanting to beat up on their already battered reputations, it would be foolhardy to walk in to an estate agency without knowledge of the market or of the selling techniques agents use to ply their trade, and to then trust them to "help" you buy a property.

If you want to tame a tiger you need to learn the rules of the jungle and if you want to tap into the wonderful network of knowledge that real estate agents can provide, you need to learn how to establish a relationship of mutual respect with agents.

DON'T UNDER-ESTIMATE THE POWER OF A REAL ESTATE AGENT

INSIDER TIP

Never take for granted the influence an agent estate has in a real estate transaction. In many cases the estate agent will be the most powerful person in the transaction and can make or break a deal.

In reality, the agent is the only person that deals with both the buyer and seller when negotiating to purchase a property so never underestimate their power in the negotiation process.

But there's more to it than most buyers realise...

To get the most leverage, it is important to deal with the "listing agent" of the particular property. This is the agent who signed up the seller on behalf of the estate agency. They really have the best relationship with, and hopefully the trust of, the seller.

I like to deal with the listing agent because I understand the office politics that goes on inside many real estate agencies. Usually the listing agent is the only person who can deal with the vendor, which means that if another agent in the company signs up a potential purchaser they must present the contract to the listing agent who will then present it to the seller.

While in theory this sounds fine, the problem is that in many estate agencies the listing agent won't instantly present your offer to the vendor. They will often announce to all the other agents that an offer has been signed up and these agents have a number of hours, sometimes even overnight, to come up with their own clients' best offer and then all offers will be presented at the same time to the vendor.

While it may not be "ethical", I have known the listing agent to use information in offers and go to one of his potential purchasers and say, "There has been an offer on this property for $600,000 and if you can better it I think I can convince the vendor into selling it to you".

Why would they do this? Now you may say because they're getting their client the best possible price. A cynic might say it's because if their purchaser comes up with the best offer, they would then get the full commission for the sale, rather than sharing it with the agent who signed up the first offer.

The lesson from this is always try and deal with the listing agent's whose name will usually be listed with the property in the Internet ad or on the For Sale board.

ARE YOU QUALIFIED?

You must remember that real estate agents are sales professionals and one commodity they have that's in short supply is not properties, but time. Agents have only eight or nine hours in the day, and they want to get the best return on their time.

They regularly meet a lot of "tyre kickers" who spend their weekends looking at real estate. These "wanna be" home buyers and investors often don't have the knowledge, money or the courage to go ahead and actually buy anything.

You can imagine how real estate agents feel about these "buyers" — the ones who waste their time, love to spend weekends pottering around the property market looking at lots and lots of properties, dreaming about the things they could and should do, but who never make serious offers and do not have the courage to finalise a purchase.

One of the first things estate agents will do when you approach them is to size you up to "qualify" you — to see how genuine you are. They've been taught how to qualify buyers without the buyers even realising they're being qualified. They just do it in their mind by asking themselves, "Is this really a genuine buyer?"

Now, from your own perspective, this is an important process because it allows agents to find out your exact needs and to help you to buy the right property. And, to be fair to them, it allows agents to make quick decisions about whether or not they're going to be wasting their time with you when they could be using it more efficiently by seeing people who are ready and willing to purchase.

So they may ask you questions such as:

- How much deposit have you got?
- How much are you able to borrow?
- What sort of property do you want to buy?
- If you find the right property, are you in a position to purchase today?

The last thing an agent wants to do is spend the whole weekend showing you around properties only to find on Sunday afternoon that you can't commit to anything "just yet" because you're still waiting for your great aunt's inheritance to come in and she's still alive and well, and holidaying in Bali!

If agents don't think you are a likely purchaser, you will find that they'll have very few properties on their books to offer you.

On the other hand, if they think you are genuine, you will be on top of their list to ring because they would much rather make a quick sale than have to hawk each property around to lots of want-to-be buyers.

After many years in business, this is the situation that we are in at Metropole. We regularly get the first call from agents because they know the types of properties we are looking for on behalf of our clients and they realise that if they have a property that meets our criteria, our clients are in the position to make quick, calculated buying decisions.

HOW DO YOU CONVINCE AN AGENT YOU ARE GENUINE?

Well first of all, let's look at what you shouldn't do.

INSIDER TIP

Don't go into their office and say, "I'm looking for a bargain". That's a big mistake!

The minute an estate agent hears that you want a bargain they will size you up and think this person isn't going to be an easy sale. Keep in mind that most estate agents don't want to be known for selling bargains — it doesn't do their reputation with sellers, who pay their commissions, any good. And if they did have a bargain on their books, they'd be unlikely to offer it to someone who just walked in off the street.

But this doesn't mean what you won't be able to find a good buy. What it does mean is that if you are going to form a relationship with an agent they have to know you are serious because they get hundreds of potential buyers approaching them every month.

So what do you say to the agent?

Be specific. Say something like, "I am looking for a well-priced investment property in the suburbs of Elwood, St Kilda or Elsternwick. I am prepared to spend between $650,000 and $700,000 and I want a property that has good growth potential and will be popular with tenants". This gives the agent the impression that you know what you want, are a serious buyer and you can make a sensible decision.

Make clear which requirements you will not change and which you are happy to be flexible about.

Let them know that you're serious and planning to invest for the long term, but also that you have realistic expectations.

Too often agents meet people who proudly proclaim, "Well, I'm going to buy five properties from you before Christmas". The estate agents can see past that and can tell by the words you use, and the suggestions you make, whether you're realistic or not.

After decades in the business I can genuinely say to agents that the Metropole Group is going to buy up to 50 properties each month because we are buying them on behalf of clients in three major capital cities. But there are really very few people in this position.

Furthermore, don't try impressing agents about all the properties you own and the things you're going to do. In general, people who have made it don't need to impress by going on and on about their successes.

While you don't need to turn up in a suit and tie don't go in your moccasins either, because unfortunately we all tend to assess people on first impressions and if you turn up looking like you can't afford to buy a property, it will be hard to convince the agent differently. Take your presentation seriously and dress in smart casual but there's no need to go over the top.

MEETING AND GREETING

Often when agents first meet you and are considering your buying potential, they may try to come across as your latest bosom buddy and best friend.

They often do this to break down the barriers and to create a more open and honest dialogue. Then they will start asking you qualifying questions, and beware — anything you say could be taken down and held against you later!

The first things they'll want to know will be your price range. Then they may ask you to give them an idea of your likes and dislikes with regards to property, but what they're really doing is trawling for an emotional chink in your armour, which could be used against you later down the track.

I'm not suggesting you should stonewall and refuse to explain what you're looking for — if you don't tell them honestly what you want, how can they help you find the right property? However,

I do suggest that you try to be aware of their tactics and the hooks they might try to snare you with later. So I give them clear parameters explaining the type of property I am looking for but I won't be telling them more than they need to know.

HOW TO GET ESTATE AGENTS TO SHOW YOU THE BEST PROPERTIES

Don't just ring estate agents — meet them in the flesh. If you want to build the type of relationship that gets the agent to think of you when he lists a good property, he has to get to see you and know a little about you. Then get to know as many agents in your investment comfort zone as you can.

Once you've introduced yourself to some agents and figured out how to present yourself in a way that will get you respect, the next question is: "How can you get shown the best properties first?"

The key to being shown the right properties is to network and to develop good working relationships with the right local estate agents. Ultimately, they will call the people they think of first and who they know are serious buyers, so it's worth spending some time on developing these relationships.

The fact that agents are business people who need to earn commissions can sometimes work in your favour. Remember that agents are often in competition against others within their own company, so if they come across someone who could potentially buy a property straight away, (earning them a commission) they will want to call that person first before other agents get a chance to sell the property.

Think of it from the agent's point of view — when they receive a new listing that's well priced they probably say to themselves, "Wow, this property's a bargain, it'll be easy to sell and snapped up quickly — I've got to show it to some genuine buyers before any of my colleagues do!"

What does an agent do first in this situation?

1. Calls his best prospect.

2. Then calls his second-best prospect as well.

3. Then calls his third best prospect just in case.

By the time he gets to his fourth best prospect, the property has probably found a buyer, so you need to be at, or very near, the top of that list.

HOW TO GET TO THE TOP OF THE AGENT'S LIST

While the estate agent works for the seller, they only get paid if they do a deal. So if you get them on your side, it can get you to the front of the queue when viewing properties. But if you are in their bad books, you can fail to get a deal.

So...

1. Don't waste their time

A lot of people mess agents around. Show them you're not a time waster.

Obviously you should have strict criteria that you can measure the property against and a process for checking the investment potential of the property. If you're offered a property that you wouldn't consider buying, then thank the agent for calling, remind him or her of the type of property you're looking for, but don't waste time viewing their dud. This way you've not only saved your time, but also their time and they'll appreciate this.

2. Give specific feedback

After each viewing tell the agent what you did and did not like about the property. This will allow the agent to build up a better picture of what it is you're looking for.

3. Be in a position to make unconditional offers

In other words, do your homework in advance by getting to know your investment comfort zone and make sure your finance is pre-approved.

4. Keep the agent updated

After inspecting the property tell the agent if you're interest or not and what your next steps will be. It's likely you'll need time to consider the deal or you may need to organise a building and pest inspection or get your solicitor to check the contract. So tell the agent what you intend to do and be specific about when they can expect to hear from you.

5. Make offers unconditional

When you're ready to present an offer, make it in writing and if possible unconditional or at least with as few conditions as possible and attach a cheque for $5,000 or $10,000 as part of the deposit to it. This will have a much higher chance of being accepted by the vendor.

Another way to get offered the best properties by selling agents is by having a professional buyer's agent working on your side to level the playing field. Let's look at this a little more closely...

CONSIDER USING A BUYER'S AGENT

While the hunt and chase of finding investments and negotiating with agents can be exciting and it would be nice to have all the skills to choose the right investment property, sometimes it's worth considering engaging the services of a good property buyer's agent to do the research and all the wheeling and dealing on your behalf. They buy and sell property and negotiate prices all the time – it's their job, whereas you've probably only done it once or twice in your lifetime.

Clearly I'm biased as I head Metropole Property Strategists, Australia's premier buyer's agency – www.metropole.com.au, but I've seen the great results our team has achieved for both beginning and experienced investors.

I've found too many investors pay a learning fee to the market when they procrastinate and miss out on good deals or when they buy the wrong property, or overpay, or don't have the right conditions in the contract. This can be very expensive. In fact I've heard this learning called a "Stupid Tax".

In my mind it's better to get the insurance of a professional buyer's agent on your side of the deal – it usually costs much less than that Stupid Tax.

Trouble is, not all buyer's agents are the same, so I'll explained what to look for in a buyer's agent in the next chapter.

HOW AN AGENT CLOSES THE SALE

Professional estate agents have had good sales training and they generally don't need to use the unpleasant high-pressure tactics that were around years ago. Nevertheless, they still know and use a collection of clever little tricks to help hook buyers emotionally and close sales.

The best estate agents are good "readers" of people and will know when a prospective purchaser becomes emotionally attached to a property. They'll often repeat positive statements that a prospective buyer has made to help anchor those thoughts in the buyer's mind.

For example, during an inspection a buyer might comment that, "The block looks a good size" and this could be recycled and repeated by the agent later with statements such as, "There's a lot of potential with a block this size, you could do anything with it later on couldn't you?"

As the agent is really only repeating an observation already volunteered by the purchaser, such statements are bound to be agreed with, which will only help to reinforce the intelligence and sincerity of the agent and the buyer's positive feelings about the property.

It is also considered useful to make the prospective purchaser keep saying "Yes" in relation to the property. So you'll find that agents using this technique will rarely make any closed statements but always ask simple questions.

This can effectively mean that every simple positive statement made by the prospect is reinforced twice. The agent recycles it and concludes with an "isn't it?" or "won't it?" inviting the prospect to reaffirm their own original remark.

You might even mistake this for casual flattery or confirmation of your own astute perception in real estate matters — don't be fooled!

TRIAL CLOSES

Eventually, like any good salesperson, the agent cautiously circle for the kill, trying to get you to agree to make an offer to purchase the property. Let's look at a couple of ways this can happen.

THE REVERSE SELL

A prospective buyer may ask, "Would the vendor accept an offer of $600,000?" Such a question may be meaningless to an untrained agent who may respond, "They probably won't", but for a professional sales person the response is, "If I can convince the owner to accept $600,000, will you buy it?"

If the prospect's answer is positive, the negotiation process has commenced. If it's negative then the agent will try to find the price at which you would buy, and effectively negotiations have begun.

Similarly, an investor might wonder "Do you think the vendor would have a problem with a 90-day settlement?" and the agent pounces with "If I can convince the vendor to take a 90-day settlement, would you buy it?"

In this technique, any question the prospect might ask can usually be recycled to put pressure back on them to buy if the answer is yes.

THE EGO-INFLATOR

This works particularly well with novice investors who have read a few books or been to a few seminars and think they know all about real estate. What the agents do is play on the prospect's ego by posing a question, which, if not answered positively, will reflect badly on the investor. For example:

"Well mate, obviously this is an outstanding buy at this price and, as I'm sure I don't need to explain to someone like you, this will be snapped up quickly by the first astute investor who sees it and is in a position to buy."

THE MINOR DECISION

Agents will rarely start by asking a prospective purchaser anything as blunt as "Well, are you ready to sign over $600,000 for this property?" Rather, they'll ask prospects to make a few minor decisions that start to lead down the path to a major result. For example:

"Will the contract be in your name only or yours and your wife's?"

"Will this sale be subject to finance or a straight-out unconditional sale?"

"Will a 30-day settlement be OK or would you prefer I try for 60 days?"

When a prospective buyer answers "Yes" to any one of these questions, it confirms to both themselves and the agent they are seriously considering proceeding with the transaction.

THE CAUTIONARY TALE

Some agents have a library of cautionary tales to suit every circumstance, but all have a common thread.

The story will go something along the lines of similar properties have made other people successful and wealthy and the prospect will join their ranks if he or she buys the property, but any hesitation will mean missing out and leading a lifetime of regret.

Something along the lines of, "Well, you know, five years ago I showed a similar property to a mate of mine and he organised a building inspection and found a few minor problems. In the end he didn't go ahead with the purchase but do you know what, this property was going to sell for five years ago? $400,000 and now it's $600,000. Imagine if he'd only spent those couple of thousand dollars doing the repairs. You know, I don't think he ever ended up buying an investment and look at the capital growth he's missed out on. It's just a shame."

THE INDUCEMENT

If an extra push is necessary, an agent will often point out some kind of a substantial benefit or saving that could be made from an immediate decision. This usually involves talk of some extraordinary circumstance that will never occur again, and can be taken advantage of right now. For example:

"The developer just needs to sell one more unit before he can commence the next project", or

"The vendor needs to sell by Wednesday so he can fund the purchase of an auction next Saturday."

SCARCITY FACTOR OR THE TIP-OFF

Agents know people desperately want things that are in short supply, so sometimes an agent will ring and speak in hushed tones, explaining that the whisper is so that others in his own office don't overhear the bargain he's about to discuss. Then he discloses that there's a chance that a contract on a property you were looking at won't go ahead and that they're looking for another buyer. Naturally this has to happen urgently before other prospects are alerted.

THE POSITIVE ASSUMPTION

If you answer all the agent's questions positively, he or she will start to use language and behave as though it's assumed you're going to go ahead and purchase the property. As though this agreement was cemented when you nodded that the property was the sort of investment you were looking for. Before long, after a few more agreements and positive statements, you may find the agent has positioned you a lot further down the purchasing path than you intended to wander.

This closing technique is often combined with the agent pulling out his contract book and asking simple questions that assume the sale is going to go ahead. Things like: "What's your full name? Who's your solicitor? Is a 10% deposit OK?"

THE "SOMEONE ELSE IS ABOUT TO BUY IT" APPROACH

What agents will often say is that another purchaser is interested or they "don't have another purchaser yet, but at the sales meeting this morning there were eight other agents in the office and they all agreed that this would be the next property to sell". The key to combating these tricks is to stick to your criteria and remember that there's always another property just around the corner!

SUMMARY

The selling agent is a pivotal person in property transaction but, of course, agents don't always have your best interest at heart. Their job is to negotiate the best price for their client – the vendor. They're professionals who've been trained in the art of negotiation and will use a variety of tricks and techniques to achieve their goals.

Be careful and be firm but don't be afraid. If you can prove you are not just another "tyre kicker" you'll soon find agents can be genuinely helpful.

One way to level the playing field is to have a property strategist and buyer's agent represent you. Let's look at how this could work in the next chapter.

WHO SHOULD YOU ASK FOR PROPERTY INVESTMENT ADVICE?

With so many mixed messages and vested interests, who do you ask for property advice and who can you really trust?

While I'm trying to teach you how to grow a substantial property portfolio (in your spare time), I'm not suggesting you do it alone. Acquiring sufficient knowledge and perspective in one particular location takes many years of experience, so make your investing a team sport and get the right people on your team.

The problem is there are many and varied sources that property investors can consult for advice. But since most property investors fail to achieve the financial freedom they deserve, and with less than 8% ever owning more than two properties, a better question to ask would be... who should you be asking for advice?

This chapter is designed to help you cut through the clutter.

Here are the people you could turn to:

1. **No One** – many beginning investors think they understand real estate because they've lived in or rented a home or an apartment.

That's a big mistake and one of the reasons around 50% of first-time investors sell up within five years. While they may know their local neighbourhood, that's very different to understanding the property market.

2. **Friends or family** – I understand why people may do this, but the question to ask is: are they financial experts? How many millionaires do you have in your family? If not, don't ask them because often their advice will be to avoid property investment because of the "risk".

3. **A real estate agent** – remember agents work for the vendor to help them achieve the best price, and they're unlikely to tell you about the other great properties for sale in the area by other agents.

4. **A mortgage broker** – while it's important to have an investment savvy mortgage broker on your side helping you through the finance maze, most don't understand the property market well enough to advise on what is an "investment grade" property.

5. **Your accountant** – they should advise you on tax matters and structuring, but most don't have the intimate knowledge of the property market required to give investment advice.

6. **Financial planners** – while financial planners are licensed to sell financial products, most are not able to advise on real estate. Not only because they lack a sound understanding of property, but the company they work for doesn't allow them to. Those who do recommend property usually have a biased view as they make commissions based on the investments they sell from their "stock list".

7. **A property marketer** – while these salespeople may seem to be on your side, they're really selling "product" for a property developer who is most likely going to make the biggest profit out of the deal.

8. **Investment seminars and workshops** – ask yourself: Is the person conducting the event an investment expert in their field? How long have they been financially secure, or do they make their money teaching others?

9. **A property mentor** – there seems to be an abundance of property mentors around, some who give great guidance, while others are really property sellers or marketers in disguise.

Let's make it clear: It's important to have mentors. They see your blind spots, give you guidance and support and expand the way you think. Just be careful who you choose and ensure they have achieved the results you want to achieve.

1. **A buyer's agent** – these can be a great help in selecting the right property, but most are just "order takers", they don't devise a plan that considers your family's future needs and your risk profile.

2. **A property strategist** – I believe Metropole Property Strategists was the first company in Australia to set themselves up as "property strategists". Today, many people (rightly or wrongly) call themselves property strategists.

When you look at this list you can now see why you need... an independent, unbiased property adviser or strategist. You need the help of someone with a holistic approach when making property investment decisions. It's just too hard to do it on your own or by trial and error, especially when starting out. There's a huge learning fee involved – of time, money, effort and heartache.

I find it interesting that while most wealthy people have, and are prepared to pay for, trusted advisors in many areas of their lives, the average person has no advisers, or they get their advice from salespeople who they perceive as advisers but are far from independent.

On the other hand, following the teachings and proven systems of those who've already achieved what you want to achieve and who've retained their wealth through a number of property cycles, while not guaranteeing your success, makes it much, much more likely.

WHAT DO PROPERTY STRATEGISTS ACTUALLY DO?

When people ask me what does a property strategist do to add value to their clients I say I've been in this game for 50 years and I'm still learning new things every day — successful property investment isn't easy. I see my role as a property advisor as helping our clients grow, protect and pass on their wealth using property as a vehicle.

While clients come to the team at Metropole for property advice, in fact they're really coming for something else. Some are looking for financial freedom; others for more choices in life like working because they want to, not because they have to; and yet others want to leave a legacy for their family or the community.

So, property is really just the vehicle they're keen on using to achieving their end goals.

While most property advisors come from a real estate background, the property strategists at Metropole come from a wealth, financial planning or banking background, but have a good understanding of property and are successful investors themselves.

You see... our property strategists' job is not to sell clients properties, but to help them safely increase their wealth over the long term.

Many years ago, when I first saw a gap in the market for sound strategic advice, I set about providing my services as a property strategist. I was the first one I knew of — today many people call themselves property "advisors" or "strategists", yet quite a few are thinly disguised salespeople, or are not really qualified to give in depth advice.

So, let's look at what a good strategist can and can't do...

Here's a list of some of the things a good property advisor can (should) do:

1. A good advisor will first start by getting to know their clients' hopes and fears and then be future-focused to help them achieve their long-term financial goals.

2. With so many mixed messages about property investing out there (many coming from parties with vested interests), a good property advisor will help remove his client's anxiety by simplifying the complex. They will provide clarity around the complicated world of wealth creation which involves much more than just property — but includes finance, tax, economics and the law. They will advise their clients about the risks as well as the rewards of property investment.

3. While most buyers' agents or property sales people are transactional and think of the current "sale" or purchase, a professional property advisor will aim to develop a long-term relationship and help their clients understand the next two or three steps even before taking the first step.

4. Many clients come to a real estate advisor looking for the next big thing — some are looking for a shortcut, or the next hotspot, or a way to get rich quickly. Instead, a property

strategist will stop their clients speculating by recommending proven strategies that have always worked.

5. An independent advisor will not have any properties for sale but will have a list of potential options and refer their clients to a buyer's agent who is part of their team to find the best opportunity in the market to suit their client's budget, plans and risk profile.

6. A strategic advisor will never put any pressure on their client to make an investment decision, but their knowledge, research and experience will help their clients select an investment property that is the highest and best use of their funds, and one that will work hard for them over the long term.

7. A strategist will help their clients avoid the big mistakes made by the average investor and will earn their fees simply by helping their clients avoid the devastating errors made by many investors such as those who lost significant amounts of money by investing in mining towns, regional locations, house and land packages or off-the-plan properties. Of course, a great advisor will do a lot more than that for their fee.

8. By being a student of history, a good strategist will be able to provide perspective, insights and often optimism at a time when the media is being pessimistic, and vice versa. They'll try and prevent you from being a pessimist in a world where pessimists almost always lose.

9. They will also advise their clients to invest their money the way they do themselves — they must be experienced investors — not enthusiastic amateurs.

10. A strategist will regularly meet with their clients to objectively assess the performance of their property portfolio and ensure they are heading in the right financial direction.

As you can see — it takes years of learning, experience and the perspective that only comes from investing through a number of property cycles to become a great property strategist.

Here are some things a property advisor can't do:

As you read on you'll find that some property "advisors" will claim to be able to do some of the things on the following list — things they really can't do. I guess they tend to do this because they're not able to deliver on many aspects on the list above — the things skilled, professional advisers can deliver.

1. Even a good advisor can't predict the future. They won't be able to tell you how the market will perform, what will happen to interest rates or what capital growth rate a particular property will achieve.

2. They won't be able to find the next hot spot for you, yet many so-called advisors suggest they can. In essence they give their clients what they are requesting, rather than what they need — sound, solid advice.

3. Even the most qualified advisor won't be able to pick the best time to purchase an investment property other than to remind you that the best time to invest was 20 years ago, and the second-best time is today.

4. A good advisor won't be able to help you get rich quickly or achieve extraordinarily high returns without taking on extra risks.

WHAT IS THE DIFFERENCE BETWEEN A PROPERTY STRATEGIST AND A BUYER'S AGENT?

There is a big difference, even though many buyer's agents will play this down, suggesting they are the right person to help investors. In my mind, it's important to have both as part of your wealth creation team.

Your property strategist will look at the big picture and formulate a strategy, a plan that makes sense to you after considering your current position, your aspirations, your time frames, your budget and your risk profile.

Buyers agents are order takers. They will fill an order given to them to find you a property and will be biased towards the areas they have expertise in, but this may not be in your best interests.

On the other hand, only a property strategist has the expertise to design that "order" to suit your specific needs.

They will be your long-term wealth creation partner, annually reviewing the performance of your property portfolio, and will provide recommendations on any opportunities as well as when it's best for you to do nothing.

A good property strategist is with you for "life" — your buyer's agent shouldn't be!

HOW DO I KNOW IF I'M GETTING RIPPED OFF?

That's a good question as you need to find someone who'll give you unbiased advice which is independent of any particular location or property.

Most so called "advisors" will only tell you about properties on their stock list or that their buyer's agents can source in a particular state.

On the other hand, a trusted advisor tailors their recommendations to your personal circumstances and warn you of the risks as well as the rewards.

Their advice is not biased by any property, products or services to be sold, so they will have their own team of on-the-ground buyer's agents in a number of states. Not ones that fly in and out and think they've nabbed a bargain, while in reality the locals know they haven't.

So one of the first questions I'd ask a potential advisor is "How are you getting paid?" This will reveal a lot.

If they are offering free advice, or they are being paid by a third party (such as a developer or property vendor) then the advice cannot be independent.

Put simply, if the advice is free then you are the product!

Your adviser should be qualified and a member of a recognised organisation such as the Property Investment Professionals of Australia and be an investor themselves.

They should have a thorough understanding of not only property, but also finance, economics and the taxation system as far as it relates to real estate investment. Similarly, your advisor should have no properties for sale, should have a number of investment options available for you depending upon your circumstances, should not make any recommendations at the first meeting and should not create a "sense of urgency".

Of course, at face value professional advice can appear to be expensive, given that there is so much free advice available.

You know... free advice from the real estate agent – but they're getting paid by the seller, or from the property marketer selling off-the-plan apartments or house and land package but they're getting paid by the developer (and often quite handsomely).

That's why in my view, you should only be taking advice from someone who doesn't have a vested interest in the outcome and therefore is working in your best interests.

WHAT IF I ALREADY HAVE A FINANCIAL PLANNER, DO I STILL NEED A PROPERTY ADVISOR?

The simple answer is almost certainly yes. You do need to speak with a property strategist, because most financial planners are unable to advise on residential real estate as an investment class.

This is a real shame as many Australians go to a financial planner seeking advice on the best investment options for their financial future, yet their planner is not going to point them towards property because their license does allow them to.

And many of those who do, tend to make significant commissions by advising their clients to buy poor performing "off the plan" properties from project marketers who provide financial incentives for the financial planner to do so.

HOW TO CHOOSE A GREAT BUYER'S AGENT

A clearly emerging trend over the last two decades is that more and more property investors are user's buyer's agents to help them secure their properties, and in my mind, this is even more important now during this slowdown phase of the property cycle when the market won't cover up buying mistakes.

That said, in an industry where every Tom, Dick and Harry knows a buyer's agent or thinks they can pick the market, how can you select the right buyer's agent for you — someone who can help you move your property goals forward?

At its very basic definition, a buyer's agent is a real estate professional that is hired by potential home buyers or investors to conduct research of potential properties, evaluate each property and, once one is chosen, handle all the subsequent negotiations during the transaction.

A buyer's agent will also bid for the buyer if the property is to be sold at auction, which is hugely beneficial for the novice, as auctions are notoriously tricky for those who aren't used to them.

Having a buyer's agent on your side will allow you to see some properties that might not be advertised on the market yet — those "off market" properties buyers love to get their hands on. This is a great way to get in before other prospective buyers, and it's something that usually can't be done without the help of a buyer's agent.

Hiring a buyer's agent will also save you time, given that you won't be doing the actual searching yourself, but simply reviewing the shortlist given to you by your agent. This is a great way to focus on the end result and minimise your efforts and stress.

At Metropole, our service is unique because when investors consult with us, they'll first see a property strategist who will help formulate their own individual Strategic Property Plan. This is how we go the extra mile to ensure that the property you buy not only suits you now, but that it will be part of your "bigger picture" plan to build wealth for the long-term.

Then you'll need a buyer's agent whose service will cover things like:

- Searching for suitable property within your desired locations, which suit your needs.
- Communicating and meeting with selling agents in these markets.
- Leveraging their research databases, network and expertise to access "off market" deals.
- Referrals to other professionals who can assist you, such as financial, accounting and legal services.
- Arranging and recommending necessary due diligence — such as strata checks, and building and/or pest inspections.
- Organisation and preparation of necessary property reports that will help you evaluate the properties.
- Importantly, negotiating over the price and conditions of your offer.
- Checking final contracts and pre-settlement inspections.

Another big benefit of engaging a buyer's agent, is the ability to make use of their industry insight and objectivity. They level the playing field (the vendor has an agent working for them) and bring a level of perspective that money can't buy.

A buyer's agent is an impartial third party, meaning they aren't going to allow their emotions — such as excitement and nervousness, the usual feelings that crop up during the property buying process — get in the way of making a clear, sensible decision.

A buyer's agent will also assist in negotiating with the seller if you do the property searching and find your desired property. This is something that is likely to make the novice and even expert buyer a bit nervous, so having it taken care of by someone who knows the industry can be a huge weight off your shoulders.

HERE ARE SOME QUESTIONS YOU SHOULD ASK ANY BUYER'S AGENT YOU'RE CONSIDERING WORKING WITH

1. What are your qualifications?

Don't be afraid to ask their credentials upfront. You can start but asking whether they are fully licensed with the relevant real estate institutes and peak industry bodies, such as Real Estate Buyers Agents Association of Australia (REBAA) and PIPA (Property Investment Professionals of Australia).

2. How experienced are you at buying within the location/s we're looking at?

By the time you're selecting a buyer's agent, you're likely to be pretty set on the locations you're wanting to purchase in. If it's your own home, you'll have a good idea where you want to live. If you're an investor, you'll have narrowed your search to a number of investment grade locations with your property strategist.

So this is a very important question to ask a potential buyer's agent right off the bat, because if they have little experience purchasing property in your desired location, they won't be able to leverage their insider knowledge and expertise for your benefit.

Local, specialised buyer's agents will know aspects neighbourhood culture, the quality of the local schools, where the most desirable lifestyle amenities are, and which strips or streets are better/worse than others. Don't engage someone who flys in and out to another State and suggests they can add value — employ a local.

3. How many years have you been in business as a buyer's agent/real estate professional?

There are many enthusiastic amateurs who've turned their hand to buying property. A buyer's agent with more years of experience is likely to have deeper market knowledge when it comes to value and performance. Their years of finely-honed negotiation expertise will also fall in your favour.

4. What sort of properties do you specialise in?

You ideally want to work with someone who specialises in the exact property type you want.

5. What resources do you have?

I wouldn't be working with a one-man-band — I'd look for someone who's part of a professional team. They should have access to a research department and other team members to leverage off their network of contacts.

6. Who has trained them?

Have they been properly mentored by an experienced industry professional or not?

7. How do you get paid?

Remember your buyer's agent should be working exclusively for you, not be selling properties part time and never take vendor or developer kickbacks.

THE BOTTOM LINE...

The cost of making a mistake — selecting an underperforming property — is significant. You can lose money, time and opportunity cost.

Think about it... there is only so much you can learn from the financial media, books and seminars. While you can gain knowledge from the Internet, you can't gain experience or perspective. That takes years to acquire and comes at a cost. It's just too difficult for beginners and even for more experienced investors to gain perspective into what's happening in today's fast-moving markets.

That's why it is suggested you leverage off the experience of a professional property adviser — a property strategist — one who is independent and unbiased.

Sound professional advice is never expensive, on the other hand most investors pay huge "learning fee" to the market by buying the wrong property, in the wrong location, at the wrong price.

Your financial success will have nothing to do with the fees you pay or don't pay. It will be all about the advice you get or don't get.

Remember Warren Buffett's great saying: "Price is what you pay; value is what you get."

HANDS UP IF YOU WANT TO KNOW MORE ABOUT AUCTIONS

Around Australia weekend property auctions have become almost a national pastime. People go along to have a sticky beak, to get an idea of the market, to fantasise about their dream homes or just to watch the street theatre unfolding before them – it's a bit like watching buskers, you see an auction and you just have to stop and gawk a while!

Auctions are a particularly popular method of selling properties when the market is strong. Melbourne has long been the auction capital of the world but over the years the other major cities around Australia have followed its lead.

For all their street theatre and entertainment value, auctions represent a lot of stress and tension for those involved. Whatever the result, you can be sure that pressures will reach boiling point with so much money at stake which means that buyers, sellers and even agents will have a tough time keeping their nervous energy and emotions under control.

After you've attended a number of auctions you'll realise that a lot of the theatre and pressure is intentionally manufactured to get results. A good auctioneer can create an atmosphere of excitement and nervous competition as well as some sneaky techniques I'm about to uncover that encourages bidders to pay a little bit more than they might have initially intended.

Given the circumstances in this emotional cauldron, it's hardly surprising that a common mistake many buyers make is the way they bid at auction.

Vendors, in particular, stand to gain excellent results if there are two or more genuine buyers putting pressure on each other and inflating the price, as they get emotional under the pressure of potentially losing their dream home to a competitor. Investors, on the other hand, need to be very wary that they keep their emotions under control.

Most purchasers hate auctions because of the pressures they're put under, but sometimes the unpredictable nature of the beast means auctions can produce good buying opportunities.

I've personally bought some great bargains at auction. If you've done your homework on the property, know its value, understand the market, attend enough auctions and know how to control an auction, you could find yourself a great deal.

One of the advantages of buying at an auction is that you can see your competition. If the property reaches its reserve and is "put on the market", as they say, you'll have a chance to see what the real "market value" is. Sure, multiple bidders may push the price up because they become emotional about the property, but that's the market talking.

Conversely, with a private sale you're flying blind. You don't really know how the rest of the market views the asking price, or what price other buyers are considering, and even if you've done your homework there could be a difference of five to ten per cent in your perception. If you think a property's worth $600,000 but everyone else thinks it's only worth $560,000 you could effectively pay $40,000 too much!

Now I know that many people are a little intimidated by the thought of bidding for a property at auction, but if you avoid properties that are up for sale at auction, you're going to miss out on a lot of good buying opportunities as usually the best properties are offered for sale by auction, particularly in Melbourne and Sydney. Currently, the team at Metropole buy many properties for our clients at auction.

But to be successful you must be aware of the little tricks the agent will use on you, so let's first look at some of the psychological principles that are used by smart agents and auctioneers before, during and after an auction campaign to get through your barriers and work on your subconscious, then I'll share some tactics to help you win at auctions:

PSYCHOLOGICAL TRICKS AGENTS USE

1. Social proof

Smart selling agents understand that the concept of "social proof" is a way of easing the minds of worried potential purchasers, so they're keen to show buyers that there are many other people similar to them who are also interested in the property.

After all, all of these people gathered at the home can't be wrong, can they?

Prior to the auction they conduct open for inspections at specific times to ensure that there are multiple interested parties going through the property at the same time. They also make sure all the neighbours know the property is for sale to ensure a large crowd gathers on auction day – again adding social proof that this must be a great property.

And of course, when you see other potential buyers bidding against you, you tend to think "this must be a good property" or "the price must be fair", otherwise other people wouldn't be bidding, and you feel reassured.

It's an extremely effective technique as we tend to look to other people for validation regarding what we should and should not buy, and this is especially the case with property.

2. Scarcity

Selling agents know that we value things that are, or at least seem to be, scarce. That's why in their preamble you'll often hear the auctioneer explain how rare it is to find a property like this. At times they will "manufacture" perceived scarcity by playing up the attributes of the property.

Another way to create scarcity is by having the property auction on site, where there's only one property for sale, rather than in an auction rooms where multiple properties are for sale, one after the other.

If it's a period property even better: they will wax lyrical about how they don't make homes like this anymore and talk about the "character" of the home, its period-era details, its uniqueness.

The auctioneer will play on purchasers' emotions by creating scarcity and F.O.M.O. (fear of missing out) suggesting the property is just about to be "knocked down" as he calls for final bids for the first, second and the third call.

Then they'll say something like: "Don't come to me on Monday and ask if I have another property like this for sale, because I don't."

They do, of course. No two properties are exactly alike, but the real fear they're playing on is that you'll never find another home that you love as much. Which is not true, obviously, but the aim is to make you panic about missing out.

Have you ever noticed the way auctioneers will talk about the successful bidder as having "won" the auction? Now that's a very clever tactic, because it makes you feel good.

3. Reciprocity

This is the behavioural principle of giving your customers something before you ask anything of them, but to jog your memory, it relies on the fact we tend to return good deeds.

I've seen agents expertly use this principle by placing coffee trucks outside the house prior to an auction offering attendees free coffee, or agents working with the auctioneer handing out chocolates, lollipops or other treats to members of the crowd or their children. These actions make you positively predisposed to talking to the agents, working with the agents and bidding at the auction.

4. Anchoring

This is that cognitive bias tendency where we rely too heavily on an initial piece of information (the "anchor") when making decisions about the quality or worth of something. Someone drops the anchor by mentioning a figure, and immediately we think the worth of the object is in this ballpark.

First impressions can be hard to shake because we tend to selectively filter, so anchoring bias can influence how much you're willing to pay. The effect works because when you're given a figure, such as the advertised asking price for a property or a suggested end sale price at auction, you are likely to, whether knowingly or not, anchor your judgement by using the number as a reference point (i.e. the anchor).

That's why the auctioneer is likely to say something like "properties like this one generally sell for $1.5 million". Now the auctioneer didn't lie, but that doesn't mean that this particular property is worth $1.5 million. However, he has anchored that figure in your mind, and it is likely to impact on how you bid. At least he hopes so!

And don't be surprised if the auctioneer repeats that anchoring price during the auction at a time when the bidding has stalled below that figure of say $1.5 million. He's just trying to trick your brain by reminding it of that initial high price it was thinking about.

Today there is legislation in each state of Australia governing how agents quote a potential selling price or how they give a price guide (as the vendor's asking price is not revealed before auction).

Yet I've found that smart agents begin the process of anchoring a potential sale price long before auction day. It starts during the selling campaign when potential purchasers ask the agent what they think the property will sell for.

You'll find the agent saying something like: "The price we're quoting is $X, but already we've already had strong interest at $Y."

The way to counteract this anchoring bias is to come to the auction prepared with your own independent research of the property's value and not be biased by what you hear the auctioneer say, or by what other's bid – remember they are unlikely to be as well-informed as you are or as skilled in negotiations.

5. Loss Aversion

Loss aversion is another form of cognitive bias where the pain of losing something is psychologically two or three times as powerful as the pleasure of gaining something. In other words, the pain we feel from losing is much more severe than the pleasure we feel from winning an equal amount.

A good auctioneer will understand your fear of losing out the opportunity to purchase a property that you've already considered yours and have possibly spent money on in the form of building and pet inspections.

They play on this fear in a number of different ways during auction.

If the auction, for example, fails to reach the reserve price required for it to sell, a good auctioneer will say "If you don't bid now you'll lose the opportunity to negotiate with us to purchase this property" framing the situation as something you are going to lose, rather than saying "If you do bid now you will have the opportunity to negotiate with us."

Other phrases I've heard auctioneers use to tug on our emotions include:

"If you let somebody else buy this property now you'll be out looking at auctions again next weekend."

"If you don't bid now you'll wake up tomorrow morning regretting that somebody else has bought your house."

"I know your wife is shaking her head saying, 'Don't bid any higher, but you know that when you get home you'll be in trouble!"

6. Recency Bias

"Recency bias" is the phenomenon of a person most easily remembering something that has happened recently, compared to remembering something that may have occurred a while back. This means buyers are inclined to make future decisions based on immediate past events, believing future outcomes will directly correlate with recent occurrences.

That's why a good auctioneer will use this principle by telling you how much properties in the area have increased in value over the past year. They won't mention that period five or six years ago when properties failed to increase much in value, but if there was some positive growth in the past few months in particular, you'll be sure to hear about it!

A few other tactics a good auctioneer will use:

Auctioneers will often encourage you to pay more by saying things like, "Owning a home in this street will be an excellent investment".

What are they getting at? Well, they're playing on the fact that you're more likely to put your hard earned money into an "investment" rather than just frivolously paying for an expensive home for your family, even if you are planning to live in the property rather than renting it out as an investment.

Auctioneers will often minimise amounts there are asking you to bid so it seems easier for you to digest. For example, if the current bid is at $750,000, then rather than asking you to bid $755,000 they will ask if you have got another $5000 in your pocket. Or even another $1,000? They are hoping by not mentioning the full amount they are asking for – the $755,000 – that you'll forget just how much you're paying.

I've also heard a smart auctioneer use the line: "It's only money. You know it will be worthless in the future."

Of course, a good auctioneer will be using many or all of these techniques to encourage you to bid more, and the potential combined effect of these statements is staggering.

To avoid falling into these traps auctioneers set for us, we should make ourselves aware of these biases and recognise that we are not the rational decision makers that we think we are.

However, once we know the tricks, understand our own bias, the fears that are played on, we can take a step back and ensure we don't fall prey to the techniques.

PREPARING TO BUY AT AUCTION

Of course, you can make an offer prior to the auction day, and I'll discuss this in a moment, but let's start with what to do if the property you want to buy goes to auction. And remember, buying at auction is an unconditional sale so here's how you should prepare, because like all other negotiations, if you're well prepared, you'll be more empowered.

THE TYPICAL AUCTION

On the day of the auction the auctioneer will usually start with a brief explanation of the contract of sale, which should have been available for display for some time before the auction. He'll outline the terms of the contract, as well as any special conditions including those related to the process of bidding, such as vendor bidding.

This will be followed by a description of the property and then he'll invite bids from the public. If no bid is forthcoming he will usually kick start the process with a vendor bid. In the old days this would have been a dummy bid from the crowd.

As many purchasers don't bid at all until they feel the auction is drawing to a close, the agent often needs to use vendor bids to try to create atmosphere and to bring the price close to the reserve.

In the meantime, the auctioneer will continue to try to elicit real bids from anyone who has declared an interest. He may do this by saying something like "Going once, going twice, for the third and final time, all done ..."

Don't be fooled and think that he's really going to sell the property at this stage of the auction. You'll know when the property's going to be sold because the auctioneer will either announce that "The property is now going to be sold" or "The property is now on the market".

When the bidding stops, the auctioneer may confer with his vendor. Depending on his instructions the auctioneer will announce either that the property is actually "on the market" to be sold to the highest bidder or that it will be passed in.

If the vendor's reserve price (the minimum price he will accept for the property) has not been reached, the property is "passed in" and it will be available for private sale. Traditionally the highest bidder will have the first right of refusal to negotiate a sale with the vendor.

PRE-AUCTION DUE DILIGENCE

1. Have your purchasing entity organised (maybe your buying in the name of a trust, a company or an SMSF etc) if you are not buying in your own name.

2. Get a finance preapproval so you know your budget and attend the auction ready to write a deposit cheque.

3. Attend many auctions to experience the atmosphere and observe different bidding strategies.

4. You should ask the selling agent who the auctioneer is going to be (it's rarely the agent you'll be dealing with) and then watch this particular auctioneer in action to learn his individual techniques and the words he uses.

5. Do your research by inspecting many properties and seeing what they sell for (not just the asking price).

6. Know the market, know the value of the property in question and be armed with that power so you can identify a 'walk-away' price – the highest price you're prepared to pay.

7. You should go to the auction with three prices in mind:

   a. The bargain price – the figure you'd really love to pay (but know this is unlikely).

   b. The fair market value – what you think the property is really worth.

   c. Your walk away price – this should be a little higher that the market value if it's a great property. Remember...the best negotiating tactic is the one where you end up buying the property.

8. Play your cards close to your chest. Real estate agents are very skilled at prying information out of potential purchasers, including the price they're prepared to pay for a property. After all – that's their job! Sometimes you can end up revealing things to them that you never intended to and that might be detrimental to your negotiation power. By keeping your cards close to your chest and revealing very little about how much you might pay for a home, you maintain an advantage and ensure the agent cannot use your information to sway another potential buyer or to help the vendor set his reserve price.

9. Organise a pest & building inspection. This way you won't get any nasty surprises. However, be realistic and recognise that minor defects will exist in most properties. You do not want to nit-pick and have a chipped paint on a door to deter you from buying.

10. Negotiate terms before the auction.

If you want to alter any of the conditions in the contract of sale, before the auction is the only time you will have room to negotiate. You may want to alter the terms of settlement, the amount of deposit or the chattels included.

I often ask for amended terms just to gauge the level of interest in the property by other potential purchasers. If I ask for longer terms or a smaller deposit and the vendor refuses, it may mean that they are comfortable that there is a strong interest in their property and the agents expect multiple bidders at the auction. Conversely, if they do accept my requests, it suggests there may not be as much interest as they would like.

George's mansion

I was asked by George to bid for him at the auction of a magnificent mansion in the inner Melbourne suburb of Armadale. It was a beautifully restored historic mansion on a double block of land. While George was able to pay a fair market price, he didn't have the funds available for five months as he was completing a property development.

I asked the agent to amend the contract to allow us to purchase the property on five per cent deposit rather than the standard 10 per cent. This would have made a huge difference to George as the expected sale price was in the order of $4 million. I also asked for a five-month settlement rather than the 60 or 90 days that was offered on the contract.

When the agent came back to me within a few hours accepting both these conditions I suspected there was very little interest shown by other potential buyers and this was borne out at the auction when we were the only interested party.

11. Consider getting an experienced buyer's agent like the team at Metropole to bid on your behalf and level the playing field. I know I've already suggested this – but having a professional, an experienced negotiator, represent you makes a huge difference

WHAT TO DO ON THE DAY

1. Arrive early – survey the landscape and see who else is there. Do they look like serious bidders or are they just onlookers? In some states bidders must register so get there early, see who registers their interest and check out your competition. In other states see who's inspecting the contract of sale that's on display and look for those saying the right things.

2. Just to make things clear, your competition is not the auctioneer, even though they will be using all sorts of psychological tricks to encourage you to bid one more time. Your real competition is the other bidders. In fact, it's only the under bidder, the one you must beat by one more bid to snare that property. Just like the auctioneer is using psychological tricks on you, you should try and "psyche out" the other bidders and convince them that you've got deeper pockets than they have and that you'll bid higher that they will. Dress like you have the means to buy the property and watch your body language. Stand proud, be assertive and don't look nervous.

3. Stand in a position where you can see everybody, and everybody can see you. Don't hide. Be out near the front where you can watch the body language of the other bidders. Are they nervous, are they conferring with their wife, are they ringing someone on the phone, are they running out of steam?

4. In a strong auction climate use the psychological advantage of projecting confidence – make the other bidders think you have deep pockets and no limit.

5. Don't be afraid to look other bidders straight in the eye and make sure you bid confidently in a loud clear voice.

6. You should always be the first bidder and show you're serious by making a firm and high bid near what you think the reserve price is. The property won't sell below this and make your bids fast and assertive. I know many people start their bidding low, but when you think are about it, the property won't be sold below its reserve, so all that happens when you bid low is you give the auction some momentum with multiple bids. I'd rather knock out the other tentative purchasers right from the start with a strong bid.

7. Procrastinating or agonising over your next bid is a sign of weakness. Call out your offer in full. In other words, say $750,000 instead of the increments – don't just say $5,000. Make your last bid as loud and assertive as the first.

8. Be prepared to miss out. Stick to your 'walk-away' price.

9. If the property is going to pass in, make sure you are the highest bidder, as this allows first right to negotiate with the vendor.

10. If you miss a property at auction, accept that it wasn't meant to be and look forward to finding something better soon.

11. While no one likes to consider themselves the "loser" in any sort of negotiation campaign, it's far better to walk away and live to fight another day than over-commit to a property you've become emotionally blinded by.

12. Don't forget if you're too nervous you can also authorise someone else to bid on your behalf. Obviously, I'm biased but having a buyers' agent like my team at Metropole represent you levels the playing field and gives you an edge.

BIDDING STRATEGIES

When it comes to bidding, you'll need to vary your tactics depending on the market. My bidding strategy varies from auction to auction. It depends on what the auctioneer does, how others are bidding and the level of bids bouncing around. This is where experience comes to the fore.

When the property market is weak, or I don't think there's going to be much competition, I tend to hold back and hope the property is passed in giving me an opportunity to negotiate a good price with a despondent vendor afterwards.

Now remember, the reserve is the amount set by the vendor under which they'll not sell their property. While this is set prior to auction, it often changes on the day depending upon how spirited the bidding is. If the bidding doesn't reach the reserve price the property is "passed in".

It's not always easy to orchestrate but I try to have the final bid when the auction falls short of the reserve, as the auctioneer will pass in the property and negotiate with the highest bidder first.

You'll usually know when this is going to occur because the auction stalls; the auctioneer will keep repeating the same bid and ask, often desperately, for any sort of bid at all. He keeps saying "Going once, going twice" but never gets to the third knockdown because he knows he can't sell the property.

In a strong market my bidding strategy is different as confidence is essential to bid successfully. I usually start off the bidding mentioning the auctioneer by name and saying something along the lines of: "Adrian, I'll start off the bidding at $550,000."

Again, a strong, relatively high bid (close to where I think the reserve will be) from someone standing up front near the agent and facing the crowd confuses and intimidates the other bidders. Remember many have come along to buy at what they believe the reserve will be and there am I making my first bid close to or above where they were planning to finish. I've snared some good buys in hot property markets using this tactic.

And when the rival bidder drops down to increments of $1,000 don't follow suit. Come back confidently with the previously bid increment, even if it's your last bid. Remember this is street theatre and appearing confident is critical.

Having said that, never deliberately put the property on the market. When a property has a reserve of, say, $900,000 and the highest bid at the auction is $880,000 an agent will sometimes come up to tap you on the shoulder and say: "I wouldn't tell anyone else but the reserve is $900,000. If you just bid another $20,000 and the property will be on the market and all yours".

Despite what the agent says, never help them put the property on the market because I've seen occasions when it looked like there were no other bidders around, but once the property was on the market the bidding took off again and zoomed up by tens or even hundreds of thousands of dollars.

Once the property is on the market, and if it's still within your price range, there are a number of bidding strategies that might help you increase your chances of success at a reasonable price.

THE KNOCK-OUT BID

A strong bid of a larger increment, say $10,000, when other people are bidding $5,000 can sometimes knock out the opposition if they are flagging.

Tell-tale signs such as a wavering of the hand, long discussions with a spouse before the next bid, or a longer than usual pause between bids could be a sign that the other bidder is near or over his or her limit.

This tactic is most effective if you look directly at the person who made the last bid and crush them with your confidence!

Make your bid confidently and call out the full price. By this I mean you don't say $10,000 or just put up your hand. Instead you say "$925,000!" – the full amount loud, clear and succinctly and look straight at the person who made the last bid.

Often the other bidders will be at their limit and, already in their minds, they will think they've bought the property and they are going to be blown out of the water. If this doesn't work and the other bidder continues then put it back in your kit bag and go on to other tactics. Only try it once or you'll end up costing yourself a lot of money. If it has not had the desirable psychological effect, I move onto the fast increment strategy.

THE FAST INCREMENT STRATEGY

Here you push the bidding up by the smallest increment, $500 or $1,000, whatever the auctioneer will allow.

So if you make your knockout bid at $925,000 and the other people come in, often after some hesitation, at $826,000 you have already worked out in your head what the next bid is and before they have even finished speaking, you place your bid at $827,000.

Always say the full amount out loud and clearly. It psyches people out; it sounds like a lot of money.

What often happens is the other party hesitates, thinks, talks with their partners or friends and eventually comes up with another bid. As soon as they do, you again come out with a fast knock-out reply, before they've even finished speaking you race ahead by another $1,000.

SLOWING DOWN THE BIDDING

Some experienced investors favour the opposite strategy, trying to reduce the increment of the bid and thereby slow the tempo of the auction. Auctioneers usually don't like this tactic and oppose having the pace of the auction slowed.

SIX AUCTION SINS

Clearly auctions can be a psychological battle, so it's important to have a strategy in place to give you the best chance of winning on the day. But this is no different to any other major negotiation is it? This means there are some things you shouldn't do at auctions – blunders that could cost you that psychological edge.

1. Not bidding at all

It's interesting that many prospective buyers just don't want to make a bid, and some even let the property pass in to another buyer. Then they'll hang around after the auction, hoping a deal isn't reached so they can jump in and negotiate the bargain of the century – alas, this is usually a terrible tactic.

The only way to be the winner at the end is to actually bid. As I said, be the first bidder and make sure you're the last one to bid because then either you end up buying the property or if it passes in, you can negotiate with the seller.

2. Deciding on a round number

Never finish your bidding on a round number, because most bidders set their limit on a round number. This means one or two more small increments could win you the property. So rather than setting an upper limit of $750,000, set yours at $753,000 – two bids above where others may stop.

Many bidders set an inflexible limit, and often a round number such as $700,000, for no valid reason. I've seen buyers miss out on a property because they're not prepared to increase their bid by as little as $500, which is silly when you think about the long-term capital growth potential they may be missing out on.

As I said, you need to set three prices. The price you'd love to pay. The price you'd be happy to pay. And the price which will really hurt, but once you've snared that property you'll look back in a few years and it won't hurt – you'll be so happy you extended yourself to buy that property.

3. Stopping and starting

Buyers who pause mid-auction to confer with their family or friends about their limit or intentions could be giving away more than they know. It's important for a buyer who's there with their partner to decide on who's actually bidding and also to determine key signs to allow you to communicate in a non-verbal fashion mid-auction.

To become more comfortable, attend as many auctions as you can to watch the theatre of how successful bidders behave, their body language and their interaction with the auctioneer.

If you're keen to buy, you need to be assertive even if they're on your last bid by making it seem like you still have several bids still up your sleeve.

4. Asking if the property is "on the market"

Auctions are a form street theatre and you'll find the initial bids are usually well below the seller's "reserve price" and the property will not sell until this figure (or an amended reserve price) is reached. That's when the auctioneer will advise the property is "on the market". Or "we're now going to sell the property".

Sometimes nervous buyers ask the auctioneer "is it on the market?" You'll know when the property is on the market. The auctioneer often will have gone inside to his vendors to confer if they are prepared to sell and he'll let you know.

However, it shouldn't matter to you if the property is officially on the market or not, whether it has reached its reserve price or not, because if the seller has gone to the trouble of putting their property to auction they are keen to sell They have invested time, money and emotion in marketing their property, so in essence it has been "on the market" for about a month. All you are now doing is negotiating the price. Don't show your hesitancy by asking this question, instead bid to your pre-set limit and hopefully you'll be the winner on the day.

5. Making ridiculous offers

Starting too low with your bidding might, in some cases, invite other bidders into the auction ring and allow momentum to build.

On the other hand, starting with a strong, confident bid could knock out several contenders early on.

If you've done your market research, and hopefully you have, then making a ridiculously low offer is usually a mistake.

6. Pretending you're not interested

It's a strange phenomenon that some buyers attend auctions and then pretend they're not interested in it at all. In my mind it can work in the buyer's favour to show interest during the entire auction campaign.

If no one bids at auction, because seemingly they're not interested, then the vendor is legally entitled to make a vendor bid on the property to help move the auction along.

This can either get things started or be used when the auction stalls because everyone is trying to "play the game".

Agents say however that they want to help a genuine buyer purchase the property, so it's important to be upfront about your intent in the pre-auction days. It's always better to be a standout potential buyer because it can help you compete better on auction day as well as be on the agent's radar.

WHAT TO DO IF YOU'RE THE HIGHEST BIDDER FOR A PROPERTY THAT IS PASSED IN AT AUCTION

At an auction, if the property doesn't meet the reserve price, it "passes in".

So imagine you turn up to an auction, keen to buy your next home or investment property, the auction stalls and the property is passed in. What do you do?

When a property passes in, the highest bidder is generally given first right to negotiate with the vendor's agent.

The first thing to do is to put yourself in the position to able to negotiate with the vendor and this means you should be the highest bidder. It's not always easy to manipulate the order of the bidding, but it's important to put yourself in that position.

What happens next is the selling agent or auctioneer usually invites you to step inside the property and commence negotiations, while other agents approach the under-bidders to explore their level of interest and keep them "hot" in case the negotiations with you fall through.

Remember, the agent is acting on behalf of the vendor and it's their job to get the best price for their client and many of them do it very, very well. You can bet your deposit they are highly skilled at emotion-based selling and will employ tactics to make you believe they are going to help you. But no matter how convincing the agent appears, remember they're not on your side.

Now it's time for your negotiating skills to come to the fore.

Unless it is pouring rain do not follow the agent inside. This puts you on their turf and isolates you from what's going on outside. I prefer to stand outside where I can assess whether there is any real competition or just friends who are pretending to be buyers hanging around.

The perceived pressure of having competition outside, breathing down your neck and waiting for an opportunity to negotiate is a powerful negotiation tool that agents use against you.

I've found the tactic of displaying strong body language, standing on my own turf (even though I still might have butterflies in my stomach) surprises the agents and returns the negotiating power to me.

Now the game begins... The first question I ask is "What is the vendor's reserve price?"

Remember, the reserve is the minimum price the vendor told the agent (prior to the auction) he or she would accept for their property. But now that the auction has failed they may, in fact, accept a lower price.

So when you hear the reserve price you should baulk (remember the flinch), seem surprised at how high it is and ask: "I understand that's the price the vendor was hoping for before the auction, but NOW what is the lowest price they will sell for?"

Your next steps will depend on what the vendor wants for their property and what you believe it is worth based on your pre-auction research.

If you're like me, you'll have an estimate of what the property is worth under low competition (what you'd really like to buy it for) and then the maximum you would be prepared to pay under intense competition (such as if the auction had continued on.)

Of course, just because the property has been passed in doesn't mean that this is the market price, it is simply a starting point for further negotiation.

The real market value is what you and hopefully the vendor have assessed it to be based on comparable sales evidence.

The key is to work within the price range you, and only you, have determined and not waver from it. What happens next really depends at which end of your price range the property is passed in for. If it is at the lower end you have more flexibility and knowing if there is any competition waiting outside will influence how flexible you are.

I would the say something like, "I've already offered you the upper end of what I think the property is worth", even if it's not the case.

Obviously, if there are no other buyers waiting in the wings you can minimise the amount you are willing to counter-offer.

Now don't fall into the trap of making the same counter increments as the vendor. Often the agent will ask you to meet the vendor halfway, but obviously you're not obliged to do so.

Stick to your guns and your own method of negotiation – that one that aligns with your interests – and don't let someone else's negotiation techniques or tactics throw you off and cause you to make a decision you'll later regret.

6 TIMES YOU CAN SNAG A PROPERTY BEFORE AUCTION

Sometimes a smart negotiating technique is to try and buy a property before it goes to auction. This works particularly well when our property markets are a little slow, when auction clearance rates are dropping, and when vendors are getting nervous.

This means that it's possible to buy good properties before they even make it to auction day. There are several reasons why vendors may be open to selling before auction day. Some of the most common ones are:

1. Nervous vendors

There's nothing quite like the energy at an auction. It's tense, exciting, atmosphere. But some vendors just can't handle it.

So to avoid auction day nerves entirely, some sellers opt to sell before the big day.

This is great news for you if you're looking to buy, because you can play into those nerves (nicely of course) and send them an offer early on.

They might be relieved to avoid the stress of the auction process altogether – and you might have your hands on the house you wanted even sooner!

2. Sensitive sellers

Selling can be a stressful time for the vendor, and if they're particularly sensitive – perhaps they're elderly, or going through an emotional time – the thought of going to auction might create too much of an emotional rollercoaster for them.

Depending on their circumstances, they might need to sell fast and move swiftly, so receiving an offer before auction could actually save them a lot of time and stress.

Remember...you're not taking advantage of the people; you're taking advantage of the situation. You'll be assisting the vendor by relieving their stress.

3. Time is running out

If the seller has already bought a house elsewhere, they could be in a bit of a panic at the thought of being unable to sell their first property in time. No one wants to be paying mortgages for two properties!

By giving them an offer to consider before auction day, you're giving them the opportunity to eliminate the very real risk of the property being passed in at auction – while allowing them to move on with confidence to their new home.

4. There just isn't much interest

No matter how hard real estate agents works to generate interest in a property, sometimes the buyers just aren't biting.

So, if there isn't much excitement or enthusiasm prior to auction, the agent may advise their client to consider any offers that come their way beforehand... which is where you can swoop in to save the day.

Of course you should take advantage of this situation – a nervous vendor and no or little competition puts you in the driver's seat. You'll be in a great negotiating position.

5. The agent is in a hurry to sell the property

You might find that the agent is very impatient to sell. This can happen if the property has been on the market and has been the agent's listing for a while, or if they're dealing with a particularly tricky seller (yes, it happens!).

Whatever the reason, a hurried agent could be a boon for you, as it means you have the upper hand when it comes to negotiating the best possible deal.

6. You have a premium offer on the table

While we sometimes wish it wasn't the case, let's be honest: money talks.

If you can slide through with a premium offer that no one in their right mind would say no to, then it could secure you the property in a hot second.

One thing to be wary of, is your money talking too much, and raising the bar so high that both the seller and their agent think other similar offers might be made at auction.

This is a risk of putting your best foot forward prior to auction – but it just might pay off.

The only way you'll ever know whether you can snag a property before it goes to auction is by putting the offer out there. The worst the vendor can do is say no, and if that's the case, you can still roll along to the auction when it occurs and try your luck once more.

SUMMARY

Clearly, the best result at any auction is that the property will be passed in, leaving you with a good understanding of the market's feeling for the property and a chance to negotiate with a despondent vendor.

Both the auction and post auction negotiations are a game of psychological warfare, so in the next chapters we'll have a closer look at negotiating skills and some techniques for managing your emotions and sticking to a calculated game plan.

TOP TIPS FOR SKILFUL REAL ESTATE NEGOTIATION

Making an offer on a property can be an overwhelming experience for many people.

A good real estate agent will be a well-trained and skilful negotiator. In fact, that's one of the core strengths they bring to the table for their clients. The agent can remain objective and calm, while pushing for the best price on the best terms.

On the other hand, most property buyers will be emotional, and this means they will struggle to make rational decisions. They are, after all, negotiating over their "dream home", their so-called "castle", and will be spending a lot of money in the hope of securing it. This makes most buyers decidedly emotional and highly vulnerable to paying too much.

This is particularly the case if you haven't engaged a buyer's agent to level the playing field for you. However, help is at hand. Let's start with...

THREE KEY INGREDIENTS

Effective negotiation needs adequate preparation and requires a combination of three ingredients – **information, time** and **power.**

It's interesting that in property negotiations, most people feel that the other party has more of each of these than they actually have.

For example, if you possess superior knowledge relating to a property transaction, then this **information** gives you a competitive edge throughout the negotiations.

The fact is, as a purchaser you probably do have a better understanding of the local property market than the vendor, because you should have done your homework and developed your investment comfort zone.

You also have all the **time** in the world if you approach investing with the right attitude. Remember you shouldn't fall in love with a property as they're a bit like buses – if you miss one, there's always another just around the corner! Yet vendors have gone through all the emotional trauma of putting their house on the market are probably very keen to negotiate a sale, although they'll never admit it.

With regards to the third major element of negotiation – **power** – there's often a perception that the other party holds the upper hand.

This is usually not true in property negotiations. If the other party is emotionally involved, especially if they are a motivated vendor and if you adhere to the rules discussed in this book, then the balance of power is with you.

INSIDER TIP

The three important elements of negotiation are information, time and power. To be a successful negotiator you must have these on your side.

---

5 QUESTIONS TO ASK BEFORE YOU START NEGOTIATIONS

We all want to buy our next home or investment property at the lowest price possible. On the other hand, the vendor wants the highest price he or she can get.

And you now know that the asking price quoted by the selling agent will usually be more than the owner is willing to take for their home. It's part of the real estate game: vendors know the asking price will come down as part of the negotiation process so they list it slightly higher than they would accept and then hope for the best.

So how much should you offer when negotiating your next investment property? Well if you ask the selling agent what price you should offer, you're asking the wrong person.

Remember, the agent is paid by the seller to represent them and to get the best price possible. Despite that, I would still ask them what they would consider was a "fair offer" and then ask them to justify it with a list of comparable sales. You don't need to respond to their ballpark figure either. In fact, I would listen without giving much away. At the very least, you should try not to respond with, "Are you joking?" if you feel the price is too high. You want to remain calm and neutral the whole way through.

If you're thinking that the agent just wants to make a sale, in many cases you are right. In reality the agent doesn't get paid unless a sale is made, so obviously they are keen to sell you the house. Most selling agents prefer an easy negotiation, knowing that sellers can get offended and take it personally when they receive low offers on their homes.

This means they will probably recommend you make an offer close to the asking price. However, in most markets (other than during boom times), houses sell for considerably less than their asking price. There is no standard discount, but as everyone knows there will be some back and forth about the price as agents tend to list the property for sale at an asking price usually about 5-10 per cent more than the market is willing to pay and the seller is willing to accept.

This means the asking price is just a starting point for the negotiations. If you pay what the seller is asking straight off the bat, you are more than likely wasting money.

The trick is to know how much less the seller will accept. So before deciding on what price to offer, here are five questions you should consider asking:

1. How did the vendor come to the asking price for their home?

Was it from the agent's suggestion or because that's how much they need to buy their next dream home? Some sellers are unrealistic and unlikely to come down from their asking price if they have to get a certain amount for a particular reason. It's good to know if this is the case so you don't waste your time and energy.

2. Have there been any other offers made?

This lets you know if you have any competition and how serious the vendor is about selling their home for a reasonable price.

3. How long has the home been on the market?

If it's just been put up for sale, the seller may not be anxious to accept the first offer. On the other hand, if the home has been on the market for several months it's more likely the seller would be ready to accept your offer.

4. Why is the vendor selling?

Are they going through a divorce? Do they have to move interstate urgently? Have they already bought another home that would put them under pressure to sell their current home?

This will let you know how motivated the seller is. I usually save this question towards the end of the conversation with the agent, once a rapport has been established. I find agents tend to open up more about the seller's reason for listing the home, once they have warmed up a little.

5. Has the asking price been reduced during the time the property has been on the market?

This will tell you whether the seller is really keen to offload their home and also let you know that you might have a motivated seller on your hands and perhaps greater bargaining power.

These questions are important because they teach you the art of listening. Remember, negotiation isn't about talking; it's about hearing the response from the other party, both verbal and non-verbal, and using that information to negotiate.

Listening carefully gives you little clues that provide an insight into the other party, and if you have poor listening skills, ultimately you will also have poor negotiation skills.

NOW LET'S LOOK AT MY TOP 21 TIPS TO SWING THE BALANCE MORE IN YOUR FAVOUR.

1. Know what you want before negotiating

It's critical to plan and know the result you want – your bottom line – before commencing negotiations. It's a bit like when you're planning your holiday. Firstly, decide your destination – where you want to end up — then work backwards to decide the best way to get there. In negotiations, as in life, if you don't have a plan of your own, you'll become part of someone else's.

2. Know their motivation for selling

Vendors sell for a variety of reasons, so it's important to understand what the other side really wants from the negotiation. And don't be surprised if it's not just about wanting as much money as possible. In fact, many sellers are happy to lower their price if their needs can be met elsewhere. Maybe they want a long settlement or a flexible settlement date?

When you determine what motivates them by asking the agent the right questions then you can give them exactly what they need so you'll be able to get more of what you want.

The reasons people sell their properties tend to fall into two broad categories. There are those that are **time-relaxed** and those that are **time-sensitive**.

Here are some examples to give you an idea of what I mean:

You discover that the seller is desperately short of money and needs an urgent sale. Here time is more important than money. The vendor may be trying to prevent the mortgagee from taking possession of his house or the finance company taking his car. If you can come up with the cash in 30 days, you may get the property at a lower price than someone who needs 90 days.

The owners of the property want to separate or divorce. You can sometimes recognise this situation because the house looks like a battlefield. Here a major motive for selling is escape. Offering a low price but a quick settlement could be attractive to the sellers who will be keen to get out and move on.

You discover the seller is building a house. How much would the sellers be prepared to drop the price if they could have the convenience of being able to rent the property from you until their house was completed? They would avoid the emotional and financial expense of moving into a temporary rental property. This type of information could be worth thousands of dollars to you.

You learn that the sellers are older and more cautious, and while they want to move, they're worried that they might sell their house and not find what they want in time. Here the dominant need of the vendor is security. If you make an offer that would allow the owners to stay in the property and rent it from you until they found what they were looking for, they'd be likely to accept a lower price in return for the increased security.

Case Study

Only recently I was looking to purchase a pleasant house on a great block of land in a prime Melbourne suburb as a future development site to build townhouses to keep as a long-term investment for ourselves.

The market was hot in Melbourne at the time and lots of owner occupiers were considering the property which was ideally situated in a top tree lined street a few doors from a park. I'd decided I was prepared to pay up to $1.8 million for the property, which I knew was a fair market price.

Knowing the selling agent, I ascertained that the vendors had lived in the property for 40 years and were downsizing and set to make a windfall as there were a number of potential purchasers ready to buy this home at auction. The trouble was the sellers had not bought their next property and were nervous about the possibility of being caught short as all the potential purchasers (other than me) were home buyers and wanted to move in within 60 days.

I asked the agent what his vendors really wanted and he explained they were looking for $1.8 million and really wanted a long settlement of 120 or more days. He also told me that there were at least two other serious home buyers who were likely to bid $1.8 million plus at the auction.

So at 4.00pm on the Friday before the auction I offered $1.7 million with a long settlement of 120 days and that I was flexible on this term but only if the vendors signed the contract before 7.00pm that night, at which time the contract would be rescinded and I'd come to the auction the next morning and bid on a 30 or 60 day settlement just like the other buyers. I also made it easier for the agent by signing a contract and giving him a deposit cheque to satisfy his vendor.

I had to wait until just after 7.00pm but I secured the property. Obviously it was a difficult decision for the vendor, but they got the certainty of their long settlement date and I bought a fantastic property at a below market price in what was a booming property market.

3. Price is not the only negotiating factor

We tend to think price is the main negotiating point in property, but there are many other important factors, such as terms and conditions, inclusions and settlement date.

Put yourself in the seller's shoes and once you understand their motivation it will help you put forward a deal that better suits their needs. If the couple is splitting and wants to get out of the house as quickly as possible, a short settlement may be more important than a few extra dollars they would have to split with the spouse they don't like anyway.

On the other hand, if the vendor hasn't purchased their next home yet, a longer settlement may suit them as it would give them the time and flexibility to search for their next home. Let me give you some examples:

1. No auction

A number of years ago I purchased a property from an elderly gentleman. He was moving house and leaving his old family home, which was now too big and had a large garden that required a lot of maintenance. Having recently purchased a small house in a country town right near where his son lived, he had listed his old house for auction with a local estate agency. Unfortunately, he found the whole process to be a traumatic ordeal.

After inspecting the property I asked the agent about the owner and why he was selling. When I found out the circumstances I took an educated guess that an easy, convenient transaction would probably have a lot of appeal to the vendor, allowing him to avoid the auction rollercoaster.

So I made a sensible but below-market offer on the property. I offered about 10% below what I thought was a fair market price but made the offer unconditional and fixed the settlement date to the date that the vendor needed to move into his new home.

Of course, the agent said the offer would not be enough to take the property off the market so early into the auction campaign, but I insisted she present the offer to her client. To create a greater level of certainty for the vendor, I signed a contract of sale and attached a deposit cheque to it.

Sure enough, with very little deliberation, the vendor accepted it and countersigned the contract note, preferring the certainty of an unconditional sale, even at a lower price, to the uncertainty of the auction process.

INSIDER TIP

Never assume you know what the vendor's motivation is. Price is not the only consideration for vendors.

---

2. The local vet's house

More proof that money is not always the motivating factor for vendors came when buying a home for my family many, many years ago. We found a lovely old two-storey home with loads of character on a big block of land with a tennis court.

The sellers were an older couple, the local vet and his wife, and their children had grown up and left home, so they were downsizing to a smaller house. I was surprised when they rejected offers from a number of property developers who wanted to build units on the large site, and were keen to sell the house to us, a young (at the time) family with children. They wanted to see their house continue as a place of joy and to see us gain happiness from living there as they had – and we did!

3. Don't let emotions get in the way

Always leave your ego, as well as your emotions, out of the equation. The better a negotiator you are, the less emotion you will show. The best negotiators must care – but not too much. Not only are they always professional in their dealings, they never take anything personally.

In other words, don't fall in love with a property and let emotion carry you away. People who let this happen often find their ideal dream home or investment property, get all excited and become willing to pay whatever it takes to make their dream a reality. Then they wait with nervous anticipation for the vendor's reply, getting even more emotional, and playing into their opponent's hands. When the agent returns with a counter offer, they're sometimes so excited that they'll sign almost anything!

Mark loses his cool and his money

Here's a real-life story that sums up the above situation. It's about a normally cool-headed solicitor named Mark and his first investment property.

Mark was a good negotiator who was used to crunching multi-million dollar deals on behalf of his clients every day. In these situations he had no trouble keeping a level head and negotiating effectively on behalf of his clients. Naturally he cared about getting his clients the best possible deal. And if he didn't get the perfect outcome of course he'd be upset … but not too much.

Now, when it came to negotiate the purchase of an investment property for himself, he did a second-rate job because he was too involved – this time he cared way too much!

Mark found a house that he wanted to buy and after inspecting it one Saturday, he did all the sums and, because it looked like a good investment property, he discussed it with his wife. They talked through all the pros and cons and agreed to make an offer.

By this stage it was Saturday night, but Mark thought he'd try to ring the agent anyway, keen to get the ball rolling. Now that he'd decided he wanted this property, he didn't want anyone else to get in and make an offer before him. Being Saturday night, the selling agent didn't answer his phone, so Mark left a message on his voicemail. He also left a message on the agent's home answering machine.

All Saturday night and Sunday morning Mark thought about the property. He imagined how, with little effort, he could fix it up and get a higher rent. He even imagined the colours he might repaint it. When the agent hadn't returned his calls by Sunday lunchtime, Mark imagined that he was probably out negotiating a deal with another buyer and selling "his" house to someone else! In reality the agent was spending some time with his family.

So Mark rang him again and left another message on his voicemail.

By the time Monday morning rolled around and the agent got around to returning Mark's calls, he knew that he had a very keen buyer. During negotiations Mark again showed how keen he was; increasing his initial offer almost immediately on being told that the sellers would never contemplate his initial offer.

If he was acting on behalf of a client, Mark would have said something like, "How do you know that they won't accept it? This is a genuine offer and we'd like it put to the vendor".

But Mark cared too much. When he heard that someone (probably an imaginary buyer) had already made an offer on the property, he made a higher counteroffer. In the end he paid $65,000 more than he'd budgeted for and had considered a fair market price.

When the stakes are high, and you are emotionally involved in negotiations, you don't think clearly. It's like a temporary state of near insanity. During the negotiations, if you hear that somebody else has made a higher offer on the property you want, the adrenalin flows and your heart will be pumping.

If you know you can't be cool, it's often useful using a middleman such as a friend or a buyer's advocate to act on your behalf and take the emotion out of negotiations.

5. Negotiation starts the moment you open your mouth

Selling agents are highly trained negotiators and they size you up from the moment they meet you. They are assessing you to ensure they don't waste time and effort on someone who is unlikely to make an offer or is merely there to "sticky beak". Remember, agents only have one commodity (other than the properties they're selling), and that's their time so they guard it preciously.

If you are genuinely interested, show it. Tell the agent you like the property. Be open, honest and transparent about the extent of your interest, but don't talk money upfront and definitely don't tell the agent the extent of your budget or finance pre-approval.

But I would add a note of caution here: do not gush if you love the home. Express your interest, but never show that you are ruled by your heart rather than your budget. Agents love buyers who do this because they're more likely to go to the top or their budget (or beyond).

On the other hand, don't go too far in the other direction, either. It's never a good move to trash a home so the agent thinks you're not interested. Not only is that bad negotiating, it's also just plain rude. And, of course, it's unlikely you'll be updated when the agent gets new listings for sale.

6. Know more than the other party

Knowledge is power when it comes to negotiation, so before you enter into any property negotiation ensure you know the local market, you've researched which properties have recently sold and for how much, and what hasn't sold and why.

Don't rely on online research as photos are deceptive and homes can look very different in reality than they do using a wide-angle camera lens.

When comparing other properties that have recently sold, focus on elements such as aspect, street appeal, elevation, finishes, quality of construction, position, and whether or not it is close, but not on, a main road. Some of these factors are invisible online, and yet they have a big impact on the value of a property.

And of course, when researching, compare like with like. Focus your attention on a market segment that is as similar to the one you are interested in buying. If you are looking to purchase a townhouse, then focus solely on this style of home. Ignore houses and apartments as they won't be relevant to your search.

Having this information gives you negotiating power.

7. Ensure you get the last concession

Remember, negotiation is a game of asking for and offering concessions. Whenever you make a concession ensure you always get something in return. The seller wants $700,000, so you offer $650,000. They counter with $675,000 so you agree as long as it's subject to finance.

8. Don't split the difference

One of the most common negotiating techniques agents will use on you is "let's split the difference".

Let's say the vendor has dropped their price to $700,000 and your offer was $640,000, they'll suggest you meet halfway at $670,000. It's tempting to accept this – it sounds fair, after all – but don't fall into this trap.

Instead say, "Thanks, but I just can't. I really can't go over $650,000." You'll be surprised how often your lower offer gets accepted.

If this doesn't work then another approach is to increase your offer by small increments. For example, after your initial counteroffer of $650,000 your next offer would be of a lower increment, say $5,000 that to be $655,000 and your offer after that to be $657,250.

Each offer should go up in decreasing amount as this suggests to the seller that you're running out of steam and they had better accept your offer.

As part of this strategy it's also wise to use the power of time and delay when making the next incremental offer. Don't rush straight back with a counteroffer, as this adds to the impression that you're running out of momentum. You really want to give the impression that you're thinking about it (which you are, after all).

9. Provide an explanation for your offer.

When you make an offer, it's always a good idea to explain your thinking because this will influence the agent and the seller's expectations about what you're prepared to pay.

It will also usually soften their response when they make a counteroffer.

You could say for example, that you're offering a lower price than what is listed to account for some renovations that you think are necessary.

For example, your first offer might be based on the lowest recent comparable sale of a property in the area, less an amount of say $20,000. You would then justify this discount based on defects in the property you're buying.

If you get to the stage of making counter offers, attempt to validate these counter offers in the same way. This will give your negotiating more credibility and force.

And if you don't think the property has any defects, you need to look harder. No property is perfect, and you should understand what the negatives are of every property you make an offer on so you can use this information to your advantage.

10. Don't go in too low

Making an offer which is too "low ball" can sometimes make the agent think you're just a tyre kicker. It also insults the seller and can prompt them to refuse to deal with you after that.

Therefore, the amount of your first offer is a balance between your desire to secure the property at the best price possible, and presenting an offer that is credible, but without being offensive to the seller so you can start a round of negotiations. This is where giving a rational basis for the offer, as discussed above, is important.

11. The higher authority trick

The tactic of having to consult a "higher authority" before moving forward with negotiations can work well when buying real estate. Our team of buyers' agents at Metropole use this strategy all of the time.

Even though we understand our client's budget and we have our client's authority to proceed, often we will stall the negotiation and say something like: "Sorry I don't have the authority to proceed higher than $600,000, I'll have to get authority from my client to go higher."

Lacking the final say in a negotiation can put you in a very powerful position. It puts a temporary pause to the negotiations and allows you some thinking time.

If you're acting for yourself, you can always blame your partner and say that you cannot act any further without clearing it with them as "you hadn't discussed a higher figure".

12. Negotiate the Conditions

Agents operate on the principle that "less is yes". That means the fewer conditions that you put in your offer, the greater the chance they have of getting a yes from the seller, and an acceptance of your offer.

But that doesn't mean you should work on the same principle.

From your perspective as a buyer, a simple offer to buy a property on a 10 per cent deposit, settlement in 45 days, cash unconditional will work against you, as the only thing you can negotiate over is the price.

Instead experienced negotiators might make their offer subject to finance, a building and pest inspection, a 120-day settlement and much smaller deposit. This will allow them the opportunity to negotiate away some of these trivial requests that they don't really want, ultimately arriving at a settlement with a 10 per cent deposit, 45-day settlement and fewer bells and whistles, but at a reduced price.

13. Protect yourself using Conditional Clauses

If you're serious about purchasing a particular property, and you don't want to let somebody else outbid you, it's often best to make your offer as simple and clean as possible.

Using the tactic above of adding a heap of conditions to your offer may give you negotiating power, but it could also frustrate the seller who will accept a simpler offer if it's available.

In these cases, a simple but very powerful condition we use is: "This sale is conditional upon the purchaser's solicitor's approval."

You'd be surprised how few vendors baulk at this clause yet, if you think about it, your solicitor will not approve the contract proceeding if the building and pest inspection is not your satisfaction, or if the bank doesn't approve your loan or in fact if you change your mind and tell your solicitor that you don't want them to approve the deal.

It's a simple-sounding clause but it covers a lot of ground and really protects you.

14. Always have an alternative

A great source of power in property negotiation is telling the agent that you are seriously looking at another property (through another agent who is going to earn the commission).

Don't be too smug about it, if you're interested in a particular property the agent should believe you are keen, but not too keen.

They may ask you for details of the property but be wary of giving too much away. Tell them it's a similar home in a similar neighbourhood, and you're "obviously weighing up the best option".

15. Patience is a virtue in negotiation

Once you've made an offer it's important to wait for the seller's response. Don't be tempted to make a further offer without hearing from the vendor.

To make another offer is to send a strong message to the seller that you're keen and they will probably take advantage of you, so stay away from your phone until you hear back.

16. Take Your Time

In all negotiations, it's important to look as if you have all day, even if you don't. Never say, "Let's cut to the chase" as this could be perceived as disrespectful to the other party's needs.

Remember, you must play the game so that the other party feels that they've gotten a good deal.

Statements like this send a clear message that you're too willing and overly keen and you could end up at the bottom of the food chain, consumed by the more experienced and sometimes predatory negotiator.

17. Never Attack the Property, the Agent or the Seller

Smart negotiators understand that even though the vendor is selling the property, it's the agent that they will be dealing with, so it makes no sense to offend them. You may secretly dislike the agent, they may have a manner or style you dislike, but you cannot let that get in the way of negotiations.

Similarly, avoid trying to put a negative spin on the property and never get personal during the negotiations. Likewise, if you are genuinely keen, don't act uninterested.

For example, don't describe the property as a "dog box", a "demolition job" or a "haven for drug dealers and prostitutes". Don't turn your nose up at the area, the quality of the appliances or the furniture.

None of these comments are likely to achieve a reduction in the price and the agent won't take you seriously if they don't think you like the property. Don't forget that sellers want to think their home will be well looked after once they have handed it over to someone else. It's a sentimental thing for them.

You're better off if you advise the seller that the property clearly has potential, but it's obviously in need of work to bring it up to its best condition (which will cost say $40,000) and your offer has been adjusted accordingly.

18. Always submit your offers in writing

I might be stating the obvious, but by putting your offer in writing with a small deposit cheque (even a few thousand dollars) formalises the offer and creates a powerful incentive for the agent to hand the seller. It's easy to throw a number around with an agent, but a written offer shows you are serious.

19. Place a time limit on your offer

Always place a time limit (say by 5pm, Friday afternoon) on your written offer. This can be a powerful negotiating strategy, which lets the vendor know they need to make a decision within that timeframe or risk losing the offer altogether.

20. Be prepared to walk away

Before entering any negotiation, always know your bottom line and the point at which you will walk away.

The most skilful negotiators are prepared to walk away if the deal doesn't go their way.

At times this is easier said than done, but the best negotiators know that there are plenty more deals out there, so they don't let themselves become emotionally attached. Be nonchalant and let the agent know you have other options.

Remember: it's important that the other side never think that their property is your favourite or that you don't have other options.

21. The best negotiation technique is...

I've outlined a few of the many strategies you could use to negotiate a better deal, but at the end of the day, the best negotiation technique is the one where you end up buying the property.

I've seen too many "smart" investors dig their heels in and lose out on buying a great property for the sake of a few thousand dollars.

Remember you make your money in the long-term not because you buy a property cheaply – that's only a once-off profit – but because you buy the right property, an "investment-grade" property that keeps delivering wealth and producing high rates of return over many years.

And that is not worth losing this long-term profit because you want to save a few dollars today.

At the same time don't be a miser, become a negotiating optimizer. Obviously smart negotiation is important as you build your **Cash Machine**, but I've seen some investors attempt to squeeze the last cent out of every deal they do. They negotiate hard and leave the other side unhappy. They push their tenants and make sure they always get the highest rents. They negotiate, haggle and plot to get the absolute lowest price on everything. They try and cut fees and commissions, resist making any concessions and look for every opportunity to cut corners to save money, as if money was the only thing of value in their property business.

In my mind you will do much better in the long run by seeking to optimise your return instead of maximising it. There is a subtle, but profound difference.

To become successful in this world you need to have an abundance mentality.

I've built my successful national businesses on the platform of keeping the other party's interest in mind, negotiating firmly but fairly and seeking win-win relationships and transactions. Sure I want to get all that I can, but not without leaving something on the table for the other party. I understand that you must give to get, you must be generous in rewarding people who have added value and I consider cost in the proper context of value received.

To build your multi-million dollar property investment portfolio you'll need to surround yourself with a good team and that's going to be hard to do if you enjoy upsetting people, burning bridges and leaving the other party angry and bitter.

Profiting from property is very much dependent on having good relationships with people who have access to the knowledge, services and opportunities you need. When you do things that agitate, infuriate and otherwise annoy your service providers, advisors and consultants, you lessen their desire to help you.

Some people make a high priority of saving money, but when you look to increase your profits by squeezing others you create unproductive outcomes. If you're serious about acquiring wealth from real estate and being in the property business for the long haul, be mindful of your reputation in the marketplace. Build it carefully and protect it jealously.

If you develop a reputation for dealing fairly then agents, consultants and business partners will line up to do business with you. If you have the reputation of trying to extract every last cent and taking advantage of others whenever you have a chance, you'll have a long hard road ahead of you.

As always – it's your choice.

TEMPORARY INSANITY

THE EMOTIONS OF BUYING AND SELLING AND HOW TO MASTER THEM

When it comes to buying or selling real estate many people suffer from a form of temporary insanity, and those who don't prepare themselves will suffer the most.

Think about it — an investment property is probably the most expensive item most of us will ever buy after our home. So when it comes time to transact a property deal it is a significant commitment and it's normal to be hit with some conflicting emotions.

On the one hand you might feel anticipation and the excitement of a potential dream about to come true. On the other hand, there will almost certainly be some doubts as to whether you're doing the right thing.

Just the thought of committing to a huge loan can be frightening. And, of course, there's always the fear that you're putting all your eggs in one basket. What if you are buying the wrong property? What if there's a better buy lurking around the corner coming up for sale the day after you sign the contract?

If you've ever watched any of the property reality TV shows, you'll have seen many entertaining examples of insanity and paranoia overcoming otherwise intelligent people.

During booms many buyers become frightened that they'll miss out on the amazing gains all around them, and that the rising market will soon be out of their reach if they don't buy — and quickly! They are driven by fear (of losing out) and greed. They also experience the disappointment of losing out when others feel the same way and are willing to pay crazy prices and outbid them.

There are also plenty of emotions on the other side of the fence — sellers can often have their hearts in their mouths and be emotionally vulnerable.

"GUILTY YOUR HONOUR!"

The reality is that you can expect to feel butterflies and fear and at times you'll be blinded by adrenalin. It's important to expect and prepare yourself for some of these powerful emotions and be equipped with strategies to cope so you don't find yourself guilty of crimes against your investing strategy, with nothing but a plea of temporary insanity to offer!

So let's take a look at a few of the unpleasant conditions experiences by both novice and seasoned property investors that could lay their best laid plans to rest.

Ailment #1: Buyer's remorse

Buyer's remorse is that feeling you get when you say to yourself, "I've done the wrong thing… I've spent too much… I should have bought the other one… I should have bought a different colour".

It is a normal psychological reaction after making any large purchase. It often happens after buying a new car, or expensive clothes, and it's particularly prevalent in property.

Forty-eight hours after you've signed the contract you'll start to hear from friends or family or see in the media that maybe you should have bought elsewhere, or perhaps you paid too much, or it was possibly the wrong time to buy.

To make matters worse, you'll probably check the Internet and notice other properties advertised that sound even better than the one you got so enthusiastic about and bought.

It doesn't seem to take much to suddenly swing your emotions from excitement to despair.

Good salespeople, and particularly good real estate agents, recognise how frequently purchasers experience buyer's remorse and try to counter it by giving them "post-purchase reassurance".

The clothing salesman will tell you "that colour really suits you… it makes you look 10 years younger". They've been taught to say this after the sale, when you figure they have nothing more to gain — they've already made the sale and their commission, so they must be telling the truth.

This is a trick all good sales people know and clever real estate agents will often try to reassure you by telling you how well you bought, or how cleverly you bid at the auction. They often send you a letter that will arrive two to three days after your purchase, just at the right time to reassure you, telling you how happy they are you bought the property and how lucky you were.

Fact is: you'll be less likely to suffer from buyer's remorse if you've stuck to your investment strategy, researched property values in your "investment comfort zone" and made a sensible offer based on this information.

Ailment #2: The desperate purchase

I've often seen buyers become so desperate that they end up buying a property that doesn't really fit of their investment criteria, or they pay more for a property than they know it is worth, just for the sake of buying something. Buying anything. It's called FOMO — Fear Of Missing Out.

You tend to see this type of behaviour during boom times, especially after the frustration of missing out on a few good deals. Investors fear they're missing out on the market gains or are just desperately short of patience and want their mad property hunt over and done with.

Ailment #3: I see opportunities!

The other interesting emotional state to watch out for is what I call "projection". It's like the budding psychiatrist who first learns about a mental disorder and begins to see it in everyone, while in truth it's merely a projection of his own focus on the condition.

In an investment context, once you've discovered new techniques, strategies or lucrative areas you may experience an overwhelming urge to grasp all the "apparent" opportunities suddenly jumping out at you.

Truth is these opportunities were always there; the only difference is that as an inexperienced investor you didn't have the ability to see them, so they went unnoticed.

When you start to see opportunities everywhere this can be dangerous. Novice investors who lack perspective often jump at the first deal that looks good, for the wrong reasons. That's why I suggest using my 6 Stranded Strategic Approach to investment — you'll be supported by a number of different pillars to minimise your risk.

Ailment #4: Stop the bus, I want to get off!

One of the worst mistakes you can make in property investing is to lose your nerve and bail out at the wrong time. At the time of writing this edition my book, there's a continual conveyor belt of negative economic commentary and negative forecasts. And I'm sure it's making some investors wonder what they should do.

But interestingly it was much the same when I wrote the fourth edition in 2012, the third edition in 2009 and the original book in 2006. Each time the media was focusing on the on the negative side of things.

Property investment is a long tern affair — so don't make long term investment decisions based on short term cyclical events, because these too shall pass.

Ailment #5: Surround yourself with support — alone and you're in trouble

INSIDER TIP

If you are the smartest person in your team you are in trouble.

If you're like me you are regularly reading comments in the media about how it's a bad time to invest in property or you've heard from friends and family how risky it is investing in property.

The problem is that you tend to get what you focus on in life and with many investors concentrating on the bad news and the financial woes, they are setting themselves up for failure. Their doubts become self-fulfilling because they have picked up their bats and balls and gone home — they have stopped playing the game.

The good news however is that the same events that have made many feel uncertain about their financial future will produce some of the best opportunities property investors will experience in their lifetime. Strategic investors are not only adapting to the change; they are exploiting it. During difficult economic times the majority of people will sit on the sidelines feeling sorry for themselves, while some investors will think counter-cyclically and look for and capitalise on investment opportunities created by the change.

If you are wondering how these successful investors remain positive in negative times, it's because they have the knowledge and experience of past property cycles; they understand the nature of economic and property cycles and they gain strength by surrounding themselves by the supportive people. There is no such thing as a self-made multi-millionaire and successful investors become so by surrounding themselves with mentors, supportive friends and a team of advisors.

Having a good team reduces your risk, increases your knowledge and gives you access to ideas, opportunities and funds you would never have on your own. I have found that collective knowledge and experience lowers risk when investing.

When first starting your journey into wealth creation, you will very likely be working alone. You'll be flying solo in learning, researching and finding investment opportunities. That's fine; you've got to start somewhere. However, putting the right team together will accelerate your learning and, more importantly, it will accelerate your wealth accumulation. As a property investor your team is likely to consist of a tax savvy accountant, a proficient mortgage broker, a smart solicitor and an independent Property Strategist.

It's going to take time and energy to put the right team together, but it's a necessary part of learning and growing as an investor. What might take the typical investor ten years or more to learn, you can learn in one or two years with the right team in place.

Successful investors also understand that having a mentor, someone who has already achieved what they want to achieve, is vital. Mentors have been critical in my success – they have helped me see things that I couldn't see. They identified my blind spots, encouraged me to think differently and made me accountable for my decisions.

I've also found one of the keys to becoming a successful investor is finding the right friends and network who can provide you with support and encouragement along the way.

It's no coincidence that our peers, the people we hang around with, have a great deal of influence over us by giving us comfort, support and security. We are social beings that like to belong to groups and if you think about it, since the people we hang around with have such a profound impact on our personal values and our priorities, it's important that we associate with supportive and optimistic people as we move along the path towards a better life.

Unfortunately, the world is full of pessimistic people who often keep us from moving forward. One of the mistakes I've seen people make on their road to investment success is listening to all the critics along the way. They put too much emphasis on the senseless advice of unsuccessful people.

It's important to surround yourself with safe and supportive people because one of the ways we process information while we're moving through our investment journey is by talking about what we're experiencing. Without safe people who are encouraging you, you won't have anyone to bounce your ideas off. The influence of supportive people who spur us on to believe in ourselves and take positive steps can make all the difference to help us transform our lives for the better.

Ailment #6: The motivated seller

Just as emotions make buyers go a little loopy at times, when somebody is super-motivated to sell, they sometimes suffer from a form of temporary insanity.

When you find property bargains you'll usually find that at their source is a highly motivated seller. If, for some reason, a seller gets really emotionally "down" on their property; reason and sound planning often seems to fly out the window as emotions take over.

When I analyse my own successes, I've found that the best property deals I've made all involved dealing with motivated sellers.

My Jaguar and my pride

In the early '90s I had a beautiful Jaguar car and, as any enthusiast will tell you, in those days as Jags got older they developed lots of problems.

When mine was a few years old things started to go wrong.

After a lot of small problems, the water pump went one week, a few weeks later it was the distributor, and after that it was the battery and I'd had enough — I decided to sell the car. Initially I wanted $50,000 for it but after advertising for a few weeks and not receiving any response I took it to a local dealer, who only offered me $40,000.

This was my Jaguar, my pride and joy; I wasn't going to sell it to just anybody for $40,000. It had cost me more than three times that amount a few years earlier!

After a few more weeks of advertising it in the paper, a few other things started to go wrong. This time the boot wouldn't unlock. I had finally reached the point where I was totally fed up.

"What a piece of junk!" I'd complain to my friends and family, "I've got to get rid of this garbage heap, it's falling apart. What I need is a new car."

I now know that the instant I began to think these thoughts I'd ceased to be objective.

My emotions were telling me the old car was nearly worthless. I went back to the dealer who was now not even prepared to offer me $40,000. He said the car was only worth $37,000. I guess I'd unknowingly set the perfect stage for the dealer to make a quick and easy profit. I sold it to him and he on-sold it to somebody else for almost $10,000 more within a few weeks.

He picked up my beautiful old Jag for a bargain because I lost the plot and he knew he'd found a motivated seller.

Interestingly today, 20 years later, I again own a Jaguar. Clearly I buy my cars with my heart rather than my head.

The same thing happens with property but the profits you can make or lose can be a lot higher.

What a dumb offer

Many years ago I saw an old house that was on the market for a month or so. It was listed for a high price but to me it was really only worth the land it was sitting on — I saw it as a potential three-unit site.

The property was listed at $270,000 (remember this was a long, long time ago) and I offered 20% less than the asking price; $230,000. Many would say that this was a dumb offer and, of course, the vendor rejected it initially. I told the agent that the offer still stood and to come back to me if anything changed.

Five or six weeks went past and the agent rang back and asked if I was still interested. I told him my offer still stood. In the intervening time the property had been put up for auction, passed in and failed to sell.

I later found out that the vendor was an elderly lady and that she had gone to a nursing home, leaving the house standing vacant.

WHEN ARE PEOPLE TRANSFORMED INTO MOTIVATED SELLERS?

When did this lady become a really motivated seller?

Obviously not when I put in my first offer. I guess not when the property was passed in at auction for a higher price than I offered her, but probably when she eventually had to go into a nursing home. I was not taking advantage of her, I made her an offer that allowed her to realise a profit on her home. It was probably the only genuine offer she received.

What this means is that if you're in the right place at the right time, you can take advantage of the eagerness of motivated sellers and possibly pick up real savings. With 10 or

15%savings representing tens of thousands of dollars, isn't it well worth your time to scout out a motivated seller?

You might think this was a rare situation, but it's not really unusual. Many of the properties I've bought have been purchased after seeking out and finding motivated sellers.

There is no substitute for doing your homework and getting to know the prices in your investment comfort zone. If you don't do this, you could be offered a super deal and never recognise it for what it is or you could end up paying too much for a property. Knowing the prices in your patch will help you know when a seller is truly motivated or just pretending to be. The hours you spend getting to know prices and values will reward you handsomely.

The first time you buy a property $25,000 or $50,000 below its value, people will call you lucky, but you'll know better. You will know you have created your own luck.

HOW DO YOU FIND THEM?

Some people pretend to be motivated sellers when they're not, and agents will often spin a line just to get a buyer's attention. Be sceptical when listening to reasons sellers give when selling. Truly motivated sellers don't usually announce that they're keen. The circumstances generally tell the full story and they try to play down their eagerness.

People are often motivated to sell quickly for personal reasons, not economic ones. There are many reasons why people are motivated to sell at less than the true value. Here are a few:

- **Death**: People who inherit property often don't want any further involvement with it. Often all they want to do is sell the property and split the proceeds amongst the beneficiaries.

- **Divorce or relationship problems**: Sometimes a home can be an emotional anchor that ties a person to a painful memory. When two people who are married or in a close relationship call it quits, it's not uncommon for a home to come up for sale — and a quick one at that.

- **Getting older**: For some older people it's necessary to downsize to a more manageable property. And when it's no longer possible to maintain a lifestyle and house because of old age and physical needs, then a new situation needs to be created quickly.

- **Relocation**: When a seller is moving and can't sell his house he's faced with potential double mortgage payments. This can make him a motivated seller and the closer it gets to a specific moving date, the more highly motivated the seller is going to be.

- **Financial difficulties**: Debt and money worries are a reality for many sellers.

- **Problems with tenants**: Another type of motivated seller is the landlord who wants out. Some just get tired of tenants, finances or property hassles and become very motivated to sell.

- **Repossession**: Mortgagee sales are typically ruthless if people hit financial problems and have their homes repossessed.

I am not suggesting that you take advantage of these people. Sometimes you'll be the only one making them an offer and this means you are helping them. There are myriad reasons and personal situations that can result in properties needing to be offloaded quickly. If you know your market values there are profits to be made from motivated sellers.

If you can find people with problems or problem properties and solve these problems, you will do well. The problem may be as simple as the vendor just wants to quit the property (like I did my car). That's easy to solve. Buy it at a bargain price.

Or the problem may be more complex as the property is run down. The solution may be a make-over or renovation that adds value.

Finding the people with problems usually means finding motivated vendors and buying below market price. Solving the problems usually means adding value to the properties and increasing its worth and your equity.

INSIDER TIP
Find motivated vendors and you could buy below market value. By solving their problems, you will be adding value and making money.

SUMMARY

It's important to realise that **most of us make the majority of our decisions emotionally rather than rationally**. We do listen, digest and react partially to facts, but under certain circumstances, such as those we've discussed in this chapter, emotions tend to over-ride our analytical minds. Many people are pushed to the point of saying, "I know I'm selling for much less than it's really worth but I just don't care. I want out and to be done with it!"

Discovering a motivated seller should not be your only reason to purchase. Obviously the property has to fit all your other selection criteria. By following the 6 Stranded Strategic Approach you take much of the emotion out of your decision-making and avoid the ailments so common among novices and undisciplined investors.

PART V

NUMBER CRUNCHING AND ADVANCED STRATEGIES

IN THE BEGINNER'S MIND THERE ARE FEW POSSIBILITIES.
IN THE MASTER'S MIND THERE ARE MANY.
– *SHUNRYU SUZUKI ROSHI*

THE TAX ADVANTAGES OF RESIDENTIAL PROPERTY

Just in case you need any further incentive to embrace real estate investing, how about this: our Government wants you to be a real estate investor, even though at times they make it hard to believe!

Luckily for us, the Government recognises that private property investors play an important role in Australia's housing market and economy — that's why there are so many tax advantages available to property investors. In this chapter we're going to investigate some of these perks and how they work.

Now I don't profess to be an expert on taxation legislation and I strongly advise that you seek professional advice from a good accountant. While it's not my intention to give you specific instruction on how to formulate and structure your portfolio in order to maximise the tax benefits, I only want to point out a few of the strategies that the rich use in order to legally reduce their tax bill.

This is because one of the big differences between the rich and the average Australian is how they use tax effective assets to accumulate their wealth. This dramatically enhances the strategies that I've already outlined in this book.

Strategic investors don't just earn compound returns, but accumulate their wealth in a tax-deferred or tax-free environment, making their property portfolio grow even faster.

DIFFERENT STROKES FOR DIFFERENT FOLKS

In Australia, the average salary earner makes their money, hands some over to the government and then gets to spend whatever is left over. The rich however, have worked out how to make their money, spend the amount they choose on legitimate expenses (such as property investment) and then pay tax on whatever is left over.

Have a look at the following figures to see what I mean:

Salary earner		Rich investor	
Income	$100,000	Income	$100,000
		Spend on legitimate expenses	$40,000
		Taxable income	$60,000
Tax paid	$32,000	Tax paid (approx)	$14,800
Net income	$68,000	Net income	$45,200
Spending capacity	$68,000	Spending capacity	$85,200

You can see by this example that simply by being able to spend money on legitimate, claimable expenses (such as investment), the strategic investor has pocketed an extra $17,200 from the same initial income as the salary earner (who handed that $17,200 over to the tax man).

THE TWO MAIN TAX TYPES

When you invest in property, there are two main types of tax that have the potential to affect your profits. The first type, and one that we all know about because we pay it whenever we earn money, is income tax. That is a portion of the income you derive from employment, or investment or any other form of taxable payment you receive from any source.

The second tax that impacts property investors is *Capital Gains Tax* (CGT). As you're aware, a good property investment will appreciate in value over time. When you sell the property, the amount it has increased by since you bought it — the capital gain — is subject to tax (Capital Gains Tax).

CGT is payable on any property you sell where the capital gain itself is more than $30,000, except when it's your own home. The applicable rate of CGT is the same as your income tax rate, however if you own the investment property for more than 12 months, you get a 50% discount on the capital gain. In other words, if you sold a property after achieving a capital gain of $50,000 more than 12 months after the initial purchase, the applicable CGT would be calculated on a capital gain of $25,000.

Of course my property investment strategy entails rarely selling your assets. By holding onto your properties for as long as possible, you will minimise your CGT obligations, as it's only when you sell that this tax is payable.

Structuring your portfolio in the correct way can greatly reduce the amount of income tax and CGT that you might have to hand over to the government. I won't be discussing the various structures in this book, but there's a whole section on this topic in my book *What Every Property Investor Needs to Know about Finance, Tax and the Law* (www.financialfluency.com.au). There is however, a lot of other tax stuff I'm going to discuss so let's start with...

THE TAXATION PROS OF PROPERTY

Property investment is privileged with many legitimate tax deductions that allow you to boost your portfolio without any tax penalties. The one piece of advice I want you to heed is that you should never make an investment to save tax. I would also like to stress that all of the tax reduction strategies you employ must be legitimate. It's very difficult to spend your money from a prison cell!

So with these words of warning in mind, let's have a look at how property can minimise your tax obligations and maximise your tax benefits.

LEVERAGE AND COMPOUNDING

I've already explained how important leverage and compounding are to growing your asset base.

Of course for leverage you must borrow and pay interest. While the interest payable on your own home mortgage is not tax deductible, the interest on your property investment is.

While some investors are keen to make a fast buck and sell their properties and make a short term gain, those who hold on to their assets for the long term don't have to pay tax on their capital gain. Yet they can access their funds by borrowing against the increased value of their property and use the money as a deposit to buy more property – leveraging.

In other words, you can have your cake and eat it too. You maximise the profit generating potential of your properties by using their increasing value to buy even more investments, and you never have to pay tax on any of those profits, unless you sell.

Now here's the thing... investing in property offers a special type of compounding – the capital growth (increase in value of your property) that you achieve is not taxed, which means you are left with a larger asset on which to base your compounding the following year.

Let's look at this principle in more detail by reviewing three examples:

Example 1: Your investment dollar doubles in value every year and no tax is payable

Let's see what would happen if you found an investment that could double in value every year. As the table below indicates, after doubling every year for 20 years with no tax payable your dollar has compounded to over $1 million.

	Year	Value
At end of year...	0 (i.e. now)	$1
	1	$2
	2	$4
	3	$8
	4	$16
	5	$32
	6	$64
	7	$128
	8	$256
	9	$512
	10	$1,024
	11	$2,048
	12	$4,096
	13	$8,192
	14	$16,384
	15	$32,768
	16	$65,536
	17	$131,072
	18	$262,144
	19	$524,288
	20	$1,048,576

> After doubling every year for 20 years with no tax payable, your dollar has compounded to over $1,000,000.

Example 2: Your investment dollar doubles in value every year and you pay 35% tax annually

Of course the example above doesn't take income tax into account and usually when you earn income, the government expects you to pay tax. So let's see what would happen with the same investment return if you had to pay tax at the rate of 35% of your earnings each year.

As you can see from the table below, after 20 years your dollar has only compounded to around $22,370 because of the effects of income tax, and it takes another seven years for you to accumulate the $1 million you made in the first example.

	Year	Pre-Tax Value	Tax Paid	Post-Tax Value	
At end of year…	0 (i.e. now)	$1.00		$1.00	
	1	$2.00	$0.35	$1.65	
	2	$3.30	$0.58	$2.72	
	3	$5.45	$0.95	$4.49	
	4	$8.98	$1.57	$7.41	
	5	$14.82	$2.59	$12.23	
	6	$24.46	$4.28	$20.18	
	7	$40.36	$7.06	$33.30	
	8	$66.59	$11.65	$54.94	
	9	$109.88	$19.23	$90.65	
	10	$181.29	$31.73	$149.57	
	11	$299.14	$52.35	$246.79	
	12	$493.58	$86.38	$407.20	
	13	$814.40	$ 142.52	$671.88	
	14	$1,343.76	$ 235.16	$1,108.60	After 20 years, your dollar has only compounded to around $22,370
	15	$2,217.20	$ 388.01	$1,829.19	
	16	$3,658.38	$ 640.22	$3,018.17	
	17	$6,036.33	$1,056.36	$4,979.97	
	18	$9,959.95	$1,742.99	$8,216.96	
	19	$16,433.91	$2,875.93	$13,557.98	
	20	**$27,115.96**	**$4,746.29**	**$22,370.66**	It takes more than another 7 years for your dollar taxed at 35% to compound to $1,000,000
	21	$44,741.33	$7,829.73	$36,911.60	
	22	$73,823.19	$12,919.03	$60,904.13	
	23	$121,808.27	$21,316.45	$100,491.82	
	24	$200,983.64	$35,172.14	$165,811.50	
	25	$331,623.01	$58,034.03	$273,588.98	
	26	$547,177.97	$95,756.14	$451,421.82	
	27	$902,843.64	$157,997.64	$744,846.01	
	28	$1,489,692.01	$260,696.10	**$1,228,995.91**	

Boy, does taxing your profits make a difference! Without paying tax (as in the first example) your investments grow much, much faster.

This means that if you can find a type of investment that increases in value (compounds) and on which you don't have to pay tax on this compounding profit, you will be way ahead of the pack. That's the beauty of residential property investment – you don't pay tax on the increasing value of your property unless you sell it.

But what if you did want to sell your properties down the track? Let's look at another example to highlight this scenario.

Example 3: Your investment dollar doubles in value every year, but your 35% tax is payable only in the final year

If you buy an investment property, your capital growth isn't taxed unless you sell that property. Using this principle and assuming you won't sell your property until the final year of the exercise, this means that you will only pay tax in the final year and in the meantime (as your property's value has been increasing), your dollar's compounding has been uninhibited.

Look at the table below and then compare it to the previous one. Between years 27 and 28, your dollar value has compounded past $200 million. After 35% tax is paid on this amount, the after-tax value equates to $130 million compared to just over $1 million in the previous example.

	Year	Pre-Tax Value	Tax Paid	Post-Tax Value
At end of year...	0 (i.e. now)	$ 1		
	1	$ 2		
	2	$ 4		
	3	$ 8		
	4	$16		
	5	$32		
	6	$64		
	7	$128		
	8	$256		
	9	$512		
	10	$1,024		
	11	$2,048		
	12	$4,096		
	13	$8,192		
	14	$ 16,384		
	15	$ 32,768		
	16	$ 65,536		
	17	$131,072		
	18	$262,144	With tax only paid in the final year, your dollar's compounding is uninhibited. Between the 27th and 28th years, your dollar value has compounded past $200 million. After 35% tax is paid on this amount, the after-tax value equates to $130 million.	
	19	$524,288		
	20	$1,048,576		
	21	$2,097,152		
	22	$4,194,304		
	23	$8,388,608		
	24	$16,777,216		
	25	$33,554,432		
	26	$67,108,864		↓
	27	**$134,217,728**	$46,976,205	**$87,241,523**
	28	**$267,435,456**	$93,952,410	**$174,483,046**

These examples clearly illustrate the benefits of using residential property to grow your Cash

Machine. It highlights the fact that, not only is compounding a powerful tool in the sense that it allows you to leverage into even more high-growth assets, it also represents tax-free profits that can accelerate your wealth accumulation to breakneck speeds.

MORE TAX BENEFITS FOR PROPERTY INVESTORS

Okay, so now that you understand the power of compounding in a tax-free environment, let's examine some other tax benefits of owning investment properties. These largely fit into four main categories:

1. **Tax deductions** – Most investors already know a lot about deductions.

2. **Depreciation allowances** – Many investors don't fully understand these benefits, but depreciation allowances can deliver up to one-third of your rental income tax-free.

3. **Negative gearing** – Often investors subsidise their loss-making properties, gaining tax breaks while capital growth works its magic.

4. **Special benefits** – Some would call these "tax loopholes" but they are really, perfectly legal advanced strategies that allow serious real estate investors to get the most from their property investments.

Let's take a look at these in more detail:

1. TAX DEDUCTIONS

If you are in the business of owning investment properties that earn you taxable income, you are able to claim legitimate costs necessary for earning that income. These include, but are not limited to:

Rental expenses

You can claim a deduction for some of the expenses you incur for the period your property is rented or available for rent. These include:

- Advertising costs to find tenants,
- Body corporate fees,
- Cleaning costs,
- Council rates,
- Electricity and gas not paid by the tenant,
- Gardening and lawn mowing,
- Insurance – including the building, contents and public liability,
- Interest on your loans,

- Land tax,
- Legal expenses,
- Managing agent's fees and commissions,
- Pest control costs,
- Quantity surveyor's fees,
- Repairs and maintenance,
- Secretarial and book-keeping costs,
- Stationery and postage expenses,
- Telephone bills,
- Tax-related expenses,
- Travel and car expenses for rent collection,
- Costs incurred in inspecting or maintaining your property (recently the government has disallowed interstate travel expenses for inspecting your investments)
- Water charges.

You can also claim your borrowing costs as a tax deduction. That is, the fee that you pay the bank when you set up your loan, loan application fees, stamp duty on mortgages, and even mortgage insurance. Plus, you can claim other loan establishment costs over the term of the loan, or five years, whichever is less.

Interest deductions

Most investors borrow against an asset they already own to fund the deposit for their investment properties, often using the equity in their own homes.

Even if you borrow using your home as collateral and this, of course, is not an income-earning property, the interest expense is deductible for income tax purposes because you're using the funds you borrow to purchase an income-producing asset.

This interest can be deducted against your total income, be it from investment properties or the salary from your day job. You see, any expense that's incurred in the process of generating income is deductible against your total income for tax purposes and interest on your loans is a major expense.

2. BUILDING DEPRECIATION

The tax deductions I have discussed so far all involve you spending money. Now let's look at a deduction that doesn't cost you anything directly out-of-pocket — depreciation allowances. These represent some of the best "tax loopholes" available to property investors, as they are legitimate tax deductions that don't cost you a cent!

Even though we know that property tends to go up in value over time, the Tax Office lets us pretend that it actually goes down in value. But on 9 May 2017, the Federal Treasurer changed what investors can claim depreciation for. In essence, plant and equipment deductions would no longer exist for second-hand properties.

To put it another way, if after that date you buy an investment property that's not brand new, you won't be able to claim deductions on blinds, carpets, cooktops, hot water systems, ovens and the like. The only way you'll receive these plant and equipment deductions is through a brand-new purchase or installing the asset yourself such as with a renovation.

The changes further complicate matters by asserting that even if you buy new, if one day you decide to live in the property, there will be zero plant and equipment deductions available from that day forward.

The good news is that there are still thousands of dollars to be claimed by property investors, as there has been no change to capital works deductions, a claim available for the structure of a building and fixed assets such as doors, basins, windows or retaining walls.

These deductions typically make up between 85 to 90% of an investor's total claimable amount.

Previously existing depreciation legislation will be grandfathered, which means investors who already made a purchase prior to this date can continue to claim depreciation deductions as per before.

A little known fact

When you eventually sell your property you'll have to add the depreciation you've claimed back to the capital base used for calculating CGT. In other words, you can't get it both ways — but don't let this put you off. Firstly, you've had benefit of the cash flow from your lower tax rate over the years. And secondly — my preferred strategy is to never sell.

---

3. NEGATIVE GEARING

Negative gearing is when your rental income doesn't cover the property expenses, such as interest payments, agent's commission, maintenance etc. This negative result — your shortfall after all deductions including interest that come off your rental income — can be applied to other income, such as your salary, to reduce your total tax liability.

In the past, negative gearing became all the rage to help reduce the tax bill of many high-income earners. These tax savings, when coupled with leveraged growth, can have dazzling results.

Watch out!

You must be cautious about negative gearing because it involves producing a loss, and even though after-tax this loss is minimised, it is still a loss and is only recaptured if the value of your property grows substantially. If your property doesn't increase in value, no amount of tax deductions will overcome the fact that you are subsidising the investment.

So how do you cope with negative cash flow?

Of course investing in negatively geared, high-growth property means you have to cover the cash flow shortfall each month.

One way of doing this is to set up the correct loan structure. An offset account or a line of credit could be used to supplement the rental, in order to pay the interest on the investment loan and property expenses. This buys an investor time.

The line of credit is often set up to cover the shortfall for three or more years, until the property's value grows sufficiently to refinance the loan out of the extra equity.

To use this investment strategy correct asset selection is critical, because to make it worthwhile you need the property's value to increase significantly more than your outstanding loan balance increases.

This means that you need to be investing in high quality assets, so that you can maximise the chances of enjoying strong capital growth.

This strategy is not without risks

The four main risks of negative gearing are:

1. *Poor capital growth* — that's why correct asset selection is so important.
2. *Interest rate increases* — which can be addressed by fixing interest rates on some or all of your debt.
3. *Poor rental growth* — which highlights the importance of owning properties that will be in continuous strong demand by a wide tenant demographic.
4. *Lack of financial discipline* — never use your financial buffers for anything other than covering your property-related expenses.

How the Tax Office will help you fund the ongoing cash shortfall

Paying the cash shortfall on a negatively geared property through the year could be a burden, even though you expect a large tax refund at the end of the year, but there is even a way the taxman will help you to do this.

There is a variation provision in the Tax Act, whereby as soon as you purchase your property you can arrange to reduce the tax being deducted from your salary.

Either you or your accountant can complete an "Income Tax Withholding Variation Form" (*Section 15/15 form*), which is a short questionnaire asking details of your salary income, the rent that you expect to receive, the expenses that you expect to pay (including the non-cash deductions) and the net loss expected on the investment.

You can simply download one from the ATO website (www.ato.gov.au).

You then mail this completed form to the Tax Office and usually within 14 days you will receive a letter, authorising the amount of tax deducted from your PAYG income to be reduced by the amount of annual cash shortfall you expect to have from your investment property, divided by the number of pay periods in a year.

All you do is hand this letter to your employer or, if you are self-employed, to your book-keeper, and he or she will immediately reduce the tax deducted from your pay by the appropriate amount.

Of course, should your estimates be inaccurate you will have to pay or be refunded the difference when you submit your annual tax return.

At the time of writing this edition of my book, the Labor Opposition party is proposing to remove negative gearing and change the level of exemptions for CGT. While this will fiddle around the edges a bit, it won't change my investment strategy which is capital growth focused and not tax focused.

4. SPECIAL BENEFITS

As you start growing your property portfolio and become a serious investor, you can begin running your investments as a business and a whole range of new "tax loop holes" will open up for you.

Your property business does not have to be your full-time occupation in order to claim these benefits either. You could still be growing your property business in your spare time, while holding down your regular day job. But you are going to have to start thinking like a business owner and not an employee.

Most employees are treated under a system in which they:

1. Earn money,

2. Pay tax, and

3. Spend what's left over.

As a business owner you can take advantage of legal "tax loopholes" to spend before you pay tax, effectively reducing your taxable income massively! The new order is:

1. Earn your money,

2. Spend on legitimately growing and improving your investing business, and

3. Deduct this amount from profits and only pay tax on what's left!

In other words, there are many items that you can purchase with before-tax dollars. Wouldn't it be great to only pay tax on the money that you've got left after you spend what you want and need?

I hope that you can see the power of this concept.

The wealthy have more to invest than the average person because they earn their income, spend and invest their money and only pay tax on what is left, as opposed to the average person who earns their income, pay tax and spend what is left.

Before you consider these suggestions, you must speak with your tax adviser. These sorts of deductions work for me because I own a number of companies and trusts that earn considerable income through property investment, and my property business is clearly my main source of income. Some of these deductions may not be available to investors who only have one property and hand out management of that property to an agent.

INSIDER TIP

The wealthy have more to invest than the average person because they earn their income, spend and invest their money and only pay tax on what is left, as opposed to the average person who earns their income, pay tax and spend what is left.

As your property portfolio becomes larger, or if you actively manage your portfolio by overseeing your property managers, then more and more deductions will apply to you. When in doubt, consult your tax adviser for clarification of which deductions are available.

Let's take a look at some of these additional deductions.

Home office

You may be able to deduct a portion of your home as a tax deduction. In order to take the home office deduction you will need to have a portion of your home used exclusively for business purposes. You can't simply use a corner of your kitchen table and call it a home office. You need to have a spot that's used only for business and a place where you regularly conduct some kind of business.

If this applies to you, you may be able to take a pro-rata portion of your home-related expenses including rent or mortgage interest, taxes, insurance, utilities and maintenance. The disadvantage of this is you would lose that same proportion of the capital gains tax exemption if you sell your home.

Car

As a serious property investor your car will be a critical part of your real estate investment business, as you do the legwork so essential to investing success. The business use of your car will be deductible in one of a number of ways; one of the simplest is to keep a logbook of business use and to calculate the proportion of use that is exclusively for business purposes. This can then be deducted. You should discuss the most suitable way of doing this with your tax accountant.

Education

A successful real estate investor is always seeking an edge and looking for educational opportunities that might create a competitive advantage or insight. You may be able to deduct the cost of seminars, magazine subscriptions and courses that help make you a better-informed investor.

Children

I have four adult children and I know that when they lived at home with us, they cost me a small fortune. Wouldn't it be great to pay some of their expenses with before-tax money by employing them to perform tasks for your business? This is also a great way to give them some meaningful employment and pass on real-life business education, as well as help them to understand what you do.

Be careful here though, because these tasks need to be legitimate and age-appropriate and, of course, you wouldn't risk handing over important work to your kids if you didn't think that they were capable of contributing.

It would be unreasonable to ask your two-year old daughter to maintain your website, but it could be quite reasonable to ask your 15-year-old son to file and maintain your paperwork and computer systems. I know my sons know more about computers than I do!

Unusual tax deductions

There are some further "loopholes" available to you once you become a serious property investor and run a property investment business. Just like many other businesses, you could give presents, or incentives, or amenities for the staff of your property investment business.

The staff and directors of your business may of course include you, your wife and your children.

Big companies like David Jones can give incentive hampers to their staff at Christmas time. Your company may also provide presents to staff, as long as they are infrequent and less than $300. It could provide them with cinema tickets as a "thank you" for their good work, or flowers for the reception of your business or gift vouchers.

Your business may need to provide newspapers for the office, or pictures and prints for display in the office area. You probably need magazines or music to brighten the office environment.

The ideas are endless, but again, please be careful and take the time to discuss them with your accountant.

Tax avoidance is illegal in Australia and, of course, there is nothing wrong with paying a fair share of tax to utilise the roads, hospitals and infrastructure that we enjoy in our society.

However, legal tax minimisation is a different story. All investors are well within their rights to look for ways to minimise taxes payable, provided they stay within the rules of our taxation system. After all, minimising taxes is an important part of maximising returns!

HIDDEN SURPRISES AND HOW TO PROTECT YOURSELF FROM THEM

Everybody loves a surprise, right? While in general life this may be true, when it comes to property investing, nothing could be further from the truth! Give me a predictable, stable environment and I'll learn to use it to my advantage. In a very real sense, unexpected surprises are the only things standing between a well-intentioned investor and an expected profit.

I'd like to share some insights with you so you can prepare yourself and eliminate many of the surprises investors encounter.

For example, when budgeting for an investment property many investors forget the hidden costs, which could easily add up to 5% of the purchase price. Sometimes you can borrow these expenses as part of your investment loan, in which case the interest will be tax-deductible. However the costs themselves are not, in most cases, tax-deductible. These will be added to the cost of purchasing your properties and accounted for in any capital gains tax if you eventually sell the property.

Here are a few of the extras you can expect to pay for.

STAMP DUTY ON THE PURCHASE

The state and territory governments charge stamp duty whenever the ownership of a property is transferred. The rate varies from state to state and is paid by the purchaser on or before settlement of the property. Stamp duty will usually be the largest of all costs associated with the purchase of your property and the amount payable is calculated on the property purchase price.

There are two other government fees to take into account:

- *Transfer of registration fee* — this is a fee charged by the government of your state to cover the transfer of the title of your new property.
- *Stamp duty on mortgage* — this is calculated on the loan amount you want to borrow, but has been abolished in some states.

LEGAL FEES AND DISBURSEMENTS

"Conveyancing" is the fancy term for the transfer of the right of ownership of a property from the seller to the buyer. It is a complicated process that is usually handled by a solicitor or conveyancer, and obviously their services will incur a charge.

I have seen problems arise from what would seem to be the simplest of conveyances. What you see isn't always what you get and the things that can go wrong are not necessarily obvious until all the documents are checked thoroughly. For example:

- I have come across properties with a covenant on the title limiting what you can build on it and even the type of materials that could be used.

- A client almost bought a property where the adjoining owner thought he had the right to use the driveway to access his own property.

- I have bought properties where many years of council fees had been left unpaid by the previous owner.

- I found a property where a government department had the right to take up some of the front yard to widen its road.

Still not convinced? Did you know that the person whose name is on the contract as the vendor may not necessarily have the right to sell the property? The ultimate buyer's nightmare would be to discover that this was the situation, after already signing a contract. And I can tell you this has really happened!

Moira's nightmare

Moira purchased an investment property at a great price, but found out through her solicitor, that two people, a mother and daughter, owned the property (in other words, they both had their names on the title).

Interestingly, only the mother had signed the contract of sale. The reason for this was that the daughter had gone bankrupt. This probably was part of the reason they were selling the property.

The problem was that the daughter had no right to sell her share of the property as she was now bankrupt and her trustee-in-bankruptcy theoretically controlled her share. Naturally, the trustee wasn't willing to sell until he'd made his own investigations into whether it had achieved a good market price.

The end result for Moira was a number of weeks of uncertainty and the bargain that she thought she'd bought almost went down the drain. Only through a clever solicitor's intervention was the settlement of this sale effected.

Your solicitor will check the contract and the various certificates for unusual or unfavourable conditions and should be able to negotiate with the vendor's solicitor on your behalf.

You can expect that legal costs on a transaction will be in the order of $1,500 plus the cost of disbursements, such as enquiry certificates, registration fees and some report fees. These could add up to another $600 to $800.

While I do suggest you check the solicitor's fees, I can't emphasise enough that this is not an area where you should skimp on costs. Proper legal representation is imperative.

FINANCE COSTS

To cover the administrative costs of setting up your loan, most lending institutions will charge you fees of some sort. Many investors choose their loans based on the interest rates and forget to consider these other costs, which tend to fall into three broad categories:

1. Application or establishment fee.

2. Property valuation fees.

3. Lender's legal fees.

With all the competition for your business some lenders will negotiate these fees and may even waive them completely.

1. Application or establishment fee

Some lenders charge this fee to compensate for the time taken to assess your loan application. Some mortgage brokers will also charge you a flat fee or percentage of the loan for helping to find the loan for you, although this is much less common than it used to be.

2. Property valuation fees

Lenders usually require a valuation before they advance you money and often charge you for this. While this may cost you in the order of $300 to $400, if you're borrowing less than 80% of the value of the property you may be able to negotiate with the lender to waive this fee.

3. Lender's legal fees

Some lenders will charge you legal fees for preparing the mortgage documents and registering the title. These costs can be in the order of a few hundred dollars.

MORTGAGE INSURANCE

If you borrow more than 80% of the valuation of your property it is likely you will be required to obtain mortgage insurance. Be warned, this charge doesn't provide you with what you might immediately think when you hear the word "insurance". Instead, it actually covers the lender so that if you default on your loan repayments the lender will get its money from the insurer, and the insurer will then seek to recover the money from you.

Your lender will organise the mortgage insurance and charge you a fee on a sliding scale depending on how much equity you have in your property. The smaller your equity the higher your rate of mortgage insurance will be. Fortunately, this is a once-off payment for the term of the loan.

ADJUSTMENT TO COUNCIL RATES

You will need to refund the vendor for the remainder of any rates and taxes they have paid in advance to the local council.

INSPECTION COSTS

In addition to the nasty surprises you might find among the paperwork, legal matters and bank charges, there are lots of places for physical problems to hide in every property. In general it is worth paying for professionals to back up your own inspections, with a detailed report on potential problems just so you don't get any big surprises. You should consider:

1. Building reports

These are usually performed by building inspectors who will check the quality of workmanship and point out any repairs or capital works required to make the building safe and sound.

When you get a report on an older property don't panic if there's a long list of defects found. Just evaluate how much the essential repairs will cost and whether, with the added expense, the property is still worth consideration. Of course you could use the report as a bargaining tool.

2. Pest reports

Don't forget to have someone check for termites, borers or other pests. You don't want to find out that your floors need replacing due to termite damage when it's too late.

3. Strata report

If you're buying a unit in an apartment building, it is important to check the records of the owners' corporation. Check for disputes within the building or with the neighbours and any major repairs or issues that have been highlighted.

4. Surveyor's report

Your solicitor may ask you to get a survey of the property to confirm that what you see is in fact what you are getting. This is to ensure that the boundary fences are in the right place and there will not be disputes with your neighbours over who owns what. Don't be surprised if boundary fences are a few millimetres out of place, this is common and shouldn't cause any troubles. Surveys are appropriate if you buy a house or land but are not usually required if you buy an apartment.

ONGOING COSTS

When analysing the feasibility of any investment property there are two classes of costs to take into account. So far we've looked at the initial purchase costs, but of course the story doesn't end the day you settle on a contract. Let's now examine the ongoing costs that you'll need to consider in any budgeting analysis.

Building, contents and landlord insurance

Remember to include insurance costs in your budgeting. If your house burns down no rent comes in but you are still going to have to make your mortgage payments and you will have lost the value of your damaged or destroyed house. Insure the building and its contents, including carpets and window furnishings — it would be taking a massive risk to not do this.

If you are buying an apartment, the owners' corporate will usually insure the building but you should still insure your contents, including carpets, blinds, curtains, light fittings and cupboards.

You should also take out landlord's insurance, which covers you for the cost of your tenants defaulting or damaging your premises.

Property management expenses

These are the fees you pay agents to find tenants, to collect the rent and to take care of all ongoing tenant and property related problems. I wouldn't even consider cutting corners by taking on some of this work yourself.

Agents charge a percentage (usually around 7%) of the rent collected for ongoing management. They also charge around two weeks' rental when they find a new tenant for your property. Sure you may find a property manager who charges less, but a good property manager will add value to your investment and not really be an expense.

Ongoing Maintenance

If you've had a thorough property inspection before you bought your property, you shouldn't receive any major unexpected maintenance bills in the short term. But there are always little outgoings such as broken hot water systems, damaged door locks and other small maintenance items. This is where property managers should do their job and take care of these promptly for you. Of course, the costs will be passed on to you.

General Maintenance

If you are trying to do your budgets before you purchase your property, these costs are really difficult to quantify because they depend on your property's age, its construction, whether it is close to the sea and how well the tenants look after it.

That's why I strongly advocate having a cash flow buffer in an offset account or similar to cover these expenses, but remember that the cost of repairs is a tax deduction so your out-of-pocket cost may be significantly less.

Land tax

This state tax is basically a "wealth tax". The more properties you own, the more tax you pay and often at higher tax rate. This tax differs from state to state and is based on how much property you own on a particular date each year, which also differs from state to state.

Each state treats properties owned by trusts differently (they pay more land tax) and has its own thresholds before the tax applies so to find out how this tax may apply to you, check out one of the following web sites:

NSW   www.osr.nsw.gov.au

Vic   www.sro.vic.gov.au

Qld   www.osr.qld.gov.au

SA   www.revenuesa.sa.gov.au

WA   www.dtf.wa.gov.au

TAS   www.treasury.tas.gov.au

DO THE NUMBERS STACK UP?

Your goal as an investor should be to maximise cash returns on your investments, so now that we've discussed some of the costs involved in property investing, let's take a look at how we can assess a final result — will it all be worth it?

In any investing situation there is a direct relationship between risk and return. That is, if you're being asked to take more risk with your money, you have to expect a better return or you simply wouldn't bother. Similarly, if you insist on the safety of a cash savings account or term deposit, you can expect a limited return.

Since there are plenty of potential unknowns or risks associated with property investment, we would expect the rate of return to be higher than if we put our money in a bank deposit.

So, how do we analyse the returns on investment from one property compared to another?

When you deposit cash in a term deposit with a bank, you know what your investment return will be. At the end of the term you will get your money back plus the interest accrued, less the tax you pay.

So the rate of return on your investment is measured as a percentage, let's say 3%. After tax this will probably leave you with a real return of more like 2% (barely enough to cover inflation).

Property returns are much more complex but should be much more impressive. However, many people still make the mistake of analysing them in a similarly simplistic manner.

They would simply say that a property is worth $400,000 and earning $15,000 a year rent, so the yield or return could be described as 3.75% before tax.

This is measuring your investment returns using a capitalisation rate. While it is OK to analyse cash invested in a bank this way, this is far too simplistic for properties.

The return on an investment property comes to you in four ways:

1. **Capital appreciation** – the increase in the value of your property.

2. **Cash flows** – the rental income you receive.

3. **Increasing your equity** by improving or renovating your property.

4. **Tax benefits** – how much after-tax money is left in your pocket is more important than your pre-tax income.

If you don't consider all four elements in your analysis, you will come up with incorrect conclusions. To provide a true picture of the investment, any analysis of your investment property must examine the effects of the following variables on these four areas.

1. The deposit you pay.

2. Your settlement costs, such as legals, stamp duty and loan acquisition costs.

3. The interest rate you are paying for finance.

4. The amortisation period of the loan, that is, over what period you are paying off your loan if you have a principal and interest mortgage.

5. Your rental income and the expected increase in your annual rent.

6. Your operating costs such as letting fees, outgoings, rates and insurance as well as the expected increase in your annual operating costs over the years.

7. A prediction of the vacancy rate for your property.

8. The property's capital growth and how long the property will be held.

9. The expected eventual selling price or revaluation if you are going to refinance your property.

When formulating Strategic Property Plans for clients of Metropole we plug these figures into a computer program to analyse the results. An excellent indicator of your results is a figure called the internal rate of return (IRR). The IRR takes into account the cash that flows in and out over a period of time and reports the total effect as a percentage rate of return.

IRR allows you to compare your real estate investments with other types of investments that are normally expressed as an annual percentage, such as savings accounts or shares. Don't worry – you don't really have to understand how the IRR is calculated in order to be a good investor. It's a bit like driving a car – you don't really need to know what goes on under the bonnet to get your licence.

If you know you get an IRR of 20% on your investment property, it means that to get the same return from money in a bank deposit, you would need to get a before-tax interest rate of say 30%, which would come to about 20% after tax.

Using this type of investment modelling program allows you to adjust possible returns using many, "what-if?" scenarios – a great tool for getting creative and thinking outside the square to improve your investment returns. You can quickly discover:

*   What if I put a bigger deposit in, what would this do to my return?

*   What if I put a smaller deposit in, what sort of return would I get?

*   What if I invested in an area that had high capital growth and therefore lower return? or conversely,

*   What if I invested in an area that gave me high returns but less capital growth?

Doing this type of analysis is critical in checking how well the numbers in any given deal really do stack up, which makes them well worth investing in!

After all, for any serious investor, these numbers are the bottom line.

BANKS AND THE SECRETS TO BORROWING

I am going to let you in on a little secret. Property, of itself, is not a particularly brilliant investment. Wait – don't throw this book away just yet! Let me explain.

On its own, property doesn't give a much better return than shares or managed funds. However, with the right **finance** property is a great investment that outperforms all other asset classes over the long term.

It's the fact that we can use other people's money to leverage our investments that can make property a fantastic wealth-building vehicle. In other words, getting the right finance is the key to unlocking property profits.

To illustrate just what I mean, let's examine a tale of two assets.

Here, Asset A is worth $500,000 and will produce 7% growth per annum and a 4% yield (rental return or income return), while Asset B, which is also worth $500,000, produces 9% growth and a 5% yield. As you can see from the following table, each year Asset B delivers a better return, leaving one to assume that Asset B is a better investment, right?

	ASSET A	ASSET B
Asset value	$500,000	$500,000
Growth % + Yield %	7% + 4%	9% + 5%
Growth + Yield $	$35,000 + $20,000	$45,000 + $25,000
Annual return	**$55,000**	**$70,000**

Well, not necessarily. Let's take this argument a step further and find out some more information to correctly compare the two. Namely – how much can you borrow against Asset A and Asset B?

Let's imagine Asset A is a house or an apartment in an Australian capital city where the banks are generally happy to lend you 80% of a property's valuation. And let's suppose that Asset B is a top-performing share for which the banks may only lend you 50% against its value. This is a key difference!

Essentially this scenario means that to purchase $500,000 worth of Asset A, you would need to invest $100,000 and a bank would lend you the balance. On the other hand, to purchase

$500,000 of Asset B, you would only be able to borrow $250,000, meaning you would have to put more of your money into the deal than if you were purchasing Asset A.

	ASSET A (property)	ASSET B (shares)
Asset value	$500,000	$500,000
Growth % + Yield %	7% + 4%	9% + 5%
Growth + Yield $	$35,000 + $20,000	$45,000 + $25,000
Annual return	$55,000	$70,000
Leverage capacity	80%	50%
Your Money	**$100,000**	**$250,000**
Borrowed funds	**$400,000**	**$250,000**

Let's have a closer look at these investments again; assuming that in both cases the banks lend the money required at the same interest rate.

It is obvious that you would have paid more interest on Asset A by the end of the year than on Asset B, because you borrowed much more money from the outset.

However, and this is the critical point I want to make about leverage, the return on your funds would also be substantially higher; you would make 35% on your initial $100,000 invested in Asset A, compared to just 23% on Asset B. In other words, the return on your funds would increase by 50%.

So (and this is a big one), the ability to finance or leverage Asset A is much more important than its return in either growth or yield.

	ASSET A (property)	ASSET B (shares)
Asset value	$500,000	$500,000
Growth % + Yield %	7% + 4%	9% + 5%
Growth + Yield $	$35,000 + $20,000	$45,000 + $25,000
Annual return	$55,000	$70,000
Leverage capacity	80%	50%
Your money	$100,000	$250,000
Borrowed funds	$400,000	$250,000
Interest rate	5% per annum	5% per annum
Interest cost	-$20,000	-$12,500
Profit	**$35,00**	**$57,500**
Return on your money	**35%**	**23%**

This is what makes residential property such a great investment – the fact that banks will allow you to borrow up to 80% (or more) of the value of your property. This means effectively, you're able to buy property using other people's money to make yourself wealthy.

This allows you to achieve the wealth generating rates of return that a Level 3 investor needs to help them grow a substantial asset base and become a Level 4 professional investor.

Of course, the more highly you are geared, the more money you have borrowed and the lower your invested capital in relation to your borrowings, the more your return on investment will be. As you can see from the examples in the table above, the higher the degree of gearing, the more leverage you achieve and the more your returns are magnified. But be warned, gearing not only magnifies your profits, if the value of your investment falls, your losses are magnified as well.

WHAT YOU'VE BEEN TAUGHT ABOUT FINANCE IS PROBABLY WRONG

Be careful – don't allow financing advice handed down from generation to generation of consumer-minded non-investors provide the framework for your investment financing decisions. Strategic investors look at debt differently than consumers do.

While the average Australian looks at debt reduction as a means of strengthening their financial position, strategic investors on the other hand, focus on accumulating assets that increase in value over time. They are not concerned with how much debt they have or how much it costs, as long as they own appreciating assets and have the financial buffers in place to buy themselves time to see themselves through the ups and downs of the economic and property cycle.

I discussed this concept of financial buffers in the section earlier on when I gave the example of Liz and Gavin.

The problem is that in the current uncertain financial climate many people have become scared of borrowing and frightened of debt. Some don't understand the concept that there is such a thing as good debt and bad debt.

Here is the most important rule you will ever hear about borrowing money: **Debt is only good if the money you have borrowed can be used to make more money**.

Using this criterion, borrowing money to invest in high-growth properties is a very different scenario to borrowing money on a credit card to spend on consumer goods.

So let me introduce an important concept; there is good debt, bad debt and necessary debt.

Good debt is borrowed against appreciating assets and is tax deductible, meaning you get a tax benefit for borrowing. Using this criterion, borrowing money to invest in capital growth properties is a very different scenario to borrowing money on a credit card to spend on consumer goods.

If you borrow money at 5% interest to invest in a rental property, which produces an average 7% capital growth, plus 4% rental return each year — in other words you are realising a 11% return by borrowing money at 5% — then you obviously come out ahead.

Remember how your parents taught you never to buy cars, electronic goods or computers with borrowed money, because these items decrease in value over time?

Well, they were right — that's bad debt. Yet banks and credit card companies will try to lend you money for these items because they know you won't pay them back quickly. If you had access to money to pay them back quickly you wouldn't need to borrow it in the first place, would you? And there is a good chance you'll pay interest at a high rate month after month. This is how the banks get wealthy from the deal.

INSIDER TIP

Using debt to buy appreciating and income-producing assets is a great way to build your personal wealth. In contrast consumer debt is a great way to reduce your net worth.

Wouldn't it be nice if you could charge something up to the bank and have somebody else make the payments? That's how buying income producing real estate works, because the rent that the tenant pays you each month helps pay back the bank and as your property goes up in value, your net worth keeps increasing while your loan balance remains the same.

Becoming comfortable with the concept of good debt and understanding that in order to make money in property, you need to borrow money, is a crucial aspect to building your own real estate empire.

Okay, what's *necessary debt*? This is the non-tax-deductible debt you take on when you borrow for your home. It's necessary because otherwise you would never be able to afford to buy a home, and while it doesn't receive a tax concession, you have borrowed against an appreciating asset, so it's really a form of good debt isn't it?

HOW THE RICH GET RICHER

Wealthy people simply access other people's money (through lenders) to make more money for themselves. Most real estate fortunes have been built on borrowed money. Even after all these years as a real estate investor, I still use borrowed money to buy my investments. Remember, debt against investment property is good debt and rich people borrow this way all the time to become even richer.

This idea is foreign to the vast majority of people who are at the bottom of the Wealth Pyramid and still working for a living and would prefer to avoid debt at all cost (regardless of whether it's good or bad). To come to terms with this idea, it's important to remember that you are trying to build a property investment business and your job is to invest and grow your asset base through the capital growth of your properties. Logically, the more money you borrow, the more properties you can own and the more capital growth you are going to get.

This step of borrowing large amounts of money to invest in real estate worries many beginning investors, because they have been told not to buy things that they can't afford and not to borrow large amounts of money from the banks. We remember that our parents taught us similar ideals, telling us to pay off our loans as quickly as possible. But things were different then and that's probably why they thought the way they did.

ISN'T DEBT RISKY?

The myth of debt is the one that seems the hardest for most people to overcome. After all, as kids we were all taught that debt is bad. But if you take a look at the *AFR Rich List* you will find that the rich use other people's money, such as banks or shareholder's funds, to grow their businesses.

Sophisticated investors use other people's money before their own. They understand that debt itself is not risky. They know that debt is only risky if you are not able to repay the interest on the debt.

While these investors use debt as a tool to build their wealth, the average Australian gets into trouble with debt. They buy depreciating assets with their credit or store cards, pay massive interest on this debt and once the cards are maxed out they are in big trouble.

However if you were still able to keep borrowing more money, without a limit on your loan size, you could afford to make your repayments couldn't you? Now you're likely to be thinking, "That would be great, but I'd end up with a massive debt," and that is true. But the wealthy have worked out that the way around this is to have their assets growing quicker than their debt, so their net asset position is improving.

YOUR RELATIONSHIP WITH DEBT

How you handle debt will vary depending on what level of investor you are.

If you are a Level 0 investor, it's likely your relationship with debt will be built around spending; it will involve consumer debt. You probably use debt to pay for your lifestyle and in the process will be mortgaging your future. You just want to get stuff and will spend money on things that decrease in value, such as consumables, cars and the latest smartphone.

Level 1, and to a lesser extent Level 2 investors, are scared of debt. Sometimes it has taken them so long to get out of consumer debt that they are scared of falling back into that hole. Their goal is to have no debt.

On the other hand, Level 3 investors want to use debt. They want to harness it and use leverage to create more wealth. They recognise that debt is a source of power as long as they control it, as opposed to having the debt control them. They are not worried about debt that pays for itself because they invest in assets that increase in value like residential real estate.

Level 4 investors have got the whole debt thing figured out. They balance their levels of debt to enable their assets to spin off sufficient cash flow to provide the lifestyle that they desire while still growing in value, and at the same time they take advantage of the tax benefits that leverage provides.

Interesting isn't it: Why does the Government tax your savings, but give you a tax deduction for being in debt?

FINANCE BROKERS AS MIDDLE MEN

One stumbling block for investors is *The Golden Rule of Banking* – he who has the gold makes the rules!

There is little room for negotiation with the banks yet there are so many lenders with hundreds of different loan products. How do you choose the right loan for you? It's a daunting task especially for Beginner Investors. That's why many investors now use the services of a finance broker.

INSIDER TIP

An investment-savvy finance broker will help you get through the maze of the hundreds of potential lenders and myriad of lending "products" saving you time, money and heartache. They are as vital a part of your investment team as a good solicitor and good accountant.

Finance brokers have the latest information on a wide range of loans, can compare different loans and work out which is the right loan to suit your financial situation. They act as your representative so that you are shielded from the banks. Their fees are paid by the banks and they only make money if they get you a loan, so they are keen to see your loan application succeed.

Because different lenders have different criteria for assessing loan applications and these "in- house policies" are not public knowledge, a good finance broker can save you a significant amount of time and heartache by not applying for a loan with a lender whose criteria don't suit you.

Once you have a number of properties your broker should also advise you how to structure your loan portfolio to maximise your borrowing capacity.

This may involve using different lenders and avoiding the mistake of cross-collateralising your loans. This occurs where one loan is secured by two or more properties. This typically happens when an investment loan is secured by both your home and the investment property.

Loan structuring is beyond the scope of this book, but is discussed in detail in my book *What Every Property Investor Needs to Know about Finance, Tax and the Law*. However, I strongly recommend you seek expert advice because a poor loan structure can be crippling. It can restrict you from growing your investment portfolio because you may have equity that you will not be able to access unnecessarily tied up in properties.

HOW DO YOU FIND A GOOD FINANCE BROKER?

You need to find somebody you can trust and who understands property investment. You would think all mortgage brokers would understand property investment, but this is not the case. Don't just fall for somebody who has the gift of the gab or wears smart suits. You need to find somebody who really knows their stuff and is a successful property investor themselves.

Find out how long they have been a broker, how long they have been with their current company and how long they have owned investment properties. Get recommendations from your friends, it's one of the best ways to find a good broker.

Find someone who asks the right questions and listens to your answers.

They should ask you about your investment goals and strategies, because they should set up your loans with the end in mind — when you own your multi-million dollar property portfolio; not just for your first investment property.

Your broker will then determine your financial capacity, in other words how much you can borrow.

They should then select the most appropriate lenders and products for you. I have seen clients whose borrowing capacity changed by over $250,000 just by changing their lenders. I have seen others extend their borrowing capacity significantly by using certain lenders in a particular order.

Your broker should then seek **pre-approval** for your loan before you go hunting for an investment property. This is an "in-principle" commitment from the lender to loan you the money. This should cost you nothing but gives you the security to make firm offers on properties, which agents love.

SOME FINANCE TIPS

There's so much to discuss about setting up an appropriate finance strategy, that I've devoted a whole section to it in my book *What Every Property Investor Needs to Know about Finance, Tax and the Law*. You can find out more and buy it online at www.MichaelYardneyBooks.com.au.

1. **Have a Financial Buffer.** Rather than gearing to the max, strategic investors take a more prudent approach by building an emergency buffer to buy themselves time to ride through the storms.

   If you are currently in a position where you have a nice little pool of equity built up in your property portfolio, then you are already ahead of the game. Maybe it's time to think about establishing a Line Of Credit (LOC) using your existing equity. In fact I would go so far as to suggest that you should draw as much equity as your bank will allow, and stash all of it away as a cash flow buffer.

   Of course you shouldn't use these funds to speculate in options or spend on a holiday. Your LOC should be viewed purely as a buffer that will give you consistent financial stability, regardless of the ups and downs of world markets and local bank's funding vagaries.

   The other beauty of being financially prepared is that when everyone else puts the brakes on and competition in the housing markets dries up, you will be in a position to nab the bargain priced opportunities that abound, by using some of your LOC as a deposit on your next property investment.

   Remember, you need to be proactive with your financial strategy and be in control of your situation before things turn sour. By doing so, you will ensure that you remain sheltered from the next world economic storm and avoid the panic that many will feel when one day again, the local or global situation worsens.

2. Choosing the **right loan product** has very little to do with interest rates which vary over time. It's more important to get flexibility, the ability to get equity redraws, fees and other features that you require for your particular structures. The lender's credit policy, their valuation process and their willingness to lend to trusts may also be important to you.

3. **Correct loan structuring is critical** if you plan to acquire multiple properties. This can affect things such as flexibility, costs, risk management and the ability to get further loans. Using multiple banks in the right sequence and avoiding cross-collateralisation are the sort of things a savvy finance broker is likely to advise you on.

4. Budgeting for cash flow and interest rate management are also an important part of your finance strategy.

SOME BANKING TERMS

Loan-to-valuation ratio

LVR, or loan-to-valuation ratio, is the percentage of loan amount to the value of a property it is mortgaged against.

For example, a loan of $600,000 on a property valued at $800,000 is at an LVR of 75%. It is really the reverse of your equity (the amount of funds you have in the property) because to have a LVR of 75% means you have equity of 25%.

All banks and finance lenders use the LVR as a guideline to determine the loan candidate's risk. The higher the LVR, the riskier they see the loan being. When lending on residential property, banks will normally lend up to 80% of the property's value (80% LVR) before they become nervous and require mortgage insurance.

Debt-servicing ratio

Apart from having sufficient equity, the banks also want to ensure that you have the capacity to "service the loan" as they say, which really means to pay the interest and principal repayments.

The banks take into account that a portion of the rent you receive will pay some of the interest, but they also consider your income and other expenses.

It is important to know that some banks are more conservative than others when calculating this figure, meaning one bank may lend you considerably more than another bank because they have a different debt servicing model.

PROTECTING YOUR CREDIT RATING

As a property investor, it's important to understand how lenders rate your credit. When making a decision on lending you funds, the bank will check your credit history by obtaining a copy of your credit file. Everyone who has ever applied for any type of finance, be it a credit card, mobile phone account, personal loan or home loan has a credit file registered against their name.

Your credit file is run by a company called Veda Advantage. The good news is you can go to their website — www.mycreditfile.com.au to request a copy of your credit file, which outlines things like:

- Any loans you have applied for in the past 10 to 15 years.
- References to bad credit you may have had in the past seven years.
- Bankruptcies or judgments.
- Current and historic directorships in companies.

- Past residential addresses.
- Historical employment data.

Interestingly this makes you pretty much transparent to the bank, with your credit file telling a detailed story about your behaviour in the world of credit.

All lenders and mortgage insurance companies have access to this file and when applying for a loan, you give them authority to delve into your credit history. This is one of the very first steps in their assessment process.

The banks check to see that you are a good "loan risk". Standard defaults on accounts you have not paid remain listed on your credit report for five years and are only removed after being paid in full. A bankruptcy stays on your file for seven years.

Simple things such as the number of addresses shown on your credit report for the past five years can make a difference to the lender as can the suburb in which you live. Continuity is considered very attractive to the banks.

Even the number of loan applications you have made could influence their decisions. If there are too many applications in a short period of time, this could go against you in obtaining a loan. They will wonder why you have approached so many lenders and why they haven't lent you the money. The type of finance companies you have applied to will also impact your application!

BOOST YOUR BORROWING POWER

In the current property climate, where opportunities abound, the last thing you want to hold you back from securing an additional asset for your portfolio is any restriction on your borrowing capacity.

But the reality is that many investors face an uphill battle to get more finance today given the banks heightened wariness around refinancing and tighter restrictions on how much money they're prepared to put up for those of us who decide to build wealth with bricks and mortar.

Don't get me wrong, real estate is still recognised as the most stable form of security by lenders, but the watchful eye of APRA has led to a more conservative borrowing stance from Aussie lenders with a more responsible lending and a greater focus around serviceability (the ability to repay interest and debt).

While the banks should and do have a legal obligation to make sure borrowers can meet their repayment responsibilities, the problem is different lenders have different benchmarks for determining an individual's ability to repay their debt.

So how do you beat the banks and borrow more (responsibly of course)? Here are eleven ways to maximise your borrowing power.

1. DON'T GET SLOPPY WITH YOUR PAPERWORK

A lot of investors (and all other mere mortals) are guilty of getting a bit lax on the odd occasion when it comes to things like handing in tax returns on time and keeping financial records up to date. But good bookkeeping can go a long way when it comes to proving your borrowing capacity to the banks.

Being able to demonstrate your combined income, from all investments as well as your day job, with your latest notice of assessment from the tax office will make the banks feel more confident about your ability to meet your repayment commitments. And let's face it; an investor who obviously runs a tight financial ship will be looked upon far more favourably by number crunching credit assessors.

2. TIDY UP YOUR DEBTS

Having lots of debts on your file can have the lenders raising their eyebrows.

Why not roll up all the smaller debts under a single loan? It would even streamline your payments and help you budget better.

Refinancing at a better rate by bringing all your loans under the refinanced loan can save you a lot of bucks over the life of the loan.

Unsecured debts (credit cards or personal loans) require repayment within a short period, which forces you to reduce your debts quickly. The result is high monthly bills. When a lender performs their servicing calculations, these debts will weigh heavily against you because they limit the amount of available funds that could be used to make payments on the proposed mortgage.

One possible solution to this dilemma is to combine your unsecured debt with your mortgage so that it won't be reflected as a financial commitment (automatically increasing your serviceability). Sure your mortgage might be a bit higher by combining the debt, but at the end of the day your application will show less unsecured financial commitments and therefore less red flags when it comes to how much credit you can manage.

Additionally, you should cut up any cards you don't really need and get rid of them entirely wherever possible.

Not only will having just one credit card make you a more attractive prospect for the banks, it will also make your wallet a lot lighter!

If you do need a credit card for life's little emergencies, keep the limit to a minimum and make your repayments on time all the time.

However if you own three credit cards with a limit of $15,000 each, the lenders will consider a potential loan of $45,000 on your hands, reducing your borrowing capacity considerably. While this may not seem fair, most lenders prefer to err on the side of caution, as it is only human to dip into the amount that is so easily available to you.

Giving up that extra credit card will save you the annual maintenance fee as well as help you avoid high interest credit that can burn a hole in your pocket. Essentially, for every extra $1,000 limit you have on a credit card you will lose about $4,000 worth of borrowing capacity.

3. CLEAN CREDIT HISTORY

Another easy and effective way to increase your borrowing capacity is to maintain a clean credit history. Paying all your utility bills on time (even the most inconspicuous ones) makes you a responsible borrower in the eyes of a potential lender and can increase your chances of approval as well as your borrowing capacity considerably.

4. UNDERSTAND YOUR LIVING EXPENSES

It is important to calculate your living expenses clearly before you file a loan application, as lenders will take this into account for determining the amount they want to lend to you.

School fees for your children, any repayments for an investment property (many lenders assume the worst-case scenario that the property may remain vacant for some time) and the expensive club membership are all taken into account while determining your repayment capacity and consequently, your borrowing capacity.

5. BE PRO-ACTIVE IN YOUR PRODUCT SEARCH

The type of loan you have applied for can have an impact on the amount you can borrow.

Lenders always calculate your repayment capacity at an interest rate that is approximately 1.5% higher than the rate at which the loan is being offered.

However, when you go for a fixed rate loan, the repayment capacity for that period is usually calculated without any buffer.

Also, if you apply for a loan jointly with your partner, more often than not you can borrow more than what you would have as a sole applicant.

And while Professional Packages can be fantastic, offering line of credit facilities, credit cards and many other bells and whistles linked to your loan, but for every extra feature some banks want to throw at you, the less money they'll be prepared to toss your way.

Get your finance broker to shop around for you to find out which lenders will provide the extra features you need, such as a line of credit or interest only repayments, without limiting your spending power on that next property investment.

Furthermore, go all out to secure a good interest rate deal. I know this sounds obvious but many borrowers are still reluctant to barter the banks down on their interest rates.

If you're one of them, consider this next time you confront your lender; reducing the interest rate payable on your loan by 0.5% on an average $400,000 loan could free up $2,000 of your annual cashflow that would otherwise be listed on your loan application as outgoing cashflow.

6. MAKE SURE YOUR RENTAL INCOME (AND EVERY OTHER CENT YOU EARN) COUNTS!

All lenders look at income streams differently. Some will accept a higher percentage of your rental profits than others as part of your income, while some might not even consider things like commissions or company profits that boost your base salary.

Essentially, for every extra dollar of income a lender acknowledges, your borrowing power increases. So be aware of what the banks will and won't accept.

7. CONSIDER REFINANCING

If the conditions of your current loan(s) are not benefiting your investing, refinancing in order to reduce your interest rate, change your loan structure or extract more equity is an option you may wish to consider.

Having a detailed discussion with your mortgage broker — they can help determine whether refinancing will be beneficial to your circumstances and help you to weigh up the pros against the cons.

For example, the longer your loan term, the smaller your monthly repayments will be. If you have multiple debts across your property portfolio, it might be worth considering taking 30-year loans as opposed to 25, thereby minimising your repayment obligations.

Additionally, you should explore what will be better for your cash flow — interest only repayments or principle and interest repayments (which often come at a lower interest rate.)

8. AVOID CROSS-COLLATERALISATION

One of the big stumbling blocks many investors face as they grow their property portfolio is hidden in the fine print of their loan documents and gives the banks more power and security than they need. This is called cross-collateralisation and occurs when more than one property is used as security to support a loan.

While this is a wide spread practice that's preferred by the banks, it may not be the most suitable way to borrow more funds for you.

9. DON'T RELY ON ONE BANK

This way you will have access to a wider range of lending products and the potential to borrow a lot more if you diversify your lenders.

Having all of your loans with one bank may result in them eventually refusing to lend you more money because as your portfolio grows and you increase your debt exposure with any one lender, you are seen to move from being what they consider a low risk borrower to a higher risk and they might begin to reduce your Loan to Value Ratios, or they may ask for you to slowly repay the principal of your loan, which eats into your cash flow and hence your loan servicing capacity.

10. SELECT YOUR LENDERS IN THE RIGHT SEQUENCE

While you may not think it makes much difference which bank you approach first, the truth is that the sequence in which you select your lenders can have a huge impact when it comes to how much money you can access.

It's just that some banks are more investor friendly than others and you need to know the "pecking order", because if you go to the banks in the wrong sequence it can make a world of difference to your borrowing capacity.

Most investors go to the friendliest bank first – the bank that will give them their loan with the least hassles – WRONG!

Think about it... once you've got that first loan you are now left with the banks that are less investor friendly.

It is advisable to start off with a bank that is not so investor friendly, meaning you initially get a loan with the bank that will be the most difficult when it comes to investor finance and then you move down the line to lenders who more readily provide money for investment because they use different (more generous) serviceability models.

Which bank do you approach first? Well this varies with time and is one of the reasons it is important to have a proficient finance broker as part of your investment team. One who knows which banks are investor friendly today.

11. BUY THE RIGHT PROPERTY

You've already learned the importance of buying the type of property that the banks are happy to lend against.

7 QUESTIONS YOU MUST ASK IF YOU'RE CONSIDERING FIXING INTEREST RATES

With interest rates at historic lows, and banks offering very attractive fixed loan rates, some investors are wondering if it's time to lock in some or all of their loans into fixed rates?

How do you decide what's the right thing to and what do you need to consider to ensure you make an informed decision?

Of course "locking into" a fixed rate home or investment loan gives you the advantage of knowing what your commitments will be for a predetermined period – the fixed term. This could be a suitable strategy if you want certainty for your cash flow commitments – especially with the likelihood that interest rates will eventually increase significantly.

However, there are also disadvantages that you need to be aware of before you make a decision.

With this in mind, let's look at some questions you should ask yourself when considering whether to fix your loan rates.

1. Will I want to sell my property during the fixed loan period? If so, there could be a penalty for breaking your loan commitment.

2. Will I want to access the equity in my property to invest further during the fixed period? Often this will come at a cost that may be prohibitive. Do I need an offset account?

3. Do I need an offset account? This is a transaction account linked to your loan.

   Many borrowers put their savings into this account and the credit balance here is offset against your outstanding loan balance reducing the interest payable on that loan. Most fixed rate loans do not allow an offset facility.

4. Can I make extra repayments off my loan? As some lenders will restrict how much extra you can repay each year when you fix your loan, if you are able to save significant amounts you may consider leaving some of your mortgage variable and maximising the use of your offset account.

5. What balance of fixed and variable rates do I need for my portfolio? Even if you only have one loan, you can usually split the facility with a portion being fixed and the rest being a variable loan, giving you the flexibility you need.

   Often beginning investors choose to lock in 50% of their loans, while investors with larger portfolios protect themselves by fixing a larger percentage of their loans.

6. How long should I fix my loan for? Now this is a difficult question, but if you believe that interest rates will remain high for a number of years then fixing for a short period such as two or three years may not make sense.

   That's because your loan facility will mature and revert to the prevailing interest rate at a time when they could be a few percentage points higher. This is an area where you should take specialist advice.

7. If interest rates don't rise too much, what will lock in today have cost me? How would you feel if you'd locked into a five-year loan facility and interest rates dropped in a year or two?

   I know when I've been in that situation I took comfort in the fact that I was not trying to beat the banks; instead I had secured my cash flow position.

   Yet I know others who have become stressed when rates turned against them.

NOW A DISCLAIMER...

I'm clearly no expert in this field (I often get the fixed vs. variable decision wrong) so please get expert advice regarding your own circumstances.

You see... There are many other issues to consider – things like your job security – and speculating on rate movements is fraught with danger and making a fixed versus variable decision for the wrong reasons can be costly.

While fixing your rate has the benefit of achieving "certainty" with your mortgage repayments, breaking a fixed rate loan can be costly as well as removing flexibility and control.

In the next chapter I'll explain some of the finance structures sophisticated investors use to help their cashflow.

THE DIFFERENCE BETWEEN A LOC AND AN OFFSET ACCOUNT

As part of their finance strategies, sophisticated investors use banking facilities called Lines of Credit facilities and Offset Accounts. In this chapter we'll look at how these different loan-related products can function to help you understand if they would suit your circumstances.

WHAT IS A LOC & HOW DOES IT WORK?

A Line of Credit (LOC) is a bit like a big credit card. It is a variable rate loan facility that is secured by a mortgage over a residential or commercial property. Since a Line of Credit is secured by a loan against a property, its credit limit can usually be much higher than a limit for a credit card, and the interest rate is generally a great deal cheaper.

Sophisticated investors set up their finance facilities before they need them and often set up their Lines of Credit in anticipation of their next property purchase or so they're ready for the inevitable rainy days. Given that interest is only calculated on funds drawn, if there is a nil balance, there is no interest for them to pay, but funds are available "at call". This means they have the convenience of having a deposit on hand to purchase their next property or funds available for renovation or repairs as and when they require them.

Some also use their Line of Credit as a financial buffer to fund their negative gearing. This preserves or improves their cash flow and buys them time until their property increases in value.

Despite their benefits, Lines of Credit may not suit every investment strategy. Depending upon the lender and whether the Line of Credit is included under a professional package, establishment and ongoing administrative fees can sometimes be higher than for term loans.

THE PROS AND CONS OF A LOC

One of the big benefits from a LOC is having what is essentially a working account that you can use to help manage your cash flow.

Let's say your investment portfolio is negatively geared and you have a shortfall between your monthly repayments and rental income of $500. That represents a substantial amount of money for you to have to personally fund each month.

But if it makes financial sense to do so, you could use the equity in one or more of your other properties to establish a LOC that would act as a cash flow buffer. For instance, you might be able to set up a $20,000 LOC using some of your portfolio's equity and run all of your property investment's income and expenses through this account.

By doing so, not only will that monthly cash flow shortfall be covered without the need to stick your hand in your own pocket, you will also have a nice, neat paper trail of all property-related incomings and outgoings for your accountant to follow at tax time.

What about the interest payable on the funds you are drawing each month from the LOC account? Well, if you are only accessing $500 out of the initial $20,000, the interest would be minimal (around $27 per month) and better yet, it's tax deductible!

SO WHAT'S THE CATCH?

Well, I have to admit I'm a little biased when it comes to Line of Credit accounts; I am a staunch advocate of their use by property investors and think the benefits far outweigh any potential drawbacks.

Having said that, if I was to play devil's advocate then I would suggest the only real negative with this type of set-up is that you are eating into some of your portfolio's equity. But if you are investing correctly – for maximum capital growth – this shouldn't be a real issue as your equity will be growing beyond what you will be spending each month.

In my opinion, you are far better off using a LOC arrangement if it will give you the confidence and financial capacity to grow your high growth portfolio, rather than be ultra conservative and fearful of tapping into your equity. Think about it – your equity is there to be used; to be leveraged so that you can buy more property and accumulate more wealth over the long-term. And a Line of Credit is the perfect tool for this very purpose.

WHAT IS AN OFFSET ACCOUNT AND HOW DOES IT WORK?

An offset account is a standalone transaction account that is specially linked to your home or investment property loan. It can be an effective tool in reducing loan interest and keeping the paper trail of funds separate for tax purposes.

The major benefit of using an offset account is rather than earning interest on any money you deposit in the account, the balance will offset daily against the home loan principal, bringing down the amount of interest you pay.

Perhaps the best way to explain it is with a diagram:

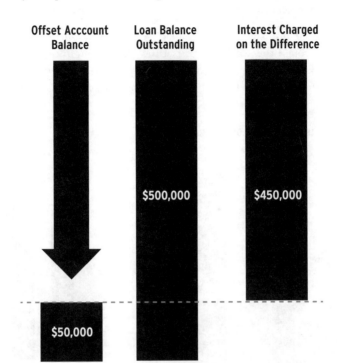

In this example your loan balance of $500,000 is offset by the $50,000 you have in your offset account, so the daily interest on your loan is calculated by the lender on a net balance of $450,000.

Another advantage is the ATO does not consider this "savings" as earning interest income and so you benefit without any additional tax expense.

If you think about it, the nett effect on the interest you are charged for having your funds in the offset account is the same as paying those funds directly into your loan account, but the big benefit is you can redraw the funds from the offset whenever you like.

But not all offset accounts are the same — there are two different types:

- **100% offset** — Every dollar in the transaction account is offset against the loan balance, working to reduce interest charges. For example, if the offset account has a balance of $20,000 and the loan has a balance of $200,000, loan interest is calculated on $180,000.

- **Partial offset** — A proportion of the transaction account balance is offset against the loan balance. For example, where the offset account has a balance of $20,000 and the loan a balance of $200,000 and there is a 40% offset capability, loan interest is calculated on a balance of $192,000.

Generally speaking, offset accounts save you more if you have a home loan because the interest on your home loan is calculated daily and is not a tax-deductible expense.

In order to gain maximum benefit from an offset account, you must direct as much cash flow as possible through the account to offset the highest amount of interest on your loan. Ideally, you would have your wages and even rental income paid directly into this account, which would be linked to your home loan rather than any investment loans to reduce your non-deductible debt.

Investment Loan Account

Interest charged only on loan balance less offset balance

Loan Balance

Salary Income

Expenses

Repayment

Offset Account

Offset accounts are generally only available with variable loan products rather than fixed term mortgages, however there are a handful of lenders who will offer this product option within a fixed term scenario. Often they are included as one of the special features found in professional loan packages.

THE PROS AND CONS OF OFFSET ACCOUNTS

While offset accounts are often promoted as the magic genie of home loans, with the ability to save you hundreds of thousands of dollars and countless years off the average mortgage, the reality is they are only as effective as the borrower who uses them and how much "spare cash" you can deposit in the account.

Yet, if used correctly, an offset can save you big bucks over the life of your loan.

For instance, if you have a $500,000 home loan and $50,000 in an 100% offset account you'll will only be charged interest on $450,000.

Now obviously the balance in your offset account will fluctuate, but for the sake of the exercise, if over a 30-year home loan term with a 5% interest rate, you maintained a balance of $50,000 in your offset account over the life of the loan you would save around $142,000 in interest and pay off your loan four years and four months earlier.

SMART OFFSET MONEY STRATEGIES

1. Diverting all your income to your offset account

One smart way some of our clients use an offset account is to manage their cash flow.

They usually have a (non-tax-deductible) home loan with an offset account attached to it plus an investment loan. They then have their salary and the rental income paid into their offset which they use as a transactional account.

As interest payable on their home loan is calculated on a daily basis, this system has the benefit of having both income sources contributing to offsetting their home loan. Then at the end of the month (when the investment loan payment is due) they'll sweep funds from their offset account into their investment loan account to meet the mortgage payment.

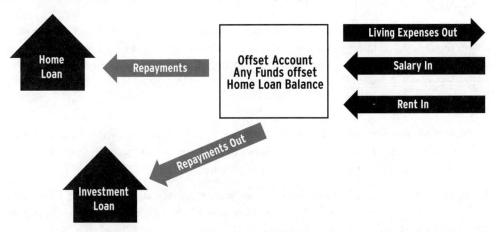

2. Using a credit card for living expenses and an offset account

Other clients go to the next level and put all their living expenses on a credit card so that the offset account balance remains as high as possible for most of the month.

Just to make things clear they always pay their credit card debt before it is due so they never pay penalty interest — in fact many banks offer a sweep facility to allow this to be done automatically.

By doing this their salary and surplus income sits in the offset account for as long as possible thereby reducing their interest bill.

3. Owner occupied property to become investment property

This is an advanced strategy, and while simple to implement, most investors get this wrong at their cost.

If you think about it, it's unlikely your first home is going to be your last home and many first-time buyers plan to turn their home into an investment property when they upgrade in the future. But they run into finance challenges.

Imagine five years down the track you've reduced your home loan and now want to use $200,000 of the equity in your first property (which will now become an investment) as security for your new home loan.

That's not a problem. The problem is the interest on this $200,000 loan will not be tax deductible, because even though the security for the loan is an investment property the purpose of the loan is to purchase a home — this loan doesn't pass the purpose test we recently discussed.

So instead of taking out a principal and interest home loan you'd be better off taking out an interest only home loan with a linked offset account. Now I know that goes against what you were probably taught by your parents — pay off your non-tax-deductible home loan as fast as you can.

The preferred strategy would be to funnel any spare cash you have into the offset account. If you're really disciplined you'd pretend you are making the higher P&I loan repayments and putting these funds into your offset account each time you make the (lower) interest only repayments.

This would do three things:

1. Having funds accumulating in your offset account (and not spending them) would effectively mean that you're not paying any extra interest on your loan. You're basically making the P&I payments — you're just making them into two separate accounts.

2. In the future when your home becomes an investment, you'd have a loan for the same amount as initially borrowed but now the interest would be fully tax deductible. This is very different to if you had made repayments off the principal of the loan as your loan balance and therefore interest claimable would be less.

3. Any funds accumulated in the mortgage offset account could at that point be used towards your next property purchase.

BE CAREFUL OF THE TAX IMPLICATIONS

As with any component of an investment strategy it's important to be well informed before making any decisions. Although funds in an offset account sit separately from the loan, there could be taxation matters to consider when converting a property from a principal place of residence to an investment property, so consultation with a qualified taxation accountant will provide clarity in this regard. Similarly, an experienced finance broker can provide valuable assistance in determining how Lines of Credit and/or offset accounts can be used to your best advantage.

In the next chapter, I'll look at how the banks and valuers decide what your property is worth and when you could refinance.

VALUATIONS AND REFINANCING

Obviously the lynch pin to growing your multi-million dollar property portfolio is obtaining more finance to allow you to buy more properties. Every time you buy or refinance a property you'll need a valuation so it will be useful to understand a few things about valuations because **the higher the valuation you can get on your property, the more the bank will lend you against it.**

In the good old days things were much easier. I used to build a good relationship with a firm of valuers, get them to value my properties and present this valuation to the bank. That meant that I, and not the bank, used to control the process.

Now things are different and the banks don't usually let their clients deal with valuers directly, instead they control the valuation process. In fact these banks don't deal directly with the valuer either but use an intermediary company, Valuation Exchange (Valex), who distributes the job to one of a panel of valuation firms. By distancing the valuer from the borrower (you), the banks have minimised the influence you can have over the final figure.

There are some exceptions: Smaller financiers often use the same valuers as the "big four", although there are many valuers who are not part of the Valex system. Often a well-connected finance broker who uses one of these smaller lenders for finance can help you choose which valuer is used.

Also when you have a very large portfolio, the banks often allow you to select a valuer from their panel and deal with them directly, which is fortunately the position I'm in today.

The first thing to understand is that what you think your property is worth, the figure a valuer will put on it and what the market will pay are likely to be three different numbers. Of course the lowest of these is usually the valuation.

WHY THE DIFFERENCE?

Well... if you default on your loan and the bank can't get back its money when it repossesses your property, the valuers carry the risk of being sued by the banks. So they err on the side of caution. Wouldn't you if you only got paid a few hundred dollars for your opinion?

I've found that if you have recently bought a property at auction, the valuation is likely to come back at your purchase price. It's hard for a valuer to say you overpaid when there were other bidders involved in a transparent sales process.

When you buy a property by private treaty I've seen valuations come in five to 10% below the purchase price. But where I see the biggest discrepancy is when investors or homeowners try and release equity from properties that they have owned for a few years. I've seen valuers suggest a property is worth 10 to 20% below the market price and I've even seen a variation of 15% between figures provided by two valuers from the same company one week apart.

HOW DO VALUERS RATE PROPERTIES?

Valuers will follow a strict process and guidelines to ensure they're on the money. The key is the definition of market value which case law defines as:

"The estimated amount for which an asset or liability should exchange on the valuation date between a willing buyer and a willing seller in an arm's length transaction, after proper marketing and where the parties had each acted knowledgeably, prudently and without compulsion."

There are arguable points within this definition, but basically the valuer is assessing what your home should sell for in its "as is" condition at a specific date and time if it had been openly and fairly marketed.

Knowing this shows why valuers won't predict future property value movements based on musings about market direction or what renovations and improvement you hope to carry out. It's a "here and now" event in their eyes.

1. The inspection

A property is typically inspected and viewed by a valuer as three interrelated elements.

- *Land* – Location, position, aspect, size, dimension and topography are all considered by the valuer. They are looking for all the pros and cons across these, and other, components.

- *Dwelling* – Age, size, construction, layout, accommodation, condition, utility. Again, the valuer is wandering through your home and taking in what a typical buyer would consider a plus, and a minus.

- *Ancillary (or site) improvements* – Fencing, landscaping, driveway, pool, shed, pathways, tennis courts and any other extra constructions separate from the dwelling.

A valuer will progressively work through these three elements of your property, taking note by sight and use of measurements to complete a comprehensive and descriptive picture of your holding. They will also rely on data from various other sources around town planning and location.

Sometimes a bank orders a **desktop or kerbside valuation** for low risk loans. This saves the lender money as the valuer is not required to enter the property but instead makes an assessment of value based on an external inspection and from information derived from a number of databases.

Clearly with this type of valuation the valuer has no idea whether you've improved your property, whether it's got air conditioning or if it is termite infested. This type of valuation returns a range of values, not a single figure and is considerably less accurate than a full valuation and it's not really what you want.

2. The sales evidence

The basic, primary method of assessment is called the Market Approach and it simply relies on comparing your property to other properties that have sold in your area recently.

By use of databases, listing portals and their local agent contacts, a valuer will gather three-to-six property sales that are nearby, recent and similar to your home and researching the attributes of those properties. The valuer's skill through their experience, art and science is determining by how much in dollar terms your property is better or worse than the comparables.

The house next door sold last week for $700,000, but is smaller, older and doesn't have a pool? Yours is worth a certain amount more than that. An identical house across the road sold for $825,000 but on a bigger block with better views? Yours is worth some figure less.

This progressive comparison across a collection of reasonable sales soon provides a tight range of value that gives a fair indication of what you should achieve.

There are other approaches to this valuation that help double check the figure, but using comparable sales is considered the preeminent legal approach.

3. The report

With all this information collated, the valuer will now send a report to the banks.

It's important to realise that along with the figure, the valuer will be asked to comment on any risks associated with the property itself or the market it's in. These include:

- *Environmental issues*: is the property flood or fire prone or near large powerlines.

- *The market*: banks sometimes ask the valuer to look into what's likely to happen to the particular property market into the near future.

- *Market Volatility*: for example, the inner-city unit market where market conditions can change quickly, might have a higher risk rating than an established "money belt" suburb.

- *The local economy impact*: This is really more relevant in areas such as mining towns or regional locations where there changing economic conditions are going to make properties harder to sell.

- *Market Segment*: The banks like to know for each different property market sub segment, what's the likelihood of a reasonable selling period. While the average home may sell in a particular location over a six-week period, if for some reason that property is unique, it may take longer to sell and this may impact on the decision-making of the bank in their lending process.

CONTROLLING THE VALUATION

To allow you to have some input, I'd suggest you make sure you are the contact person for the valuer, not the selling agent or your property manager.

This means the valuer will contact you to organise an inspection of the property and you can attend armed with some helpful information, but don't be disappointed if you get less than 10 minutes of their time. Make sure the property is well presented and submit any recent comparable sales in a document ranking your property against these sales as inferior or superior.

Briefly put your case to the valuer, but don't badger him. He'll come to his own conclusion.

VALUATION FOR DEVELOPMENT PROJECTS

Valuers look at development projects differently to buy and hold investments. The valuation for a development project is a **property risk report** and this is the primary resource used by banks for lending purposes.

Development finance usually requires an indication of the end value of the properties (even before the project commences) as well as the current value. To help valuers, I give them complete details of the specifications of fitting and finishes, and photos of similar projects that I have completed so that they can get an idea of what is going to be built.

I also give them feasibility studies, budgets, a list of expenditures and comparable sales and rental values.

AN EASY-TO-APPLY REFINANCING FORMULA

How do you know when you have enough equity in your property to allow you to refinance and use the funds as a deposit for further properties?

I've developed a simple four-step process that's helpful in determining how much capital you may be able to obtain by refinancing and then deciding if it is practical to do so. Let's take a quick look at it.

Step 1   Determine the current fair market value of your property. Not what you paid for it, but what you could sell it for today.

Step 2   Subtract your current mortgage balance to determine how much equity you have in the property.

Step 3   Assume you can obtain an 80% mortgage on your property. What is 80% of the current market value?

Step 4   Determine how much it will cost to refinance and how much cash you will actually end up with after mortgage application costs are paid.

This figure you have come up with is your available equity — the money you have available to use as a deposit on your next investment.

To get a feel for what this all means, let's walk through the process with some real-life numbers.

Katherine and George

Katherine and George bought their first property, their family home, seven years ago. Keen to begin growing their assets, they're interested in buying an investment property.

Naturally they will require a significant deposit for their purchase so they are considering refinancing their home. George is conservative and doesn't believe that they've built up enough equity but Katherine disagrees. Here are the numbers:

Step 1	Current market value of their home	$700,000
Step 2	Current mortgage balance	$300,000
	Equity $400,000	
Step 3	80% mortgage (80% of $700,000)	$560,000
Step 4	Cost of refinancing	
	Say estimated fees are	$1,000
	Proposed mortgage	$560,000
	Existing mortgage	$300,000
	Gross proceeds	$260,000
	Less loan costs	$1,000
	Balance for refinancing	$250,000

They could now use this **$250,000 as a deposit** to buy an investment property. On the one hand this money is debt, on the other hand it is like cash to them because they can use this money as a deposit for another property or two.

Of course, this assumes they could afford the repayments on the extra loans, but remember they would have the assistance of the rent they would receive from the new properties.

WHEN SHOULD I PAY OFF MY MORTGAGE?

A question I'm commonly asked is, "If we keep refinancing whenever we have equity and are in a position to do so, when do we ever pay off our mortgages and will we ever own these properties?"

Now I am not talking about your home mortgage here, because the interest on a home mortgage is not tax-deductible and it needs to be considered differently. But when it comes to residential investment properties my opinion is clear — why on earth would you want to pay them off?

I can probably best explain my reasoning as follows.

Imagine you had an investment property worth $600,000 with a mortgage of $480,000 against it. Let's say you suddenly got hold of a lump sum of $100,000 in cash. It could be a lottery win, an inheritance or a bonus.

Why would you apply that $100,000 to paying down your $480,000 mortgage when you could use it as a deposit on another property that would give you greater exposure to the market and should produce more gains?

Paying off your mortgage would reduce the leverage you have on your investment and therefore reduce the return you receive on the equity in your investment. In fact, it reduces the return on your funds by around a third.

The yield on your property won't change; the rental income and the value remains the same, but the internal rate of return on your funds) goes down. The situation is even stranger if you consider that after a number of years you will probably refinance the property to release some equity so that you can buy even more properties, and you will pay the bank more fees to borrow again.

Let's have a look at the figures:

	Don't pay off mortgage	Pay $100,000 off the mortgage
Property value	$600,000	$600,000
Growth + Yield per cent	7% + 3.5%	7% + 3.5%
Growth + Yield $	$42,000 + $21,000	$42,000 + $21,000
Annual return	$63,000	$63,000
My money	$120,000	$220,000
Borrowed funds	$480,000	$380,000
Interest rate	5%	5%
Interest cost	-$24,000	-$19,000
Profit	$39,000	$44,000
Return on money	32.5%	20%

When I explain this the response I usually get is: "Fine, but I don't have a lump sum of cash; can I just use a principal and interest mortgage and pay off the loan slowly over time?"

Sure you can. There is nothing wrong with doing that, but it is really achieving the same thing, isn't it? At the end of the day, you can either pay off your debt or use the surplus funds to save up a deposit to buy further properties.

If you have a home loan that is not tax-deductible it makes more sense to put any surplus income into an offset account which will reduce your non-tax-deductible home mortgage payment and then, when you have enough equity, draw these funds out as the deposit for your next property.

I guess the final decision comes down to how comfortable you are with debt and how much exposure you want to the property market. But you can probably use your money more wisely than paying off your home loan. I'll show you how in a minute.

"BUT MICHAEL, REDUCING THE PRINCIPAL INCREASES EQUITY..."

Some see an advantage in reducing the principal as a form of increasing equity in their property. Sure it's a form of forced saving, but it doesn't actually create new value for you. You are simply transferring money from your pocket into the property. Only capital growth of the property can create new wealth for you without you having to contribute time or money to the deal. And the best way to access the most capital growth is to own a larger number of properties or add value to your properties through renovation or development.

"BUT THEN... HOW DO WE EVER OWN IT?"

Now this is the final question that these discussions usually lead to. My response is that a paradigm shift is required in investors' thinking if they feel they need to own all their properties outright.

If we borrow only for investment purposes the aim is not to own our properties outright, but to maximise the use of our available assets to own as much property as we reasonably can, and to receive the future benefit of capital growth and live off our increasing equity.

At the end of the day if you have a lot of loans but lots more equity in multiple properties, what does it matter?

"SHOULD I PAY OFF MY HOME LOAN OR SHOULDN'T I?"

If you are like me, you were probably taught by your parents to go to school, get a good education, get a good job, buy a home and then repay your home loan as quickly as you can because it's bad debt — it's non-tax-deductible debt. So most Australians try and pay off their home loan as soon as they can. You've probably guessed by now that I disagree with this concept. I don't think we should be scared of home loan debt even though it is not tax-deductible.

Let's look at the figures I have shown above in a different way.

Imagine you have received $20,000 as a bonus. You could use this windfall to pay off some of your home loan. At 5% interest you would save $1,000 each year.

On the other hand, if you took that $20,000 and used it as a deposit to purchase a property, you could buy $100,000 worth of property using 80% debt. Now of course you cannot buy any decent sort of property for $100,000, but if you just follow my example – for every $20,000 you have, you could buy $100,000 worth of property by borrowing 80% of the value of that property.

If you bought a well-located property in any capital city your property would increase in value by about 7% per annum and you would get about 3.5% rental return. This means you would get a total investment return of 10.5%. At the same time you would have to pay about 5% interest on your money and maybe 1% of the value of the property would go in outgoings such as rates, taxes and insurance and managing agents' fees.

This means that you would have 10.5% return coming in (some in cash and some in capital growth) and 6% going out, leaving you a net return of 4.5%. In other words, for every $20,000 you invest in property you would make $4,500. But if you used the same $20,000 to pay off your home loan you would save $1,000 in interest.

I would rather make $4,500 than save $1,000 any day, which means that I would rather not pay off my home but use any available cash to help purchase an investment property.

LIVE THE LIFE OF A
PROPERTY MULTI-MILLIONAIRE

Now it's time to understand the end game — how you convert the high-growth assets you have accumulated as a Level 3 investor, into your *Cash Machine* as a Level 4 investor.

If, like many readers of this book, your retirement is 10 to 15 years away let's get a few things clear...

The rules have changed considerably since I wrote the first edition of this book and recommended my *Living Off Equity Strategy*. More restrictive lending criteria since the Global Financial Crisis means that while this strategy still works for a few high net worth property investors, it's likely to be difficult for many investors to use this strategy moving forward.

And it's likely there will be many more changes moving forward.

I don't know if the government of the day will allow negative gearing or not. I really have no idea what interest rates are going to be then. Will you still be able to negatively gear properties or borrow in yourself and superfund? Will there be capital gains tax exemptions if you plan to sell some properties to release funds?

No one knows what the banks' lending policies will be or whether they'll allow you to have interest only loans or whether you'll have to pay down principal. And we don't know how they'll assess your serviceability which will affect your ongoing borrowing capacity.

But what I do know is that if between now and then you grow a substantial asset base (a multi-million-dollar property portfolio plus your superannuation) you'll have choices.

And along the way you'll have to formulate a debt reduction strategy, because holding a significant amount of debt in retirement is not advisable. While there's no exact formula, the end game I'd like to see is that you own your own home with no debt against it as well as a portfolio of investment grade properties with an LVR of less than 40% as well as some income producing assets such as shares or managed funds which might be held in your superannuation fund.

The further away your retirement, the easier this will be to achieve this because the capital growth of your properties over time will lower the overall Loan to Value Ratio of your portfolio.

If however your planning to retire in the next five to 10 years, unless you've already got a significant property portfolio or significant funds in your superannuation, it's almost impossible that you'll be able to live off your property portfolio. Which leads to the question…

HOW MUCH INCOME DO YOU WANT?

When I ask clients how much income they think they will need to fund retirement almost everyone says "$100,000 per year after tax". Yet when asked how they arrived at that figure, there is rarely any real thought put to it.

To work out how much money you will need you should start with how much you spend today on living expenses and make some adjustments from there. It's likely that you will have fewer mouths to feed once your kids leave home – but don't count on that. Adult children still seem to get themselves into trouble and needing help.

Also it's probable that you'll want to holiday more often or pursue certain hobbies or pastimes that you don't currently do. And unfortunately, there will be medical and other expenses you're not having to pay today.

While it's difficult to accurately assess your life expectancy as it will probably be impacted by medical technologies and treatments that haven't even been discovered yet, meaning many Australia's will live well into their '80s or '90s, you're likely to have to fund 25 years or more of living expenses in your retirement phase.

WON'T MY SUPER BE ENOUGH TO FUND RETIREMENT?

All working Australians contribute a portion of their income to superannuation and many hope this will see them through their golden years however, for most people, super will not be enough to fund the kind of comfortable lifestyle they're aiming for. This will of course depend on your superannuation balance and the type of lifestyle you hope to enjoy.

The problem with relying on superannuation is that the Government can (and do) change the laws and move the goal posts. They decide when and how you can access the funds in your super. I don't know about you, but I'm not comfortable with putting my retirement plans in the hands of the Government.

HOW MANY PROPERTIES DO YOU NEED TO RETIRE?

As you've been reading this book, have you wondered how many properties you would need to quit your day job and live comfortably?

The simple answer...*It depends.*

OK that's not what you wanted to hear, but in fact it's the wrong question to ask. It doesn't really matter how many properties you own. What is more important is the value of your asset base and how hard your money works for you.

Why do I say this? Because I'd rather own one Westfield Shopping Centre than 50 secondary properties in regional Australia.

HOW WILL YOU LIVE OFF YOUR PROPERTY PORTFOLIO?

While investors know they want their properties to replace their income, I've found most don't actually think about how they'll actually achieve financial freedom. Many just think that they'll live off their rental income, yet I rarely see this happen. It's just too hard to grow a portfolio of cash flow positive properties to a sufficient size to replace your income.

On the other hand, the wealthy investors I deal with have built a *Cash Machine* by growing a substantial asset base of high growth properties, and other income producing assets and then lowering their loan to value ratios so they can transition into the next phase of their lives.

WHY CAN'T I JUST LIVE OFF THE RENT?

Here's why...

Let's say you want an annual after-tax income of $100,000. How are you going to achieve that? How many properties do you need?

If you plan is to eventually pay down your debt and live off the rent, you'll probably need to own your home outright (without a mortgage) and at least $6 million worth of properties *with no mortgage* to get that $100,000 after-tax income.

DON'T BELIEVE ME?

The average gross yield for well-located properties in Australia is around 3% per cent.

This means if you eventually own $1 million worth of properties with *no* debt (you've paid off all the mortgages), you'll receive $30,000 rent each year. But you'll still have to pay rates, land tax, agents' commissions and repairs, leaving you with less than $30,000 a year. And then you'll have to pay tax on this income.

When you do the sums you'll see that you need an unencumbered portfolio worth $5-6 million to earn that $100,000 a year after outgoings and tax.

Remember that's $5-6 million worth of property and no mortgage debt, otherwise you cash flow will be lower. And as I said, you'll also need to own your own home with no debt against it. And those values are in today's dollar value.

Let me ask you a question...Will you ever be able to save $6 million? Will you ever build a portfolio of that size on a few dollars a week positive cash flow from your rentals?

In my mind the only way to become financially independent through property is to first grow a substantial asset base (by owning high-growth properties) and then transition to the next stage — the cash flow stage — by lowering your loan to value ratios. In other words, reducing your debt, but not paying it off completely.

Now you can see why most property investors fail to build a sufficiently large property portfolio to be able to live off its fruits.

Many start too late in life, they don't take advantage of their peak income earning years to trap spare cash and invest it. Others don't stay in the market long enough. The power of compounding takes time to build wealth. It may take 20 or more likely 30 years to allow capital growth to build a large enough asset base.

Yet others don't buy the right assets to get sufficient capital growth. I hope by know I've made it clear that you cannot expect to invest in average properties (non-investment grade assets) and expect above average returns. Therefore, if you are going to invest you better make sure that you invest in the highest quality properties you can find. And this means properties that grow at above average rates of return. Capital growth must be your main focus. Everything else is a distant second.

Now remember the three stages of wealth creation I've mentioned before:

1. The asset growth — this requires leverage

2. Transitioning to lower LVR — where you slowing pay down your debt

3. Living off the Cash Machine of your property portfolio

CAN'T I JUST BUY HIGH YIELDING RESIDENTIAL INVESTMENTS?

Yes you can! Last year the best-yielding area in Australia was the Queensland mining town of Blackwater, where there was an average return of 11.8 per cent for a median price house worth $120,000.

But I wouldn't invest in a mining town – would you?

I'd rather put my money into a well-located property in a gentrifying inner or middle ring suburb of our three big capital cities where there are multiple growth drivers including economic growth, jobs growth, population growth and infrastructure spending. And I would look for a suburb which has a large percentage of owner occupies who are earning higher wages so that they can afford to and prepared to buy houses in this location.

Sure these locations will provide lower rental yields, but they will have low vacancy rates, more stability of property values and stronger long-term capital growth potential.

Don't try and fight the trends. Residential real estate is a high growth relatively low-yield investment. After all expenses, your net yield may be less than 3%. But when you consider the capital growth, you'll achieve from a well located 'investment grade" property, the overall returns are very good, especially in today's low interest rate environment.

And as this capital growth is not taxed unless you sell your property (and why would you do that?) this enables you to reinvest your capital to generate higher compounding returns. On the other hand, rental income is taxed, leaving less to be reinvested.

This means for investors in the asset accumulation stage of their journey, the more capital growth you achieve (even at the cost of lower rental income) the more wealth you will accumulate in the long term.

When investors eventually transition to the cash flow stage of their journey, adding higher yielding commercial properties to their portfolio makes sense.

BUT HOW ARE YOU GOING TO REPAY ALL YOUR LOANS BEFORE YOU RETIRE?

Once you've built a substantial asset base you'll need to start thinking about lowering your debt levels, but it all begins long before that — you have to have a plan.

By now I've shown you that part of successful investment is having a strategy — a strategy for property purchases, a strategy for asset protection, a finance strategy and now I'm explaining you need an exit strategy knowing how you're going to repay your debt before you retire.

Just to be clear you don't need to fully pay off all your debt before you retire but, considering current lending practices, you must assume that the banks won't be comfortable extending you further debt unless in retirement unless you can prove serviceability.

They won't just keep lending you more money because you have equity like they did in the past. You'll need to prove serviceability which could come from your rental income (meaning you'll need a very low loan to value ratio) or from dividends from your share portfolio.

Since your ability to service debt will be very dependent upon interest rates at the time, it will therefore be important to go into your retirement years with a level of debt that is easily manageable, and which would not choke you financially if interest rates rise.

With that in mind, an ideal situation to be to own a mixture of growth and income producing assets look a little like this:

- You would own your own home with no debt against it

- You'd have a substantial superannuation fund which should be delivering you regular income

- You would own a multi-million-dollar property portfolio which is no longer negatively geared and, if it does have debt against it, the LVR would be such that the portfolio generates income. This would not need to be a lot of income, but needs to be sufficient so that your property portfolio is not draining your cash flow.

I know many financial planners suggest you should go into retirement with no debt at all, but in my mind entering retirement with a conservative amount of leverage works well for those investors who have set themselves up correctly.

These investors often live off their superannuation assets and income for the first 10–15 years of their retirement allowing their property portfolio to once again double in value which allows their already low loan to value ratio to fall even further enabling their property portfolio to spin off even more cash flow.

Others achieve their cash flow in retirement through the dividends from shares or from the positive cash flow of commercial property investments.

SO HOW DO I TRANSITION TO THE CASH FLOW PHASE OF MY INVESTING?

1. Grow your portfolio at a slower pace

Once you've grown a substantial asset base, one option is to slow down the pace at which you grow your property portfolio.

In other words, rather than refinancing and buying more properties as the value of your properties increase, just sit tight and allow your Loan to Value ratio to progressively fall as the value of your loans becomes a smaller proportion of the total value of your property holdings. With lower levels of borrowings, your properties would start generating positive cash flow and passive income that you could then use to enjoy your lifestyle.

2. Convert to a principal and interest loan

In the asset accumulation stage of your investment journey your borrowings should be interest only loans if economically possible, thus lowering your monthly payments, allowing you to borrow more and accumulate surplus funds in an offset account.

As you transition to the cash flow phase of your investing, you could convert some of your loans to principal and interest, allowing your tenants to slowly pay off your mortgages, thereby putting you in a stronger cash flow position. Remember that while paying interest on investment loans is tax-deductible, paying off the principal portion of the loan is not. However, this is a common strategy that investors use to reduce their debt and increase their cash flow.

3. Investing in commercial properties.

Different to residential real estate, commercial properties tend to have strong cash flow but less capital growth (this is linked to the rent increases which tend to be linked to the CPI). So adding commercial properties to your portfolio once you already have a strong asset base may be appropriate for you.

4. Use part of your Super or savings to pay off debt

When you reach the official age you may, if your advisor believes it's appropriate for your circumstances, choose to sell some assets in your Self Managed Super Fund, which under current legislation would not attract capital gains tax and then distributing the proceeds tax-free to help pay off debt outside the SMSF.

5. Redevelop a property or two to repay debt

It's possible that one of your investment properties has unrealised redevelopment potential. You can develop this property, make a profit selling the new dwellings and repay some of your debts, or even better — you could keep the new units and enjoy the rental income from two or three properties on the allotment where previously there was only one.

6. Sell a property or two and repay debt

You know I prefer to hold properties for the long term, but the purpose of owning these properties is to give you the lifestyle you want. This means sometimes the right thing to do is sell off one or two investments and use the proceeds to reduce your portfolio debt and increase your cash flow.

It will be important to consider the impact of capital gains tax (CGT) from the proceeds of your sale, but this could be avoided if you own the property in an SMSF and it is sold while you are in pension phase.

However, my favourite strategy is living off the increasing equity of my property portfolio. This allows me to retain my high-growth assets, avoid having to pay CGT and essentially, have my cake and eat it too. Let me explain this concept in more detail...

HERE'S HOW IT WORKS:

Fast forward 15 years and imagine you own your own home plus $5 million of well-located investment properties.

If you had a typical 80% Loan to Value Ratio (LVR), you would be highly negatively geared. On the other hand, if you had no debt against your property portfolio you would have significant positive cash flow, but would forego the benefits of leverage.

Somewhere in the middle, maybe at 40% LVR, your property portfolio would be self-funding. And if you lower your LVR further you'll have sufficient cash flow to prove serviceability to the banks.

If you think about it, it will be much easier to amass a $5 million property portfolio with $2 million of debt than the same size portfolio with no debt.

You could then go to the bank and explain that you've got a self-funding portfolio that isn't reliant on your income and in fact, provides surplus cash for serviceability. You would also have your other income producing assets (shares etc) to bolster your serviceability.

You would then ask for an extra $100,000 loan, so you increase your LVR slightly.

The good news is that because it's a loan you don't have to pay tax on this money because it's not income. But you would have to pay interest, which would not be tax deductible if you use the money for your living expenses.

This means after the interest payments you're left with around $95,000 to live on.

CRUNCH THE NUMBERS...

At the end of the year, you've "eaten up" your $100,000; but in a good year, your $5 million property portfolio would increase in value by say $400,000. In an average year it will have increased in value by $300,000 and in a bad year it may have only gone up by $150,000 or $200,000.

Of course, your rents will also have increased because your properties have grown in value.

Sure you've used up the $100,000 you borrowed, but because your portfolio has risen in value, along with rents, your LVR is less at the end of the year than the beginning, so you finish off the year richer than you began it. You truly have a Cash Machine, and then you can do this over and over again.

DOES THIS REALLY WORK?

In the old days living off equity was easy. You just had to go to the bank and get a low doc loan and as long as your properties increased in value it was smooth sailing.

Yes it's harder today, much harder. But it's definitely do-able if you own the right type of property and lower your LVR to show substantial serviceability to the banks.

Needless to say, you can't achieve this overnight. It takes time to build a substantial asset base and a comfortable loan-to-value ratio. But if you take advantage of the magic of leverage, compounding and time, it happens.

Of course this strategy depends on the growth in your property portfolio and your ability to ride the property cycle by having financial buffers in place.

To help you understand this concept better, I have included a spreadsheet to help you undertake these calculations on the special resources web page you can access when your register your copy of this book at www.TheBookOnPropertyInvestment.com.au You can use this to run the numbers for your own personal circumstances.

WILL THE BANKS KEEP LENDING ME MONEY?

Before I answer this, remember that if you follow this model you still are earning income – in fact you're getting it from a number of sources:

1. The *Passive Income* you receive from the growth in value of your property portfolio. Of course banks don't recognise this capital growth as income. They want to see wages or rents or dividend income to cover the mortgage payments. However, the good news is you don't pay tax on this income.

2. Your *Rental Income:* Remember I suggested that you lower your loan to value ratio so that your rental income at least covers your property expenses and your mortgages? Depending upon your returns, this means your LVR will have to be substantially less than 40%.

3. *Share, or dividend or superannuation income.*

At the time of writing banks are cautious and reluctant to refinance property portfolios based purely on the prospect of capital growth. What this means is that as you become a Level 4 investor you are going to have to lower your Loan to Value ratios (decrease your debt as a proportion of your portfolio) using one of the strategies that I mentioned at the beginning of this chapter.

And as you do, your property portfolio *Cash Machine* will start producing more cash flow. And if you substitute a commercial property or two for some of your residential properties this will increase your cash flow even more.

Of course a by-product of not being as highly leveraged is that your asset base will not grow in value as fast, but that's okay because as a Level 4 investor you are now in the cash flow stage of your investment life, not the asset accumulation stage.

DO YOU HAVE AN ASSET PROTECTION PLAN?

Remember this strategy depends on the growth in your property portfolio and your ability to ride the property cycle. This means that as you build your asset base, buying high-growth properties and adding value, you will need an asset protection plan to see you through the highs and lows that you'll experience.

After all, over the next ten years we'll have good times and bad. We'll have periods of strong economic growth, but there will also be downturns. And while interest rates are low at present, they may rise again — not that I'm expecting this any time soon.

Savvy investors count on the good times but plan for the downturns by having an asset protection plan, as well as a finance and tax strategy to make sure they set up their structures in the most efficient way. They recognise that market downturns are a "fee of admission" rather than a fine for getting it wrong. The short term fall in the value of their properties is the cost of being in the market. It is the cost of long-term success.

DON'T GET ME WRONG

While I've just made gaining financial freedom from property investing sound simple, it's not easy.

If you want financial freedom from property investment to fund your dreams, you're going to have to do something different to what most property investors are doing. You're going to have to listen to different people to whom most Australian property investors listen. You're going to need to set yourself some goals and follow a strategy that's known, proven and trusted.

Then you grow your property investment businesses one property at a time and of course you need to buy the right type of properties.

But that's what we've been talking about throughout this book — isn't it?

PROPERTY MANAGEMENT

DON'T LET YOUR PROPERTIES MANAGE YOU!

This chapter was originally written with the assistance of my wife Pamela Yardney, who established metropole's property management department in 2002. She has since retired and enjoys playing golf while living off the cash machine we have created from our property portfolio.

If you treat your property investing as a serious business and grow a multi-million dollar property portfolio, you will soon come to realise the importance of efficient property management.

So far we have looked at the processes of acquiring the right type of property. What we haven't really examined is how to manage the day-to-day running of your property investment business. Tenants need to be qualified and selected, condition reports completed, repairs organised — believe me, there is a long list.

As a property investor you have the choice of managing your investment properties yourself or delegating the day-to-day issues to a managing agent. In my mind there is no choice — this is a task for a professional property manager.

DOING IT YOURSELF BRINGS DANGERS

Until you have extensive experience, it can be risky to take on the management responsibilities yourself, and by the time you've built up a reasonable portfolio of properties you won't want to bother.

A good property manager will be a critical part of your team as you build your property portfolio.

Sure, quality management comes at a cost. Agents usually charge around seven to 8% plus GST of the rental to manage a property. Then they take a further commission, usually equivalent to about one or two weeks' rental to find new tenants and lease the property for you.

But the results should justify the expense of paying someone else who is better qualified than you to manage your property. Good property managers tend to pay for themselves by keeping your investments on track. This means quickly finding you good tenants who pay market rents and don't damage your property, keeping vacancies to a minimum and shielding you from the day-to-day hassles.

Even if you want to be actively involved in the management of your property, you can still stay involved without being responsible for every little detail. For example, if you are handy and can take care of the minor repairs yourself, your instructions to your agent would be to contact you when repairs are necessary or washers need changing, rather than calling a tradesman and passing on the costs.

MANAGING AGENTS ASK THE HARD QUESTIONS FOR YOU

Let's consider a real life example of how managing agents can save you money through professional practices.

Maurice's story

Maurice wound up getting himself very emotionally involved with a townhouse he bought as his first investment property.

Wanting to save money and be a "hands on" investor, he decided to have a go at managing the property himself. He simply placed an advertisement in the weekend paper and let his property quickly. What's more, everything seemed to be going quite well from a distance as his tenant stayed put for many years.

When I caught up with him about five years later and asked him how his property was going, he complained that the rent had not been raised since he first bought it and he felt he was missing out on the rental growth he deserved.

When I asked why he had allowed this situation to occur, he told me that the tenant was "a good payer and trouble-free" and he was embarrassed to put up the rent.

On further investigation it appeared that he had tried to bring up the idea of increasing the rent to the tenant, who complained how she was having trouble affording the current rent and said she just couldn't afford to pay more.

So Maurice resolved to wait until the tenant moved out to put up the rent and, of course, the tenant didn't move out!

Why would she, when she was in such a great situation?

When Maurice and I had this conversation he was receiving 30 to 40% below the market rental. My guess was that the property was let so quickly because the optimum rent hadn't been identified and set, and with no regular inspections, lease renewals and orderly small, incremental rent increases, the situation had got out of hand.

I'm sure the tenant had no intention of ever leaving and probably could not afford to move and pay market rent elsewhere.

By the way, Maurice now uses a property manager!

WHAT DOES A PROPERTY MANAGER REALLY DO?

If you manage your own properties you will have to attend to most of the following, but if you employ an agent, they should do these tasks for you.

Find prospective tenants

After finding tenants, your agent will need to thoroughly screen them before recommending them to you. This means scrutinising their references, confirming their employment history and checking with the agent for their last place of residence to ensure that their rent was paid promptly and the property was kept in good condition.

To help with their checks, agents have access to national tenancy databases not available to private landlords.

To help your agent in selecting tenants, you may choose to give them guidelines as to the type of tenant you would not accept. However, in today's legislative environment, qualifying tenants is particularly tricky, as you cannot discriminate against people on the basis of certain criteria.

Prepare the lease documentation

Your agent will prepare a lease that protects both you and your tenant.

I suggest you never lease your property for less than 12 months. This minimises management problems as well as re-letting fees for you and gives the tenant certainty and protection from rental increases.

I also try not have leases end at quiet letting times like just before Christmas or in the depths of winter when there are fewer prospective tenants looking for properties.

Bond

This is usually the equivalent of four weeks' rent and legislation requires the bond to be placed with a rental bond authority. The agent handles the documentation for this and any disputes regarding the bond arising at the end of the tenancy.

If tenants are up-to-date with their rent at the end of their tenancy and have left the property in the same condition as when they moved in (expect for what is considered "fair wear and tear"), then they should get their whole bond returned to them.

Unfortunately disputes often arise as to what is considered property damage and what should be considered fair wear and tear. Misunderstandings can be minimised by a well-documented lease and condition report with photos of each room of the property at both the beginning and the end of the tenancy.

Offer up-to-date advice on rentals

A good property manager knows the local market well and should advise you of the market rent for your property. If there is an oversupply of rental properties on the market, don't be greedy. A slightly lower rent, even $5 to $10 per week, should attract more tenants. It's far better to have a choice of candidates than to feel compelled to take anyone who comes along. I would rather have a guaranteed lower rental than a potential problem!

Administer rent reviews

At the end of the lease, or every 12 months, your property manager should advise you whether the rent being paid is still appropriate or whether you should ask for an increase. There are now regulations as to the incremental size of increases that can be asked or how frequently you can increase the rent, so it's important to keep the rent at market rates. If you slip too far behind it can take a long time to catch up in small increments!

Pass on the rental payments promptly

Agents deposit your rent directly into your bank account within days of them receiving them.

Provide regular statements

By furnishing you with a fully itemised monthly statement and a comprehensive statement at the end of the financial year to give to your accountant, your managing agent can save you time and trouble keeping track of your accounts.

Regularly inspect the property

Your agent can minimise disputes when your tenant vacates by conducting full internal and external inspections at the beginning and at the end of each tenancy. The tenants should be sent a written report together with photographs. The tenant then countersigns these reports to show that they reflect the true condition of the property.

Regular inspections during the tenancy should also be carried out, followed by written reports. This lets the tenants know that you take the proper care and maintenance of your property seriously and should pinpoint problems early, minimising the risk of having a "tenant from hell" who causes damage. Once the tenant has proven themselves, I am happy to have less frequent inspections, allowing the tenant peaceful enjoyment of their home.

Charles' story

I remember one friend, Charles, who had a rental property let to a group of young students. Although he employed a property manager, this agent did not have a policy of regular inspections. At the end of the tenancy, much to the agent's and Charles' horror, they found that every room in the house had been painted BLACK.

This is a true story. Every wall in every room was black and the ceilings too.

Sure Charles had a bond, but the whole house needed painting and because the paint had to cover black, an extra two coats were required. The bond was nowhere near enough.

Now Charles uses a different agent, insists that his properties are inspected regularly and gets a written inspection report with photographs.

Handle arrears

One of the unpleasant tasks you could have as a landlord is to confront tenants who are in arrears with their rent. This is especially so if it is due to genuine hardship, such as loss of a job or illness. Your property manager will shield you from this and know the correct action required if the tenant is in default. They will issue the relevant notices and follow through until the rent is up to date.

Advertising

Today the vast majority of rental enquiries come through the Internet which means prospective tenants do their "first inspection" over the Internet. They then create a short list of properties they physically visit. This means it's really important for your property manager to present your property professionally on major property portals.

Maintenance

When it comes to maintenance of your property, a good managing agent will have a team of qualified tradespeople who do a good job at a reasonable cost — often saving you money in the process.

Your agent can attend to maintenance requests by the tenant on your behalf. Usually you would advise the agent of how much involvement you want with these matters. You could ask to be notified of every request or ask your manager to take care of the whole thing. This could include instructing the tradespeople, arranging quotations, advising you and inspecting the work and passing the cost on when you receive your monthly rental statement.

Pay authorised account and statutory charges

At your request your agent can pay bills on your behalf out of the rent they receive. These could include owners' corporation fees, insurance premiums, and water and council rates.

HOW TO CHOOSE A PROPERTY MANAGER

When looking for a property manager you need to look out for the following things:

1. **The number of years of experience the property manager has in the industry.**

   Note that I said property manager and not the agency!

   Don't go to an agency just because it has a brand name — it doesn't mean the service is going to be any better.

   Just to expand on this even further, most agencies have a sales department and a rental department. Generally speaking the business owner has a sales background and not a rental background.

   Now, most business owners look after the sales department because it has high income and high turnover. And don't look after their rental department as much because of its relatively lower income and higher maintenance.

   Since the rental department is often seen as a headache, the owner will leave everything to other staff members, who are happy to collect their weekly wage. As they do not suffer or benefit directly from the services they provide or don't provide to their landlords, why should they really give a damn? Some will, some won't. You need to qualify them.

2. **How long has the property manager been with the agency?**

   Due to the stresses involved in property management, staff turnover tends to be quite high, but ideally you want stability in your property manager. You'd like someone who will know your property inside and out. You want to pick up the phone and talk to that person today, and a year later you want to be able to talk to that same person.

3. **Does the property manager give you a written proposal?**

   If they just look at your property and say, "OK, we'll put it on our books" they're not demonstrating much of a commitment to servicing your needs. Look for people who have put in the time and effort to present a professional image to you. If they have made that effort, they will make the extra effort when looking after your property.

4. **Ask property managers what they think of tenants!**

   I know this may sound dumb, but one of the interesting lessons I've learned over the years is that to get a good tenant and to get them to do what you want, you need to treat them well.

5. **Make sure they have a proactive approach**

   Basically this means that they actively do tenant reference checks, they undertake thorough ingoing and outgoing inspection reports, regular periodic inspections and regular drive-by inspections too; and that you receive a written report with photos after each inspection.

6. **Check whether the property managers just hand out keys or accompany prospective tenants on inspections**

    If they hand out keys and let tenants inspect properties alone, move on to another agency. I've seen too many things go wrong with this approach, including one extreme case where a prospective tenant made a copy of the key and returned it, later using the copy to move in and squat on the premises without paying rent. It took weeks to get him out!

    Also walking around the property with prospective tenants gives the agent a chance to promote the property and get to know the tenant a little better. It's amazing what can come up in a general chat that would never be written on an application form!

7. **Ask how many properties the manager looks after**

    The rule of thumb used to be that 200 properties was a full load for a full-time property manager, but this depends upon the support staff they work with.

LOOKING AFTER YOUR BEST ASSETS — THE TENANTS

The relationship you have with your tenants, either directly, or through your agent, is important. Always attend to repairs and maintenance promptly and treat your tenants fairly and with respect and it is likely that they will reciprocate by treating you and your property in the same way.

WHAT ABOUT PETS?

Since around 40% of Australian households have dogs, 26% have cats and, of those of those who don't own a pet, 53% would like one in the future, I recommend you accept tenants who have pets. While many landlords would prefer not to have the complications of animals on their properties, in many states it is illegal to forbid a tenant to own a pet. A sensible pet policy would be to allow pets in a rental property as long as all damage is repaired at the end of the lease period and protect your interest with a special "pet clause" inserted into the lease.

THE SECRET TO GETTING THE BEST TENANTS

When I ask investors what qualities they are looking for in a tenant, they usually come up with a list that looks something like this:

"I want a tenant who pays on time. I also want a tenant who takes care of my property. Then I want a tenant who is going to stay forever, and one who never calls with problems."

So who are these ideal tenants and, more importantly, how do we attract them? How do we tempt the tenant who will look after your property and you the landlord?

The best way to answer this is to flip the question on its head, and ask "What are THEY (the tenants) looking for?"

Here is a list that any good tenant would compile:

First, they want a property in a great position. Next, they look for a property that's big enough to hold all their "stuff". Then they want a property that's clean and in good repair and a property manager who will listen to their needs and pass their requests onto their landlord. Speaking of which, they want a landlord who will maintain the property.

Of course, they also want privacy, a fair rent and reasonable rent increases. And when they find these things, their final wish is for a long-term tenancy, which means a property that is not likely to be for sale.

As a property investor, when you look at that list, is there anything that you would find difficult to provide?

At the current vacancy rates, tenants are spoiled for choice of rental properties, so how do you attract top tenants?

The secret is simple: provide what they want — the *right type of property in the right location*. And of course these are exactly the things we have spoken about in the previous chapters of this book.

BEING THE BEST LANDLORD

OK — you now know how to get good tenants — how do you become a great landlord? Here are four tips:

1. **Keep your distance:** Forming friendships with tenants is rarely a good idea, for anybody.

2. **Keep your distance emotionally:** Try not to become too attached to your property. This can be a particular problem with owner-occupiers who move out of a property and decide to rent it out. It's no longer your home — allow the tenant to live how they want, as long as they're not damaging your property.

3. **Don't turn up unannounced:** There are rules in place to prevent this happening, but some owners still feel as though they can simply pop round and let themselves in whenever they want. This is unacceptable, often illegal, and means you're crossing the boundary into someone's home. Stick to the law when it comes to giving notice of visits and respect the whole property — including the garden — as somebody else's territory.

4. **Sort out issues promptly:** There's little that will annoy a tenant more than reporting a problem with the property and nothing being done about it. And don't simply opt for the cheapest tradesman to get the job done — this benefits neither you nor the tenant.

SHOULD I FURNISH MY INVESTMENT PROPERTY?

If you think you will get better returns by furnishing your property, think again: in general, this has not proven to be the case. I don't recommend furnishing rental properties, I've found it more trouble than it's worth.

Furnished apartments are more likely to attract transient tenants who tend not to be as stable and usually end up giving landlords more headaches. I like to know that tenants have managed to save enough money to afford their own belongings. When they rent an apartment and furnish it with their own furniture it makes it that much harder for them to just up and leave.

Every time there is a turnover in your tenants there is a cost to you. Each time they move out you have a few days, or more likely weeks, of vacancy and you pay management fees to re-let your property. These costs, plus the cost of replacing furniture, soon eat away at your investment yields. In fact there is not a lot of demand for furnished rental properties in many suburbs.

THE HABITS OF SUCCESSFUL PROPERTY INVESTORS

Success is not a miracle. Nor is it a matter of luck. Everything happens for a reason, good or bad, positive or negative.

And it's the same with success in property investment. While real estate is generally considered a sound investment, as I've already explained a few times, only a small number of those who get involved eventually develop financial independence.

It probably won't come as a surprise that when you study those who have achieved financial freedom through property investment, you will find they come from a variety of backgrounds, walks of life and educational standards, but there are certain traits shared by all of these successful investors.

By now you know that most property investors fail, with less than 10% ever owning more than two properties and close to 50% selling their properties within five years. The inconvenient truth is that close to 95% of investors never reach their objective of financial independence. This means to become successful you must do the opposite of what the vast majority of investors do.

If you want to join their ranks you need to model those who have achieved the success you desire. So as we come towards the end of this book, let's consider some of the traits that successful property investors have in common. They:

1. HAVE A STRATEGY

Successful investors have defined goals and a wealth creation plan to help them achieve those goals, allowing them to visualise the big picture and maintain focus.

Every property purchase they make is based on proven investment criteria rather than emotions. This allows them to say *"no"* more often, bypassing the mediocre investments to take advantage of great investments. Real estate investing can be complicated and demanding and a solid plan can keep investors organised and on task.

2. TREAT THEIR INVESTMENTS LIKE A BUSINESS

Successful investors realise it's not how much money they make that matters, it's how hard their money works for them and how much they keep that counts. For this reason, they treat their investments like a business.

They are financially fluent and understand "the system" of finance, tax and the law. They get the right type of finance and set up financial buffers to buy themselves time through the ups and downs of the property cycle. They establish the correct ownership and asset protection structures and know how to legally use the taxation system to their advantage.

Devising a business plan allows investors to establish and achieve their short and long-term goals, identifying objectives and determining a viable course of action to attain them.

3. CONTINUE TO EDUCATE THEMSELVES

Most Australians want to improve, grow, and lift their personal ceilings of achievement. However they think they can do this through trial and error, learning from their mistakes. Sure you can learn this way — but only so far and so fast.

In contrast, seeking out and learning from mentors who have achieved what you want to achieve can help raise your level of success dramatically and in a relatively short period of time. That's why sophisticated investors are prepared to invest in their education and never stop learning. They keep reading, attending seminars and learning from mentors and mastermind groups.

They make the effort to stay educated, adapting to market and regulatory changes as well as economic trends; recognising this as an investment in the future of their business.

4. THINK BIG

While the average Australian is content on buying a home and slowly paying it off, those who become financially free paint a much bigger picture for themselves. They see themselves building a substantial property investment portfolio that will one day replace the income from their day job.

There is nothing new about this; one of Donald Trump's favourite sayings has always been *"Think Big"*.

5. KNOW THEIR MARKETS

Effective property investors gain an unfair advantage by acquiring an in-depth knowledge of their selected markets. The more they understand a particular market, the more qualified they will be to make sound business decisions.

Successful investors like to invest in an imperfect market. This means they are more likely to buy an investment at a price below its true value. Being familiar with specific property markets allows successful investors to predict when trends are going to change; creating opportunities for those who are prepared and can think three or four steps ahead of everyone else.

6. DEVELOP A NICHE

Because there are so many ways to invest in real estate, it's important for investors to develop a niche in order to gain the depth of knowledge essential to be a success. This involves learning everything about a certain type of investment and becoming confident in that arena.

Once a particular market is mastered, savvy investors keep doing the same thing over and over again, recognising that it's better to do one thing well rather than five things poorly.

7. UNDERSTAND THE RISKS

Prudent investors understand the risks associated with the business of property including fluctuating cycles and interest rates and the inevitable "X factors" that come out of the blue to undo the best laid plans. They take precautions to reduce their risks.

8. TAKE FULL RESPONSIBILITY

Successful people know they are the pilot of their own lives. I believe everything that happens to you is a result of your thoughts, feelings and actions.

By taking responsibility for both the good and bad things that happen in your life, you will reduce the number of bad situations that occur and increase the number of good things.

9. ARE DECISIVE

Great investing is about taking action while average investing is about reacting to the media, the market place, the news etc. While the average person tends to wait for the right time, opportunity or price, successful investors take action.

Learn from them and become decisive. Once you have made a decision, stand by it. Don't question it, even if others around you do. Obviously you won't always make good decisions, but accept them, follow through and then deal with any problems that arise immediately.

10. FIND OPPORTUNITIES WHERE OTHERS SEE PROBLEMS

Some people see the cup half full, while others see it as half empty.

When confronted with opportunities, the average person will find reasons not to do something, yet successful people look for reasons to take action. Find ways to make the situation work.

This is particularly true in property. If you can find hidden opportunity that others fail to recognise — such as adding value to a tired property through renovations or solving a vendor's problems — you will make money.

11. EMBRACE CHANGE

It's often said "the only constant in life is change". See change as an opportunity and take advantage of the prospects that change presents.

Property markets, interest rates, market sentiment and supply and demand all change, but whenever change occurs it opens up fantastic possibilities. If you are committed to moving forward, you'll have to step out of your comfort zone.

12. THEY INVEST AND DON'T SPECULATE

Speculation is based on hope. Investment is based on facts. Speculators look for the next "hot spot", big thing, or latest fad and *hope* things will work out.

Successful investors recognise that it's not very exciting to buy property and wait for it to increase in value, but they don't look for excitement in their investments. They don't speculate.

Rather than trying to pick the next hot spot, investors ask questions like *"what has worked well over the last 20 to 30 years?"* and follow a strong longstanding trend.

13. BUILD A COMPETENT TEAM

Successful investors surround themselves with people they trust, who know more than they do. They don't expect to do everything themselves and are not afraid to pay for good advice. I've often said *'If you're the smartest person in your team you are in trouble'*.

14. HAVE LEARNED TO USE DEBT WISELY

Successful investors are not scared of taking on debt. They have learned how to use other people's money to grow their own substantial property portfolio. While beginning investors use finance to buy properties, sophisticated investors understand that once they have a property portfolio they can borrow against it and use finance to fund their lifestyle.

15. BELONG TO A MASTERMIND GROUP

Successful investors have learned to hang out with 'winners' not 'whingers.' Find a group of like-minded people and meet with them regularly to help you in your investment endeavours. Learn what makes winners and copy their habits.

16. ACT WITH INTEGRITY

If you commit to do something, always make sure you do it. I have seen many people in the investment business who tell you they will do something then create all sorts of excuses why it hasn't happened. Some of them are acting as honestly as they can. Some of them never had any intention of keeping their commitments.

To stand out from the crowd you must do what you commit to do.

17. SEE THE BIG PICTURE

Successful investors think of the big picture; recognising that the value of their property, if well positioned, will double in value every seven to 10 years. Yet the average investor will worry about fluctuations in interest rates, land tax changes or other minor details; they become paralysed when analysing the situation, failing to act.

Of course part of the reason successful investors look at the big picture is that they have a plan and know where they're heading.

18. THINK DIFFERENTLY TO AVERAGE INVESTORS

I once read that if you want to be successful, you should look at what everybody else is doing and then do the opposite. It's much the same with property investment...

LET'S LEARN A FEW THINGS FROM WARREN BUFFET, THE WORLD'S MOST SUCCESSFUL INVESTOR

Warren Buffet is arguably the greatest investor of all time. He has a great track record of creating and maintaining his wealth through share investments, but many of his principles also apply to property investors.

He would teach you that bad times will come and go with surprising frequency over our investing lifetimes, but if we have a plan and stay focused on sound financial strategies, we can gain financial independence through prudent investing.

So let's look at eight of Mr. Buffet's investment principles and see how we can apply them to our property investing.

1. ADHERE TO A PROVEN STRATEGY

Buffet's success has often been put down to his extraordinary patience and discipline, never deviating from his proven investment strategy even when faced with short term changes in the market.

This is a great lesson for property investors, as most don't have a plan or adhere to a proven strategy. In fact they spend more time planning where they're going to holiday than they do planning their financial future.

If you don't have an investment strategy to keep you focused, how can you hope to develop financial independence? It's too easy to get distracted by all the "opportunities" that keep cropping up. Unfortunately many of these supposed opportunities don't work out as expected. Look at many of the investors who bought off the plan or in the next "hot spot", only to see the value of their properties underperform.

2. INVEST COUNTER CYCLICALLY

Buffet is a renowned countercyclical investor, advising: "We attempt to be fearful when others are greedy and to be greedy only when others are fearful." This is also the investment strategy of many successful property investors and has proven to be a winning formula for many who invested in property last year when many predicted that property prices would fall further.

So be sceptical of conventional wisdom — not because the crowd is always wrong but because the crowd is always late.

3. SOMETIMES IT'S BEST TO DO NOTHING

A great quote from Warren Buffett is "The trick is, when there is nothing to do — do nothing." Yet many investors get itchy feet and want to do more, put another deal together or buy another property. There are stages in the property cycle and times in your investment journey when it is best to sit back and wait for the right opportunities because wealth is the transfer of money from the impatient to the patient.

4. INVEST FOR VALUE

Buffett is a value investor who says "It's far better to buy a wonderful company at a fair price than a fair company at a wonderful price" and it's the same with property. You make your money when you buy your property but not by buying a bargain. You lock in your profits by buying the "right property" — one that will outperform the averages in the long term because of its scarcity or the potential to add value.

In today's strong property market don't look for a bargain. Remember, the price you pay for a property isn't the same as the value you get. Successful investors know the difference.

5. INVEST FOR THE LONG TERM

Buffett admits he can't predict which way the markets will move in the short term and he is quite certain no one else can either. So instead, he takes a long-term view of the market saying if you don't feel comfortable owning a stock for 10 years, you shouldn't own it for 10 minutes.

Similarly those who have created wealth out of property took a long-term view. This doesn't mean buy and forget — you should regularly reviewing your property portfolio.

When was the last time you checked to make sure you were getting the best rents or that your mortgage was appropriate for the current times? Maybe it's time to refinance against your increased equity and use the funds to buy further properties? And sometimes it is appropriate to consider selling an underperforming property to enable you to buy a better investment.

6. DON'T INVEST IN ANYTHING YOU DON'T UNDERSTAND

During the boom years investors' hunger for returns took them into exotic terrain, whether they realised it or not. Promoters often promised large profits using opaque schemes, and the same is starting to happen again as the new property cycle rolls on. Warren Buffett never invests in anything he doesn't understand — nor should you.

7. MANAGE YOUR RISKS

Many investors don't fully understand the risks associated with property investment and therefore don't manage them correctly.

One common error is not having sufficient financial buffers to see them through from one property cycle to the next. Smart investors have financial buffers in their lines of credit or offset account to not only cover their negative gearing but to see them through the down times like we experienced in the last few years. They don't only buy properties; they but themselves time.

Another way smart investors minimise risk is to buy their properties in the correct ownership structures to legally minimise their tax and protect their assets.

8. SPECIALISE – DON'T DIVERSIFY

Buffet has adopted a focussed investment philosophy investing the bulk of his funds in a few companies. However, most advisers suggest diversifying. This is really just playing the game of investment not to lose, rather than playing the game to win and leads to average results. On the other hand, successful investors specialise. They become an expert in one area or niche and reproduce the same thing over and over again getting great results.

A BIT MORE ABOUT DIVERSIFICATION

Most financial experts recommend, "Diversify, diversify, diversify." Yet, the best investors in the world do not diversify.

Warren Buffet says, "Diversification is protection against ignorance. It makes little sense for those who know what they are doing."

Robert Kiyosaki asks: "Who's ignorance are you being protected from? Yours... or your financial advisor's?"

To me one of the keys to being successful at anything is to know what you are doing. When you know what you are doing, you make more money because you buy only great investments... not a basket of wishful thinking.

I've found most successful investors, business people and entrepreneurs don't diversify. They specialise – they find one thing they're good at and do it over and over again. That's how they become experts. You don't become an expert by doing a hundred things once, you become an expert by doing one thing a hundred times.

Now this needs a little further clarification. To consistently achieve wealth-producing rates of return you are going to have to specialise. You are going to have to become an expert in your niche, and I believe for most people it should be residential investment property. But as you build up your property portfolio, you then need to diversify.

Considering the cost of investment properties, you can't diversify when you first start off, but over time you should by owning a number of properties, a number of different types of properties, properties in different areas, and properties in different states. For example, I own residential, commercial, industrial, and showroom properties, as well as apartments, houses and townhouses and I own properties in a number of different geographic locations. So while I specialise in property, I'm diversified within that asset class.

SUMMARY

Despite abundant advertisements claiming that property investing is an easy way to wealth, it is in fact a challenging business requiring expertise, planning and focus.

Though it may be relatively simple to enjoy short-lived profits from property, developing a viable, long term investment business that provides you and your family with financial independence requires additional skill and effort.

Those who become highly effective real estate investors all share these 18 essential habits.

WHAT'S NEXT?

The trouble with so many investment books is that when you've finished them, you're finished with what they have to tell you. What happens after that? Readers are often left to their own devices to try to take the next step and put the theory they have learned into action. This book is going to be a little bit different.

Now that we've covered a lot of ground in terms of theory the next step in your journey is going to involve putting this into practice and there are a number of ways that you can keep in touch with me and my thoughts on the market.

One of the first things you should do is subscribe to my daily newsletter at www.PropertyUpdate.com.au where all Australia's leading experts and I discuss property, money management and success.

Then go to Apple Podcasts or your favourite podcast app or www.MichaelYardneyPodcast.com and subscribe to my weekly podcast – The Michael Yardney Podcast.

Next please go to www.TheBookOnPropertyInvestment.com.au. There you will be able to download a number of gifts and resources including a special **bonus chapter** *How to outperform the property markets by becoming a property developer.* There is also a spreadsheet to accompany the chapter about living off the equity of your properties and a number of other templates, reports and resources.

Be patient – creating wealth takes time so don't be in a rush and don't become greedy. Warren Buffet wisely said: *"Wealth is the transfer of money from the impatient to the patient."*

You must give your property time to increase in value and allow leverage, compounding and growth to work its magic. As the value of your portfolio increases you will have the ability to build on your wealth one property at a time. This means after buying your first property you're likely to have to wait a few years until you get sufficient capital growth to borrow your next deposit.

YOUR FUTURE IS IN YOUR OWN CAPABLE HANDS!

My property investment system is sometimes too simple for intelligent people — they look for something more complex. But I wrote this book to teach readers how to gain financial freedom through growing their own multi-million dollar property portfolio. I know the information in this book works — in has for me and it has for hundreds of thousands of Australians who've read this book, been to my seminars or become clients of Metropole.

In fact I was wrong when I said the information in this book works. The power of the information is not in the knowledge; the power is in its implementation and unfortunately many people have read this book, enjoyed the content and done nothing with it.

Why don't some people invest in real estate? After all it's easy to do. I guess because it's also easy not to do.

You can read more, learn more, attend seminars or you could take action. If you're scared of doing it on your own, give us a call at Metropole on 1300 METROPOLE and we'll help you.

Remember where you are right now is the result of the decisions you've made up until now. Where you will be in ten years' time will be the result of the decisions you make from now on.

The bottom line is ten years from now will be 10 years from now — whether you take action and build your Cash Machine or not. You are now equipped with new knowledge, ideas and perspective to give you a sense of what's possible.

Sure there will be obstacles along the way, they are part of what makes success possible. I wish you tremendous personal growth, financial success and that you build your own multi-million dollar property portfolio. And I hope to see you along the way.

Please email me and let me know about your successes. Since I wrote the first edition of this book I've enjoyed hearing many success stories from investors and I look forward to adding yours to the list.

Spend your time... wisely,

Michael Yardney
Michael Yardney
Michael@metropole.com.au